Oceanic Linguistics Special Publication No. 16

SYNTACTIC DERIVATION OF TAGALOG VERBS

by

Videa P. De Guzman

The University Press of Hawaii

Honolulu

Library of Congress Cataloging in Publication Data

Guzman, Videa de.
  Syntactic derivation of Tagalog verbs.

  (Oceanic linguistics special publication ; no. 16)
  Bibliography: p.
1. Tagalog language--Verb. 2. Tagalog language--Word
formation. 3. Tagalog language--Inflection. I. Title.
II. Series: Oceanic linguistics special publications ;
no. 16.
PL6053.G8   499'.211'5   78-11029
ISBN 0-8248-0627-1

TO MY BELOVED

PAPÁ AND MAMÁ

TABLE OF CONTENTS

CHAPTER III: TAGALOG VERB INFLECTION AND PRIMARY VERB STEM
             SUBCATEGORIZATION

LIST OF ILLUSTRATIONS

LIST OF CHARTS

ACKNOWLEDGMENTS

I am very grateful to the members of my dissertation committee -- Dr. Ruth H. Crymes, Dr. George W. Grace, Dr. Byron W. Bender, and, in particular, Dr. Howard P. McKaughan, who initially stimulated and encouraged me to venture on this task, and, most of all, Dr. Stanley Starosta, who guided me rigorously and faithfully, and without whose unstinting generosity this work could not have been accomplished. My special thanks to Dr. Lawrence A. Reid for reading this work critically and for giving some helpful comments.

To all the members of my family who provided support and inspired me to strive for a higher goal and to all my Christian friends who help me up in their prayers, my sincere appreciation.

And above all, to our Lord Jesus Christ, Who comforts me with His love and grace, my faith and trust.

CHAPTER I

INTRODUCTION

1.1 Aim and Scope

This study investigates the intriguing problem of Tagalog verb
formation. Although there have been a significant number of works
written on Tagalog verbs and on verbs in other Philippine languages, the
relevant questions pertaining to their inflection and derivation are
far from settled. There is no consistent agreement as to what the
categories of inflection are and how they are distinguished from
derivation. Neither is there a clear and concise description of the
relations existing between verb stems manifesting identical roots,
particularly in regard to their syntactic relations. It is the purpose
of this study to distinguish the two morphological processes of inflection and derivation as they operate in Tagalog verb formation. By
identifying the inflectional features and the corresponding affixes
which a verb stem type takes and showing the various kinds of verb
stems which can be created by derivation, we can account systematically
for the elaborate affixation of verbs and at the same time identify the
lexical relations obtaining between lexical items.

To fulfill this goal, the analysis explores and makes use of the
interrelated syntactic, semantic and morphological features of the verb
which serve to subcategorize the verbs. Syntactic features refer to the
cooccurring nominal expressions which bear specified case relations to
the verb and which are manifested in specified case forms. Semantic
features are unifying properties of meaning of classes of verbs which
have corresponding syntactic and/or morphological consequences. Lastly,

morphological features identified here are abbreviatory features that serve to identify verb stem classes according to their morphological structure which is in turn related to their voice paradigms and the particular voice affixes that mark them.

The verbs analyzed here are morphologically simple verbs, that is, there is only one instance of a root in every form. They may be labelled in general terms as state verbs and non-state verbs.[1] Verbs with compound or phrase bases have been excluded from the analysis.

The study includes the following topics:

(a) Chapter II describes the case relations and case forms in Tagalog. It deals with the case features of nominal expressions which cooccur with verbs. These features are central to the analysis of verbs. They are the identifying contextual features of verbs which serve as one way of subcategorizing verbs. They also play a significant role in stating relations between classes of lexical items expressed in the form of general derivational rules. Chapter II also includes a skeletal framework of the phrase-structure rules for Tagalog.

(b) Chapter III presents the major subcategorization of verb stems according to their syntactic and semantic features cross-classified by the verb stems' morphological-voice features. It is prefaced by a discussion of the distinction between inflection and derivation and an account of Tagalog verbal inflection.

(c) Chapter IV describes the syntactic derivational processes involved in the various stem forms including those subcategorized in the preceding chapter. A syntactic derivation involves a syntactic change either in lexical category feature or in case frame subcategory and/or morphological-voice related features.

1.2 The Lexicase Framework

The theoretical framework adopted in this study is called 'lexicase'. It has been developed by Stanley Starosta and some of his students and colleagues at the University of Hawaii in several articles and dissertations. (See Bibliography.) It was first applied to the analysis of Japanese by Harvey Taylor (1971), and then to Rukai by Paul Li (1973), to Thai by Pranee Kullavanijaya (1974), to Kusaeian by Keedong Lee (1974), to Vietnamese by Marybeth Clark (1975), and to Melayu Betawi by Kay Ikranagara (1975). In all these works, the lexicase model has been shown to be a workable grammatical framework with much promise.

A lexicase grammar is a generative syntactic model which consists of a set of phrase structure rules (PSR), a lexicon and a phonological component. The context-free phrase structure rules generate labelled trees indicating hierarchical and attributional relations between sentence constituents. They refer only to categories that dominate single surface structure constituents whose members are surface words and not morphemes or formatives. Unlike the Aspects (Chomsky, 1965) model, the category nodes here do not develop into complex symbols. Instead, lexical items from the lexicon are inserted freely under the corresponding category symbols.[2]

The lexicon consists of three types of lexical rules and a list of lexical entries representing roots and stems. Each entry has a phonological representation and a corresponding matrix of features which are not assignable by subcategorization rules nor predictable by redundancy rules. A lexical entry represents one or more fully

specified lexical items based on the applicable lexical rules. The
significant features included in each lexical item are: a) lexical
category features such as [+N] for noun, [+V] for verb, [+Adj] for
adjective; b) case features of case relations such as [+OBJ] for
objective, [+AGT] for agentive, and case forms such as [+NM] for nominative, [+AC] for accusative, [+B] for benefactive; c) contextual
or case frame features (particularly for verbs) such as [+[+OBJ]] for
cooccurring with an objective case relation, [-[-AC, +INS]] for cooccurring with an instrumental case relation expressed only in the
accusative case form; d) semantic features associated with either
syntactic or morphological consequences, e.g., [+caus] for causative,
[+dir] for direction, [+af] for affected; e) morphological features
on verbs associated with constraints on voice inflection such as
[+erg] for ergative, [-pot, +act] for non-potential, active; and
f) other idiosyncratic features, including a dictionary meaning or
definition.

There are three types of lexical rules that apply to each entry
where appropriate. They are called subcategorization rules (SR),
redundancy rules (RR), and derivation rules (DR). As the name implies,
subcategorization rules identify the subcategories of the lexical
categories. They are characterized by the symbol '±' before a
specific feature in the output of the rule. The symbol is read
'either plus or minus' which means that one subcategory marked with a
'+' indicates having the specified feature and another subcategory
marked with a '-' is marked negatively for the feature. For example:

SR: [+V] $\longrightarrow$ [±pot]

The rule states that the lexical category V, for verbs, is subcategorized into those that are specified as potential, [+pot], and those that
are non-potential, [-pot]. Each of these subcategories may still be
further subcategorized according to certain other related features. At
the same time, V's may also be subcategorized on the basis of a
different relevant feature. For example, [+V] $\longrightarrow$ [±[+AGT]] shows a
subcategorization based on a contextual feature. A verb is either
positively marked for cooccurring with an agent actant, [+[+AGT]], or
negatively marked, [-[+AGT]], to mean the verb does not cooccur with
this particular actant.

Redundancy rules, on the other hand, add or predict certain
features on the basis of another specified feature. The predictable
feature in the output is marked with either a '+' or a '-' symbol
before it. For example, a redundancy rule which applies to verbs
marked with the feature [+strict] acquires the feature [+[+LOC]] as
stated as follows:

RR: $\begin{bmatrix} +V \\ +strict \end{bmatrix} \longrightarrow$ [+[+LOC]]

This means that all verbs marked [+strict] are also marked with the
feature which is on the right hand side of the rule. In this case, the
added feature means that a [+LOC] actant must overtly cooccur with the
verb.

The third set of rules known as derivation rules is of a different
kind. They relate lexical items to other lexical items or a lexical
class to another lexical class. By means of these rules, new lexical
entries are created from already existing ones. The new item is marked
with the feature [+Derv] to indicate that it is derived and that a

derivation rule accounts for its general feature specifications which
are features carried over from the source item or introduced by the
rule. These rules formally and historically relate lexical classes.
For example:

DR: $$\begin{bmatrix} +V \\ -[+AGT] \\ -[+DAT] \\ -[+INS] \\ +[+OBJ] \end{bmatrix} \longmapsto \begin{bmatrix} +V \\ +Derv \\ +[+AGT] \\ -[+DAT] \\ +[+OBJ] \end{bmatrix}$$

The above rule, stated generally, says that a verb with cooccurring
agentive and objective actants may be derived from verbs that allow
only an objective actant. In common traditional terms, a transitive
verb may be derived from an intransitive verb, as may be illustrated
by the verb ta?ob 'turn over' and the derived verb ta?ob 'turn something over'. From the rule, it will be observed that the primary
change in the matrix of features of the output is the introduction of
an agentive actant while the [+OBJ] remains unaltered. This syntactic
change has a morphological consequence in terms of the range of the
verb's voice paradigm and its corresponding voice affixes. Whereas the
intransitive verb is realized with the active voice affix um-, the
derived transitive takes the affix i-, giving the forms tuma?ob and
ita?ob, respectively, in their objective voice inflected non-finite forms.

All three rules capture linguistically significant generalizations
pertaining to lexical categories or subcategories. By employing these
rules, all morphological processes, particularly derivation and inflection, are treated in the lexicon. As they apply to each individual
lexical entry, the corresponding lexical item or items become fully
specified qualifying them ready for lexical insertion at the terminal

nodes of the trees generated by the phrase structure rules. After lexical insertion, the resulting string is a fully specified syntactic representation.

The third component of the grammar, the phonological component, operates on the syntactic representations giving them the necessary full phonological representation.[3] It may be stressed that since the lexical items in the string are each expressed in phonological representations--some phonological changes being handled in the lexicon by morphophonemic rules corresponding to derivation and inflection rules-- this component operates only across word boundaries but within the bounds of the sentence. Any syntactic representation then may be considered virtually as a phonological representation. As a general rule, each syntactic representation which has met all the syntactic cooccurrence conditions is a grammatical or well-formed sentence.

The attached diagram, Figure 1 (adapted from Taylor, 1971:10), shows the interrelationships of the components of a lexicase grammar. Note that semantic interpretation lies outside the boundary of the model. It restates or reinterprets all the semantic information provided by the content of lexical items and the relations between them in a given syntactic representation in the light of a particular context of situation (COS). But the context of situation is likewise outside the realm of this grammar. In other words, the 'intrinsic' semantic representations of the string generated by the grammar is what is contained in the syntactic representations. The semantic representations derived by the semantic interpretation component (SIC) in which some extra-linguistic information has interacted with the supposed rules operating on the input from the grammar are conceivably matters of performance. On the basis of such interaction between these two components, a sentence may be judged acceptable or not. Take as an illustration the following English nursery rhyme:

1. Hey, diddle-diddle,
   The cat and the fiddle,
   The cow jumped over the moon,
   The little dog laughed to see such sport,
   And the dish ran away with the spoon.

Leaving out the phonological component, the sentence represents a perfectly grammatical structure which means just what it says. However, this sentence, given its semantic interpretation from the input of the grammar and the COS, can only be acceptable in an imagined world. This situation could not constrain the grammar from generating well-formed sentences such 1. It is not at all unreasonable or inconceivable to think of a competence grammar as generating grammatical sentences regardless of whether they match with a real or an imagined context.

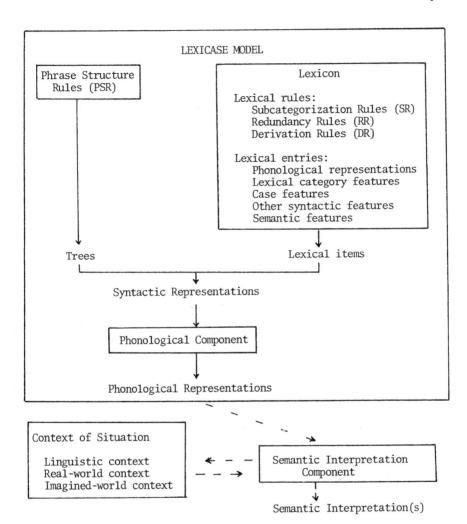

Figure 1.   Components of a lexicase model and its relationship
            to semantic interpretation (Adapted from
            Taylor, 1971: 10)

1.3 Similarities and Differences Between Lexicase and Some
Other Generative Grammars

The lexicase model as a form of generative grammar is more narrowly
restricted compared with the enormously powerful transformational types
of generative grammars. Bordering between Chomsky's model in Aspects 1965
and Fillmore's case grammar of 1968, lexicase is similar to these two
grammars in certain characteristic ways but is, at the same time,
different in other significant respects.

1.3.1 Chomsky 1965

The two syntactic-related components shared by lexicase with Chomsky
1965 are the Phrase Structure Rules and the Lexicon. Lexicase PSR's, however, are different in that they use only category symbols that dominate
individual lexical items or constituent symbols which are also composed
of category symbols dominating lexical items, e.g., V, NP, PP, N, Adv, etc.
They exclude Chomsky's grammatical categories or items which have only
relational or semantic content such as Place, Manner, Direction, Predicate-
Nominal, Tense, etc. By using the latter symbols, we go against the
essential function of PSR's which is to identify constituency. For
instance, the PSR which rewrites:

"(v) Prep-Phrase $\rightarrow$ Direction, Duration, Place, Frequency, etc."
(Chomsky, 1965:107) gives no information as to the constituent structure
of the symbol identified on the left side of the arrow. Furthermore,
it is unclear how the categories listed to the right of the arrow are to
be matched by appropriate lexical items. It is rather unlikely that these
categories refer to lexical categories if they are manifested by adverbs
or nouns occurring as object of the preposition. In a strict sense, then,
lexicase PSR's represent a more realistic and consistent way of expressing

constituency.

Lexicase handles Chomsky's categories such as Tense, Aspect, IMP, NEG, or Q as features of lexical categories and as such they are treated in the lexicon before lexical insertion occurs. These features appear as inherent or contextual features which are assigned either by SR's or RR's. In the manner of Chomsky's alternative proposal, lexicase eliminates the subcategorization rules from the component containing the PSR's and assigns them to the lexicon (Chomsky, 1965:120). The grammatical properties expressed as features affect the form of the lexical items and all these corresponding changes in morphological forms take place in the lexicon which stores all existing, and defines possible, lexical items in the language. Thus, the base component or what is referred to here as the set of PSR' is no longer encumbered with grammatical formatives and complex symbols.

Chomsky 1965 has a separate semantic component which determines the semantic interpretation of a sentence. The semantic features introduced in the lexicon are again introduced in the semantic component. Lexicase, which does not have a semantic component as part of the grammar, makes use of semantic features in the lexicon, and other grammatical features specified in the terminal string to give the output sentence its semantic interpretation. In effect, the syntactic representations, or, if we want to go further, the phonological representations are themselves the semantic representations. However, a semantic interpretation component which lies outside the realm of the lexicase model may operate on the phonological representations as input with the context of situation also contributing to the assignment of possible semantic interpretations.

One other significant difference between lexicase and Chomsky 1965 is the exclusion of transformational rules in the former model. Positing a deep structure level and a surface structure one in Chomsky 1965 necessitates this type of rules to relate them. Lexicase does not recognize the existence of a deep structure which supposedly determines the semantic interpretation of a sentence. It considers just one level of structure. Every sentence is specified with syntactic and semantic features, and if there happen to be two identical strings which by Chomsky's analysis are considered ambiguous, these two are shown to be different sentences as given by their different syntactic representations. For example:

2.   ibibili   niya   ito   ng damit
       buy   he   this   dress

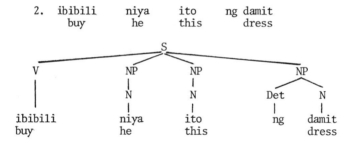

The same string can have the following sets of features which differentiate two syntactic representations, hence, two different sentences:

2.a.   ibibili   niya   ito   ng   damit

$$\begin{bmatrix} +V \\ -[-AC, +AGT] \\ -[-AC, +OBJ] \\ -[+NM, -BEN] \end{bmatrix} \begin{bmatrix} +N \\ +pro \\ +AC \\ +AGT \end{bmatrix} \begin{bmatrix} +N \\ +pro \\ +NM \\ +BEN \end{bmatrix} \begin{bmatrix} +Det \\ +AC \end{bmatrix} \begin{bmatrix} +N \\ +AC \\ +OBJ \end{bmatrix}$$

'He will buy a dress for this one.'

2.b. ibibili   niya   ito   ng   damit
$$\begin{bmatrix} +V \\ -[-AC,\ +AGT] \\ -[-AC,\ +OBJ] \\ -[+NM,\ -INS] \end{bmatrix} \quad \begin{bmatrix} +N \\ +pro \\ +AC \\ +AGT \end{bmatrix} \quad \begin{bmatrix} +N \\ +pro \\ +NM \\ +INS \end{bmatrix} \quad \begin{bmatrix} +Det \\ +AC \end{bmatrix} \quad \begin{bmatrix} +N \\ +AC \\ +OBJ \end{bmatrix}$$

'He will buy a dress with this.'

Similarly, the argument that two sentences may be related only by transformation, e.g., active and passive sentences, in that one is derivable from the other is not thoroughly convincing (Freidin, 1975). Lexicase can capture the relationship between two constructions not necessarily by showing that they have the same deep structure but again by referring to the features of the lexical items, particularly to their case features. For example:

3.a.

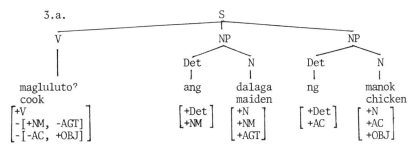

'The maiden will cook chicken.'

3.b.

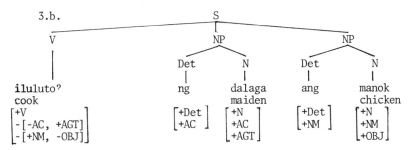

'The chicken will be cooked by the maiden.'

The two sentences above are related since they are made up of identical trees and partially identical lexical contentives. The first N, dalaga 'maiden', is marked in both sentences as having the agentive case relation to the verbs magluluto? and iluluto?. Similarly, the second N, manok ' chicken', has the objective case relation in both sentences. The difference, however, is in the case form in which each of the two N's is manifested in each sentence. In 3.a, the [+AGT] actant is realized in the nominative, [+NM], and the [+OBJ] in the accusative, [+AC], whereas in 3.b, the [+AGT] is in the accusative and the [+OBJ] in the nominative. Corresponding to the selection of which case relation is realized in the nominative or as the grammatical subject of the sentence is the difference in morphological form in terms of stem structure and affix of the cooccurring verbs. These two verb forms are considered separate but related lexical items by virtue of derivation. Both share the same root luto? 'cook' and the relation is formally statable in the form of the following derivation rule:

$$\text{DR:} \quad \begin{bmatrix} +V \\ +[+AGT] \\ -[+DAT] \\ +[+OBJ] \\ +erg \\ \alpha F_i \end{bmatrix} \longmapsto \begin{bmatrix} +V \\ +Derv \\ +[+AGT] \\ -[+DAT] \\ +[+OBJ] \\ -pot \\ +act \\ \alpha F_i \\ \beta F_j^1 \end{bmatrix}$$

$$\text{MR:} \quad {}_V[\quad \longrightarrow \quad {}_V[\ \text{pag}$$

The derivation rule states that a verb with cooccurring [+AGT] and [+OBJ] marked with the feature [+erg] can create a verb with the same case relations but marked with the features [-pot, +act]. By a redundancy rule, a verb marked [+erg] is restricted from cooccurring with a nominative agentive actant but it allows a nominative objective. On the other hand, a redundancy rule allows just the opposite cooccurrence restriction when the verb has the features [-pot, +act]. The derived verb acquires all other features specified as αF_i from its source. It undergoes a morphophonemic change as stated by the accompanying morphophonemic rule (MR) which prefixes it with pag-. The associated voice affix of the source is i- and that of the derived one is m-. Thus, the verbs of sentences 3.a and 3.b, which may be labelled active and passive, respec-tively, are related via a verb derivation rule.

Lexicase grammar, then, is able to account for facts about struc--tural and lexical relations at least as adequately as, if not more than, that of a transformational grammar of the Chomsky 1965 version. It can do this task without positing a deep structure level and, hence, using no powerful transformational rules. It eliminates certain redundancies such as requiring complex symbols in the base as well as in the lexicon and semantic features in both the lexicon and the semantic component, by incorporating subcategoriztion rules in the lexicon and by defining a grammar without a separate semantic component. The PSR component of the lexicase grammar is simplified by relegating morphological processes to the lexicon. And, most importantly, lexicase uses derivation rules, a much more narrowly restricted type of rules than transformational rules, to relate lexical items or classes of lexical items and to show in some cases syntactic relations as well.

These characteristics of the lexicase model are not shared either by Fillmore's case grammar nor by the generative semanticists' grammar. The following comparisons treat the specific points with which lexicase differs from these two other grammars.

1.3.2 Fillmore's Case Grammar (1968; 1971)

The use of case relations in lexicase is attributable to Fillmore's
(1968) revival of the notion of case and description of its place in a
transformational grammar. It will be recalled that in the grammar he
proposes, he incorporates case relations as categories dominating NP's in
the base component. By applying transformational rules such as nominative
marking, accusative marking and preposition selection, the deep case
relations are mapped onto surface structures. Later, Fillmore concedes
(1971) that his use of labelled nodes for case dominating NP's or S is
problematic. He recognizes that cases are clearly not categories, but,
so far, he has not found an acceptable notation which can handle them with
fewer complications.

The solution which lexicase adopts for this perplexing problem is to
mark case as features on lexical items. As features on lexical items, case
includes both case relations and case forms. Both of these features are
drawn from a limited set of relations and forms posited for all languages.
Case forms other than Fillmore's nominative and accusative have been
introduced by lexicase, e.g., [+L] for locative, [+B] for benefactive,
[+C] for comitative, etc. (see others in Taylor, 1971; Li, 1973;
Kullavanijaya, 1974). It may be pointed out that lexicase considers it
important not only to determine the ways in which case relations are
realized but also to explain why certain sets of case relations tend to
be manifested in one single form. Starosta (1973b) observes that in a
variety of languages, certain groups of case relations take identical
case forms. This type of information can possibly be useful in explaining
historical change, in making typological classification and in postulating
some universal characteristics in language. He presents several

justifications for the value of positing not only universal case
relations but case forms as well.

1.3.3 Generative Semantics (Lakoff, 1971; McCawley, 1968 and 1972)

Compared with the stream of transformational grammar known as
generative semantics, lexicase shares many fewer features than what it
does with the two generative grammars discussed above. In its claim
that "semantic representations and syntactic phrase-makers are formal
objects of the same kind" (Lakoff, 1971:269), generative semantics
states semantic representations of sentences and lexical items in terms
of atomic predicates. From McCawley's classic example (1968:73; 1972:60)
<u>John killed Harry</u>, the semantic representations are as follows:

(a)

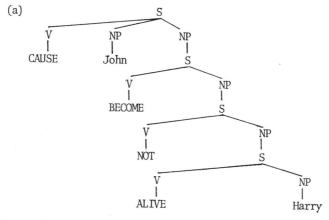

By the application of the predicate-raising rule, the predicate from
the innermost node combines with that of the next higher node in each
cycle until it reaches the topmost predicate giving the output:

(b)

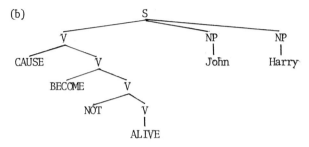

With this derived verb construct, the lexical item **kill** can now be inserted.

One basic difference pointed out by Starosta between the two systems is that features in lexicase are unordered bundles, while atomic predicates are arranged hierarchically. This suggests that lexicase makes the claim that "it is impossible for two lexical items to differ solely in the ordering of features or in the iteration of a single feature" (Starosta, forthcoming, p.184), and since any necessary constraints on feature domination are part of the basic definition of features, the simpler feature system is preferable.

Finally, the semantic structure of generative semantics is so abstract there are only two terminal node labels, namely, predicates and indices. The differences among N,V, Adj, P and Conj do not exist; they all correspond to the single semantic category identified as predicate. It seems that what is emphasized by this categorization are only the feature similarities shared by the various lexical categories which features can be expressed in the matrices of lexical items. As a consequence, the transformational rules and derivational constraints that relate the deep semantic structure to surface structure have been invested with more and more power, until they can do practically anything. This is rather unfortunate because the extremely powerful rules can in principle accommodate any form of deep structure, thus emptying the theory of any claim about the nature of language in general.

In all these contrasts between lexicase and the other generative grammars, the significant points of differences are as follows:

(a) it has a single level of structure that is simultaneously the syntactic and semantic representations;

(b) it makes use of features on lexical items which provide syntactic, semantic and phonological information; and

(c) it uses derivation rules, which rely heavily on features, to state significant generalizations about syntactic and lexical relations.

Under these stringent conditions imposed by lexicase, this study attempts to show lexicase to be a viable and promising framework for the description of another natural language. It is believed that if a less powerful framework can account adequately for a broad range of linguistic facts, it is to be preferred in that it provides a narrower characterization of the nature of language.

Footnotes to Chapter I

[1]The term state is equivalent to Lakoff's stative (or non-activity) verbs (1970:121) and not to Chafe's state verbs (1970:98-99), which are identified here as adjectives.

[2]The same principle is used by Jackendoff in his model (1972:21-22).

[3]The phonological component is beyond the scope of this study, hence, the representations given here are the phonological representations of individual lexical items.

[4]To interpret a double negative marking on contextual features, see Chapter II, p. 30.

CHAPTER II

CASE RELATIONS AND CASE FORMS IN TAGALOG

2.1 Case

One of the fundamental notions in a lexicase grammar is <u>case</u> as an inherent feature of lexical items. As Blake points out, case is commonly understood in a limited sense as referring "to form and has to do with meaning only insofar as that is denoted by the form" (1930:34). He clarifies the meaning of the term by distinguishing between case (called case relation, CR, in this study) as the semantic relationship a nominal expression holds with its cooccurring predicate, and case form (CF here) as the realization or manifestation of the case. Depending on the language, various devices are used to express case relations. It may be through affixation or suppletion of nouns or pronouns, use of particles or prepositions/postpositions, constraints on word order, or verbal affixation(Fillmore, 1968:21, 32). Thus, a case relation always has an associated case form marked by the particular mechanism the language adopts. This being the system, it is possible for a CR to be realized in more than one CF, and for a CF to represent a neutralization of more than one CR. For instance, German has various case forms which manifest a noun perceived as having an objective case relation with its cooccurring verb, such as shown in the following sentences (Kufner, 1962:43) which have been marked here with case features:

1.a. ich   sehe   den Mann
      I   see   man
                       $\begin{bmatrix} +AC(cusative) \\ +OBJ(ective) \end{bmatrix}$

'I see the man.'

1.b. ich   helfe   dem Mann
     I   help   man
$$\begin{bmatrix} +D(\text{ative}) \\ +OBJ \end{bmatrix}$$

'I help the man.'

1.c. ich   gedenke   des Mannes
     I   remember   man
$$\begin{bmatrix} +G(\text{enitive}) \\ +OBJ \end{bmatrix}$$

'I remember the man.'

The noun marked with the feature [+OBJ] means that it has an objective case relation with its verb. In 1.a, this noun is realized in the accusative case form [+AC], in 1.b, in the dative case form [+D], and in 1.c, in the genitive case from [+G]. In contrast, to show one CF manifesting different CR's we can cite the following familiar examples in English (Fillmore, 1968:27):

2.a. The door opened.
$$\begin{bmatrix} +NM\ (\text{nominative}) \\ +OBJ \end{bmatrix}$$

2.b. John opened the door.
$$\begin{bmatrix} +NM \\ +AGT\ (\text{agentive}) \end{bmatrix}$$

2.c. The wind opened the door.
$$\begin{bmatrix} +NM \\ +INS\ (\text{instrumental}) \end{bmatrix}$$

The nominative case form [+NM] in the above sentences realizes an objective [+OBJ], an agentive [+AGT], and an instrumental [+INS] case relation. This form is identified by its occurrence before and agreement with the finite verb. From the two sets of examples above, it will be observed that a case form does not only realize CR's. It also characterizes the grammatical function of a given CR in the sentence. Thus, for the first set, the designated CF's show different functions of a noun which has an objective case relation to the verb while that of the second set shows that each noun specified with a different case relation is the subject of the sentence, as indicated by [+NM].

Following Blake's and Fillmore's assumption that case relations are basic to the structure of sentences in any language, this study analyzes the case relations and case forms in Tagalog which cooccur with verbs. In this connection, another assumption held in this study is that the verb has both inherent contextual (case frame) and semantic features. As Chafe asserts, "the nature of the verb determines what the rest of the sentence will be like; in particular...what nouns will be semantically specified" (Chafe, 1970:97). This characteristic of verbs suggests that they can be subcategorized according to these cooccurring case relations and case forms which comprise what is called the verb's case frame. It will be recalled that lexicase, unlike Fillmore's case grammar, does not have a deep structure wherein the case relations are generated. Since there is only a single level of structure in lexicase, both features are marked in that level. They are assigned to lexical items, in general, by redundancy and subcategorizational rules. Otherwise, they appear as idiosyncratic features of certain lexical items. The difference in formulation of the case frame features between lexicase and Fillmore's case grammar may be illustrated by the following examples:

3.a. Fillmore

open
[+[__ O(I)(A)]]

3.b. Lexicase

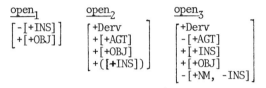

$$\text{open}_1 \quad \begin{bmatrix} -[+\text{INS}] \\ +[+\text{OBJ}] \end{bmatrix} \qquad \text{open}_2 \quad \begin{bmatrix} +\text{Derv} \\ +[+\text{AGT}] \\ +[+\text{OBJ}] \\ +([+\text{INS}]) \end{bmatrix} \qquad \text{open}_3 \quad \begin{bmatrix} +\text{Derv} \\ -[+\text{AGT}] \\ +[+\text{INS}] \\ +[+\text{OBJ}] \\ -[+\text{NM}, -\text{INS}] \end{bmatrix}$$

The latter formulation has the following advantages:

(a) By registering each contextual feature separately, we can manipulate one independently of the others such that a rule, for instance, may state a generalization that refers only to the case form of the [+INS] when cooccurring with a [+AGT] without referring to other CF's or CR's that cooccur.

(b) Rules predicting the occurrence of one case feature based on the presence of another can be easily formulated, thus, simplifying the specifications in the entry.

(c) By using the notation of the form [+[+OBJ]] to denote either [+[+OBJ]___] or [+___[+OBJ]], we can formulate universal rules of case cooccurrences without reference to word order which can be handled by language-specific redundancy rules.

(d) The use of parentheses means only optional overt manifestation, hence, a [+INS] may or may not be present only with open$_2$ under 3.b. No [+INS] cooccurs with open$_1$, but it must be the subject in open$_3$ where there is no cooccurring [+AGT]. By Fillmore's notation, both instrumental and agent actants are shown to be optional.

(e) Finally, especially for stating lexical relations in terms of DR's, this type of configuration shows precisely the features that carry over, those that get altered, and those that are introduced.

2.2 Case in Tagalog

Working on Fillmore's hypothesis that there exists a finite and universal set of case relations and on Starosta's claim to a corresponding universal set of case forms and, consequently, to the necessity of accounting for the system of case expression to achieve explanatory adequacy (Starosta, 1973b), we will identify the case relations which Tagalog distinguishes and, concomitantly, the system it adopts in expressing them. The CR's and CF's identified will be used for marking N's, Det's and P's.

Tagalog, like other Philippine and some other Austronesian languages, has an interesting, although seemingly peculiar, way of expressing case in both verbs and cooccurring nouns. This characteristic is not at all a new observation in Philippine linguistics. As early as 1906, Blake had described this phenomenon in his article 'Expression of Case by the Verb in Tagalog.' His account centers on the case-indicating function of the verbal affixes which he identifies as voice. The active voice, he says, denotes the case of the agent and the passive expresses not only the accusative, but also the dative, instrumental, locative, and ablative, with the noun whose case is to be indicated being made the subject of the passive verb (Blake, 1906:183-4). One important fact he recognizes is that "sometimes two forms are used to express what is ordinarily considered one case, sometimes one form expresses two or more cases" (1906:188).[1] For example:

4.a. lulutu?in   niya   ang manok
       cook   he   chicken
                     $\begin{bmatrix} +AC \\ +AGT \end{bmatrix}$ $\begin{bmatrix} +NM \\ +OBJ \end{bmatrix}$

      'He will cook the chicken.'[2]

4.b. ilulutu?   niya   ang manok
                  $\begin{bmatrix} +AC \\ +AGT \end{bmatrix}$ $\begin{bmatrix} +NM \\ +OBJ \end{bmatrix}$

'He will cook the chicken.'

5.a. bubuksan   ng diyanitor ang kandado
     open   janitor   lock
                 $\begin{bmatrix} +AC \\ +AGT \end{bmatrix}$ $\begin{bmatrix} +NM \\ +OBJ \end{bmatrix}$

'The janitor will open the lock.'

5.b. itata?ob   niya   ang bangka?
     turn over   he   boat
                 $\begin{bmatrix} +AC \\ +AGT \end{bmatrix}$ $\begin{bmatrix} +NM \\ +OBJ \end{bmatrix}$

'He will turn over the boat.'

5.c. tatabasin   niya   ang tela
     cut out   she   cloth
                 $\begin{bmatrix} +AC \\ +AGT \end{bmatrix}$ $\begin{bmatrix} +NM \\ +OBJ \end{bmatrix}$

'She will cut out the cloth.'

In sentences 4.a and 4.b, the verb stem luto? can be marked with either the affix -in or i- indicating the subject [+NM] as having the [+OBJ] case relation. In sentences 5, each verb stem is marked by the only affix it can take to identify its cooccurring subject as having the [+OBJ] case relation. All these show that different affixes may mark one case relation. On the other hand, compare the following:

6.a. ihahatid   niya   ang   bata?   sa   paaralan
     take to   he   child   school
              $\begin{bmatrix} +AC \\ +AGT \end{bmatrix}$ $\begin{bmatrix} +NM \\ +OBJ \end{bmatrix}$ $\begin{bmatrix} +L \\ +LOC \end{bmatrix}$

'He will take the child to school.'

6.b. ibibili   niya   ang   bata?   ng   laru?an
     buy   he   child   toy
              $\begin{bmatrix} +AC \\ +AGT \end{bmatrix}$ $\begin{bmatrix} +NM \\ +BEN \end{bmatrix}$ $\begin{bmatrix} +AC \\ +OBJ \end{bmatrix}$

'He will buy a toy for the child.'

6.c. <u>i</u>sasalok   niya   ng   tubig   ang   timba?
     fetch   he   water   pail

$$\begin{bmatrix} +AC \\ +AGT \end{bmatrix} \qquad \begin{bmatrix} +AC \\ +OBJ \end{bmatrix} \qquad \begin{bmatrix} +NM \\ +INS \end{bmatrix}$$

'He will fetch some water with the pail.'

Note that in sentences 6, a single verbal affix <u>i</u>- is able to mark a nominative [+OBJ], a nominative [+BEN], and a nominative [+INS]. Supporting evidence for the lack of a strict one-to-one correspondence between a verbal affix and a case relation has been given previously (see example 2) and its syntactic representations 2.a and 2.b on pp. 11-12, Chapter 1 where one verb stem takes the same affix but each time marking a different case relation as its subject.

Further on, Blake states that aside from verbal modification, case relations between nouns and verbs may also be indicated by the case forms of those words which have case inflection such as the various pronouns and pronominal adjectives.[3] The cases of words that are uninflected, such as common nouns and personal names, are indicated by the forms of the articles or determiners (labelled Det) placed before them. However, a similar form of overlap and diffusion observed in verbal affixes also obtains in determiners which mark the case relations which occur in non-nominative forms. For example:

7.a. maghihintay   siya   ng   magpeperyodiko   sa   kanto
     wait for   he   newspaperboy

$$\begin{bmatrix} +Det \\ +AC \end{bmatrix} \begin{bmatrix} +N \\ +AC \\ +OBJ \end{bmatrix} \qquad \begin{bmatrix} +Def \\ +L \end{bmatrix} \begin{bmatrix} +N \\ +L \\ +LOC \end{bmatrix}$$

'He will wait for a newspaperboy at the street corner.'

7.b. maghihintay   siya   sa   magpeperyodiko   sa   kanto

$$\begin{bmatrix} +Det \\ +L \end{bmatrix} \begin{bmatrix} +N \\ +L \\ +OBJ \end{bmatrix} \qquad \begin{bmatrix} +Def \\ +L \end{bmatrix} \begin{bmatrix} +N \\ +L \\ +LOC \end{bmatrix}$$

'He will wait for the newspaperboy at the street corner.'

The [+OBJ] actant in 7.a is marked by the accusative determiner
ng while the same actant in 7.b is marked by the locative determiner
sa. The difference suggested by these case forms does not mean a
necessary distinction in the case relation of the noun following
them. The difference in semantic content between the two forms
of [+OBJ] NP's is one of definiteness, [+AC, +OBJ] means indefinite
and [+L, +OBJ], definite.

In the sentences below, the determiner with the accusative case
form feature marks either the non-nominative [+OBJ] or [+AGT].

8.a.　humiram　　ang　　estudyante　　ng　　libro　　sa　　guro?
　　　　borrow　　　　　　student　　　　　book　　　　　teacher

$$\begin{bmatrix} +Det \\ +NM \end{bmatrix} \begin{bmatrix} +N \\ +NM \\ +AGT \end{bmatrix} \quad \begin{bmatrix} +Det \\ +AC \end{bmatrix} \begin{bmatrix} +N \\ +AC \\ +OBJ \end{bmatrix} \quad \begin{bmatrix} +Det \\ +L \end{bmatrix} \begin{bmatrix} +N \\ +L \\ +LOC \end{bmatrix}$$

'The student borrowed a book from the teacher.'

8.b.　hiniram　　ng　　estudyante　　ang　　libro　　sa　　guro?

$$\begin{bmatrix} +Det \\ +AC \end{bmatrix} \begin{bmatrix} +N \\ +AC \\ +AGT \end{bmatrix} \quad \begin{bmatrix} +Det \\ +NM \end{bmatrix} \begin{bmatrix} +N \\ +NM \\ +OBJ \end{bmatrix} \quad \begin{bmatrix} +Det \\ +L \end{bmatrix} \begin{bmatrix} +N \\ +L \\ +LOC \end{bmatrix}$$

'The book was borrowed by the student from the teacher.'

8.c.　hiniraman　ng　　estudyante　　ng　　libro　　ang　　guro?

$$\begin{bmatrix} +Det \\ +AC \end{bmatrix} \begin{bmatrix} +N \\ +AC \\ +AGT \end{bmatrix} \quad \begin{bmatrix} +Det \\ +AC \end{bmatrix} \begin{bmatrix} +N \\ +AC \\ +OBJ \end{bmatrix} \quad \begin{bmatrix} +Det \\ +NM \end{bmatrix} \begin{bmatrix} +N \\ +NM \\ +LOC \end{bmatrix}$$

Lit.:　'The teacher was borrowed-from a book by the student.'

The same determiner can also mark a [+INS] as in:

9.　hiniwa?　　ng　　bata　　ng　　kutsilyo　　ang　　tinapay
　　slice　　　　　child　　　　knife　　　　　　bread

$$\begin{bmatrix} +Det \\ +AC \end{bmatrix} \begin{bmatrix} +N \\ +AC \\ +AGT \end{bmatrix} \quad \begin{bmatrix} +Det \\ +AC \end{bmatrix} \begin{bmatrix} +N \\ +AC \\ +INS \end{bmatrix} \quad \begin{bmatrix} +Det \\ +NM \end{bmatrix} \begin{bmatrix} +N \\ +NM \\ +OBJ \end{bmatrix}$$

'The bread was sliced by the child with a knife."

With these seeming discrepancies in the correspondence between case relations and case forms, no description of Tagalog grammar which treats only the cooccurring CR's or only the cooccurring CF's can ever be adequate. We will, therefore, seek to explain the system formally in light of case frame features referring to both CF's and CR's as well as to some other inherent semantic features that subcategorize the verbs.[4] In this connection, the term voice is adopted from Blake to designate the various forms the verb stem takes to identify the case relation of its subject.[5] The terms case relation and case form are used only for identifying nouns, determiners, and prepositions.

2.3 Case Marking in Tagalog

The three kinds of case-related features that are marked on lexical items are case relation, case form, and case frame features. The verb as center or head of the sentence requires its nominal 'subordinates' to play specified roles and this character of the verb is reflected in its case frame feature specification. The nominal expressions governed by the verb may be either a noun phrase, NP, or a prepositional phrase, PP. The construction NP has a noun, N, as its head with sister determiner, Det, while the PP has two heads, the preposition, P, and the N of its sister NP.[6] By convention, each N in these constructions is marked for CR and CF. Det's and P's are marked only for CF, and their obligatory sister category N carries the CR of the entire nominal expression. There are only a few lexical items belonging to the

class of Det's and P's and each one is permanently marked in the
lexicon for the CF feature that it manifests.

For example:

10.   pumitas   ang   binata?   ng   bulaklak   para
      pick   bachelor   flower   for

$$\begin{bmatrix} +\text{Det} \\ +\text{NM} \end{bmatrix} \begin{bmatrix} +\text{N} \\ +\text{NM} \\ +\text{AGT} \end{bmatrix} \begin{bmatrix} +\text{Det} \\ +\text{AC} \end{bmatrix} \begin{bmatrix} +\text{N} \\ +\text{AC} \\ +\text{OBJ} \end{bmatrix} \begin{bmatrix} +\text{P} \\ +\text{B} \end{bmatrix}$$

              sa   dalaga
                        maiden

$$\begin{bmatrix} +\text{Det} \\ +\text{L} \end{bmatrix} \begin{bmatrix} +\text{N} \\ +\text{L} \\ +\text{BEN} \end{bmatrix}$$

'The bachelor picked a flower for the maiden.'

Interestingly, it will be noted that in Tagalog the object of the
preposition is realized in the locative case form [+L] instead of
the accusative [+AC] as in most languages that lack case inflectional
modification on nouns.

To distinguish a CR feature from a CF feature, we use three
capital letters representing the abbreviation of the CR and one or
two capital letters representing the CF. Using two letters, instead
of adhering to only one, to symbolize CF's avoids confusing the
feature with other identical symbols representing a different
feature, e.g., if N is used for the nominative CF and at the same
time it is used for the category of nouns. These features like all
others are enclosed in square brackets.

For marking case frame features on verbs (V), we follow the
notation of the form [+__[+X]], [-__[+X]], or [+__([+X])] to indicate
contextual features. If [+X], which may be a CR, a CF or both, is
the case feature environment of the V, the first case frame states

that a V must occur before this specified case feature; the second
means it cannot occur before that case feature; and the third means
that it may or may not be followed by that case feature. The blank
shows positional order and if the V requires that it occur after the
case feature, then the specification is [+[+X]__]. On the other
hand, if there is no requirement on order, the feature may be stated
simply as [+[X]] which is interpreted as 'must occur either before
or after [+X].' The simpler notation without the blank can still
be used despite cases where a strict order is required if this
requirement is stated in the form of a redundancy rule. For
Tagalog, a RR applying to verbs will state, unless otherwise marked,
that [+[+X]] is always to be interpreted as [+__[+X]]. For N's,
Det's, or P's, the proper positional environment may be similarly
marked.

One other type of notation used here is called double negative
marking. A verb which is marked [-[+NM, -OBJ]] is interpreted as
having the contextual feature of a nominative but which can only be
realized by an objective case relation. Should the verb cooccur with
a nominative manifesting a case relation other than an objective,
then the sentence becomes ungrammatical. If the verb is marked
[-[-AC, +AGT]], it means that its cooccurring agentive case relation
can be realized only in the accusative case form. This system of
negative marking is economical because it does not only indicate
the required cooccurring feature but also specifies the corresponding
constraint on cooccurrence.

The category V is not the only one that requires case frame

specifications. Prepositions as heads of PP's are marked not only
for case form which indicates the case form of the entire phrase,
but also for case relations they require of their sister NP's.
In the above example, the preposition para 'for' has to include
[+[+BEN]] in its matrix of features. Since the cooccurring case
form of the N following a P is predictable in the locative case
form, except when P is in the comitative case from [+C], a redundancy
rule such as follows will simplify the case feature specifications
of P's in the lexical entry:

$$\text{RR:} \quad \begin{bmatrix} +P \\ -C \end{bmatrix} \rightarrow [-[-L]]$$

Stated negatively, the rule means that a preposition which is not
in the comitative case form cannot occur with a specified case
feature other than a locative case form. With this rule, the entry
for para only contains [+P, +B, +[+BEN]]. An entry with these
kinds of features may be further simplified by eliminating the
contextual feature if, in the language, it is the case that for
all P's marked with a particular case form they cooccur only with
a single corresponding case relation. It may be mentioned that
a few prepositions permit a sentence S after them instead of a NP.
In such a construction, the S is not marked for case since, by
definition, only N's carry case relations.

2.4 Case Relations

The CR's set up in this study are only those required by a
verbal predicate V. In positing them for Tagalog, two guidelines
have been observed: a) each distinctive role occurs only once in

each sentence (Fillmore, 1971:38), and b) two instances of the same case relation can occur in the same simple sentence only if they are coreferential or conjoined (Starosta, 1973b:136). Some of these cases are required obligatorily by the verb, others only optionally. This will become evident in the subcategorization and redundancy rules that assign case frame features.

The CR's set up by Ramos (1974:20, 34) may be compared with those in this study as listed below.

CR's in Ramos:

(a) Inherent   (b) Non-inherent

   1. agentive (A)   1. instrumental (I)

   2. objective (O)   2. benefactive (B)

   3. directional (Dir)   3. affected (Af)

   4. locative (L)

   5. instrumental (I)

CR's in this study:

   1. Objective (OBJ)

   2. Agentive (AGT)

   3. Dative (DAT)

   4. Locative (LOC)

   5. Instrumental (INS)

   6. Benefactive (BEN)

   7. Reason (RSN)

   8. Comitative (COM)

In this analysis, Ramos' directional and locative cases fall together under a single case relation, the locative; her inherent and non-inherent instrumental case can also be mentioned once with certain collocational restrictions stated in the verb; her afected case is identified here as the Dative which is required by other verbs not covered in her study. In addition to these changes and the other cases shared by both studies, two other CR's are introduced, the Reason and the Comitative case relations which will be shown as CR's cooccurring with Tagalog verbs.

2.4.1 Objective Case Relation [+OBJ]

The objective case relation is "the semantically most neutral case, the case of anything representable by a noun whose role in the action or state identified by the verb is identified by the semantic interpretation of the verb itself" (Fillmore, 1968:25). Fillmore further restricts the concept to things which are affected by the action or state identified by the verb. This definition is expanded here to include animate beings, things resulting from the action or state, and even those indirectly involved or remaining unchanged in the course of the action. The objective case relation is basic in that if a verb takes any CR at all, it takes at least a [+OBJ]. If it occurs by itself, it takes the nominative case form; if it cooccurs with a locative, a dative, an agentive or an instru= mental, it can be realized in either the nominative or the accusative case form. With an instrumental case relation and without an agentive, however, the [+OBJ] is always manifested in the nominative case form. Certain verbs which cooccur with an objective and an agentive case relation require a third actant, which is either a locative, a dative or a comitative case relation, the last two being required only by derived verb forms under secondary verb subcategories. The following examples show some of these occurrences:

11. gumalaw   ang   bata?
    move   child
$$\begin{bmatrix} +NM \\ +OBJ \end{bmatrix}$$

'The child moved.'

12. gumawa? si Angel ng tugtugin
    make   music piece
$$\begin{bmatrix} +NM \\ +OBJ \end{bmatrix} \qquad \begin{bmatrix} +AC \\ +OBJ \end{bmatrix}$$

'Angel composed a music piece.'

13. natapon ang sabaw sa sahig
    spill   soup   floor
$$\begin{bmatrix} +NM \\ +OBJ \end{bmatrix} \qquad \begin{bmatrix} +L \\ +LOC \end{bmatrix}$$

'The soup got spilled on the floor.'

14. tinupok ng malaking sunog ang sambayanan
    burn   big   fire   whole town
$$\begin{bmatrix} +AC \\ +INS \end{bmatrix} \qquad \begin{bmatrix} +NM \\ +OBJ \end{bmatrix}$$

'The big fire burned down the whole town.'

Fillmore's restriction that only a single case relation can occur in every simple sentence necessitates his positing two distinct cases, namely, Objective and Factitive (1968:25), the latter being absorbed into the Goal case (1971:42). The difference is that the Objective refers to the thing affected whereas the Goal is that which results from the action or state identified by the verb. An object of result or Goal case cooccurs with creative verbs such as gawa? 'make', tahi? 'sew', sulat 'write', tayo? 'build' while an Objective cooccurs with non-creative verbs. Since the distinction between these two cases can be predicted by the semantic features, say [±create], of the verb, then both can be subsumed under one case relation. A problem arises when a creative verb occurs with apparently two objective cases in the same sentence, one as a result and the other as a source, as in:

15. gumawaʔ ang nanay   ng punda   sa tela-ng natira
    make   mother   pillowcase   cloth   left
         $\begin{bmatrix} +NM \\ +AGT \end{bmatrix}$ $\begin{bmatrix} +AC \\ +OBJ \end{bmatrix}$ $\begin{bmatrix} +L \\ +OBJ \end{bmatrix}$

'Mother made a pillowcase out of the left-over piece of cloth.'

Starosta (1973a:135-37) proposes to deal with this problem by applying the criterion of coreference. This principle allows both the result and source actants to be marked by the same case relation and occur in the same simple sentence if the referent of one actant is identical to or included in the referent of the other. This suggests that there are verbs that permit the optional cooccurrence of an actant which is coreferential to one that is required by the verbs. The same principle can be shown to account for relations other than source-result. For instance, Fillmore's sentence 'I hit him on the leg' (1970:126) is translated as follows:

16.a. hinampas ko   siya sa binti?
      hit   I   he   leg
           $\begin{bmatrix} +AC \\ +AGT \end{bmatrix}$ $\begin{bmatrix} +NM \\ +OBJ \end{bmatrix}$ $\begin{bmatrix} +L \\ +OBJ \end{bmatrix}$

'I hit him on the leg.'

In this sentence, the actant <u>binti?</u> marked by the locative case form indicates the specific location of <u>hitting</u> done on the more general object <u>siya</u> marked by the nominative case form. Semantically, logically and pragmatically one cannot hit <u>binti?</u> without also hitting

<u>siya</u> since the former is contained in or part of the latter. The
coreferentiality that can be alluded to here expresses the relation
between a possessor and an inalienably possessed actant. To attest to
this relation, the same verb in sentence 16.a can cooccur with the
[+OBJ] <u>binti?</u> realized in the nominative case form:

16.b.　hinampas　ko　ang　binti?　niya
　　　　hit　　　　I　　　　leg　　　his
　　　　　　　　　　　　　　　$\begin{bmatrix} +NM \\ +OBJ \end{bmatrix}$

　　　'I hit his leg.'

In 16.b, the relation possessor-possessed is marked more directly by
the use of the possessive pronoun <u>niya</u>, which will be marked with
[+DAT] in the accusative case form according to Fillmore's analysis
of possessive N's (1968:49-50). It will be noted that this possessive
pronoun is an attribute of the [+OBJ] noun and not a sister of the
verb, hence, it is not marked here with case features.

　　　Besides the occurrence of a [+OBJ] in the locative case form in
instances such as 16.a, there is also a class of verbs which expresses
its [+OBJ] as [+L] when the cooccurring [+AGT] is [+NM]. For example
(cf. the German sentence 1.b, p. 21, which is the exact analogue of 17):

17.　tumulong　siya　sa　mga　nasunugan
　　　help　　　　he　　　　　　fire-victims
　　　　　　　　$\begin{bmatrix} +NM \\ +AGT \end{bmatrix}$　　　$\begin{bmatrix} +L \\ +OBJ \end{bmatrix}$

　　　'He helped the fire-victims.'

The other occurrence of a [+L, +OBJ] as exemplified in 7.b (see p. 27)
indicates definiteness in contrast to indefiniteness marked by [+AC].
It may be noted that a similar situation obtains in Spanish where a
personal or personalized direct object of a verb, except for the verb

tener 'have', is marked by <u>a</u> which can be related to the preposition
<u>a</u> 'to'.

In the preceding examples, we have NP's being marked [+OBJ] with
either the more common [+AC] or the [+L] case form. However, there are
also PP's which contract an objective case relation when cooccurring
with what may be identified as verbs of communication. Some of the
words which are analyzed as prepositions (Institute of National
Language, 1950:416-7) or as introducers (Otanes, 1966:132-3) are
<u>tungkol, hinggil</u> 'about', <u>ukol</u> 'with regard to', and <u>laban</u> 'against'.
They introduce a following [+OBJ] actant in the [+L] form, and they
may be marked accusative [+AC]. Thus, Otanes' sentence (1966:138) may
be given the following feature specifications:

18. nag?usap tungkol sa eleksyon ang mga lalaki
    talk about election men
$$\begin{bmatrix} +P \\ +AC \end{bmatrix} \qquad \begin{bmatrix} +L \\ +OBJ \end{bmatrix} \qquad \begin{bmatrix} +NM \\ +AGT \end{bmatrix}$$

'The men talked about the election.'

Words classified as P such as <u>tungkol</u> in sentence 18 present two
problems: (a) The PP above may also occur as a NP in the accusative
case form as follows:

18.a. nag?usap ng tungkol sa eleksyon ang mga lalaki
$$\begin{bmatrix} +AC \\ +OBJ \\ +[+OBJ] \end{bmatrix} \qquad \begin{bmatrix} +L \\ +OBJ \end{bmatrix} \qquad \begin{bmatrix} +NM \\ +AGT \end{bmatrix}$$

in which <u>tungkol</u> is a noun which requires a related NP attribute.
The two phrases may be contrasted more vividly in the following tree
diagrams:

(a) <u>as PP</u>

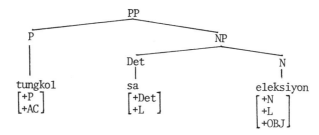

(b) <u>as NP</u>

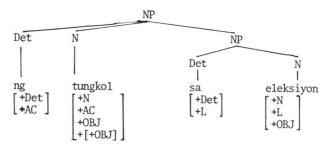

The complex NP analysis seems tenable especially when we compare it with similar NP's such as <u>sa pamamagitan ng palakol</u> 'by means of an ax', which, incidentally, is a 'true' NP in that it never occurs without the determiner, and <u>ang asawa ng guro?</u> 'the spouse of the teacher' in which the head N's require a following attributive NP.

(b) Unlike other PP's as in sentence 10 (see p. 30), this type of PP in question may occur in full in the nominative case form:

18.b. pinag?usapan ng mga lalaki ang tungkol sa eleksyon

'The matter on elections was discussed by the men.'

which strongly supports the NP analysis. In contrast, the same verb in sentence 10 never allows the cooccurrence of the P when the [+BEN] is in the nominative case form:[7]

10.a *ipinitas ng binata? ng bulaklak ang para sa dalaga
     pick   bachelor   flower   for   maiden

In view of the evidence supporting a N analysis instead of a P
for the words concerned, the explanation could be that these words are
derived P's from original N's and both forms exist under separate
categories. This is accomplished through a general process of deriving
P's from certain N's which may be called a preposition DR. This
particular type of word derivation is well attested to in Indo-
European languages.

2.4.2 Agentive Case Relation [+AGT]

By Fillmore's definition, the agentive case relation is "the
typically animate perceived instigator of the action identified by
the verb" (1968:24). In a lexicase grammar, the presence of an
agentive case relation is assumed to require a cooccurring objective
case relation. In addition, certain classes of verbs also require
the cooccurrence of a locative, a dative, or a comitative case
relation. This means, then, that there are at least two case
relations cooccurring when a [+AGT] is present. In general, the
presence of a [+AGT] also allows the potential occurrence of an
instrumental, a benefactive, or a reason case relation. Of these
peripheral cases, the instrumental case can serve as a condition for
distinguishing the agentive case relation from the objective or
dative which do not normally cooccur with an instrumental case relation.

The case forms in which the [+AGT] may be realized are either
the accusative [+AC] or the nominative [+NM]. The basis for selecting
one form over the other is not determined by a kind of hierarchy based

on cooccurring actants (see Fillmore, 1968:33). The restriction on
the selection of subject depends on the classification of the verb.
One class may prohibit a particular cooccurring case relation from
being realized in the nominative case form whereas another class of
an identical case frame may allow the same case relation to be either
subject or non-subject. In view of this, the definitions commonly
associated with the labels accusative or ergative language do not
hold for Tagalog as a whole, but rather for individual verb classes.

The following examples illustrate some occurrences of the
agentive case relation:

19. naghanda? si Irma ng isang programa para sa mga
    prepare   one   program   for
             [+NM]   [+AC]   [+B]
             [+AGT]   [+OBJ]

    bisita **niya**
    guest her
    [+L]
    [+BEN]

    'Irma prepared a program for her guests.'

20. gagawaran ng hukom ang bilanggo? ng parusa bukas
    lay on   judge   prisoner   sentence tomorrow
              [+AC]   [+NM]   [+AC]
              [+AGT]   [+LOC]   [+OBJ]

    'The prisoner will be given a sentence by the judge tomorrow.'

In comparison with the agentive case relation in Ramos
(1974:20-23), the present analysis does not see the necessity of
subcategorizing this case relation, or any case relation for that
matter, into the classes [+undergoer], [-undergoer, +goal], and
[-undergoer, -goal] which are designated as subcase features. In
her semantic feature analysis of the verbs, the classes of verbs

specified with the features [-ext], [+ext, -cf], and [+ext, +cf]
imply the three classes of cooccurring [+AGT], respectively. Since
the semantic features on the verb already provide the semantic
interpretation of its cooccurring actant or actants, it would be
redundant to set up two separate sets of features each implying the
other. It suffices to identify only those features that subcategorize
the verbs.

2.4.3 Locative Case Relation [+LOC]

As defined by Fillmore (1968:25), the locative case relation
identifies the location or spatial orientation of the state or action
identified by the verb. He also points out that locational and
directional elements do not contrast. In Tagalog, there is evidence
that these two elements are complements and their differences can
be determined by the character of the associated verb. Hence, we
can distinguish locational and directional (source or goal) uses of
the locative case depending on verb class and case form. (See also
Anderson,1971:100-18 .)

By some semantic features on the verb, we can determine whether
the locative case relation required by the verb is a directional
or a non-directional which may be simply a locational, and if it is
the former, whether it is a destination or a point of origin. This
characteristic may be captured by the following subcategorization
and redundancy rules:

SR-i: [+V]   ⟶   [±loc]

SR-ii: [+loc] ⟶ $\begin{bmatrix} ±strict \\ ±dir \end{bmatrix}$

RR-i: [+strict] ⟶   [+[LOC]]

RR-ii: [-strict] ⟶   [+([+LOC])]

SR-iii: [+dir]   ⟶   [±goal]

The first rule means that a verb may or may not be a locative
verb. By SR-ii, a locative verb may be either strict or non-strict
and directional or non-directional. A [+strict] verb, by RR-i,
requires the cooccurrence of a [+LOC] actant whereas a [-strict], by
RR-ii, permits the cooccurring LOC to be manifested optionally.
SR-iii states that directional verbs are further subclassified into
those which designate the cooccurring or the implied [+LOC] as
either a goal or a non-goal, which means source. With these inherent
semantic features identifying the meaning of the locative verb and
its cooccurring locative actant, Tagalog finds no need for using
prepositions, say as in English, to designate in, on, into, onto, to,
from, at, etc. It can function adequately using only its single
locative determiner sa, since the verb already specifies the
information that is otherwise contained in the preposition. Thus,
locative verbs in Tagalog can be given a more accurate translation
by indicating its associated preposition, e.g., punta 'go-to',
alis 'depart-from', tira 'reside-in/at'. Indeed, these features
explain the seeming lack of prepositions in the language. However,
Tagalog is not completely devoid of prepositions. In fact, there are
a few indicating direction which are available if one desires to be

more specific, e.g., mula?, buhat, galing which can be equated with
'from' and patungo or tungo, papunta, hanggang, indicating 'to'
broadly. Another device used to specify locations is complex locative
noun phrases, e.g., sa ibabaw ng mesa 'on top of the table'.

In terms of distinguishing between what Fillmore (1968:26ff.)
calls 'optional' and 'obligatory' locative expressions, it is useful
to consider the distinctions made by Platt (1971:30-33) among inner,
outer, and far outer locatives. Platt defines "an inner Locative as
a Locative which is obligatory (as with put) and/or directional (as
in the case of: Tom walked to town): Outer Locatives... as Locatives
optionally co-occurring with certain predicate fillers and with the
Agentive..." A far outer Locative, on the other hand, is one which
may cooccur with any verb and, thus, "plays no part in the selection
of verbs". The following examples from Platt identify these
three 'degrees of location', respectively:

a. John keeps his car in the garage.

b. John washes his car in the garage.

c. In that town, people know their neighbors.

Another criterion which he identifies as distinguishing the first
two types of location has to do with the location of the cooccurring
Agent. He states that with an inner locative, the Agent is usually
located at the specified location.

In this study, the terms inner and outer locative have been
adopted with a modification of certain conditions. An inner locative
is one that is required by the verb to indicate the location of the
[+OBJ] and not necessarily that of the [+AGT]. It may be obligatorily

or optionally manifested, and even if it is not expressed overtly, it is implied in the lexical content of the verb. Kullavanijaya (1974:56) marks this distinction by the features [+strict], where the inner [+LOC] must be grammatically expressed (see RR-i), and [-strict], where the inner [+LOC] may not be overtly present (see RR-ii). By these definitions, the three subcategories of locative verbs identified above by the features [+goal], [-goal] and [-dir] are all inner locative verbs and are further specified as [+strict] or [-strict].[8] Some examples which illustrate the various classes of verbs that take inner locatives are as follows:

21. inilagay   niya   ang mga bulaklak sa mesa
    put   she   flower   table
    $\begin{bmatrix} +V \\ +goal \\ +strict \end{bmatrix}$ $\begin{bmatrix} +AC \\ +AGT \end{bmatrix}$ $\begin{bmatrix} +NM \\ +OBJ \end{bmatrix}$ $\begin{bmatrix} +L \\ +LOC \end{bmatrix}$

    'She put the flowers on the table.'

22. itatapon   niya   ang basura (sa hukay)
    throw   he   garbage   pit
    $\begin{bmatrix} +V \\ +goal \\ -strict \end{bmatrix}$ $\begin{bmatrix} +AC \\ +AGT \end{bmatrix}$ $\begin{bmatrix} +NM \\ +OBJ \end{bmatrix}$ $\begin{bmatrix} +L \\ +LOC \end{bmatrix}$

    'He will throw away the garbage (in the pit).'

23. nanggaling siya sa ibang bansa?
    come from   he   other country
    $\begin{bmatrix} +V \\ -goal \\ +strict \end{bmatrix}$ $\begin{bmatrix} +NM \\ +OBJ \end{bmatrix}$ $\begin{bmatrix} +L \\ +LOC \end{bmatrix}$

    'He came from a foreign country.'

24. humingi?   siya ng payo   (sa guro?)
    ask for   she   advice   teacher
    $\begin{bmatrix} +V \\ -goal \\ -strict \end{bmatrix}$ $\begin{bmatrix} +NM \\ +AGT \end{bmatrix}$ $\begin{bmatrix} +AC \\ +OBJ \end{bmatrix}$ $\begin{bmatrix} +L \\ +LOC \end{bmatrix}$

    'She asked for advice (from the teacher).'

25. tumira   sila   sa bahay namin
    reside   they   house our
    $\begin{bmatrix} +V \\ -dir \\ +strict \end{bmatrix}$ $\begin{bmatrix} +NM \\ +OBJ \end{bmatrix}$ $\begin{bmatrix} +L \\ +LOC \end{bmatrix}$

'They lived in our house.'

On the other hand, an outer locative expresses the location of
the entire action. It is one which can be selected by any verb,
either a locative or a non-locative verb. It is always optional.
For example:

26. kuma?in sila ng hapunan (sa bagong restawrang
    eat   they   dinner   new   restaurant
    $\begin{bmatrix} +V \\ -loc \end{bmatrix}$ $\begin{bmatrix} +NM \\ +AGT \end{bmatrix}$ $\begin{bmatrix} +AC \\ +OBJ \end{bmatrix}$ $\begin{bmatrix} +L \\ +LOC \end{bmatrix}$

    ito) kagabi
    this last night

'They ate dinner at this new restaurant last night.'

27. sumakay   sila sa 'cable car' (sa San Francisco)
    ride   they
    $\begin{bmatrix} +V \\ -dir \\ +strict \end{bmatrix}$ $\begin{bmatrix} +NM \\ +OBJ \end{bmatrix}$ $\begin{bmatrix} +L \\ +LOC \end{bmatrix}$ $\begin{bmatrix} +L \\ +LOC \end{bmatrix}$

'They rode on the cable car in San Francisco.'

28. nagluto? siya ng litson sa kawali? (sa kusina?)
    cook   he   roast   frying pan   kitchen
    $\begin{bmatrix} +V \\ -dir \\ -strict \end{bmatrix}$ $\begin{bmatrix} +NM \\ +AGT \end{bmatrix}$ $\begin{bmatrix} +AC \\ +OBJ \end{bmatrix}$ $\begin{bmatrix} +L \\ +LOC \end{bmatrix}$ $\begin{bmatrix} +L \\ +LOC \end{bmatrix}$

'He cooked a roast in the frying pan in the kitchen.'

Needless to say, this type of locative is not relevant to the
subcategorization of verbs, and, hence, it is not marked as a feature
of the verb. The locative feature on the verb, then, refers only
to inner locatives. When cooccurring with outer locatives, inner
locatives can be distinguished by being closer to the verb in

terms of position. Where only one locative actant is overtly manifested, it is always subject to either inner or outer locative interpretation.

There are some interesting and significant observations which can be made of locative actants in relation to their cooccurring verb forms as well as to other cooccurring actants, namely:

(a) The inner locative actant of strict or non-strict locative verbs can occur in the nominative case form marked on the verb by an affix different from that which requires a [+AGT] or a [+OBJ] subject. Note the difference in verbal affixes in the following sentences which correspond to those in sentences 21 to 25:

21.a. linagyan niya ng mga bulaklak ang mesa
       put   she   flowers   table

$$\begin{bmatrix} +V \\ +goal \\ +strict \end{bmatrix} \quad \begin{bmatrix} +AC \\ +AGT \end{bmatrix} \quad \begin{bmatrix} +AC \\ +OBJ \end{bmatrix} \quad \begin{bmatrix} +NM \\ +LOC \end{bmatrix}$$

Lit.: 'The table was laid-on some flowers by her.'

22.a. tatapunan niya ng basura ang hukay
       throw   she   garbage   pit

$$\begin{bmatrix} +V \\ +goal \\ -strict \end{bmatrix} \quad \begin{bmatrix} +AC \\ +AGT \end{bmatrix} \quad \begin{bmatrix} +AC \\ +OBJ \end{bmatrix} \quad \begin{bmatrix} +NM \\ +LOC \end{bmatrix}$$

Lit.: 'The pit will be thrown-into some garbage by her.'

23.a. pinanggalingan na niya ang iba't ibang bansa?
       come from   he   other   country

$$\begin{bmatrix} +V \\ +goal \\ +strict \end{bmatrix} \quad \begin{bmatrix} +AC \\ +OBJ \end{bmatrix} \quad \begin{bmatrix} +NM \\ +LOC \end{bmatrix}$$

Lit.: 'Other countries have been traveled/visited by him.'

24.a. hiningi?an niya ng payo ang guro?
       ask for   she   advice   teacher

$$\begin{bmatrix} +V \\ -goal \\ -strict \end{bmatrix} \quad \begin{bmatrix} +AC \\ +AGT \end{bmatrix} \quad \begin{bmatrix} +AC \\ +OBJ \end{bmatrix} \quad \begin{bmatrix} +NM \\ +LOC \end{bmatrix}$$

Lit.: 'The teacher was asked for some advice by her.'

25.a. tinirahan   nila ang bahay namin
      reside   they   house our
      ⎡+V   ⎤   ⎡+AC ⎤   ⎡+NM ⎤
      ⎢-dir   ⎥   ⎣+OBJ⎦   ⎣+LOC⎦
      ⎣+strict ⎦

Lit.: 'Our house was lived in by them.'

The sentences express what action is done on the [+LOC] subject or

what event ensues from it. It may be mentioned that if obligatory

occurrence of the [+LOC] is made the criterion for identifying a

locative case, we cannot account for the many instances of optionally

cooccurring inner locatives.

(b) Outer locatives generally occur in the locative case form

and usually after the inner locative, if any occurs. However, there

are instances where they can appear in the nominative with a

particular derived verb form which means approximately 'V-ing place

or place for V-ing'. They are usually prefixed with the derivational

affix pag-. For example:

26.a. kina?inan   nila ng hapunan ang bagong restawrang
      eat   they   dinner   new   restaurant
      ⎡+V   ⎤   ⎡+AC ⎤   ⎡+AC ⎤   ⎡+NM ⎤
      ⎢+Derv   ⎥   ⎣+AGT⎦   ⎣+OBJ⎦   ⎣+LOC⎦
      ⎣-[+NM, -LOC]⎦

      ito   kagabi
      this last night

Lit.: 'This new restaurant was eaten dinner at by them last night.'

29.   pinagpahingahan niya   ang lilim ng punong-kahoy
      rest   he   shade   tree
      ⎡+V   ⎤   ⎡+AC ⎤   ⎡+NM ⎤
      ⎢+Derv   ⎥   ⎣+OBJ⎦   ⎣+LOC⎦
      ⎣-[+NM, -LOC]⎦

      'He rested in the shade of the tree.'
Lit.: 'The shade of the tree was where he rested.'

30. pinagkumpunihan niya ng bisikleta ang garahe ni Pedro
    repair   he   bicycle   garage
    $\begin{bmatrix} +V \\ +Derv \\ -[+NM, -LOC] \end{bmatrix}$ $\begin{bmatrix} +AC \\ +AGT \end{bmatrix}$ $\begin{bmatrix} +AC \\ +OBJ \end{bmatrix}$ $\begin{bmatrix} +NM \\ +LOC \end{bmatrix}$

'He repaired a bicycle in Pedro's garage.'

The verbs in the above examples come from non-locative verbs

ka?in 'eat', pahinga 'rest' and kumpuni 'repair', respectively.

Some locative verbs also manifest similar derived verb forms, but

others do not. For example:

31. pinangpintahan niya ng larawan sa 'canvas'
    paint   he   picture
    $\begin{bmatrix} +V \\ +Derv \\ -[+NM, -LOC] \end{bmatrix}$ $\begin{bmatrix} +AC \\ +AGT \end{bmatrix}$ $\begin{bmatrix} +AC \\ +OBJ \end{bmatrix}$ $\begin{bmatrix} +L \\ +LOC \end{bmatrix}$

    ang 'den' ng tatay
    $\begin{bmatrix} +NM \\ +LOC \end{bmatrix}$

'He painted the picture on canvas in father's den.'

27.a. *sinakyan   nila sa 'cable car' ang San Francisco
      *pinagsakyan

The verb form sinakyan cooccurs only with an inner locative subject

and pinagsakyan with an inner locative subject and a [+AGT]. Note

that 27.a does not have an inner locative subject or a cooccurring AGT.

(c) Directional verbs marked either [+goal] or [-goal] have

the option to cooccur with another inner locative actant which

expresses the point of origin of a [+goal] verb or the destination of

a [-goal]. The restriction is for this locative actant to be

expressed as a prepositional phrase with its preposition specifying

a directional feature opposite that of the directional feature of

the verb. This may be expressed in the form of the following negatively stated redundancy rule:

RR: [αgoal] ⟶ $\left[\begin{bmatrix} +P \\ +L \\ \alpha goal \\ -[+[+LOC]] \end{bmatrix}\right]$

For example:

32. pumunta siya sa aklatan mula? sa klase
    go-to   he   library from   class

$\begin{bmatrix} +goal \\ +strict \end{bmatrix}$ $\begin{bmatrix} +NM \\ +OBJ \end{bmatrix}$ $\begin{bmatrix} +L \\ +LOC \end{bmatrix}$ $\begin{bmatrix} +P \\ +L \\ -goal \\ +[+LOC] \end{bmatrix}$ $\begin{bmatrix} +L \\ +LOC \end{bmatrix}$

'He went to the library from class.'

33. umalis siya (sa bahay) patungo sa tindahan
    leave he   house   towards   store

$\begin{bmatrix} -goal \\ -strict \end{bmatrix}$ $\begin{bmatrix} +NM \\ +OBJ \end{bmatrix}$ $\begin{bmatrix} +L \\ +LOC \end{bmatrix}$ $\begin{bmatrix} +P \\ +L \\ +goal \\ +[+LOC] \end{bmatrix}$ $\begin{bmatrix} +L \\ +LOC \end{bmatrix}$

'He left (the house) for/towards the store.'

When the directional verb is marked [-strict] and the locative
noun phrase is not expressed overtly, the optional locative
prepositional phrase may still cooccur with the verb. The preposition
in this phrase must obligatorily occur, otherwise, the actant receives
the interpretation as provided by the directional feature on the
verb. For instance, sentence 33 has a [-strict] feature, and as such
the locative phrase sa bahay may be absent.

    33.a. umalis siya patungo sa tindahan

        'He left for/in the direction of the store.'

If the prepositional phrase is not marked by the preposition patungo
'to, toward', the noun phrase sa tindahan will be interpreted as
the place of origin. Hence, observe the following sentence:

33.b. umalis siya sa tindahan

'He left the store.'

Similarly, compare the following pair of sentences with a verb marked [+goal, -strict]:

34.a. dumating siya sa paaralan ng alas siyete
      arrive   he   school   seven o'clock
$\begin{bmatrix} +goal \\ -strict \end{bmatrix}$ $\begin{bmatrix} +NM \\ +OBJ \end{bmatrix}$ $\begin{bmatrix} +L \\ +LOC \end{bmatrix}$

'He arrived in school at seven o'clock.'

34.b. dumating siya galing sa paaralan ng alas siyete
                     from
$\begin{bmatrix} +goal \\ -strict \end{bmatrix}$ $\begin{bmatrix} +P \\ +L \\ -goal \end{bmatrix}$

'He arrived from school at seven o'clock.'

The above cooccurrence restrictions show the relevance of the features [+goal] and [-goal] specified in both verbs and prepositions.

(d) By postulating one locative case relation and some semantic features which give the [+LOC] a proper interpretation, we can capture the relations and generalities expressed by what others have identified separately as directional and locative cases (Ramos, 1974:33).

(e) The close connection between what in other languages would be considered the [+DAT] actant cooccurring with what is commonly called ditransitive verbs and the [+LOC] with what is commonly identified as locative verbs is quite striking in Tagalog. Both actants indicate either the goal or the source of the [+OBJ] referent involved in the ditransitive or locative verb. Consider, for instance, the parallels between ditransitive and locative verbs which can be subclassified into [+goal] and [-goal] such as follows:

Ditransitive verbs:		Locative verbs:	
[+goal]	[-goal]	[+goal]	[-goal]
bigay 'give'	kuha 'take'	lagay 'put'	pitas 'pick'
alay 'offer'	hiram 'borrow'	tapon 'throw'	alis 'remove'
abot 'hand over'	bili 'buy'	sabit 'hang'	bunot 'extract'

It has been found that there are no discernible syntactic or semantic differences between the supposed [+DAT] and the [+LOC] actant cooccurring with the verbs listed above. Hence, the four types of verbs have been classified here into [+goal] and [-goal] verbs with the actant representing the goal or the source of a cooccurring [+OBJ] identified as the [+LOC] actant.[9] Supporting evidences for this analysis are: (a) the supposed [+DAT] of ditransitive verbs and the [+LOC] of locative verbs, with a cooccurring [+AGT], are realized in the same non-nominative case form, the locative [+L]:[10]

(b) the verbal affix which marks the supposed [+DAT] and the [+LOC] as being realized in the nominative case form is the same affix -an. With causative verbs, however, a distinct contrast exists between the affix that marks what is identified here as [+DAT] and that which marks the [+LOC] or the supposed [+DAT] of ditransitive verbs as subject. Compare the following examples of non-causative [+goal] ditransitive and locative verbs, which are both marked here as taking a [+LOC], with corresponding causative verbs where the [+DAT] means the actant that is ordered to perform the action indicated by the causative verb:

35. binigyan niya si Rosa ng regalo
    give   he   present
    $\begin{bmatrix} +V \\ +goal \end{bmatrix}$ $\begin{bmatrix} +AC \\ +AGT \end{bmatrix}$ $\begin{bmatrix} +NM \\ +LOC \end{bmatrix}$ $\begin{bmatrix} +AC \\ +OBJ \end{bmatrix}$

    'Rosa was given a present by him.'

36. linagyan niya ang bata? ng laso
    put   she   child   ribbon
    $\begin{bmatrix} +V \\ +goal \end{bmatrix}$ $\begin{bmatrix} +AC \\ +AGT \end{bmatrix}$ $\begin{bmatrix} +NM \\ +LOC \end{bmatrix}$ $\begin{bmatrix} +AC \\ +OBJ \end{bmatrix}$

    'She put a ribbon on the child.'

35.a. papagbibigayin niya si Buddy ng regalo kay Rosa
      give   he   gift
      $\begin{bmatrix} +V \\ +caus \end{bmatrix}$ $\begin{bmatrix} +AC \\ +AGT \end{bmatrix}$ $\begin{bmatrix} +NM \\ +DAT \end{bmatrix}$ $\begin{bmatrix} +AC \\ +OBJ \end{bmatrix}$ $\begin{bmatrix} +L \\ +LOC \end{bmatrix}$

      'Buddy will be asked by him to give a gift to Rosa.'

36.a. papaglalagayin niya si Mel ng laso sa bata?
      put   she   ribbon child
      $\begin{bmatrix} +V \\ +caus \end{bmatrix}$ $\begin{bmatrix} +AC \\ +AGT \end{bmatrix}$ $\begin{bmatrix} +NM \\ +DAT \end{bmatrix}$ $\begin{bmatrix} +AC \\ +OBJ \end{bmatrix}$ $\begin{bmatrix} +L \\ +LOC \end{bmatrix}$

      'Mel will be asked by her to put a ribbon on the child.'

35.b. pabibigyan niya kay Buddy ng regalo si Rosa
      give
      $\begin{bmatrix} +V \\ +caus \end{bmatrix}$ $\begin{bmatrix} +AC \\ +AGT \end{bmatrix}$ $\begin{bmatrix} +L \\ +DAT \end{bmatrix}$ $\begin{bmatrix} +AC \\ +OBJ \end{bmatrix}$ $\begin{bmatrix} +NM \\ +LOC \end{bmatrix}$

      'Buddy will be asked by him to give a gift to Rosa.'

36.b. palalagyan niya kay Mel ng laso ang bata?
      put
      $\begin{bmatrix} +V \\ +caus \end{bmatrix}$ $\begin{bmatrix} +AC \\ +AGT \end{bmatrix}$ $\begin{bmatrix} +L \\ +DAT \end{bmatrix}$ $\begin{bmatrix} +AC \\ +OBJ \end{bmatrix}$ $\begin{bmatrix} +NM \\ +LOC \end{bmatrix}$

      'Mel will be asked by her to put a ribbon on the child.'

If such fusion of ditransitive and locative verb classes is taken, we arrive at two classes of what may be labelled location verbs, namely, [+goal] and [-goal], with cooccurring [+OBJ], [+AGT] and [+LOC] actants. These classes are comparable with the corresponding

classes of locomotion verbs which are non-agentive.[11] For example,
the following verbs express the same [+goal] and [-goal] features:

Locomotion verbs:

[+goal]	[-goal]
punta 'go to'	alis 'leave from'
pasok 'enter'	labas 'get out of'
akyat 'climb to'	hiwalay 'dissociate one's self from'

Both location and locomotion verbs are locative directional verbs.

2.4.4 Dative Case Relation [+DAT]

The [+DAT] actant in this study is the same as Fillmore's
Experiencer case, the animate being affected by a psychological event
or mental state expressed by the verb (1971:42). In addition, it is
also, in Taylor's terms (1971:44), the case of the normally human
entity indirectly involved in the activity described by the verb. It
is not, however, to be equated with the dative case form of traditional
grammar which marks the goal or destination of the object in such
verbs as give, sell or return. Neither is it to be identified
with the dative or ablative in some case grammars which is associated
with the source of the object of verbs such as buy, borrow or remove.
These two instances have been identified in the preceding section as
manifesting a locative case.

The distinction between a [+DAT] and a [+OBJ] case seems to be
obscured when the two are not cooccurring in the same simple sentence.
Thus, some linguists have suggested that they be conflated and
considered as [+OBJ]. The subjects in the following sentences, if we

follow the suggestion, are both marked [+OBJ]:

37. naḃaliʔ ang lapìs
    break   pencìl
               $\begin{bmatrix} +NM \\ +OBJ \end{bmatrix}$

    'The pencil broke.'

38. nagalìt   ang dalaga
    was angered   maìden
                     $\begin{bmatrix} +NM \\ +OBJ \end{bmatrix}$

    'The maiden became angry/was angered.'

It may be countered, however, that although these two verbs may be
satisfied with the presence of just a single actant, their syntactic
possibilities differ. Sentence 38 with a supposed [+OBJ] feature may
allow another actant which means the object of the maiden's anger
and which may be properly identified as [+OBJ]. On the contrary,
sentence 37 with the neutral [+OBJ] does not allow a similar actant.
Thus, the following marking for 38 is considered to be the correct
analysis:

38.a. nagalit ang dalaga   (sa   tsuper)
                     maiden   driver
                     $\begin{bmatrix} +NM \\ +DAT \end{bmatrix}$ $\begin{bmatrix} +L \\ +OBJ \end{bmatrix}$

    'The maiden became mad (at the driver).'

Moreover, similar psychological experiences expressed by the verb are
paralleled by verbs of perception or sensation and of emotional or
mental states. These verbs require the cooccurrence of the same
actants as those in 38.a where the designated [+OBJ] is unaffected
and indifferent to the experiencer marked [+DAT]. For example:

39. nakita namin ang palabas sa plasa
    see   we   show   town square
    $\begin{bmatrix} +AC \\ +DAT \end{bmatrix}$ $\begin{bmatrix} +NM \\ +OBJ \end{bmatrix}$

    'The show at the town square was seen by us.'

40. nakarinig kami ng kaluskos sa ibaba?
    hear   we   scuffing   downstairs
    $\begin{bmatrix} +NM \\ +DAT \end{bmatrix}$ $\begin{bmatrix} +AC \\ +OBJ \end{bmatrix}$

    'We heard a scuffing downstairs.'

The class of state verbs exemplified in the sentences above shows
the necessity of establishing a dative case relation distinct from
the objective since 'we' and 'scuffing' are not coreferential.

Another occurrence of the [+DAT] is with state or potential verbs
that express leaving an adverse effect on the experiencer, who is
somehow intrinsically related to the [+OBJ] whose state has been
affected. With these verbs, we find another support to Fillmore's
assignment of a [+DAT] to an actant who is the possessor of something.
(See pp.36-37.) For example:

41. nawala? ang pera   ng bata?
    lost   money   child
                 $\begin{bmatrix} +NM \\ +OBJ \end{bmatrix}$

    'The child's money got lost.'

41.a. nawalan ng pera ang bata?
                  $\begin{bmatrix} +AC \\ +OBJ \end{bmatrix}$ $\begin{bmatrix} +NM \\ +DAT \end{bmatrix}$

      'The child lost some money.'

The noun bata? which is the possessor of pera that was lost in 41
becomes prominently the affected actant when the cooccurring verb
requires it to be realized in the nominative case form in 41.a. It

suffers from the event or state or process designated by the verb involving an object which it owns or possesses. This particular occurrence of the [+DAT] is referred to in Ramos (1974:40) as the "Affected" case, but we can avoid positing an extra case relation and capture syntactic and semantic generalities by treating this case relation as a [+DAT].

One other relevant environment in which the [+DAT] occurs is with some subclasses of causative verbs. These verbs require at least a cooccurring [+OBJ] and a [+AGT] besides the [+DAT]. With such verbs, the [+DAT] can occur either in the nominative or the locative case form. (For examples, see 35.a, 35.b, 36.a, and 36.b on p. 53.)

The [+DAT] as possessor or owner of an object, alienable or not, poses an interesting puzzle in the analysis of the existential verb may and its derived form mayroon or its corresponding negative wala?. Either form carries the meaning 'have' or 'there exist'. With the first meaning, the verb cooccurs with a [+OBJ] in the accusative case form and a [+DAT] or a coreferential [+OBJ] as subject. The second instance does not require the cooccurrence of a nominative actant with the accusative [+OBJ]. The [+OBJ] may occur by itself, particularly in exclamations, or with a locative, a benefactive or a coreferential objective realized in the form of a prepositional phrase. For example:

42. may   sakit   si Heneral Castro
     have   illness
     $\begin{bmatrix} - \begin{bmatrix} +Det \\ +AC \end{bmatrix} \end{bmatrix} \begin{bmatrix} +AC \\ +OBJ \end{bmatrix}$ $\begin{bmatrix} +NM \\ +DAT \end{bmatrix}$

     'General Castro is ill.'

43. may   pakpak   ang   balita?
    have   wings   news
    $\begin{bmatrix} - \begin{bmatrix} +Det \\ +AC \end{bmatrix} \end{bmatrix}$ $\begin{bmatrix} +AC \\ +OBJ \end{bmatrix}$ $\begin{bmatrix} +NM \\ +OBJ \end{bmatrix}$

   'News has wings.'

44. may   sunog
    there exists   fire
    $\begin{bmatrix} - \begin{bmatrix} +Det \\ +AC \end{bmatrix} \end{bmatrix}$ $\begin{bmatrix} +AC \\ +OBJ \end{bmatrix}$

   'There is fire!'

45. wala?   ang   nanay   dito
    not exist   mother   here
                      $\begin{bmatrix} +NM \\ +OBJ \end{bmatrix}$ $\begin{bmatrix} +L \\ +LOC \end{bmatrix}$

   'Mother is not here.'

46. walang   balita?   tungkol   kay   Pete
    there is none   news   about
                        $\begin{bmatrix} +AC \\ +OBJ \end{bmatrix}$

   'There is no news about Pete.'

The only justification for positing a [+DAT], as in 42, is that the cooccurring [+OBJ] referent is viewed as an alienable or inalienable possession of the designated [+DAT] referent. Otherwise, both actants may be analyzed as coreferential OBJ's, with the one in the accusative form being a part of or included in the other actant marked subject, as in 43. As for sentence 46, the PP is an attribute of the preceding N. This problem, however, is beyond the scope of this study.

2.4.5 Instrumental Case Relation [+INS]

The instrumental case relation expresses the force or object causally involved in the action or state identified by the verb (Fillmore, 1968:24). It also embraces the concept of means for the

occurrence of what is expressed by the verb. It may occur as a tool
implicated by an agent in the performance of an action or as a means
that brings about an event. While the potential occurrence of an
instrumental case can be predicted by the occurrence of a [+AGT], the
presence of a [+INS] is not a sufficient condition for the presence
of a [+AGT]. There are verbs that allow the instrumental case to
cooccur with an objective case alone and a few, with an objective and
a dative case.

The instrumental case relation exhibits a few peculiarities in its
various occurrences. First, when it cooccurs with an agentive case,
it may be realized either in the nominative or the accusative case
form. In the latter form, the [+INS] may be optionally manifested
in either a simple NP structure or a complex one depending on the
type of verb it cooccurs with and the case relation which occurs
as the subject of the sentence. The simple NP structure consists of
the determiner marked with the feature [+AC], accusative, and the
head noun representing the tool or force involved. In the complex
NP structure, the [+INS] actant is an obligatory attribute of the
specific head noun pamamagitan 'means, way'. The structure is
represented in the following tree-branching diagram:

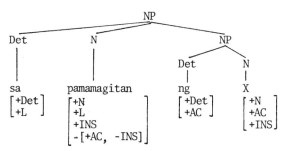

The head noun <u>pamamagitan</u> is permanently marked with the identical [+INS] feature but with a different case form [+L]. The obligatory cooccurrence of another [+INS] attribute is also specified. The complex [+INS] actant then ·is realized in the locative case form following the marking of the case form on the head N and not the marking on its attribute. The gloss for this NP is 'by means of X'. For example:

47.a. nagputol si Pablo ng damo (sa pamamagitan) ng karit
       cut   grass   means   sickle
                    $\begin{bmatrix}+NM\\+AGT\end{bmatrix}$ $\begin{bmatrix}+AC\\+OBJ\end{bmatrix}$ $\begin{bmatrix}+L\\+INS\end{bmatrix}$ $\begin{bmatrix}+AC\\+INS\end{bmatrix}$

'Pablo cut grass (by means of) with a sickle.'

47.b. pinutol ni Pablo ang damo (sa pamamagitan) ng karit
                 $\begin{bmatrix}+AC\\+AGT\end{bmatrix}$ $\begin{bmatrix}+NM\\+OBJ\end{bmatrix}$ $\begin{bmatrix}+L\\+INS\end{bmatrix}$ $\begin{bmatrix}+AC\\+INS\end{bmatrix}$

47.c. ipinangputol ni Pablo ng damo ang karit
                      $\begin{bmatrix}+AC\\+AGT\end{bmatrix}$ $\begin{bmatrix}+AC\\+OBJ\end{bmatrix}$ $\begin{bmatrix}+NM\\+INS\end{bmatrix}$

47.d. pinutulan ni Pablo ng sanga ang punong mangga
       cut from   branch   tree   mango
                   $\begin{bmatrix}+AC\\+AGT\end{bmatrix}$ $\begin{bmatrix}+AC\\+OBJ\end{bmatrix}$ $\begin{bmatrix}+NM\\+LOC\end{bmatrix}$

(sa pamamagitan) ng itak
   means   bolo
$\begin{bmatrix}+L\\+INS\end{bmatrix}$ $\begin{bmatrix}+AC\\+INS\end{bmatrix}$

'Pablo cut off some branches from the mango tree with a bolo.'

Second, without a cooccurring [+AGT], the [+INS] may cooccur with a [+OBJ] or, rarely, with a [+OBJ] and a [+DAT]. In these environments, the [+INS] with only a [+OBJ] is always realized in the [+AC] form. However, when the verb is marked potential, to mean either ability or accidental, the [+INS] may be either in the [+AC] or the [+NM].[12] It plays the role of an involuntary, non-responsible

agent that brings about the event. With non-agentive verbs,

instrumental tools usually cooccur with [+pot] verb stems and

instrumental forces with either [+pot] or [+erg] verbs. They are

always in the [+AC] case form. For example:

48.a. giniba? ng bagyo ang bahay
      destroy   strom   house
      [+V]   [+AC]   [+NM]
      [+erg]   [+INS]   [+OBJ]

      'The house was destroyed by the storm.'

48.b. nagiba? ng bagyo ang bahay
      [+V]   [+AC]   [+NM]
      [+pot]   [+INS]   [+OBJ]

      'The house was destroyed by the storm.'
  Lit.: 'The storm was able to destroy the house.'

49. nahiwa? ang bata? ng kutsilyo
    cut   child   knife
    [+V]   [+NM]   [+AC]
    [+pot]   [+OBJ]   [+INS]

  Lit.: 'The child happened to be cut by/with a knife.'

With a cooccurring [+DAT], the [+INS] is realized in either the [+AC]

or the [+L] in a complex NP structure.

50. nakita ko ang buong nangyari ng mga mata ko
    see   I   whole event   eye my
           [+AC]   [+NM]   [+AC]
           [+DAT]   [+OBJ]   [+INS]

    'I saw the whole event with my eyes.'

51. nakaramdam siya ng ginhawa sa pamamagitan ng hipnotismo
    feel   he   relief   means   hypnotism
    [+NM]   [+AC]   [+L]   [+AC]
    [+DAT]   [+OBJ]   [+INS]   [+INS]

    'He felt some relief through hypnotism.'

From the foregoing occurrences, it appears that a pattern of case forms emerges. There seems to be an effort on the part of the language to realize the cooccurring case relations in distinct case forms to the extent necessary to avoid ambiguity. For instance, verbs with a cooccurring [+AGT] distinguish a nominative, an accusative and a locative case form. When a case relation is non-nominative, the [+AGT] and the [+OBJ] are realized in the [+AC] while the [+LOC] and the [+DAT] are manifested in the [+L]. There is no confusion between the two accusative actants when they occur as non-subject because of certain distinctive features such as [+animate] usually associated with [+AGT] and [-animate], with [+OBJ]. Between a [+LOC] and a [+DAT], the latter is easily recognizable not only because it is typically [+animate], but, also, because it is selected by identifiable types of verbs, again, designated by certain semantic features. Thus, a normal construction with an agentive verb may consist of one [+NM], one [+AC] and one [+L]. It can allow an outer [+L, +LOC] which can be distinguished from the inner [+LOC] by the features on the verb as discussed earlier. When all three case forms as pigeon holes are full and an optional instrumental case is taken, it has to occur in a case form that will distinguish it from the case relation that it closely resembles, which is the [+OBJ]. It is not realized, generally, in the [+AC] when the [+OBJ] is also in that form. Hence, we find it taking the [+L] form as manifested by the unique complex noun phrase. However, if the [+OBJ] is in the nominative, the [+INS] can freely assume the accusative case form since it can just as well be distinguished from the accusative [+AGT].

Without a cooccurring [+AGT], the non-nominative [+INS] can
be manifested in the [+AC] since it does not compete with the cooccurring
[+OBJ] which has to be in the [+NM]. When it occurs with verbs of
sensation or perception, the [+INS] may be either [+AC] or [+L].
With a cooccurring [+NM, +OBJ], it is [+L]. With a [+DAT] it usually
expresses the sense organ used for what is indicated by the potential
verb or the means through which the state is achieved.

2.4.6   Benefactive Case Relation [+BEN]

The relation of the animate or inaminate element for whose
benefit an action is performed or for the benefit of which a state
exists is the benefactive case relation. It can also indicate the
entity in whose place an action is performed or the purpose for
which an action is undertaken (Starosta, 1973a:139-40). It may be
realized in the nominative or the benefactive case form with agentive
verbs, and only in the benefactive case form with non-agentive verbs.
It does not cooccur with verbs of sensation or perception. For
example:

52. bumili áko ng silya para sa nanay
     buy   I   chair for   mother
     $\begin{bmatrix} +NM \\ +AGT \end{bmatrix}$ $\begin{bmatrix} +AC \\ +OBJ \end{bmatrix}$ $\begin{bmatrix} +P \\ +B \end{bmatrix}$ $\begin{bmatrix} +L \\ +BEN \end{bmatrix}$

     'I bought a chair for mother.'

53. ipinagluto ko ang nanay
     cook   I   mother
     $\begin{bmatrix} +AC \\ +AGT \end{bmatrix}$ $\begin{bmatrix} +NM \\ +BEN \end{bmatrix}$

     'I cooked for mother.'

54. namatay   si Rizal   para/alang-alang sa kaniyang bayan
    die   for /for the sake of   his   country
             $\begin{bmatrix} +NM \\ +OBJ \end{bmatrix}$ $\begin{bmatrix} +P \\ +B \end{bmatrix}$ $\begin{bmatrix} +L \\ +BEN \end{bmatrix}$

'Rizal died for his country.'

The [+BEN] actant in the benefactive case form as recipient
is usually manifested by a prepositional phrase consisting of a P
and a NP, where NP is generally a [+L] Det and a head noun N. With
the meaning 'purpose', the [+BEN] actant is a prepositional phrase
consisting of a P and either a NP with a nominalized verb as head N
or a sentence S whose head V is always non-finite. The nominalized N,
like any underived N, is marked for both case relation and case form
whereas the S, not being a noun, is marked neither for case relation
nor case form. The only indication that the phrase is a benefactive
actant is the case form marking on the preposition, which at the
same time functions as a complementizer of the embedded S. For
example:

55. nag?ipon   siya ng pera   para sa pamimili ng aginaldo
    save up   he   money   for   buying   presents
            $\begin{bmatrix} +NM \\ +AGT \end{bmatrix}$ $\begin{bmatrix} +AC \\ +OBJ \end{bmatrix}$ $\begin{bmatrix} +P \\ +B \end{bmatrix}$ $\begin{bmatrix} +L \\ +BEN \end{bmatrix}$ $\begin{bmatrix} +AC \\ +OBJ \end{bmatrix}$

    sa Pasko ^{13}
       Christmas
       $\begin{bmatrix} +L \\ +LOC \end{bmatrix}$

    'He saved up some money for the purchase of some gifts
    at Christmas.'

56. kumaka?in   ako ng bitamina   para lumakas
    eat   I   vitamins   for   become strong
            $\begin{bmatrix} +NM \\ +AGT \end{bmatrix}$ $\begin{bmatrix} +AC \\ +OBJ \end{bmatrix}$ $\begin{bmatrix} +P \\ +B \end{bmatrix}$ $\begin{bmatrix} +V \\ -fin \end{bmatrix}$

    'I take vitamins to be strong.'

In some analyses (Platt, 1971:48-49; Kullavanijaya, 1974:51),
the benefactive case relation has also been associated with the
indirect object of verbs such as <u>give</u> obviously because it 'benefits'
from the action. As has been mentioned previously, verbs of
transportation or location in this study require a [+LOC] as goal.
The indirect object cannot be a [+BEN] because it can be shown that
an optional [+BEN] can cooccur with it. Compare the following pair
of sentences:

57.a. binigyan ko ng pera si Nena para sa simbahan
      give   I   money   for   church

$\begin{bmatrix} +AC \\ +AGT \end{bmatrix}$ $\begin{bmatrix} +AC \\ +OBJ \end{bmatrix}$ $\begin{bmatrix} +NM \\ +LOC \end{bmatrix}$ $\begin{bmatrix} +P \\ +B \end{bmatrix}$ $\begin{bmatrix} +L \\ +BEN \end{bmatrix}$

'I gave Nena some money for the church.'

57.b. ipinagbigay ko ng pera si Nena sa simbahan
      give

$\begin{bmatrix} +AC \\ +AGT \end{bmatrix}$ $\begin{bmatrix} +AC \\ +OBJ \end{bmatrix}$ $\begin{bmatrix} +NM \\ +BEN \end{bmatrix}$ $\begin{bmatrix} +L \\ +LOC \end{bmatrix}$

'I gave some money to the church for Nena.'

2.4.7 Reason Case Relation [+RSN]

The nominal which indicates the reason for doing an action or
the cause of the occurrence of an event or state expressed by the
verb has been labelled reason case relation. It occurs optionally
with almost all verbs whose semantic features are compatible with
a reason or cause that explains why the agent performs an action, why
an object undergoes a process, or why/how a certain state comes
about. It is realized either in the nominative or the reason case
form. With state or emotion verbs, the [+RSN] may optionally be in
the reason case form or the locative. For example:

58.a. nagtrabaho ang dalaga dahil sa pagkamatay ng tatay
  work   maiden because death   father
        $\begin{bmatrix} +NM \\ +AGT \end{bmatrix}$ $\begin{bmatrix} +P \\ +R \end{bmatrix}$ $\begin{bmatrix} +L \\ +RSN \end{bmatrix}$

  niya
  her

  'The maiden worked (took on a job) because of her
  father's death.'

58.b. ikinapagtrabaho ng dalaga ang pagkamatay ng tatay niya
        $\begin{bmatrix} +AC \\ +AGT \end{bmatrix}$ $\begin{bmatrix} +NM \\ +RNS \end{bmatrix}$

  'Her father's death caused the maiden to work.'

59.a. natumba siya (dahil) sa matinding init
  fall/faint she because intense heat
  $\begin{bmatrix} +NM \\ +OBJ \end{bmatrix}$ $\begin{bmatrix} +P \\ +R \end{bmatrix}$ $\begin{bmatrix} +L \\ +RSN \end{bmatrix}$

  'She fell/fainted because of the intense heat.'

59.b. ikinatumba niya ang matinding init
     $\begin{bmatrix} +AC \\ +OBJ \end{bmatrix}$ $\begin{bmatrix} +NM \\ +RNS \end{bmatrix}$

  'The intense heat caused her to faint.'

With potential verbs cooccurring with a non-nominative [+RSN],

the preposition that marks the reason case form may be optionally

unexpressed leaving only the [+RSN] actant realized in the [+L]. The

resulting construction as in 59.a becomes superficially identical

with that manifested by a potential verb with a [+OBJ] and a [+DAT]

in its case frame.

60. natakot siya sa kulog
  afraid she   thunder
  $\begin{bmatrix} +NM \\ +DAT \end{bmatrix}$ $\begin{bmatrix} +L \\ +OBJ \end{bmatrix}$

  'She became afraid of the thunder.'

By simply looking at the cooccurring case forms, 59.a. without dahil is apparently identical to 60. The two sentences differ, however, in their cooccurring case relations. Where the potential verb in 59.a takes a [+OBJ] subject and a [+RSN], that of 60 takes a [+DAT] subject and a locative [+OBJ]. It may be mentioned that sentence 60 is analyzed differently by Ramos (1974:37). She gives the same sentence as cooccurring with kulog 'thunder' marked either by the accusative determiner ng or by the locative determiner sa. With ng, the sentence is glossed 'She was frightened by the thunder' and with sa, it is 'She was frightened of the thunder' and the subject siya is identified as having the objective case relation and the non-nominative actant kulog, the instrumental. Although she considers the sa in this sentence as possibly a reduced form of dahil sa marking a "causal case", Ramos was prevented from pursuing this line of analysis due to the limitation of her study. Two questions can be raised about her analysis: (a) Her first sentence possibility -

    "natakot siya ng kulog 'She was frightened by the thunder.'"
          0   I

is rejected on the ground of unnaturalness. The acceptable form is the non-potential form which has no [+NM, +INS] counterpart:

        tinakot siya ng kulog

It is claimed here that the potential forms of the class of emotion verbs do not cooccur with an instrumental actant in the accusative case form. (See pp. 60-61 for occurrences of the INS actant.)
(b) Her second sentence possibility -

    "natakot siya sa kulog 'She was frightened of the thunder.'"
          0   I

forces a locative case form realization of the instrumental actant,

which would be restricted to this subclass of verbs, and thus,
loses the generalizations made previously about instrumentals
(see 2.4.5, pp.58-63). Moreover, the meaning carried by the actant
kulog is that to which fear is directed. This meaning can be
compared with the following examples used previously:

38.a. nagalit ang dalaga (sa tsuper) (From p.55)
     got angry   maiden   driver
               $\begin{bmatrix} +NM \\ +DAT \end{bmatrix}$ $\begin{bmatrix} +L \\ +OBJ \end{bmatrix}$

'The maiden got mad (at the driver).'

49. nahiwa? ang bata? ng kutsilyo (From p.61)
   cut   child   knife
            $\begin{bmatrix} +NM \\ +OBJ \end{bmatrix}$ $\begin{bmatrix} +AC \\ +INS \end{bmatrix}$

'The child got cut by/with a knife.'

Apparently, the sentence in question is closer to 38.a than to 49;
their verbs belong to the same subclass of emotion verbs and their
non-nominative actants kulog and tsuper play the role of the object
of fear and anger, respectively, built up in the experiencer actant.
Hence, with the meaning given for the sentence in question, the proper
analysis should be that it has a cooccurring [+DAT] subject and
a locative [+OBJ] instead of a [+OBJ] subject and a locative [+INS].

Having justified the analysis of 60, we can proceed to compare
it with 59.a without dahil. One way of showing the difference
between the two sentences is by expanding 60 to include a [+RSN], and
we may get something like the following:

60.a. natakot siya sa kulog   dahil   sa pagkamatay
   afraid   she   thunder because death
     [+NM]   [+L] [+P]   [+L]
     [+DAT] [+OBJ] [+R]   [+RSN]

   ng aso niya na tinama?an ng kidlat
      dog her   struck   lightning

   'She was afraid of thunder because of the death of her
   dog that was struck by lightning.'

Another way is by comparing the verb form in 59.b, where the
cooccurring [+RSN] is the subject, with the following sentence in
which the [+OBJ] in 60 is [+NM]:

60.b. kinatukutan niya ang kulog (dahil sa pagkamatay
          [+AC]   [+NM] [+P]   [+L]
          [+DAT] [+OBJ] [+R]   [+RSN]

   ng aso niya....)

and with the sentence in which the [+RSN] is [+NM]:

60.c. ikinatakot niya sa kulog ang pagkamatay ng aso
       [+AC]   [+L] [+NM]
       [+DAT] [+OBJ] [+RSN]

   niya na tinama?an ng kidlat

It will be observed that in 60.a where the locative [+OBJ] is present,
the [+RSN] retains its preposition to mark it unambiguously.
Sentences 60.b and 60.c show the difference in corresponding verb
forms to show that the cooccurring [+OBJ] in the former and [+RSN]
in the latter are in the nominative case form. Note the identical
affix i- used in 58.b, 59.b and 60.c to mark [+NM, +RSN].

One other point that may be stressed in connection with 60 is
that a class of verbs exemplified by natakot with only a cooccurring
[+OBJ] can be derived from the class which requires both [+DAT] and
[+OBJ]. (See SVDR-3, p.318, Chapter IV.) This suggests that if no

[+DAT] is present and a [+RSN] cooccurs without its preposition, the construction will be superficially identical to 60, but with a different feature specification:

60.d. natakot siya (dahil) sa kulog
$$\begin{bmatrix} +NM \\ +OBJ \end{bmatrix} \qquad \begin{bmatrix} +L \\ +RSN \end{bmatrix}$$

'She became afraid because of the thunder.'

Whatever semantic commonality there may be between 'be/become afraid of' and 'be/become afraid because of' has not been explored here. A fairly reasonable explanation for the cooccurrence possibility of the [+DAT] with a [+OBJ] and a [+RSN] with this verb, or any other verb in this subclass, is that we can speak of someone's feeling what is expressed by the verb toward some object for a certain reason.

2.4.8 Comitative Case Relation [+COM]

Taylor defines the comitative case relation as "that which is somehow associated in a parallel way with the referent of another actant in the verbal activity or state described" (1971:42). There are three types of verbs in Tagalog which permit the occurrence of a [+COM] actant, namely:

(a) Non-potential verbs whose subclassification is not affected by the presence of a [+COM] which expresses the notion 'in company with' or 'at the same time with' one other actant in the action or process designated by the verb. The [+COM] is realized in the comitative case form [+C] through the preposition kasama or kasabay, whose respective meanings are as indicated above. Both prepositions are presumed to have been derived from nouns of the

same shape meaning 'companion'. The status of the category of the
source, however, lies beyond the scope of this study. For example:

61. nag?aral ako ng pagmamaneho kasabay ni Mercy
    study   I   driving   same time
$$\begin{bmatrix} +NM \\ +AGT \end{bmatrix} \begin{bmatrix} +AC \\ +OBJ \end{bmatrix} \begin{bmatrix} +P \\ +C \end{bmatrix} \begin{bmatrix} +AC \\ +COM \end{bmatrix}$$

    'I studied driving at the same time with Mercy.'

62. pumunta ang pamilya ni Titong sa Missouri
    go to   family
$$\begin{bmatrix} +NM \\ +OBJ \end{bmatrix} \qquad \begin{bmatrix} +L \\ +LOC \end{bmatrix}$$

    kasama   ng pamilya ni Mel
    in company with   family
$$\begin{bmatrix} +P \\ +C \end{bmatrix} \qquad \begin{bmatrix} +AC \\ +COM \end{bmatrix}$$

    'Titong's family went to Missouri along with Mel's family.'
It will be noted that the comitative prepositional phrase is different
from the previous type of prepositional phrase discussed in terms of
the accusative marking on the head N rather than the locative.

(b) Verbs identified as 'social' require a cooccurring [+COM]
expressing the nominal that has been performing or is in the process
of undergoing something indicated by the verb before another actant,
usually a [+AGT] or a [+OBJ], 'joins in' the same activity or process.
In other words, the verb indicates that an actant does or undergoes
what the verb states imitating or following the model set by the [+COM]
actant. The [+COM] with this class of verbs is usually manifested
in the locative case form, but it may also appear in the nominative.
For example:

63. nakipanood siya ng TV sa amin
    watch   he   us
$$\begin{bmatrix} +V \\ +soc \end{bmatrix} \begin{bmatrix} +NM \\ +AGT \end{bmatrix} \begin{bmatrix} +AC \\ +OBJ \end{bmatrix} \begin{bmatrix} +L \\ +COM \end{bmatrix}$$
    'He joined us in watching TV.'

64. pinakisakyan ni Del ang kaibigan niya sa kotse
    ride   friend   her   car
    $\begin{bmatrix} +V \\ +soc \end{bmatrix}$ $\begin{bmatrix} +AC \\ +OBJ \end{bmatrix}$ $\begin{bmatrix} +NM \\ +COM \end{bmatrix}$ $\begin{bmatrix} +L \\ +LOC \end{bmatrix}$

'Del joined her friend in riding in the car.'

(c) A small class of verbs which expresses social-reciprocal action requires the cooccurrence of at least a [+AGT] or a [+OBJ] with a [+COM]. The [+COM] is realized in the locative or nominative case form. For example:

65. nakipagkasundo? siya sa kalaban niya
    come to terms   he   opponent his
    $\begin{bmatrix} +V \\ +soc-rec \end{bmatrix}$ $\begin{bmatrix} +NM \\ +OBJ \end{bmatrix}$ $\begin{bmatrix} +L \\ +COM \end{bmatrix}$

'He came to terms with his opponent.'

66. pinakipagkita?an niya ang guro tungkol sa
    meet with   he   teacher about
    $\begin{bmatrix} +V \\ +soc-rec \end{bmatrix}$ $\begin{bmatrix} +AC \\ +AGT \end{bmatrix}$ $\begin{bmatrix} +NM \\ +COM \end{bmatrix}$ $\begin{bmatrix} +P \\ +AC \end{bmatrix}$

    kaniyang marka
    his   grade
    $\begin{bmatrix} +L \\ +OBJ \end{bmatrix}$

'He met with the teacher about his grade.'

2.5 Case Forms

A description of the case system in a language would be incomplete without any reference to the system by which the various case relations are realized and marked. As stated earlier in this chapter, the system of marking case relations in Tagalog involves two devices: a) by case-marking determiners or prepositions occurring before the nominative and non-nominative nouns; pronouns are permanently marked for their individual case forms; and b) by verb inflection to mark the case relation of the actant realized in the nominative case form which is the grammatical subject of the sentence. (See McKaughan, 1973:208.) The case-relation-marking affixes in the verb are referred to as the verb's voice. It may be emphasized that a single voice inflectional affix does not necessarily mark one and only one case relation subject. Depending on the verb's syntactic (case frame subcategory), semantic and morphological features, a voice marker identifies a corresponding case relation as subject. This means that a particular voice affix with a verb in one subcategory may mark, say a [+OBJ] case, and the same voice affix with a verb from another subcategory may mark another case relation, e.g., [+AGT]. Conversely, a given case relation in the nominative case form may be marked by one or more voice affixes according to the particular class of the verb it cooccurs with.

As stated previously, case forms are treated in lexicase as lexical features on nouns, prepositions, and determiners. Each of these categories is marked for a single case form feature. There are six case forms identified in this study that realize the eight case relations posited. They are the nominative [+NM], accusative [+AC], locative [+L], benefactive [+B], reason [+R], and comitative [+C]. The first three case forms are realized by determiners [+Det] and the remaining three by prepositions [+P]. However, there are also a few prepositions that may realize the [+AC] and [+L] case forms. The presence of a preposition and a determiner both carrying a case form feature in a prepositional phrase does not pose any conflict in identifying the case form of the entire constituent, The principle of dominance applies to the different categories. In a complex noun phrase, for instance, the case relation of the head noun is the case relation of the whole constituent and the case form of the marker in the highest node governs the marker under it; whereas, the case form of a prepositional phrase is the case form of · the preposition (its lexical head) and the case relation is the case relation of the head noun of the noun phrase.

The discussion which follows deals first with the non-nominative case forms and their corresponding case form markers. The nominative case form, which realizes all the case relations marked variously in the verb, will come after.

2.5.1 Accusative Case Form [+AC]

Most accommodating of the non-nominative case forms is the accusative case form. It can realize the [+AGT], [+OBJ], [+DAT], and [+INS] case relations. Excluding phenomenal, existential and impersonal verbs, every verb, in general, cooccurs with at least one case relation which is realized in the nominative case form. This implies that an accusative case form can appear only when the nominative slot has been filled by a case relation, and one other actant in the case frame of the verb is one that is allowed to be realized in the accusative case form.

Unlike the nominative case form, the accusative may occur more than once in a simple sentence. Each of these occurrences manifests a distinct case relation. Verbs normally allow one or two occurrences of the [+AC], unless a third optional actant may also be realized in the same case form. Sometimes, this third actant is modified in some ways that will distinguish it from the two other accusative case forms. (See discussion on Instrumental Case Relation, 2.4.5, pp.58ff.)

The accusative case form is marked by the accusative determiner nang (here abbreviated ng to conform to standard orthography) when the actant is a common or abstract noun. If it is a personal name, the personal accusative determiner that marks it is ni with a singular meaning and nina with a plural meaning. In general, the whole actant can also be manifested by members of the accusative class of pronouns, either personal or demonstrative, which bear any of the case relations allowed to be realized in the [+AC].

Some of the case relations that occur in the accusative form have to obey certain restrictions. They are discussed below.

2.5.1.1 Accusative Objective [+AC, +OBJ]

In Tagalog, there are certain constraints on the case form realization of N's that are assigned the objective case relation feature. As a general rule, any case relation can be manifested in either a nominative or a non-nominative case form. When non-nominative, the actant may be realized either in the accusative or the non-accusative case form following the subcategorization below:

SR: [-NM] $\longrightarrow$ [±AC]

If the actant is non-accusative, the following redundancy rule marks it with the locative case form:

RR: [-AC] $\longrightarrow$ [+L]

A [+OBJ] actant, when non-nominative, is realized in either the accusative or the locative case form. Each of these forms corresponds to the semantic feature indefinite and definite, respectively.[14] These semantic features are added by the following redundancy rule:

$$\text{RR:} \begin{bmatrix} \alpha AC \\ +OBJ \end{bmatrix} \longrightarrow [-\alpha def]$$

The usual non-nominative form of a [+OBJ] is the accusative, but where the locative form is permitted, it expresses a definite objective referent. When the [+OBJ] actant is a personal name or a personal pronoun, it can only be realized in the locative case form when non-nominative. Thus, the following redundancy rule applies:

$$\text{RR:} \begin{bmatrix} \begin{Bmatrix} +pers\ name \\ +Pro,\ +pers \end{Bmatrix} \\ -NM \\ +OBJ \end{bmatrix} \longrightarrow \begin{bmatrix} +L \\ +OBJ \end{bmatrix}$$

The above rule accounts for the ungrammaticality of the following sentence:

67. *naghintay   ni Maria   ang   nanay
                 niya
     wait for   Mary/her   mother
                 $\begin{bmatrix} +AC \\ +OBJ \end{bmatrix}$ $\begin{bmatrix} +NM \\ +AGT \end{bmatrix}$

and the grammaticality of the following:

67.a. naghintay   kay Maria   ang   nanay
                  sa kaniya
                  $\begin{bmatrix} +L \\ +OBJ \end{bmatrix}$ $\begin{bmatrix} +NM \\ +AGT \end{bmatrix}$

'Mother waited for Maria/her.'

It is important to note that demonstrative pronouns behave like the common nouns in being realized in either the [+AC] or the [+L] form

when occurring with the [+OBJ] role. Besides denoting definiteness,
since both forms are lexically definite, the demonstrative pronoun
marked [+L] is more emphatic than that which is marked [+AC]. For
example:

67.b. naghihintay nito   ang nanay
       wait for   this   mother
                     $\begin{bmatrix} +AC \\ +OBJ \end{bmatrix}$ $\begin{bmatrix} +NM \\ +AGT \end{bmatrix}$

'Mother is waiting for this.'

67.c. naghihintay dito   ang nanay[15]
                     this
                     $\begin{bmatrix} +L \\ +OBJ \end{bmatrix}$ $\begin{bmatrix} +NM \\ +AGT \end{bmatrix}$

'Mother is waiting for this very particular thing.'

Although not expressed formally, a similar observation pertaining
to the surface realization of the objective case is made by Ramos
(1974:100-1). She indicates that the objective phrase is not marked
by ni nor ng pronouns and, instead of ni-marked phrases and ng-pronouns,
kay-marked phrases and sa-pronouns are used. It can also be replaced,
she adds, by ng-demonstratives. What these statements fail to account
for, however, is the possibility of realizing a [+OBJ] case relation
expressed by a common noun or a demonstrative in the locative case
form (a common noun marked by sa or a sa-demonstrative in Ramos' terms).

This 'irregularity' in the case form realization of the [+OBJ]
has not passed unnoticed in some other works on Tagalog. Two authors,
in particular, state a similar restriction as follows:

(a) "Also, in a verbal predicate, the nominal in the object
complement cannot be a name or a pronoun" (Otanes, 1966:70).

(b) "Pronouns and personal names cannot be objects of agentive

verbs; they are always in a dative relationship to these verbs"
(Stevens, 1969:4).

One problem with the preceding statements is the vagueness of
the terms 'object complement', 'objects of agentive verbs', and
'dative relationship'. It is not clear whether the authors are
referring to case relations or case forms when they use such terms.
Perhaps, it would be reasonable to interpret the terms as case
relations rather than case forms. Following Otanes' restriction in
a, the complement kay Maria/sa kaniya in sentence 67.a cannot be an
object complement (a [+OBJ] here), and neither can nito nor dito
in 67.b and 67.c, respectively. Our prediction is that she must mark
these as directional complements (our [+LOC]), even if they differ
semantically from her directional complements in general. To
Stevens, these complements will be assigned a dative case, except
nito. However, if the complement cooccurring with the same verb
maghintay 'to wait for' were not a name or a pronoun such as follows:

67.d. naghintay ng bus ang nanay
       wait for   bus   mother

       'Mother waited for a bus.'

then, it would be considered by both Otanes and Stevens as being an
object complement or as having an object relationship to the verb.
It is rather curious that a verb which presumably determines what
case relations must cooccur with it should change one case for
another on account of selectional differences between the elements that
manifest it, e.g., common versus proper nouns, common nouns versus
pronouns, definite versus indefinite. When we compare 67.a - 67.c
with 67.d, we note that the [+OBJ] case relation in all four sentences,

regardless of form or inherent features, plays the same role in
relation to the verb. To this list may be added a definite [+OBJ]
form corresponding to the indefinite [+OBJ] form in 67.d as follows:

67.e. naghintay sa bus ang nanay
      wait for   bus   mother
                   $\begin{bmatrix} +L \\ +OBJ \end{bmatrix}$ $\begin{bmatrix} +NM \\ +AGT \end{bmatrix}$

'Mother waited for the bus.'

In all instances, it can be said that the verb takes the same case
relation features. What we observe changing are the case forms with
a corresponding change of feature referring to either definiteness or
emphasis, as the case may be. This change is considered reasonable
since actants are to a certain extent free to occur in at least two
different case forms. To say that the case relations contracted by
a verb change with a change in case forms loses semantic and syntactic
generalizations. Until a more arguable position than the one claimed
here is presented, we will continue to regard CR's as invariant
within the same verb and CF's more flexible. In view of these
arguments, we find the importance of making CR and CF distinctions.

There is another marker besides ng which applies strictly to
the objective case relation. These are the expressions tungkol or
hinggil 'about', ukol 'with regard to', and laban 'against' which
have been classified here as members of a limited set of prepositions.
They are marked with the accusative case form feature and with a case
frame feature requiring a cooccurring [+OBJ] actant interpreted
by the verb as topic of conversation or subject of information in
verbs of information. For example:

68. nag?ulat siya sa amin tungkol sa aksidente
    report   he   us about   accident
    $\begin{bmatrix} +NM \\ +AGT \end{bmatrix}$ $\begin{bmatrix} +L \\ +LOC \end{bmatrix}$ $\begin{bmatrix} +P \\ +AC \\ +[+OBJ] \end{bmatrix}$ $\begin{bmatrix} +L \\ +OBJ \end{bmatrix}$

'He reported to us about the accident.'

2.5.1.2 Accusative Dative [+AC, +DAT]

When the [+DAT] does not cooccur with a [+AGT], it may be
realized in the accusative case form. In this case form, it cooccurs
with a [+OBJ], [+LOC] or [+RSN] realized in the nominative. For
example:

69. nakita ni Jim ang 'air show' (sa bukid)
    see   field
         $\begin{bmatrix} +AC \\ +DAT \end{bmatrix}$ $\begin{bmatrix} +NM \\ +OBJ \end{bmatrix}$ $\begin{bmatrix} +L \\ +LOC \end{bmatrix}$

'The air show was seen by Jim in the field.'

70. kinatakutan ng bata? ang malaking aso
    fear   child   big   dog
              $\begin{bmatrix} +AC \\ +DAT \end{bmatrix}$ $\begin{bmatrix} +NM \\ +OBJ \end{bmatrix}$

'The child feared the big dog.'

2.5.1.3 Accusative Instrumental [+AC, +INS]

The [+INS] almost always occurs in the accusative case form.
When it occurs in the case frame [+[+AGT, +[+OBJ]]], its form may be
modified into a complex noun phrase in the [+L] case form, to mark it
explicitly as having the instrumental case, especially when there are
already two or more identical [+AC] forms. Often, an ambiguity occurs
when the objective case is unexpressed. For example:

71. nagguhit siya ng lapis
    draw   he   pencil
         $\begin{bmatrix} +NM \\ +AGT \end{bmatrix}$ $\begin{bmatrix} +AC \\ +OBJ/+INS \end{bmatrix}$

'He drew a pencil/with a pencil.'

The same sentence may be realized unambiguously as follows:

71.a. nagguhit siya sa pamamagitan ng lapis
                          means   pencil
$$\begin{bmatrix} +L \\ +INS \\ +[+INS] \end{bmatrix}$$ $$\begin{bmatrix} +AC \\ +INS \end{bmatrix}$$

'He drew by means of a pencil.'

2.5.2 Locative Case Form [+L]

The locative case form can host a locative, a dative, an objective or a comitative case relation. A simple, underived agentive verb of location can have two instances of the [+L] case form, excluding outer locatives, optional prepositional phrase locatives, and coreferential locatives. These two [+L] constituents must be a [+LOC] and a definite [+OBJ]. However, when the verb is causative, the possibility of realizing a third actant in the [+L] case form can be attributed to the presence of an additional [+DAT] in the verb's case frame. One other verb type which can compound the occurrence of [+L]'s in a sentence is the social verb in which a [+COM] case relation may also be realized in this case form. For example:

72. nakipagpasalin ako (sa Mama) (kay Cricket) sa
     transfer   I   mother
     [+soc-caus] $$\begin{bmatrix} +NM \\ +AGT \end{bmatrix}$$ $$\begin{bmatrix} +L \\ +COM \end{bmatrix}$$ $$\begin{bmatrix} +L \\ +DAT \end{bmatrix}$$

     pabangong ito sa aking 'atomizer'
     perfume   this   my
     $$\begin{bmatrix} +L \\ +OBJ \end{bmatrix}$$ $$\begin{bmatrix} +L \\ +LOC \end{bmatrix}$$

     'I joined Mother in having Cricket transfer some of this
      perfume to my atomizer.'

This sentence can look forbidding especially if we consider the notion of 'free' ordering of constituents in Tagalog. There are bound to be as many readings here as there are permutations of the case

relations than can be realized as [+L] matched with each lexical
item. However, these readings can be narrowed down on the basis of
some semantic features expressed by the definition of [+OBJ] and
[+LOC]. Perhaps, the crucial distinction is between the [+COM] and
the [+DAT], since both, like the [+AGT], are typically animate.
Failing support from semantic features to make a clear-cut distinction
between these two case relations, we can refer to possible 'preferred'
ordering conditions on constituents. As many linguists would not
contest, the preferred ordering for the case frame requiring [+AGT],
[+OBJ] and [+LOC] in Tagalog is as appears in this sequence. With an
additional [+DAT] in the preceding case frame, the preferred order
is [+AGT], [+DAT], [+OBJ] and [+LOC]. If, in addition to the
preceding four actants, a [+COM] is permitted to cooccur, the order
is identical to the preceding with the [+COM] appearing between the
[+AGT] and the [+DAT], as shown in sentence 72.

The determiner sa marks the locative case form of common nouns.
Before personal names, the determiner is kay indicating a singular
meaning or kina indicating a plural meaning. The [+L] marked
locative set of pronouns can also be assigned any of the case relations
enumerated above which may be realized in [+L]. Directional verbs,
as has been mentioned, may express their locative case relation
through a prepositional phrase. The prepositions galing, mula? and
buhat indicate 'from', hence, [-goal] or source and patungo or
tungo 'toward' and hanggang 'until; up to' refer to [+goal].[16]

2.5.3 Benefactive Case Form [+B]

There is only one case relation which the benefactive case form realizes and that is the benefactive case. The [+B] case form is identified by the preposition para 'for; for the sake of' and as in most prepositional phrases, it governs the [+L] case form of its cooccurring noun phrase. (See examples 52 and 52, pp. 63-64.)

2.5.4 Reason Case Form [+R]

The reason case form realizes only the reason case relation. It is marked by the preposition dahil 'because of' and is followed by the [+L] marked nouns, including names and pronouns. Certain verbs, particularly potential verbs, allow the preposition to be omitted, creating an opportunity for the remaining [+L] marked phrase to be given a different possible case interpretation. (See examples 58.a, 59.a, 60.a, pp.66, 69-70.)

The behavior of the preposition dahil is identical to that of the preposition tungkol 'about' which occurs before a [+OBJ] noun phrase. (See pp. 38-39.) That is, the prepositional phrase as a whole can be preceded by the accusative case form determiner ng rendering dahil a noun, as in the following:

73. na?inis   ang   dalaga   ng   dahil   sa   kaniya
    annoy   maiden   because   him
                    ⎡+NM ⎤   ⎡+N   ⎤   ⎡+L   ⎤
                    ⎣+OBJ⎦   ⎢+AC   ⎥   ⎣+RSN ⎦
                                   ⎢+RSN   ⎥
                                   ⎣+[+RSN]⎦

'The maiden got peeved because of him.'

Unlike the tungkol phrase, however, the full dahil phrase cannot occur in the nominative case form; only the nominative noun phrase can,

84

as in:

73.a. ikina?inis siya ng dalaga
       [+NM]   [+AC]
       [+RSN]   [+OBJ]

'He was the reason for the maiden's being annoyed.'

2.5.5 Comitative Case Form [+C]

The comitative case form which is identified by the preposition

kasama 'in company with' or kasabay 'along with; at the same time as'

realizes only the comitative case relation. Further studies on

prepositions may reveal other derived words with the affix ka- as

possible markers for the [+C] case form, e.g. kasunod 'after;

following', ka?agapay 'shoulder to shoulder with; arm to arm with'.

Moreover, such studies may explain why the following NP of this

preposition is marked [+AC] instead of the widespread [+L]. One

explanation that may be attempted here is that the preposition we

have isolated is possibly a noun or an adverb functioning as predicate

of a non-verbal sentence. This sentence is embedded in the NP

associated with it, thus creating a complex NP. Following this

treatment, sentence 61 on p.71 may have the structure represented

schematically as follows:[17]

61.a.

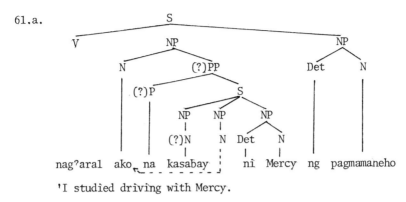

'I studied driving with Mercy.

Two evidences that support this analysis are as follows:

(a) The complementizer na, marked here as a P, which occurs with other types of embedded sentences may also occur before the posited embedded sentence.

(b) Following a, this particular concept of 'togetherness' in the action or event is also expressed by a complex NP structure where the attribute is no longer a sentence but simply a NP, and the head N in order to incorporate the idea of an expressed or unexpressed associate has to be realized in the plural pronoun, thus:

6.b.

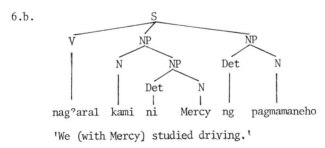

'We (with Mercy) studied driving.'

2.5.6 Nominative Case Form [+NM] and Voice Marking on the Verb

It is a characteristic feature of the case system of Tagalog and the other Philippine languages to realize all verbal case relations in general in the nominative case form which corresponds to the grammatical subject of the sentence. With the exception of the small classes of special verbs which include phenomenal, time, event and existential verbs, one case relation always occurs in the nominative form of every simple verbal sentence. The nominative case form is identified by the determiner ang, marked [+NM], when the actant is a common or abstract noun and by si when it is a personal name, singular in meaning, and sina with the meaning plural. The set of pronouns marked [+NM] realizes any of the case relations compatible with the role identified.

Although the nominative case form neutralizes all case relations it manifests, the identity of the case relation is recoverable through the verb by means of a system of affix marking. Depending on the case relations the verb takes, the verb is marked by a particular affix to indicate which of its cooccurring case relations is realized in the nominative case form. This feature is called voice. Thus, a verb marked with an affix that signals a cooccurring [+AGT] as the grammatical subject is said to be in the agentive voice; with one that indicates a [+OBJ] in the nominative, the verb is in the objective voice; with one that indicates a [+LOC] as subject, the verb is in the locative voice, and so forth. The analysis here shows that there are sets of affixes that identify the voice paradigm of verbs. They are manifested by classes of verbs subcategorized according to their case frame, semantic and morphological-voice features. In the following are identified the case marking affix or

affixes with which each case relation realized in the nominative is
signified. The six voice marking affixes are um-, m-, -in, i-,
-an and ∅.

2.5.6.1 Nominative Agentive [+NM,+AGT]

The agentive case relation manifested in the nominative case
form is marked by the active affix um- or m-. At this point, it
must be emphasized that the approach taken in this study considers
the classification of verb stems rather than verb roots, the latter
being the normal practice in all previous works in Tagalog. (See
detailed discussion in Chapter III.) This means that with the roots
bigay 'give' and kuha 'take', we can also have stems such as
pagbigay, pamigay, pangbigay, kapagbigay, pagpabigay, etc.,
correspondingly. While um- marks the [+AGT] subject for the class
of verbs exemplified by the root-stem kuha, identified here as
belonging to the non-ergative class, [-erg], m- marks the [+AGT]
subject of the stem classes exemplified by pagbigay in one subclass
and panguha in another subclass, both of which share the morphological-
voice features [-pot, +act] read as non-potential active verbs. All
verb stems belonging to these two subclasses have initial p's and
when they are marked by the voice affix m-, the initial p of the
verb stem is fully assimilated to the voice marker m-. Thus,
m-+pagbigay becomes magbigay, and m-+panguha becomes manguha.
It will be shown later how this type of classification and marking
can express more significant generalizations than a root classification
and marking with affixes such as mag-, mang-, and ma-, as in mano?od

'watch' and <u>makinig</u> 'listen', and why this analysis is preferable or desirable.[18]

2.5.6.2 Nominative Objective [+NM,+OBJ]

Of all case relations, the object cooccurs with the greatest number of verb subclasses, and it is marked in the verb with a voice affix according to the type of verb it cooccurs with. Being this basic, it is not surprising to find that it can be marked by all types of voice marking affixes available in the language. It can be marked by either of the active affixes <u>um</u>- and <u>m</u>- and by any of the passive affixes -<u>in</u>, <u>i</u>-, or -<u>an</u> or by Ø which means no affix at all. (The specific case frame, semantic and morphological-voice marking of each verb subclass with the corresponding affix will be discussed in detail in the next chapter.)

2.5.6.3 Nominative Dative [+NM,+DAT]

The dative case relation occurs in two major subcategories of verbs, namely, information and psychological verbs and in one type of secondary derived verbs--the causative verbs. Information verbs marked with the affix -<u>an</u> and subclasses of psych verbs marked by Ø and another subclass marked by -<u>an</u> signify that the cooccurring [+DAT] is realized in the nominative case form. With causative verbs with a cooccurring [+DAT] as subject, the voice affix is -<u>in</u>.

2.5.6.4 Nominative Locative [+NM,+LOC]

The inner locative case relation when realized in the nominative case form is always marked in the verb by the affix -<u>an</u>. The problem

of ambiguity with one affix marking two different case relations
arises when -an marks a nominative objective case and a nominative
locative case in identical verb stem forms. For example:

74.a. papahiran niya   ang mesa
       mop   he   table
                  [+AC]   [+NM]
                  [+AGT]   [+OBJ]

'He will mop the table.'

74.b. papahiran niya ng barnis   ang mesa
       apply   he   varnish   table
                  [+AC]   [+AC]   [+NM]
                  [+AGT]   [+OBJ]   [+LOC]

'He will apply varnish on the table.'

With some subclasses of non-strict locative verbs, the root forms
of stems, particularly those that are marked by -an to indicate a
[+NM,+OBJ], do not manifest a locative case in the nominative at all.
Instead, the related stem characterized by either the affix pag- or
pang-, signifying an active verb stem, is marked by -an to express a
locative voice. For example:

75.a. {linabhan}
       {nilabhan} niya ang damit na naputikan sa palanggana
       launder   she   dress   soiled   basin
                   [+AC]   [+NM]   [+L]
                   [+AGT]   [+OBJ]   [+LOC]

'The soiled dress was washed by her in the basin.'

75.b. pinaglabhan niya ng damit na naputikan ang palanggana
                    [+AC]   [+AC]   [+NM]
                    [+AGT]   [+OBJ]   [+LOC]

'The basin was used by her to launder the soiled dress in.'

As mentioned earlier, there is a class of derived locative verbs
which indicates outer locatives as being the cooccurring subject.
Being identical in form and marked by the same affix -an as the

location verbs that indicate an inner locative subject, these

derived verbs can be easily confused with inherent location verbs in

the locative voice. (See pp. 48-49.) For example:

76. paglalaru?an nila ng 'pingpong' ang aming 'basement'
    play in   they   our
    $\begin{bmatrix} +AC \\ +AGT \end{bmatrix}$ $\begin{bmatrix} +AC \\ +OBJ \end{bmatrix}$ $\begin{bmatrix} +NM \\ +LOC \end{bmatrix}$

'Our basement will be used by them to play pingpong in.'

The distinction is more apparent in the case of a derived locative

verb which comes from one with a locative voice form. Compare the

following:

77.a. pinagbigyan ni Clara ng regalo kay Rosa ang
      given-to   gift
      $\begin{bmatrix} +AC \\ +AGT \end{bmatrix}$ $\begin{bmatrix} +AC \\ +OBJ \end{bmatrix}$ $\begin{bmatrix} +L \\ +LOC \end{bmatrix}$

      katulong nito
      maid   this
      $\begin{bmatrix} +NM \\ +LOC \end{bmatrix}$

'The maid was handed a present by Clara for Rosa.'

77.b. binigyan ni Clara ng regalo si Rosa
      give
      $\begin{bmatrix} +AC \\ +AGT \end{bmatrix}$ $\begin{bmatrix} +AC \\ +OBJ \end{bmatrix}$ $\begin{bmatrix} +NM \\ +LOC \end{bmatrix}$

'Rosa was given a gift by Clara.'

The meaning of the derived verb in 77.a differs from that of the

source verb in 77.b. The former indicates that the locative subject

is not the intended goal or terminal of the objective referent. It

expresses only 'place of giving'. The latter means that the locative

subject is the end goal or recipient of the objective referent.[19]

2.5.6.5 Nominative Instrumental [+NM,+INS]

The instrumental case relation ordinarily occurs in the nominative
case form only when it cooccurs with a [+AGT]. It is identified in
the verb with the affix i- and the verb stem is a derived form with
the affix pang-. When the verb root-stem does not employ the i- affix
to designate a nominative objective, the root-stem with i- may also
signify the [+NM,+INS]. For example, either of the following
sentences is acceptable:

78.a. ipangbubungkal niya ng hukay ang asarol na ito
       dig   he   pit   hoe   this
       $\begin{bmatrix} +AC \\ +AGT \end{bmatrix}$ $\begin{bmatrix} +AC \\ +OBJ \end{bmatrix}$ $\begin{bmatrix} +NM \\ +INS \end{bmatrix}$

       'This hoe will be used by him to dig a pit.'

78.b. ibubungkal niya ng hukay ang asarol na ito
       $\begin{bmatrix} +AC \\ +AGT \end{bmatrix}$ $\begin{bmatrix} +AC \\ +OBJ \end{bmatrix}$ $\begin{bmatrix} +NM \\ +INS \end{bmatrix}$

2.5.6.6 Nominative Benefactive [+NM,+BEN]

The benefactive case relation in the nominative case form is
marked in the verb by the voice affix i-. The verb stems which require
the cooccurrence of a [+NM,+BEN] are the same verb stems that allow a
cooccurring [+NM,+AGT]. When the agentive subject is realized by
either a root-stem or a derived active stem, a benefactive may also
be realized by the same stem. For example:

79. iginawa? ng nanay ng damit ang manika? ni Melissa
     make   mother   dress   doll
     $\begin{bmatrix} +AC \\ +AGT \end{bmatrix}$ $\begin{bmatrix} +AC \\ +OBJ \end{bmatrix}$ $\begin{bmatrix} +NM \\ +BEN \end{bmatrix}$

     'Mother made a dress for Melissa's doll.'

80. ipagdidilig   niya   ng   halaman   ang   nanay
    water   she   plants   mother
                  [+AC]   [+AC]   [+NM]
                  [+AGT]   [+OBJ]   [+OBJ]

'She will water the plants for mother.'

The agentive voice forms of 79 and 80 are gumawa? and magdilig whose

stems are the root gawa? and the derived stem pagdilig, respectively.

There are instances in which root-stems of non-locative or

even non-strict locative verbs are used with the affix -an instead of

i- to indicate a benefactive subject. They have become acceptable,

although the element of ambiguity in the verb as marking also a

[+NM,+LOC] remains. For example:

81. binilhan   ng   nanay   ng   damit   ang   kaibigan   niya
    buy   mother   dress   friend   her
                    [+AC]   [+AC]   [+NM]   [+NM]
                    [+AGT]   [+OBJ]   [+LOC] or [+BEN]

'Mother bought a dress from/for her friend.'

Because of its limitations, this particular form with the -an marker

is considered an 'irregular' benefactive voice form.

2.5.6.7   Nominative Reason [+NM,+RSN]

The case relation here labelled [+RSN], which refers to the

cause or reason for the occurrence of an action, event or state, when

realized in the nominative case form is marked in the verb by the

affix i-, too. The verb stem, however, is a derived form with the

prefix ka-. For example:

82. ikinapagluto? kaagad   ng nanay   ng pagka?in
    cook   immediately   mother   food
                                       $\begin{bmatrix} +AC \\ +AGT \end{bmatrix}$ $\begin{bmatrix} +AC \\ +OBJ \end{bmatrix}$

    ang pagdating ng mga bisita
         arrival   visitors
         $\begin{bmatrix} +NM \\ +RSN \end{bmatrix}$

    'The visitors' arrival caused mother to cook food immediately.'

83. ikinata?as ng presyon niya ang pagkawala? ng
    rise   pressure his   loss
                $\begin{bmatrix} +AC \\ +OBJ \end{bmatrix}$ $\begin{bmatrix} +NM \\ +RSN \end{bmatrix}$

    kaniyang anak
    his   child

    'The loss of his child caused his blood pressure to rise.'

2.5.6.8 Nominative Comitative [+NM,+COM]

Of the verbs that may allow the occurrence of a [+COM], only

the derived secondary social verbs can allow it to be realized in

the nominative case form. This manifestation is marked by the affix

-an appended to a derived social verb stem identified by the prefix

paki-. For examples, see 64 and 66, p.72.

2.6 Summary of Case Relation and Case Form Correspondences

The following charts show in summary the correspondences

between case relations and case forms with their case markers, and

those between case relations in the nominative case form and their

voice affix markers in the verb.

Case Relation	OBJ	AGT	LOC	DAT	INS	BEN	RSN	COM
Case Form; Case Marker								
+NM : +Det, ang	x	x	x	x	x	x	x	x
+AC : +Det, ng	x	x		x	x			
: +P, tungkol hinggil	x							
+L : +Det, sa	x		x	x	x			x
: +P, +goal patungo hanggang				x				
: +P, -goal mula? buhat galing				x				
+B : +P, para						x		
+R : +R, dahil							x	
+C : +P, kasama kasabay								x

Chart 1. Tagalog case relations and case forms with corresponding case markers

Voice Affix in Verb: \ Nominative Case Relation	UM-	M-	-IN	I-	-AN	Ø
1. [+NM, +AGT]	x	x				
2. [+NM, +OBJ]	x	x	x	x	x	x
3. [+NM, +LOC]					x	
4. [+NM, +DAT]			x		x	x
5. [+NM, +INS]				x		
6. [+NM, +BEN]				x		
7. [+NM, +RSN]				x		
8. [+NM, +COM]					x	

Chart 2. Tagalog case relations in the nominative case form and the corresponding voice affixes that mark them in the verb

The analysis of CR's and CF's in this study inevitably led to the distinction between determiners and prepositions, i.e., Det is a sister category of N whereas P is a sister category of NP; both categories are marked for CF; the CF of the P is the CF of the entire PP. The distinctions arrived at lend clarity to the otherwise confused status of particles, noun markers, prepositions and similar categories that have been used in relation to noun phrase and prepositional phrase constructions. The problem of whether the complement marker consists of "a particle or a particle phrase" (Constantino, 1965:80) has, to my knowledge, not yet been satisfactorily described. This problem is recognized by Constantino himself (1965: footnote 13, p.80), but the paper he intends to write (or probably has written) on this particular problem (1965: footnote 14, p.81) has unfortunately not reached my attention. Even in Otanes (1966:133), the constituent labelled 'Intro(ducer)' which occurs before a NP to make up an adverbial complement is expressed by various syntactic forms such as <u>para sa</u>, <u>dahil sa</u>, <u>sa pamamagitan ng</u>, <u>sa</u>, <u>nang</u>, <u>tungkol sa</u>. A similar description is found in Ramos (1974:99) where the case marking particles may be the simple ones, e.g., <u>ng/ni</u> and <u>sa/kay</u> (<u>ang</u> being identified apart as a subject marker), or "compound forms incorporating them: e.g., <u>para sa/ para kay</u> 'for', <u>dahil sa/dahil kay</u> 'because of', and <u>sa pamamagitan ng</u> 'by means of'."

The present analysis profits quite significantly from the system of sorting out PP's and NP's in their simple and complex forms. By the account that has been explicated here, we are no longer forced to group 'simple and complex' particles under one category label, and neither are we compelled to set up various kinds of nominal phrases beyond NP's and PP's. The distinction made between Det's and P's, based on their syntactic relation with N and NP, respectively, and on the case forms each class may be specified with, gives a clearer picture of case-marking of nominal phrases.

In connection with verbs, it has been noted at various points in this chapter that some of the verb forms identified here as signifying a cooccurring [+NM,+LOC] with <u>pag-</u> and <u>ka-</u> stems, a [+NM,+RSN] or, perhaps, even others such as a [+NM,+BEN] and a [+NM,+INS] with <u>pang-</u> stems have not been thoroughly established as verbs. Capell, along with

Müller and Lopez, treats the passive forms of the verbs as nouns on the basis of the occurrence of the possessive forms (accusative case form) of pronouns which mark the 'actors' (1964:239). This reason is not totally convincing because the possessive forms in Tagalog, as well as in Indonesian and Formosan languages (Starosta, personal communication), have a very broad range of uses which makes the 'evidence' for the claim weak. For purposes of this study, we will leave this question open, and provisionally assume that they are verbs. At some later time, some of these forms may turn out to be nominals, in which case the DR's posited here have to be modified or supplemented accordingly.

2.7 Phrase structure Rules for Tagalog

2.7.1 PS Rules

The Phrase Structure Rules (PSR's) component of the lexicase grammar generates bracketed strings of grammatical categories to which corresponding lexical items from the lexicon are inserted. The rules are context-free and they apply to category symbols. The bracketed strings contain general information of syntactic categories and of ordering and hierarchical relationships of constituents necessary for the insertion of lexical items. A lexical item is allowed to be inserted if the syntactic category feature marked on it is identical to the syntactic category labelling the node under which the lexical item is to be inserted. The contextual features in the lexical entry are stated in terms of sister categories and thus, the hierarchical information the phrase structure rules give is indispensable. These contextual features must be compatible with the environment given by the string. They must match with the terminal category nodes, and there must be no contextual features violated.

Strings of simple grammatical sentences in Tagalog are formed following the rules stated below:

$$\text{PSR-1:} \quad S \longrightarrow (\text{Modal})(\text{Neg})(\text{Modal}) \left\{ \begin{array}{l} \left\{ \begin{array}{l} \text{NP} \\ \text{AdjP} \\ \text{PP} \end{array} \right\} \text{NP} \\ \text{V } (\text{NP})^n (\text{PP})^n (\text{S}) \end{array} \right\} (\text{Adv})$$

$$\text{PSR-2:} \quad PP \longrightarrow P \left\{ \begin{array}{l} \text{NP} \\ \text{S} \end{array} \right\}$$

$$\text{PSR-3:} \quad AdjP \longrightarrow Adj \ (\text{NP})$$

$$\text{PSR-4:} \quad NP \longrightarrow (\text{Det}) \ N \ (\left\{ \begin{array}{l} \text{NP} \\ \text{PP} \\ \text{S} \end{array} \right\})$$

The symbols are to be interpreted as follows:

$\longrightarrow$: The symbol to the left of the arrow consists of the constituents to the right of it.

$(\ )$: Parentheses indicate optionality of occurrence.

$\{\ \}$: Braces indicate obligatory choice of one of the elements within them.

X^n : Superscript $\underline{n}$ means any number of actants allowed by the cooccurring verb.

S   : Sentence

NP   : Noun phrase

AdjP   : Adjective phrase

PP   : Prepositional phrase

Modal   : Modal includes optative words such as <u>kahimanawari?</u> <u>nawa?</u> 'would that,' indeterminate particles such as

baka? 'may; probably', marahil 'perhaps', tila 'seem',
quotative particles such as daw 'so it is said', and
other types of modals. (The order restrictions are
specified on each item.)

Neg   : Negative words such as hindi? 'not', huwag 'don't'.

V   : Verb

Adv   : Adverb

P   : Preposition

Adj   : Adjective

Det   : Determiner

N   : Noun

2.7.2 Some Basic Sentence Types

PSR-1 generates two major types of basic sentences, namely,
non-verbal and verbal sentences. Both types may cooccur with optional
constituents such as modal, negative and adverb. Because this study
centers on verb forms and the cooccurring actants that subcategorize
them, no attempt will be made to explain the conditions on these
optional constituents. These constituents are not relevant environments
to the modification of verb forms and their corresponding subcategorization. They have been identified in the portion of the rule that
generates non-verbal and verbal sentences only to indicate the
possible position of their occurrence.

2.7.2.1 Non-verbal Sentences

The non-verbal sentences are identified by their predicate
constituent construction (the first constituent) as a) equational,

with a NP, b) descriptive or impersonal, with a AdjP, and c) locational, with a PP. The two NP constituents of an equational sentence have the same referent. For example:

84. guro? ang tatay ko
    teacher   father my

    'My father is a teacher.'

85. laru?an ito
    toy   this

    'This is a toy.'

86. Linggo bukas
    Sunday tomorrow

    'Tomorrow is Sunday.'

The descriptive or impersonal sentences are classified further into two subtypes according to their adjectival constituents: a) The special descriptive type consists of either an existential adjective or an impersonal adjective such as may/mayro?on 'have; there is', wala? 'don't have; there is none' and gusto 'like; enjoy; want', ayaw 'don't like; don't enjoy; don't want', respectively. These adjectives are special in that they obligatorily cooccur with a following NP. They may or may not occur with a grammatical subject, that is, a NP marked with a nominative determiner. For example:

87. may lamat ang baso-ng ito
    have crack   glass   this

    'This glass has a crack.'

88. may miting sa plasa
    have meeting   town square

    'There is a meeting at the town square.'

89. gusto niya ang bago-ng bahay nila
    like he   new   house their

    'He likes their new house.'

90. ayaw ng kapatid ko ng 'abstract painting'
    don't   sister my
    like

'My sister does not like abstract painting.'

b) The simple descriptive type does not require a cooccurring NP complement in the AdjP and it always cooccurs with a grammatical subject. For example:

91. matalino   ang anak nina En Jin at Harry
    intelligent   child

'En Jin and Harry's child is intelligent.'

The third type of non-verbal sentences labelled locational is further distinguished by the kind of PP it manifests into: a) temporal location, marked by the preposition na followed by a locative noun phrase, b) reservational, marked by the benefactive preposition para followed by a locative noun phrase, and c) possessive, unmarked by any preposition and identified by a noun phrase in the locative case form (marked by sa or kay/kina) expressing ownership of the subject referent. When the locative noun phrase is a personal pronoun, the sa-marker may be omitted. Each of these subtypes is exemplified below:

92. na sa sala   ang mag?anak
      living room   family

'The family is in the living room.'

93. para sa kuya ang regalo-ng ito
    for   eldest present   this
         brother

'This present is for eldest brother.'

94. (sa) kaniya ang trabaho-ng iyan
       his   work   that

'That work is his.'

2.7.2.2 Verbal Sentences

The second portion of PSR-1 which requires the occurrence of at least a V constituent in the string generates the verbal type of sentences. As will be discussed in Chapter III, the primary verb stem subcategories based on their case frame features manifest corresponding subtypes of verbal sentences. Seven major types are established. They are a) information, b) location, c) simple transitive, d) locomotion, e) calamity, f) simple intransitive, and g) psych verbs. Each subclass of verbs reflects its corresponding sentence structure in terms of number and types of NP's and/or PP's the verb allows. The structure of strings with secondary verb stems will be treated in Chapter IV.

FOOTNOTES TO CHAPTER II

[1]This view is shared by De Guzman (1968), Constantino (1971), Schachter and Otanes (1972) and Ramos (1974).

[2]Lawrence Reid (personal communication) pointed out that his informant claims that the only meaning of this sentence is 'He will cook-well/over-cook the chicken.' This is not necessarily so. It is only another meaning. In fact, the adverb mabuti 'well; thoroughly' usually cooccurs with the verb in this sense.

[3]An alternative analysis adopted in this study is that pronouns and pronominal adjectives are not inflected in the usual sense but rather are marked with inherent inflectional case form features. (See Appendix A.)

[4]By employing syntactic and semantic features in the analysis of verbs, this study shares some similarities with the work done by Ramos (1974). However, as will be pointed out later, there are substantial differences between these two studies.

[5]This term is also used by Bloomfield (1917), Lopez (1937), McKaughan (1958:1962), Wolfenden (1961), Constantino (1965), and Llamzon (1966: 1968). Others prefer to call it focus. Among them are the linguists from the Summer Institute of Linguistics, Capell (1964), Otanes (1966) and Schachter and Otanes (1972).

[6]These constructions and constituents are taken up under the section on Phrase Structure Rules. For a thorough discussion of grammatical relations between constituents, refer to Starosta (forthcoming).

[7]To make the sentence grammatical, only the head noun dalaga must occur after the nominative Det ang.

[8]This distinction refers to [+LOC]'s in the non-nominative case form only since if it is in the nominative, it has to occur grammatically. Its absence as [+NM] is considered to be a matter of performance, or a restriction on the verb subclass.

[9]This analysis is in agreement with Schachter and Otanes' (1972) and Ramos' (1974) classification of directional verbs.

[10]In other languages such as Melayu Betawi, some Formosan languages, Japanese, and Vietnamese, the [+DAT] as the goal or the source in ditransitive verbs is also realized, although only partially in some, in the locative case form. See Ikranagara (1975), Starosta (1974), Taylor (1971), and Clark (1975), respectively. If the two actants are distinguished in case form, it may suggest that a split has occurred.

[11]Other linguists have maintained that the [+OBJ] identified here as cooccurring with [+LOC] is a [+AGT]. However, it has been found fruitful in terms of stating generalizations if the lexicase analysis of this actant as [+OBJ] is followed. (See Chapter III on verb subcategorization.)

[12]Despite the phonological feature distinctions between an ability and an accidental verb form, which in many cases are no longer kept by native speakers, these two types have been treated here as one designated by the feature potential, [+pot], for the purposes of this study.

[13]The marking of the actant sa Pasko 'at Christmas' with [+LOC] should be considered tentative because it could also be marked with a time case relation, if such is posited. In view of the adverbial nature of many time elements and their restricted capacity for occurring only in non-nom-inative case form, which means that no verb form realizes them as subject, the possibility of their being actants with a Time case relation was not explored in this study. For the same reasons, expressions of Manner are also excluded.

[14]The distinction between definite and indefinite goals (OBJ here) is adopted from Constantino (1965:80).

[15]The use of the pronoun dito marked [+L, +OBJ] should be distinguished from dito marked [+L, +LOC].

[16]The class of prepositions set up here may be divided into inherent or underived prepositions and co-verbs or derived prepositions. This is another interesting unexplored area of study in Tagalog.

[17]Note the tentativeness of the analysis of the prepositonal phrase PP and the non-verbal embedded sentence marked by the symbol (?). The system of marking the missing complement subject of the embedded sentence pointing to the corresponding complement in the matrix sentence is adopted from Kullavanijaya (1974:254).

[18]It may be pointed out that the voice affixes discussed here are those that mark verb roots and verb stems which are syntactically derived. Se-mantically derived verbs such as abilitatives or accidentals from [-erg], [+erg] and [-pot, +act], e.g. makakuha 'able to get', mabigyan 'able to be given to', are not covered in this study.

[19]It may be mentioned that another derived verb of the form pagbigyan has the meaning 'to give in'.

CHAPTER III

TAGALOG VERB INFLECTION AND

PRIMARY VERB STEM SUBCATEGORIZATION

3.1 Inflectional and Derivational Affixes in Verbs in Previous
      Works on Tagalog

In this study, voice as the case-indicating feature of the verb
realized as an affix is described as inflectional. It is
inextricably linked with the case frame and semantic features of the
verb. On the other hand, affixes that have nothing to do directly
with marking the nominative case form of a particular case relation
are considered derivational. Before proceeding to a more detailed
discussion of the terms inflection and derivation, it will be
instructive, at this point, to review briefly how some of the most
important works on Tagalog grammar treat verbal affixes. Some of
them make explicit distinctions while others merely imply them. On
the basis of this presentation, we can determine in what respects
the present analysis is similar to previous analyses and, more
importantly, in what fundamental respects it differs from them.

Of all Philippine languages, major as well as minor, Tagalog
has received the widest attention from Philippine linguists. The
study of the verb, in particular, has been so fascinating that even
to this date, attempts at refining past descriptions abound. The
most widely known scientific grammars are those written by Bloomfield
(1917), Blake (1925) and Lopez (1941). According to Constantino
(1971:42), Bloomfield's grammar is considered superior to the other

two. He also states that Lopez's grammar shows the influence of
Bloomfield's analysis. Despite this recommendation, we will consider
both Bloomfield's and Blake's works for comparison because of the
valuable insights contained in their treatment of verbal affixes.
The other significant studies represent two more recent major
approaches: a) a modified structural framework by Wolfenden (1961)
and by Llamzon (1968); and b) a generative transformational framework
by Otanes (1966) and by Ramos (1974).[1] Each of these works is
presented in the sequence it has been cited.

3.1.1 Bloomfield (1917)

Bloomfield's grammatical analysis of Tagalog is considered
to be "by far the most well-known and by far the most influential
work on any Philippine language" (Constantino, 1971:28). It became
the model for many succeeding descriptive studies of various
Philippine languages and dialects. His use of new grammatical
terms in place of traditional, established ones to stress the
difference between Tagalog and primarily any other Indo-European
language, however, offers no special advantage to the analysis.[2]

Bloomfield labels verbs transient words and classifies them
into four types "according to the four relations which a subject may
bear to them when they are used as predicates" (1917:153-4). He
designates these classes with the following names: 1) active: the
subject is viewed as an actor; 2) direct passive: the subject is
viewed as an object fully affected or produced; 3) instrumental
passive: the subject is viewed as a means, an instrument, something

given forth or parted from; and 4) local passive: the subject is viewed as an object partly or less fully affected, as a place or sphere (1917:154).

In his discussion of transient formation, he describes each active and passive form as existing in "two modes, actual and contingent, and each of these has two aspects, punctual and durative" (1917:217). This system gives rise to four different forms of each active or passive type each of which corresponds to the following more common terms in Philippine linguistics and in grammar in general indicated in parentheses:

(a) actual-punctual (past or completed), e.g. nag?aral 'studied';

(b) actual-durative (progressive or continuing; present), e.g., nag?aaral 'is or was studying; studies';

(c) contingent-punctual (infinitive), e.g., mag?aral 'study';

(d) contingent-durative (future or not begun or contemplated), e.g., mag?aaral 'will study'.

He further identifies each active and passive verb according to the affix it takes as follows:

(a) active with -um-, e.g., pumutol 'cut'

(b) active with mag-, e.g., maglako? 'peddle'

(c) active with mang-, e.g. mamili 'shop'

(d) direct passive with -in, e.g., putulin 'cut'

(e) instrumental passive with i-, e.g., iputol, use for cutting'; ipagdiwang 'celebrate'; ipagputol 'cut for'; ipangharang 'use for holding up'

(f) local passive with -an, e.g., putulan 'cut from',
bakuran 'fence', bigyan 'give to'
It will be noted that each type of passive has only one characteristic
affix. Each is described as corresponding to forms in the active
with either the -um-, mag- or mang- affix. Bloomfield mentions
that some passive forms corresponding to actives with mag- are
prefixed with pag- and others corresponding to those with mang- are
prefixed with pang-.[3]

The above set of verbs belongs to what Bloomfield refers to as
primary formations. Verb forms which take affixes different from or
in addition to those in the primary formations belong to secondary
formations. The affixes of secondary forms which generally combine
with those in primary forms are -si-, paki-, ka-, pa- and pati-.
Certain secondary forms with ka- are said to have varied meanings.
They are identified as involuntary if ka- is without an accent and
as accidental if ka- is accented. The active form of these verbs
takes the full affix maka- while the direct passive form takes only
ma-, e.g., makagawa? 'be able to make', mabasag 'can be broken; to
get broken'. It may be noted that the direct passive forms, like the
active ones, express various types of subjects. Furthermore, the
direct passive forms may or may not correspond to an active form.
Thus, we find verbs such as mabali? 'get broken', magambala? 'get
disturbed' although expressing "an object which undergoes or has
undergone a process due to an inanimate actor or to no actor in
particular" (1917:284) and verbs such as maawa? 'pity someone',
maginaw 'get or be cold', mahiya? 'feel embarrassed' denoting "the

animate performer of an involuntary act, which, then, is looked upon rather as an undergoing than as a performing" (1917:285) falling under the same class.

According to Bloomfield, the instrumental passive of the above set of verbs seems to occur only with pag- and pang- with the i-affix following the ma- (1917:287). The locative passive has the prefix ma- and the suffix -an or it can occur with the explicative pag- as in mapaglagari?an 'place available for sawing'. The set of forms with ka- expressing accidental actions or events are formed with identical affixes as above, except for the difference in accent.

Bloomfield's exhaustive enumeration of the possible verb forms extends beyond the secondary formations. Under primary formation, he describes other modified forms that have identifiable meanings such as a) mutual or concerted action, b) plentiful or diverse action, and c) repeated action at intervals. In this account of special verb formation, he did not fail to describe the accent shifts necessary in some of these forms. Other verb forms included are those whose roots or stems are derived from other words, particularly nouns and adjectives, phrases or compound words.

Although Bloomfield is non-committal with regard to the identification of inflectional and derivational affixes in verbs, the distinction he makes between active and passive forms is considered significant. To a certain extent, it implies that there is a relation existing between an active form and a passive form that share a common root. Unfortunately, the nature of the relation is not clearly established. His reference to the passive forms as corresponding to certain active forms may also give the wrong impression that for every active form there is a corresponding predictable passive form in three different types. The correspondence is only true for verbs that allow the cooccurrence of certain case relations which in turn can be permitted to occur in the nominative case form. Furthermore, with verbs that allow only one case relation, the verb form can only be either active or passive and not active and passive. For example, the verb bumagsak 'fall' is in the active form and takes only a cooccurring [+OBJ] case relation. This form can appear in no other underived passive form with only the same case relation. It can occur in the potential form with the derivational affix ma- as in mabagsak 'accidentally drop; fall unexpectedly' which is of a different semantic and morphological class from the primary form with um-.

Bloomfield isolates pag- and pang- as important affixes in word formation in general. However, he sets up mag- as a different affix from pag- and, likewise, mang- as different from pang- either of which pairs may be affixed to a verb root or a verb stem.

The case relation of the subject identified by each of the four types of verbs postulated by Bloomfield is not clearly defined. For example, his active form with um- expresses "the actor in a simple action or process" (1917:226). Thus, transitive verbs such as umagaw 'snatch', pumutol 'cut' which cooccur with an actor (or agent) and an object are classified together with intransitive verbs such as bumaba? 'go down', bumaluktot 'bend, curl up', uminit 'become hot' which require no actors but simply objects. Concerning the direct passive, there is no problem of one affix marking more than one case relation as subject. The direct passive marked by the affix -in always signifies that the subject is "an object viewed as fully affected, taken in by the actor, or created by a simple action" (1917:243). However, the two other passive types, the instrumental and the local passive, denote case relations other than what the labels indicate. As Bloomfield states, the instrumental passive "denotes, transiently, an object given forth, parted from, or used as instrument or the person for whom in such and such an action or process" (1917:248), and the local passive "denotes the thing affected as place in which or the person to whom" (1917:250). Without these individual definitions, it is easy to associate the instrumental passive or local passive only with the case relations suggested by the labels.[5]

In connection with the last two types of passive voice forms, two questions may be raised: (a) With the object, benefactive, and instrument relations neutralized by the instrumental passive form of the verb, how can the following pairs of sentences be distinguished without marking the case relation of their subject:

```
1.a.   ipuputol  niya  ito   ng   tubo
       cut       he    this       sugar cane
                       ⎡+NM ⎤
                       ⎣+INS⎦
```

'He will cut sugar cane with this.'

1.b. ipuputol niya ito ng tubo
$\begin{bmatrix} +NM \\ +BEN \end{bmatrix}$

'He will cut some sugar cane for this.'

2.a. ipinangbahay niya ang bagong tsinelas
use for house he   new   slippers
$\begin{bmatrix} +NM \\ +OBJ \end{bmatrix}$

'He used the new slippers for house-wear.'

2.b. ipinanghiwa? niya ng mansanas ang lansita
use for cut- he   apple   jack knife
ting
$\begin{bmatrix} +NM \\ +INS \end{bmatrix}$

'He used the jack knife for cutting an apple.'

(b) As shown in a, the classification of verbs exclusively according
to the affix i- which marks the general label instrumental passive
does not only obscure the differences between two case relations as
subjects that can be marked identically in the verb; it also seems to
place a minor importance on the syntactic requirements of each type
of verb stem that may be marked by the same affix (see examples 2.a
and 2.b).

3.1.2 Blake (1925)

Although Blake completed his grammar of Tagalog in 1902 and
revised it in 1910, it did not get published until 1925 (Constantino,
1971:24). This means that this grammar actually antedates
Bloomfield's. The most important feature of the Tagalog verb as
analyzed by Blake is the recognition of the expression of case by
the verbs and by the case forms of the articles placed before common
nouns or personal names or of the pronouns and pronominal adjectives.
As far as voice is concerned, he comes up with practically the same

classes of verbs as Bloomfield. He sets up an active voice form and
three passive ones, labelled, in-passive, i-passive, and an-passive.
To him, the use of these forms depends on the relative importance of
the various elements, the most important or the most emphatic idea
being made the subject of the sentence. If this is the agent of the
action expressed by the verb, the active voice is used; if it is
any other element of the sentence, then one of the three passives
is employed (1925:140). Blake's identification of the general uses
of the passives slightly differs from Bloomfield's; "the in-passive is
used when the object of the action towards the agent (e.g., to take)
is made the subject; the i-passive when the subject is the object of
an action away from the agent (e.g., to give), or the instrument or
cause of the action; the an-passive, when a place or anything regarded
as place, stands as subject" (1925:141-2). In connection with the
case relation of the noun that is made subject of the verb as
indicated by the verbal affixes, the same shortcomings noted above in
Bloomfield's analysis may be said of Blake's.

Similar to Bloomfield's mode-aspect categorization, Blake
distinguishes four mode and tense forms for every stem as follows
(1925:40):

    (a) modal (subjunctive, imperative, infinitive)

    (b) future

    (c) preterite

    (d) present

He identifies verbs, then, as being inflected to express voice and
tense (1925:13). However, he does not give any definite statements

as to which of the verbal affixes he considers inflectional and which are derivational.

The most valuable insight in Blake's analysis of the verb derives from his classification of verbal affixes, which he calls verbal particles, into principal and subsidiary types. The principal particles are employed to form the ordinary finite verb, the subsidiary ones make certain special verbal forms. It will be instructive to present below the seventeen classes of principal particles Blake sets up according to the active particle so that we can identify the pattern of structure the verb stems manifest. These classes fall into five groups as follows (1925:38):

	I	II	III	IV	V
a	um	mag	man	ma	pa
b		magsi	manhi	maka	magpa
c		magsa			magpaka
d		magka			
e		maki			
f		magin(g)			
g		magkan			
h		magkapa			
i		magpati			

Correspondingly, Blake states that all of these classes with the exception of I, have a special passive particle which is used instead of the active particle when the verb is passive. He lists these special passive particles as follows (1925:39):

	I	II	III	IV	V
a		pag	pan	ka, ma, maka	pa
b		pagsi	panhi, hi	ka, ma	pa, pagpa
c		pagsa, sa			paka, pagpaka
d		pagpa			
e		paki			
f		pagin(g)			
g		pagkan			
h		pagkapa			
i		pagpati			

Recognizing the exceptions in some of these classes, Blake accounts
for the formation of the special passive particles, in general,
by changing the initial m of the active to p.

In view of this account, two important observations can be made:

(a) Blake's classification of principal particles (affixes)
into active and passive, the former consisting of the affixes in
the first list above and the latter requiring the combination of
the special passive particles, except IV, and one of the essential
passive particles i-, -in or -an with a given root, appears to be
rather unbalanced. Firstly, each active particle is complete and
ready to be affixed to a root to form an active verb, whereas the
special passive particle, in most cases, has to be combined with
another so-called essential passive particle in its occurrence with
a root to form a passive verb. Secondly, whereas the active roots
of class I are marked by um- and those of the other classes by
active affixes with initial m-, except V.a, their passive counterparts
are all marked by any one of the essential passive particles i-,
-in, or -an.

(b) The affixes ma- and maka- behave differently from the affixes
with initial m or p. They remain unaltered in either the active or
passive set. This strongly suggests a separate class for verbs
marked by these affixes which contrasts with all the other groups of
stems.

The importance of Blake's grouping of particles is the indication
of the verb's capacity to take on various forms in the active or passive
voice, marked by a corresponding active or passive affix. Another

significant lead provided by Blake's analysis is his account of
secondary and tertiary derivation whereby the principal verbal
particles of the various classes are combined in the same verb, the
second particle, either active or passive, being regularly prefixed
to the 'passive' stem of the primary verb, except in certain cases
(1925:50), e.g., maka-pag-laro? 'be able to play', pa-pag-labas 'have
taken out', i-ka-pagpati-hulog 'cause to throw oneself downward'.
This will be referred to in detail in the next chapter on verb
derivation.

3.1.3 Wolfenden (1961)

Wolfenden's grammar presents an analysis of the verb structure
which is different in certain respects from the two works discussed
in the preceding sections. He identifies quite definitely the
various inflectional categories of the verb and their corresponding
affix realizations. To him, Tagalog verbs are inflected for four
aspects, five modes, and five voice-modes (1961:13-14). His voice-
mode category is comparable with the active and passive distinctions
made by Bloomfield and Blake. The major difference lies in the
identification of the active affixes which mark the subjective
(actor or agent) relation. Instead of -um, mag-, mang- as set up
by Bloomfield (and partly by Blake), Wolfenden lists them as follows
with corresponding modal descriptions:

(a) -um- 'causal'

(b) -ag- 'comprehensive'

(c) -ang- 'iterative or habitual action'

To all purposes, the objective, locative and implicative (instrumental) voice-modes marked by -in, -an, and i-, respectively, are identical to the three passives in Bloomfield's and Blake's works. One voice added to the voice-mode category is called aptative, marked by -a-. It is defined as showing "the topic (subject) to be able to undergo the action named by the verb stem; modally, it shows 'state of being'" (1961:15). This particular voice may be questioned since its cooccurring subject does not manifest a unique relation different from those contracted by the three passive forms.

Wolfenden's description of the aspect category as consisting of two cooccurring subcategories, namely, start of action which indicates either 'begun' or 'not begun' and state of action which is either 'continuing action' or 'punctual action' reminds us of Bloomfield's mode-aspect system. However, Wolfenden assigns the 'begun' aspect to the affix n- and the 'not begun' to m-. This is the only explanation which can be gleaned for positing -ag- and -ang- active affixes and -a- aptative affix. The position that m- is an aspect affix is unconvincing in view of its limited range of applicability: root stems that are marked by -um-, -in, and -an never use m- to mark aspect.

The third category of verbal inflection is labelled mode. It shows "a five-way contrast in manner of performance as indicated by the affixes ka 'inversive, reciprocal', pa 'injunctive', pang 'iterative, habitual', pag 'comprehensive;, and # (zero affix) 'indicative', and six kinds of action modification contributed by voice-mode morphemes under certain conditions" (1961:20). One major objection that can be raised here is the presence of the 'comprehensive'

and 'iterative, habitual' modes marked by pag- and pang-, respectively.
They are identical in meaning with the active or subjective affixes
identified as -ag- and -ang-, and to treat them under separate inflectional
categories does not seem to be warranted. Moreover, the possibility of
two different modes cooccurring simultaneously in the same verb stem,
e.g., ka and pag or pa and pang, poses a serious question on the
criteria used for determining categories of inflection, and, consequently,
in whatever ways these criteria differ from those used for derivation.

Finally, one other problem with this system of verbal inflection
is the implication that any verb stem can be inflected for all the
categories set up. There are no restrictions to indicate that that
is not so.

3.1.4 Llamzon (1968)

The description given by Llamzon of the 'verba' in Tagalog is
more complex than the preceding accounts. He has a network of
categories, some of which seem unnecessary, others overlapping. His
description follows (1968:124-5):

> "The categories of the verba are either: (a) proper states,
> or (b) modalities. There are five proper states of the verba,
> namely: (i) the non-finite, (ii) the finite, (iii) the brusque
> command, which is an interjection; (iv) the gerund, and (v)
> the absolute... The non-finite proper state is used when the
> action is viewed as possible, commanded, hypothetical, or
> dependent on the action of another. It is used for: (a)
> imperative sentences, e.g., matulog ka! 'go to sleep'; (b)
> subordinate clauses with certain conjunctions, e.g., pumunta aŋ
> tao sa bukid upaŋ hanapin aŋ kaniya ŋ kalabaw 'the man went to
> the field to look for his carabao'; (c) with certain adverbs, e.g.,
> sana y umulan! 'I wish it would rain'... The finite proper state
> requires an indication of the aspect under which the action is
> viewed... The finite brusque command proper state consists of the
> bare root of the verb, which is an interjection, e.g., suloŋ

'forward!' The gerund is a verbal-noun formation... e.g.,
aŋ pagbibili naŋ manga 'the selling of mango'. The absolute is
a subordinate sentential nexus form, and commutes with the
adverbs in the sentential nexus, e.g., pagdatiŋ naŋ guro y
batiin mo 'when the teacher arrives, greet him'."

Analyzing these five proper states, the last two can be dismissed
since they are non-verbs. The gerund is a derived noun and the
absolute may be categorized as a derived adverb. The three remaining
ones may be related to aspect, where non-finite expresses no aspect
while finite expresses one of three (or four in Llamzon's analysis)
aspectual forms. The brusque command which is another form of
expressing an imperative may be accounted for by a rule which states
that an imperative may or may not be marked by a voice affix. These
features may be incorporated with the other category labelled
modalities.

Llamzon's modalities consist of two main groups, the 'actualizing
functors and the accidental functors'. The latter is accessory to
the combination of the former and the 'argument' (taken to mean the
verb root). The four kinds of actualizing functors are (a) voice,
(b) tension, (c) emphasis, and (d) aspect. The four voices identified
as active, passive, local, and instrumental are identical to the
four voices defined in the works cited above. The aspects listed are
imperfect, perfect, future, and immediate past. The first three
are equivalent to the general terms present, past, and future,
respectively. The last one is a form which is also referred to as
recent past.[6] Tension is defined as "each set of 1 non-finite, 1
finite (with 3 aspects), 1 immediate past aspect, and 1 absolute mode
form" (1968:126). The active voice is described as having two

tensions, the subitive and the executive, whereas each of the three
other voices has only one; the subitive uses the affix -um- and
the executive uses mag-. The only tension in the passive voice is
expressed by the suffix -(1)(h)in, (1968:155), that in the local voice
by -(1)(h)an, (1968:160), and that in the instrumental voice by
the prefix i- (1968:169).[7] The actualizing variable functor
emphasis has two values, namely, (a) emphatic and (b) non-emphatic.
The emphatic is formed by adding the prefix pag- to the non-emphatic
forms of the verb (1968:126-7). It may be recalled that in Wolfenden,
we find this same pag- introduced by the modal category labelled
'comprehensive ' in order to account for non-simple verb forms
such as magsipagtago? 'to hide, plural subject', magsipagpakabait
'exert effort to behave, plural subject', makipaglaro? 'play with',
or papaglampasuhin 'have s.o. mop/wipe s.t.'. Setting up a category
'comprehensive' or 'emphatic' to account only for the manifestation
of pag- in a complex formation would appear insufficient because it
excludes similar formations with pang- or pa- as in magsipamili
'shop, plural subject', makipabili 'join in having s.t. bought',
or pagpatahi?an 'make s.o./s.t. be the place for having s.t.
sewed'. Bloomfield accounts for this type of formation under his
description of secondary affixes which are attached to either roots,
pag-stems or pang-stems according to the corresponding forms in the
active, i.e., -um-, mag-, mang-, respectively (Bloomfield, 1917:
262-314). In Blake's description, such forms are described as
secondary or tertiary derivations (Blake, 1925:50-52).

What may be considered significant and attractive in Llamzon's analysis is his recognition of what he labels accidental functors as resulting in the formation of derived stems, with each variable corresponding to a stem-forming affix or 'stem-formant' (Llamzon, 1968:178-86). In his summary of the formation of the realizations of the various accidental functors of the verb, he distinguishes between inflectional affixes and stem-formants. His inflectional affixes include -um, mag-, ma-, ma- -(1)(h)an, and maŋ- in the active voice; -(1)(h)in, pa- -(1)(h)in, pag- -(1)(h)in, paŋ- -(1)(h)in, ka^1- -(1)(h)in, ma- (potential) and ma- (accidental) in the passive voice; -(1)(h)an, ma- -(1)(h)an, pa- -(1)(h)an, pag- -(1)(h)an, paŋ- -(1)(h)an, ka^2- -(1)(h)an (local intensive) and ka^2- -(1)(h)an (local intensive-accidental) in the local voice; and i-, i- -(1)(h)an, mai- (potential) and mai- (accidental) in the instrumental voice. All other simple and complex affixes are listed as stem-formants. In connection with the distinction made between the inflectional and stem-forming affixes the following observation can be noted:

(a) There appears to be no criteria for determining which affixes are inflectional and which ones are derivational. Certain affixes, for instance, pa-, pag-, or paŋ- are either stem-formants or parts of complex inflectional affixes, having identical meanings in both functions.

(b) The list of stem-formants or derivational affixes shows some redundancies which can be formalized to express more generalities. For instance, each of the following groups of stem-formants although apparently related are treated individually: 1) -si-, -sipag-,

-sipagpa-, -sipagpaka-, -sipaŋ-, -sipa-, etc.; 2) -ŋa-, -ŋapa- or
-ŋag-, ŋagsi-, -ŋagsipag-, -ŋagsipagpa-, -ŋagsipagpaka-.

3.1.5 Otanes (1966)

Using the generative-transformational approach of Chomsky 1965,
Otanes (1966) gives a different presentation of the verb structure.
A striking deviation from the verb composition in past studies is
the isolation of the inflectional category of aspect from the verb
marked V which is defined as the basic form of a verb (1966:50). The
rule that generates a verbal predicate is stated as follows (1966:50):

$$
\text{B-12.} \quad \text{Vb1} \quad \longrightarrow \quad \text{Asp} \left\{ \begin{array}{l} V \left\{ \begin{array}{l} \text{Comp} \\ \text{(Adjc)} \end{array} \right\} \quad (\text{Comp}_{\mathbf{Adv}}) \\ \left\{ \begin{array}{l} \underline{\text{pa-}} \\ \underline{\text{maki-}} \end{array} \right\} S \end{array} \right\}
$$

The constituent aspect Asp cooccurs with another constituent which
is either a basic verb form V followed by either a complement Comp
or an adjunct Adjc, or the indirect-action affix pa- or the social-
participation affix maki- and an embedded string S. The verb form
that takes a complement may or may not cooccur with an adverbial
complement Comp$_{\text{Adv}}$. The two affixes pa- and maki- followed by an
embedded sentence are described as generating an indirect-action
verb and its complementation and a social verb and its complementation,
respectively. Based on the rule above, there is no way of telling
that the Asp constituent is more directly related to the constituent
V than it is to the constituent Comp or Adjc, in that it is realized
in the lexical category V itself. On the other hand, the constituent
Comp is a syntactic component and does not express aspect. Also, the

use of the affix symbols pa- and maki- as a constituent class
conceals the fact that the category expressed by them is also a V.

Otanes further describes the basic form of a verb V as consisting
of a verbal affix and a base, with the former constituent being made
up of other identifiable constituents. She expresses them by the
following rules (1966:51, 58):

B-13. V   ---) Af B

B-18. Af   ---) (Mod) Foc

B-19. Foc --) (DerF) MajF

From rule B-19, the obligatory focus constituent Foc of the verbal
affix Af may be either a major focus affix MajF or a major focus
constituent combined with a derived focus constituent DerF. Either
of these possible realizations, by rule B-18, may in turn be
combined with any of the features listed under the optional
modification constituent Mod. These rules, in effect, subcategorize
the verbs according to the focus affixes they take into:

(a) major verbs, those that take only the major focus constituent;

(b) derived-focus verbs, those that have derived-focus features
in their affixes;

(c) modified verbs, those that manifest a modification constituent
in addition to the focus constituent.

Otanes' focus constituent is the analogue of voice in previous
analyses. It "determines the semantic component to be made the
center of attention and expressed in the topic ('subject' in this
study) of the sentence" (1966:59). The difference between focus and
voice as used by Bloomfield, Wolfenden and Llamzon is that Otanes

allows focus to cooccur with a derived-focus feature and/or a
modification feature which in a way resembles some of Blake's
passive voice forms and secondary or tertiary derivations. To
determine the interplay between the constituents MajF and Mod, let
us consider the other rewrite rules given for the MajF constituent
as follows (1966:58):

B-20. MajF $\longrightarrow$ $\begin{Bmatrix} [\pm\text{Actor}] & \text{in env.} & \text{Asp}\underline{\quad}B_t \\ [+\text{Actor}] & \text{in env.} & \begin{Bmatrix} \underline{\quad}B_i \\ \text{DerF}\underline{\quad} \end{Bmatrix} \end{Bmatrix}$

B-22. $[-\text{Actor}]$ $\longrightarrow$ $\begin{Bmatrix} [+\text{Object}] \\ [+\text{Direction}] \end{Bmatrix}$

By rule B-20, the choice of the major-focus constituent is restricted
to [+Actor] in the environment of a derived-focus feature. The DerF
constituent may be any of the following features as stated (1966:132):

B-57. DerF $\longrightarrow$ [+Ben(efactive)]
[+Cau(sative)]
[+Ins(trumental)]
[+Loc(ative)]
[+Mea(surement)]
[+Ref(erential)]
[+Res(ervational)]

To show how the rules operate, Otanes gives the example _ipagluto_
'cook for', a derived-focus verb analyzed as containing three
morphemic constituents: "(1) _i_-, the benefactive-focus affix
(belonging to the "DerF" constituent); (2) _pag_-, the transformed
variant of the actor-focus affix _mag_- (belonging to the "MajF"...);
and (3) the base _luto_ 'cook'" (1966:130). Interestingly, Otanes
further requires the rules that supply the actual affix morphemes
to apply cyclically, "the rule that supplies the "MajF" affix applies,

forming the major-focus verb, and then the rule that supplies the
"DerF" affix applies, forming the derived-focus verb. The reason for
prescribing such an order of derivation is that the shape of the
derived-focus affix is determined by the major-focus affix in certain
derived focuses" (1966:131). From her last statement, we can glean
that the derived-focus affix changes according to the major-focus
(actor-focus) affix taken by the verb base. Thus, she directs the
reader to compare the benefactive-focus affix i- in ibili 'buy for'
and ipag- in ipagluto 'cook for' whose major focus affixes are
-um- as in bumili 'buy' and mag- as in magluto 'cook', respectively.
Referring to the analysis of the derived-focus verb ipagluto above,
where the benefactive-focus affix identified is i-, it is no longer
clear whether ipag- should be identified as the benefactive-focus
affix based on the corresponding major-focus affix mag-. While it
may be correct to say that the form of a derived-focus verb may
depend on the form of the actor-focus verb, it is rather questionable
to say that the shape of the derived-focus affix of certain derived
focuses is determined by the major-focus affix. It may be argued
rather that for the forms ibili and ipagluto, the benefactive-focus
affix is invariably i- and the difference between the two forms lies
in the distinction between their corresponding stem forms; the
active stem in the former is a root, whereas it is a derived pag-stem
in the latter. Where the active stem has a derivational affix pang-,
as in pamili 'shop', the benefactive-focus verb is ipamili 'shop for'.

With a modification constituent in the verbal affix, based on
rule B-18, the verb is a modified verb. Quite significantly, Otanes

describes a modified verb as corresponding to a simple (major) verb with which it is identical in focus and in base classification, and to which it has a morphological relationship (1966:156-7). Further on, she states that a modified verb "may be characterized as a verb whose morphological structure and syntactic behavior can be predicted from the morphological and syntactic behavior of a simple verb" (1966: 159). The present analysis agrees fully with Otanes that what she describes as a modified verb is a morphological derivation. However, it does not recognize the modified verb as being generated by base rules if they are derived. Rather, they are created from simple verbs by means of semantic derivation rules whose effect on the simple verb is a change in semantic feature and a corresponding morphophonemic change.

Another important aspect in Otanes' description is the classification of the verb bases B into transitive B_t and intransitive B_i verbs based on their cooccurring complements. In addition, she also mentions in a footnote (p. 62) that the bases are further classified into affix classes, based on the actual affix morphemes that they combine with.[8] Each verb is marked by the set of major-focus affixes it takes to focus on a topic which has a particular semantic relationship with the verb, e.g., object, directional goal, or actor. From the examples given, however, we find mag- as one of the actor-focus affixes, and, in this case, the same objection raised in the previous analyses reviewed concerning the identification of the affix mag- or mang- instead of m- also applies to Otanes' description.

Since this study, according to the author, is not concerned with morphological derivation, she says that the rules involving the various verb derivations are not formulated. This statement seems to be a curious contradiction to what some of the base rules are generating. Indirectly, the modified verbs and the pa- and maki- verbs are described as being derived from simple verbs, and their formation is in fact accounted for by base rules that generate them. Thus, the rules in the base component do not only deal with sentence formation but also with category inflection and derivation. In part, this treatment results in a mixture of syntactic, semantic and lexical category labels. Of course, it is still an interesting theoretical question whether morphology and related semantic categories properly belong to the base component, the semantic component, or the lexicon component, or to any two or all components.

3.1.6 Ramos (1974)

Recognizing the futility of classifying verbs exclusively according to the affixes they take, Ramos (1974) approaches the problem by adopting a case grammar type of the generative transformational framework which focuses on semantic-syntactic features. She formulates a semantic feature system for verbs wherein the semantic features trigger the case frame or case cooccurrence restrictions of the verb (1974:10). The semantic features are assigned by subcategorization rules contained in both the constituent structure subcomponent and the lexicon subcomponent, while the case frame features with corresponding subcase features under each case relation feature are provided by selectional redundancy rules. In her system, she requires a deep structure level which indicates the case relationships existing between the verb and the rest of the sentence. Using a set of transformational rules, the deep structure manages to manifest itself in the surface structure. To avoid Fillmore's problem of having the case relational terms dominate categorial elements, the author resorts to Starosta's and Taylor's system of marking case on nominal constituents in the lexicon.

In this work, Ramos limits her treatment to basic simple verbs. Those that involve modifications of any kind such as those previously discussed are excluded. Hence, we can only refer to her account of the structure of 'major' verbs. Ramos follows Chomsky's model of having the categorial nodes develop into complex symbols. Her verb V takes two basically distinct features: one marks the verb for aspect and the other marks it for the types of case relationships it can enter into (1974:44). With a few modifications, the aspect features in Otanes' analysis have been adopted by Ramos. With respect to case frame features, Ramos marks only the cooccurring case relations of verbs and, following Fillmore (1968), she treats subjectivalization as a surface phenomena described as a late transformation. Depending on which nominal expression is chosen as subject, the verb form acquires an affix that marks the case relation of the subject chosen. This might seem to imply that voice or focus is not an inherent feature of the verb. On the contrary, however, it is acquired through a process called case feature incorporation assigned by a transformation rule (1974:118-9). The rule explains that the case feature of the particle which cooccurs with the actant marked as subject is

transferred to and incorporated in the verb. "The incorporated K
case feature comes to the surface in combination with aspect and
other features of the verb as a verbal affix" (1974:119).[9] She
identifies the affixes um-, mag-, and ma- as marking the agentive
subject; i-, -in or -an marks the objective subject if an agentive
case cooccurs, otherwise, the affix is um-, mang- or ma-; the
directional subject is marked by -an only; the locative by either
pag- -an or -an; the instrumental force by um-, but the instrumental
with agentive involvement by ipang- or i- and by maka- without
agentive involvement; the benefactive subject by i- or ipag-; and
the affected by ma- -an. To a large extent, the affixes identified
here are similar to those described in other works. As such, the
same questions, observations or agreements, as the case may be, which
have already been pointed out also apply to Ramos' analysis.

As a whole, the complex of semantic features which develops from
the basic case feature of the verb presented by Ramos provides some
valuable insights into the character of each verb as it relates to
its cooccurring actants. For any further semantic feature analysis
of verbs, this study can serve as a springboard. As for the problem
of inflection versus derivation, no mention is made of it. It
remains a question, then, how this approach treats various types of
lexical relations.

3.2 Inflection and Derivation

As can be noted in the preceding section, the previous works on
Tagalog, generally, have not made a clear-cut distinction between

inflectional and derivational categories or processes. Although voice and aspect (or tense) may have been described as inflectional categories of the verb in some works, together with some other categories which may also be considered inflectional in some others, the precise affixes manifesting voice are still problematic. The identification of the voice inflectional affixes in contrast with the derivational ones has important consequences on the description of the morphological structure of the verb stems, especially on the various affix combinations in many verb forms. The contention in this study is that if inflection and derivation are properly distinguished, we can provide a more satisfactory account of the lexical relations among verb forms and of the ramifications of verbal affixes in a variety of complex forms.

Classical grammars make a fundamental distinction between inflection or accidence and derivation or word formation. In discussing such grammars,Lyons (1971:195) says that inflection is defined as "a change made in the form of a word to express its relation to other words in the sentence." Derivation, on the other hand, covers the process "whereby new words are formed from existing words or roots". The problem with the first definition is the vagueness in the meaning of "to express its relation to other words in the sentence." This condition for the change in form can equally well apply to derivation. For instance, the undoubtedly derived form beautiful from the base form beauty expresses an attributive relation to the noun that follows it in a sentence. Perhaps, the kind of relation that is intended by Lyons in the above definition needs to be clarified. In the definition of the second term, the problem is in identifying the criterion for a 'new' word. What makes a 'new' word? Why are inflected forms not considered new words?

The problem of distinction becomes more acute when one realizes that the two processes have a good deal in common. In terms of meaning, both processes modify the semantic content of the base in some way. Based on formation, both can involve a root or stem and normally a corresponding phonological modification. A further problem of analysis arises when a given form may be considered as consisting of either a complex affix plus a root or a simple affix plus an affixed stem. For example, the verb ipagluto? 'cook for someone' has been analyzed variously as: a) a complex affix i- plus pag-, each representing an inflectional or verbal category plus the root luto? (Wolfenden, 1961; Llamzon, 1968); b) the affix i- plus the stem pagluto? consisting of the root luto? and the affix pag- which is considered the alternant form of mag- (Bloomfield, 1917; Otanes, 1966); and c) a single complex affix ipag- plus the root luto? (Institute of National Language, 1950; Schachter and Otanes, 1972). In these accounts, the affixes i- and pag-, whether taken as individual units or as a composite affix, appear to be considered inflectional. The view held in this study, on the contrary, is that the affix i- is inflectional, marking the benefactive actant as the subject of the sentence, and the affix pag- is derivational, forming the stem pagluto? which is derived from the root luto?.

In the current lexicase framework, the following criteria serve to distinguish inflection and derivation:

(a) "Inflection is a modification in the phonological representation of a lexical entry which corresponds to the choice of a particular inflectional feature. An inflectional feature is a semantic feature which can be freely varied within a single lexical entry" (Starosta, 1974:11). Inflectional features characterize all members of a given lexical category, hence, they need not be specified in each lexical entry. Rather, general rules that apply to the entire category specify these general properties. In this framework, such rules are expressed in the form of subcategorization rules (SR's) and/or some redundancy rules (RR's). With the full specification of inflectional features, every resulting lexical item from a lexical entry becomes unique and is thereby restricted in its syntactic functioning. The few exceptions to the rules which may occur are marked individually for one of the values of the inflectional feature, e.g., English trousers, [+plural], mud [-plural].

Starosta (1974:11) defines derivation as "the creation of a lexical entry in a given syntactic category in accordance with a systematic analogy with a lexical entry in another syntactic category. A syntactic category is a set of lexical entries defined by a unique category feature and/or a set of case frame features." In general, it is true that derivation changes the syntactic category or subcategory of a given lexical entry. However, this cannot be made the sole criterion because there are instances of purely semantic derivations. What a semantic derivation does is simply to introduce a non-variable semantic feature to the lexical entry. Thus, the definition above may be revised to allow for both syntactic and

semantic derivations. Every derived lexical entry from a different
lexical category is subject to the inflection rules of its new
category.

(b) With inflection, the form, meaning, and other syntactic and
semantic properties are generally predictable. With derivation, these
properties are often sporadic although there may be certain types of
derivation whose semantic properties are quite predictable, e.g.,
gerundive nominalization in English and abstract noun formation
in Tagalog.

(c) Derivation relates two lexical entries, the source and the
derived forms, by means of a derivation rule (DR) which, among others,
shows the changes in either semantic content or syntactic features,
particularly that of the case frame, or both. Either change may
entail a corresponding change in morphological structure.

The first distinction is crucial. Whereas an inflectional
feature can be freely varied within a lexical entry, a derivational
feature cannot be. Akhmanova (1971:108) expresses the same criterion
for an inflectional category as being "constituted by the opposition
of no less than two mutually incompatible grammatical forms."
Thus, in English, the inflectional categories person, number and
tense in verbs take the forms first, second or third person, singular
or plural number, and past or non-past tense. The forms, differing
in at least one inflectional feature, contrast in a particular
syntactic environment. For instance, the two non-past forms of the
verb go, namely, goes (third person singular) and go (non-third-person-
singular) reflect their grammatical contrast by requiring their

cooccurring subject actant to be one which is specified with the same person and number features indicated in the verb. In contrast, a derivational feature is not made up of an opposition and, consequently, there are no opposing forms that constitute a paradigm to speak of. The derivational feature refers to a single instance of a lexical entry or a class of lexical entries. While inflection is typically 100% productive, derivation is typically not.

Implicit in the first criterion is the obligatory application of inflectional rules to every member, underived or derived, of a lexical category. This requirement is not true of derivation rules. The extent to which a derivation rule applies may be an entire category, a subcategory, a subtype or just a few items or even just one lexical entry. The creation of a new word in accordance with a derivation rule (DR) is a distinct historical event, and at any given point in time, there will generally be in the lexicon a large number of lexical items eligible for derivation for which no derived forms have as yet been formed.

Using the second distinction, the English nominal suffix -s indicating plural number of count nouns such as book, map, bat is an inflectional form which is completely predictable. In Tagalog, verbs derived from nouns can have varying meanings conditioned in varying degrees by the meaning of the nouns, e.g., magsapatos 'wear shoes' from the noun sapatos 'shoes'; magdoktor 'study to become a doctor' from the noun doktor 'physician'; mag?itlog 'eat an egg; sell eggs' from the noun itlog 'egg'. In such cases, predictability, particularly of meaning, is fairly limited.

The last distinction implies that derived lexical items must be listed separately in the lexicon (with the possible exception of those derived through completely productive DR's), and that lexical items abbreviated in a lexical entry are related by inflection while lexical entries themselves are related by derivation.

Following these criteria, we can show the different inflectional affixes in Tagalog and distinguish them from the derivational affixes on the verb stems if there are any.

3.3 Inflectional Features and Inflectional Affixes of Tagalog Verbs

3.3.1 Inflectional Features

A verb in Tagalog marked [+V] is characterized by syntactic, semantic and morhpological properties. Its syntactic properties are expressed in terms of case frame features which indicate the permissible actants which may cooccur with the verb. These actants bear certain case relations with the verb and are realized in certain case form. In this connection, the verb also has the property of requiring one of its cooccurring actants to be realized in the nominative case form which is the grammatical subject of the sentence. It signals the case relation of the nominative actant by means of a particular affix. This property is referred to as voice feature and the verbal affix as voice affix. Simply put, voice is a syntactic feature marked on a verb which pertains to the case relation of the verb's subject. Thus, a verb with a feature [-[+NM,-OBJ]] is in the objective voice, one with [-[+NM,-AGT]] is in the agentive voice, another [-[+NM,-DAT]] is in the dative voice, and so forth, according to which cooccurring actant is permitted by the verb to occur as subject. Since the voice feature corresponds to a specific phonological modification of the verb stem and it can be varied freely within each given verb stem depending on its cooccurring actants, and since a characterization of voice is part of a full description of the properties of every verb in every occurrence, this feature is identified as an inflectional feature. Voice is manifested overtly in the verb by one of the voice affixes um- or m-, -in, -an, i- or Ø.

The other inflectional feature that identifies verbs is aspect. Unlike languages that have tense as a feature of the verb, Tagalog has aspect. Aspect is not a system of time-oriented events. It expresses the contrast between starting or not starting, and, if started, between completing or continuing what is expressed by the verb. The aspect feature is realized in the form of morphophonemic changes operating on the verb stem of a given class. These morphophonemic modifications may be in the form of affixation, reduplication, sound replacement or a combination of these modifications.

The voice and aspect features of inflection modify the single phonological representation of a verb stem. According to each type of inflection, a verb stem manifests a set of forms which in traditional grammar is called its paradigm. Thus, we can speak of a verb stem's voice paradigm and aspectual paradigm. Following are the redundancy and subcategorization rules which assign the voice and aspect features on verb stems.

3.3.1.1 The Voice Feature

As a general rule, every verb [+V] implies the occurrence of

a grammatical subject. This concept is expressed by the following
voice redundancy rule (VRR):

VRR-1: [+V] $\longrightarrow$ [+[+NM]]

The rule states that a verb cooccurs with a nominative or subject
actant. Certain verbs such as phenomenal, time and event verbs that do
not require a cooccurring subject are marked in the lexicon with the
feature [-[+NM]] to indicate this prohibition. In some instances
where the subject is not overtly expressed with verbs that are not
marked for non-occurrence of a subject, the grammatical absence of the
subject is considered a matter of performance. In such cases, the
unexpressed subject is always recoverable from context. For example:

1.a.   bumibili   dito   ng   alahas
       buy   here   jewelry
$$\begin{bmatrix} +L \\ +LOC \end{bmatrix} \quad \begin{bmatrix} +AC \\ +OBJ \end{bmatrix}$$

    'Jewelry is bought here/ (We) buy jewelry here.'

1.b.   bumibili   kami dito ng alahas
                   we
$$\begin{bmatrix} +NM \\ +AGT \end{bmatrix}$$

    'We, here, buy jewelry/We buy jewelry here.'

Related to the above rule is the restriction that only one
nominative case form can occur in a simple sentence. This constraint
is stated as follows:

VRR-2: [+V] $\longrightarrow$ [-[+NM][+NM]]

The occurrence of an actant as subject in a given case frame can
be expressed by the following general voice subcategorization (VSR)
and voice redundancy rules (VRR):

VSR-1: $\begin{bmatrix} +V \\ +[+NM] \end{bmatrix} \longrightarrow \begin{bmatrix} \begin{bmatrix} +NM \\ \pm OBJ \end{bmatrix} \end{bmatrix}$

VSR-2: $\begin{bmatrix} \begin{bmatrix} +NM \\ +OBJ \end{bmatrix} \\ - \end{bmatrix} \longrightarrow \begin{bmatrix} \begin{bmatrix} +NM \\ \pm DAT \end{bmatrix} \\ - \end{bmatrix}$

VSR-3: $\begin{bmatrix} \begin{bmatrix} +NM \\ +DAT \end{bmatrix} \\ - \end{bmatrix} \longrightarrow \begin{bmatrix} \begin{bmatrix} +NM \\ \pm LOC \end{bmatrix} \\ - \end{bmatrix}$

VSR-4: $\begin{bmatrix} \begin{bmatrix} +NM \\ +LOC \end{bmatrix} \\ - \end{bmatrix} \longrightarrow \begin{bmatrix} \begin{bmatrix} +NM \\ \pm AGT \end{bmatrix} \\ - \end{bmatrix}$

VSR-5: $\begin{bmatrix} \begin{bmatrix} +NM \\ +AGT \end{bmatrix} \\ - \end{bmatrix} \longrightarrow \begin{bmatrix} \begin{bmatrix} +NM \\ \pm BEN \end{bmatrix} \\ - \end{bmatrix}$

VSR-6: $\begin{bmatrix} \begin{bmatrix} +NM \\ +BEN \end{bmatrix} \\ - \end{bmatrix} \longrightarrow \begin{bmatrix} \begin{bmatrix} +NM \\ \pm INS \end{bmatrix} \\ - \end{bmatrix}$

VSR-7: $\begin{bmatrix} \begin{bmatrix} +NM \\ +INS \end{bmatrix} \\ - \end{bmatrix} \longrightarrow \begin{bmatrix} \begin{bmatrix} +NM \\ \pm RSN \end{bmatrix} \\ - \end{bmatrix}$

VRR-3: $\begin{bmatrix} \begin{bmatrix} +NM \\ +RSN \end{bmatrix} \\ - \end{bmatrix} \longrightarrow \begin{bmatrix} \begin{bmatrix} +NM \\ -COM \end{bmatrix} \\ - \end{bmatrix}$

It will be noted that the rules are stated negatively. To interpret this kind of rule, let us take VSR-1. This rule subcategorizes
verbs into a class marked [-[+NM, +OBJ]] which means that the verb does
not cooccur with a [+OBJ] as subject, and a class marked [-[+NM, -OBJ]]
which means that the verb does not cooccur with a subject except that
this actant be identified as [+OBJ]. Rather than simply say that the
verb cooccurs with an OBJ, [+[+NM, +OBJ]], the feature [-[+NM, +OBJ]]
carries more information. Besides indicating what the required case
relation of the subject is, this type of marking also prevents the
cooccurrence of another subject which has another case relation, say
a LOC subject.

Rules VSR-1 through VSR-7 and VRR-3 give eight voice subcategories
of verbs, namely, 1) objective, [-[+NM, -OBJ]], 2) dative, [-[+NM,
-DAT]], 3) locative, [-[+NM, -LOC]], 4) agentive, [-[+NM, -AGT]],

5) benefactive, [-[+NM,-BEN]], 6) instrumental, [-[+NM,-INS]],

7) reason, [-[+NM,-INS]], and 8) comitative, [-[+NM,-COM]]. This

set of rules means that all verb stems, regardless of their derivation-

al or morphological structure, express a particular voice. However,

it does not imply that every verb stem occurs with noun phrases in

eight different case relations or allows each one of its possible

cooccurring actants to be realized as [+NM]. Some verbs permit only

one particular cooccurring case relation to take on the [+NM] case

form, others allow more than one. With certain other verb stems, a

particular cooccurring case relation is prohibited from occurring except

it be realized in its non-nominative case form. This is one major

difference between classifying verb roots in contrast to classifying

verb stems. With a verb root classification, as done in most studies,

the verbs generally take at least four types of voice forms (identified

as the active um-, mag-, mang- or actor class, the passive -in or object

class, the passive i-, ipang-, or ipag- or instrumental or benefactive

class, and the passive -an, pag- -an, or pang- -an or the locative

class). The result is a confusion among some of the inflectional and

derivational affixes. For instance, a verb root such as luto? 'cook'

has been described as taking the inflectional affixes mag- in the active

or actor, -in in the direct passive or objective, pag- -an in the

locative, ipang- in the instrumental, and ipag- in the benefactive.

By this approach, the generalization that can be stated about the iden-

tity of the derivational affix pag- present in the affixes mag-,

pag- -an and ipag- were m-, -an, and i- analyzed, respectively, as the

inflectional affixes of the verb stem pagluto?, is unfortunately missed.

Similarly, a verb root classification will always fail to account for the invariant inflectional affixes for the locative, benefactive and instrumental voice. (See Section 3.3.2, p.145 for a more exhaustive discussion.)

3.3.1.2 The Aspect Feature

Each verb stem with a given voice feature is also specified for aspect. With some modifications introduced, the following aspect sub-categorization rules (ASR) have been adopted from Otanes (1966: 54, 1970: 36-37):

ASR-1:   [+V]   ⟶   [±fin]

ASR-2:   [+fin]   ⟶   [±beg]

ASR-3:   [+beg]   ⟶   [±comp]

The first rule states that a verb is either finite [+fin] or non-finite [-fin]. The feature [-fin] indicates lack of aspect. Generally, the verb form marked with this feature occurs in imperative sentences, such that the following subcategorization rule applies:

SR :   [-fin]   ⟶   [±imp]

The rule means that a verb marked [-fin] is either an imperative [+imp] verb or a non-imperative [-imp] one.

Non-finite verbs also occur in embedded sentences as obligatory verbal or predicate complements. As such, they never precede the main verb. The subclass of verbs that takes a sentential complement is therefore marked with the contextual feature [-[+fin]] to indicate that the verb of the sentential complement cannot cooccur with the verb specified unless the verb of the embedded sentence is in the non-finite form.[10]

For example:

2. sinikap niya-ng sumulat ng tula?
   try   he   write   poem
   [+fin] $\begin{bmatrix} +AC \\ +AGT \end{bmatrix}$ [-fin]

   'He tried to write a poem.'

3. natuto si Cricket na tumugtog ng piyano
   learn   play   piano
   [+fin] $\begin{bmatrix} +NM \\ +DAT \end{bmatrix}$ [-fin]

   'Cricket learned to play the piano.'

Another obligatory occurrence of a [-fin] verb is as a sentential complement to adjectives functioning as predicates.[11] For example:

4. madali-ng lutu?in ang adobo
   easy   cook   braised-dish
   [+Adj]   [-fin]

   'To cook adobo is easy.'

By ASR-2, a verb marked [+fin] is further specified as either begun [+beg] or not begun [-beg]. If it is marked [+beg], then by ASR-3, the verb is identified as either completed [+comp] or not completed [-comp] in which case it is continuing.

One of the changes introduced in the present rules is the introduction of the subcategorization [±fin]. This distinction is rather important to maintain because it suggests the opposition between two types of sentences governed by each category of verb. Moreover, the verb form occurring as a predicate complement if marked with the feature [-fin] signals its different function in relation to the main verb while it indicates at the same time its predicate function within the embedded sentence. Finally, by considering the [-fin] category as a member of the aspectual paradigm, we can show more efficiently the morphological relationship existing between this form and the [+comp] form which relationship parallels that of the two other members, the [-beg] form and the [-comp] form. To illustrate these relationships, observe the forms exemplified under the following tree-diagram which shows the development of the aspectual categories:

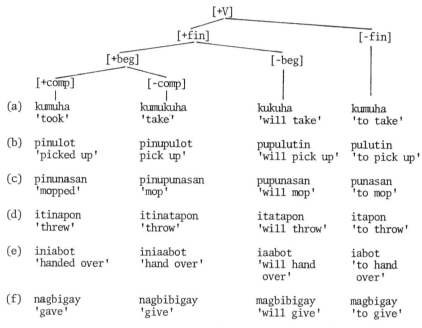

	[+comp]	[-comp]	[-beg]	[-fin]
(a)	kumuha	kumukuha	kukuha	kumuha
	'took'	'take'	'will take'	'to take'
(b)	pinulot	pinupulot	pupulutin	pulutin
	'picked up'	'pick up'	'will pick up'	'to pick up'
(c)	pinunasan	pinupunasan	pupunasan	punasan
	'mopped'	'mop'	'will mop'	'to mop'
(d)	itinapon	itinatapon	itatapon	itapon
	'threw'	'throw'	'will throw'	'to throw'
(e)	iniabot	iniaabot	iaabot	iabot
	'handed over'	'hand over'	'will hand over'	'to hand over'
(f)	nagbigay	nagbibigay	magbibigay	magbigay
	'gave'	'give'	'will give'	'to give'

The [-fin] and the [+comp] forms have identical non-reduplicated stems while both the [-beg] and [-comp] forms take the same partially reduplicated stem.

The other deviation from previous analyses of aspect taken in this study is the elimination of the aspectual subcategory identified as [+recent] which refers to a recently completed action.[12] This deviation is based on the following facts:

(a) The [+recent] form exhibits a syntactic behavior which is quite unique to itself, that is, totally different and unrelated to the other finite forms of the verb.

(b) Not one of its cooccurring actants is realized in the nominative case form, resulting in a subjectless sentence and, thus, syntactically patterns with impersonal adjectives such as gusto 'like; want' and ayaw 'don't like; don't want'; the verb form does not take a voice affix and this is a plausible reason for not cooccurring with a subject.

(c) This feature has a more restricted range of application than the other finite features. It does not apply to the various classes of inchoative nor of non-perception verbs. In this connection, it may be mentioned that the restriction which Otanes (1966:60) gives for the recent-perfective aspect as applying to Actor-focus verbs may be questioned on two counts. (1) It is not clear why the actor-focus feature is isolated as the conditioning environment when the [+recent] form does not show any overt manifestation of its being in the actor-focus. In fact, no actor-focus affix appears to identify it as such, e.g., "kabibili ' have/had just bought,'" and neither is there a cooccurring topic (subject) which can be identified as actor, e.g., "kabibili pa lang ng bata ng kendi 'The child has just bought some candy'" (Otanes, 1966:54). What appears to be relevant to the structure of the [+recent] form of verbs which cooccur with an actor or agent actant is the type of verb stem they are, whether it is a root, as in kabibili from the root-stem bili, a pag-stem as in kapagpapakulo? ' have just boiled s.t.,' etc. (2) Following her definition of Actor-focus which is extended to include not only the performer of the action, but also "any entity primarily involved in the action expressed by the verb" (Otanes 1966:93) in the case of intransitive verbs, there are various types of intransitive verbs which cannot form the [+recent] aspect, although by her definition they should all be able to, e.g., nilanggam 'attacked by ants,' gumanda 'get pretty,' bagalan 'make slow,' mahuli 'be late', etc.

(d) Immediately following the [+recent] form, a particle lang or the combination of the particles pa and lang which approximately means 'just' or 'just now' must be introduced; something not true of the other aspectual forms.

(e) Finally, this form has a unique morphophonemic rule of its own, completely unconnected with the other forms. For example:

5. katatapos pa lang ng parada
   finish   just   parade
                          $\begin{bmatrix} +AC \\ +OBJ \end{bmatrix}$

   'The parade ended just now.'

6. kakikita ko lang sa bago-ng bahay ni Heather
   see   I just   new   house
            $\begin{bmatrix} +AC \\ +DAT \end{bmatrix}$ $\begin{bmatrix} +L \\ +OBJ \end{bmatrix}$

   'I have just seen Heather's new house.'

The above peculiar syntactic and morphological characteristics strongly indicate that the [+recent] form cannot be justifiably considered a member of the aspect inflection. Any suggestion for its possible inclusion has to be rejected on these grounds. The unavoidable conclusion is to consider the form in question as a set of derived verbs created by a derivation rule and characterized by the semantic feature [+recent] and by all the other properties described above, (b,c,d, and e) including those features carried over from the base.

3.3.2 Inflectional Affixation or Modification

To distinguish the inflectional from the derivational affixes of verbs,
it will be necessary to define certain terms such as stem, root and base
which are used in the process of verb formation. A _stem_ is that element
to which only inflectional affixes are added. It may be in the form of
a root or a derived stem. A _root_ is a minimal unanalyzable form. A derived
stem is that form which is created from an already existing stem. It is
usually identified by the addition of a derivational affix. The source
is called the _base_ of the derived stem. Without their inflectional affixes,
verb stems may take the form of a root, an affixed stem derived from a root,
or an affixed stem derived from another affixed stem. Two or more verb
forms share the same stem only if they differ from each other only in
inflectional affixation. The set of inflected forms of a given verb stem
is its inflectional paradigm. It is, however, possible to have two or
more homophonous but different stems. To illustrate some morphological
types of verb stems and their corresponding voice inflectional paradigms,
we have the following examples:

(a) Root-stem [-erg]	(b) PAG-stem [-pot,+act]	(c) PANG-stem [-pot,+act,+dist]	(d) PANG-stem [+ins]
1. hiram 'borrow'	∅	2. panghiram	3. panghiram
humiram [-[+NM,-AGT]]		manghiram [-[+NM,-AGT]]	ipanghiram [-[+NM,-INS]]
hiramin [-[+NM,-OBJ]]		panghiramin [-[+NM,-OBJ]]	
hiraman [-[+NM,-LOC]]		panghiraman [-[+NM,-LOC]]	
ihiram [-[+NM,-BEN]]		ipanghiram [-[+NM,-BEN]]	

(e) Root-stem
[+erg]

4. bigay   5. pagbigay   6. pamigay   7. pambigay
   'give'   [+dist,+erg]

   ibigay   magbigay   ipamigay   ipambigay
   [-[+NM,-OBJ]]   [-[+NM,-AGT]]   [-[+NM,-OBJ]]   [-[+NM,-INS]]

   bigyan   ipagbigay   pamigyan
   [-[+NM,-LOC]]   [-[+NM,-BEN]]   [-[+NM,-LOC]]

                      pagbigyan
                      [-[+NM,-LOC]]^{13}

(f) PA-stem
[+caus]

8. pabigay   9. pagpabigay   ∅   10. pampabigay
   [+caus,+erg]   [-pot,+act,+caus]   [+ins,+caus]

   ipabigay   magpabigay   ipampabigay
   [-[+NM,-OBJ]]   [-[+NM,-AGT]]   [-[+NM,-INS]]

   pabigyan   ipagpabigay
   [-[+NM,-LOC]]   [-[+NM,-BEN]]

                      pagpabigyan
                      [-[+NM,-LOC]]

(g) PA-stem
[+caus,+dat]

11. papagbigay

    papagbigayin
    [-[+NM,-DAT]]

Based on stem forms, there are four classes of verb stems
exemplified above, namely, Root-stem, PAG-stem, PANG-stem, and PA-stem.
They are further identified by their respective morphological-voice
features and certain other semantic features, as the case may be.[14]
Depending on the particular type of Root-stem, other affixed stems
can be derived. The two derived PANG-stems are distinguished from
each other by their morphological-voice features [-pot,+act] versus

[+ins] and the semantic feature [+dist] specified in c. It will
be observed that the non-potential active distributive PANG-stem
exemplified by items 2 and 6 have a voice paradigm corresponding to
the paradigm of their bases, the Root-stems hiram and bigay, whereas
the instrumental [+ins] PANG-stem is limited to the instrumental
voice only. Given the PANG-stem [-pot,+act,+dist] as base, it is
possible to form another PANG-stem [+ins] by prefixing the [+dist]
stem, say panghiram with the instrumental derivational affix pang-
which is then marked with the instrumental voice affix i-. This
gives us the form ipangpanghiram, and ipangpamigay in the case of
item 6 as base. Performance skill, however, prohibits the use of
items with a sequence of identical derivational affix forms, and
thereby modifies the items by dropping one of the affixes or by deleting
the final consonant of the first affix. Thus, the first becomes either
ipanghiram or ipapanghiram which are homophonous to the simple [+ins]
form and the causative instrumental, respectively.[15] The productivity
of verb stem derivation can be appreciated by comparing items 2 and 3
with their source which is item 1; items 5, 6, 7 and 8 with their
source item 4; items 9 and 10 with item 8; and item 11 with source
item 5.

Turning now to the voice paradigm manifested by each morphological
class, we find that one class may have different voice paradigms and
different classes may exhibit identical ones. For instance, compare
Root-stem class a with Root-stem class e distinguished by the features
non-ergative [-erg] and ergative [+erg], respectively. The former class
is inflected for four voices whereas the latter is inflected for only

two. Similarly, the PA-stem class f marked with the features causative and ergative [+caus,+erg] differs from the PA-stem class g marked causative and dative [+caus,+dat] in their respective voice paradigms. On the other hand, note that the pairs PA-stem class f and Root-stem class e and the PAG-stem b.5 and b.9 and the PANG-stem d.7 and d.10 share the same voice paradigms. This identity in voice paradigms suggests the presence of a common syntactic-semantic feature. These unifying features for the two pairs mentioned are [+erg] which means that the verb disallows its cooccurring [+AGT] to be realized in the nominative case form, and [-pot,+act] to mean that the PAG- and PANG-stems are active and their cooccurring [+AGT] can take the nominative case form. Note also that the [-erg] Root-stem class allows an agentive voice form, and, consequently, it does not have or need a corresponding PAG-stem to accommodate the agentive and benefactive voices.

From the above illustration, we observe that a Root-stem class can be the source of various types of derived stem classes and a derived stem class has the potential of being rederived into another stem class. Thus, it is possible for one derived stem class to have different types of morphological bases as can be seen in the PAG-, PANG- [+ins] and PA-stem classes. This is also true of the other derived stem classes marked by the derivational affixes ma-, maka-, ka-, paki- and the other variants of the PAG- and PANG- active stems. Again, each of these other stem classes has its own semantic feature and corresponding voice paradigm. All the major classes of root and derived stems will emerge as we subcategorize them according to their syntactic semantic and morphological voice-related features.

3.3.2.1 Voice Inflectional Affixes

Given a verb stem with its matrix of syntactic, semantic and
morphological-voice-related features, along with its phonological
representation, the voice affix which realizes the voice inflectional
feature of each member of its paradigm can be predicted. The eight
voice features identified as objective, dative, locative, agentive,
benefactive, instrumental, reason, and comitative are each realized
by one of the six voice affixes um-, m-, -in, -an, and ∅. The
first two affixes are referred to as the active affixes because the
verbs manifesting either of them more or less choose a subject in
accordance with Fillmore's (1968:33) subject choice hierarchy, i.e.,
if there is an agent, it becomes the subject; otherwise, the subject
is the object. They are in complementary distribution, um- occurring
primarily with [-erg] Root-stems and their semantically derived reduplicated Root-stem counterparts, and m- with [-pot, +act] PAG-
and PANG-stems, as well as the PAKI- and the petrified PA-stems.
The next three affixes are the non-active or passive affixes. Their
verb stems which may be a root or a derived stem indicate that the
subject is voluntarily, involuntarily or circumstantially affected.
The zero ∅ affix posited here means that a significant absence of any of
the voice affixes in a particular verb stem can also identify a corresponding voice feature. Among the major verb stem classes, it marks
psychological verb stems as well as simple intransitive verbs.

Of the six voice affixes identified here, the active m- and ∅
are introduced for the first time. In previous analyses the active

affixes besides um- are generally identified as mag- and mang-
not to mention maki- and ma- as in mano?od 'watch' and makinig
'listen'. These four affixes correspond to pag-, pang-, paki- and
the petrified pang-, respectively, in the passive form. Without the
inflectional affix m-, the verb stems in the active form are exactly
the same as the uninflected verb stems in the passive with the
affixes pag-, pang- or paki-. This indicates that in the same manner
that a Root-stem may be inflected for both active and passive forms,
certain derived stems are also capable of taking both active and
passive inflection with the verb stem remaining constant. Thus,
as shown in items 2. panghiram, 5. pagbigay, 6. pamigay and
9. pagpabigay above, only one type of stem serves both active and
passive inflection in the paradigm. By describing the inflectional
active voice affix as m-, which in the examples above mark the agentive
voice, the generality of its application to the active PAG- and
PANG- stems, and even to PAKI-stems not exemplified above, is captured.
Such an analysis also establishes a phonologically closer relationship
between the two active affixes um- and m-. It may be said that the
relationship of these two affixes can be explained diachronically
with the least difficulty.

The present analysis further indicates that as the verb stems
that admit voice inflection are invariant, so are the general forms
of the inflectional affixes. To show that the voice affixes of root
and derived stems are the same simple affixes, we can consider the
benefactive voice forms ihiram 'borrow for', ipanghiram 'borrow for,
[+dist]', ipagbigay 'give for, [-pot,+act]', ipagpabigay 'ask s.o.

to give s.t. on behalf of s.o. else, [-pot,+act,+caus]'. The
benefactive case relation whose occurrence is dependent on the
presence of a cooccurring agentive also reflects this dependency on
the verb form which requires the behefactive to be the subject.
The verb stem inflected for [-[+NM,-BEN]] is always the same stem
inflectable for [-[+NM,-AGT]], and the benefactive voice affix is
always i-. By identifying verb stems instead of verb roots as the
elements that are inflected, the unnecessary, dubious and completely
redundant practice of listing mag-, magpa-, mang-, etc. and, correspondingly, ipag-, ipagpa-, pag- -an, pagpa- -an, pang -an, etc.
as other voice inflectional affixes is avoided.[16] In contrast to
previous studies, the analysis of verb stems and m- as an active affix
in this study makes the grammar capable of stating significant
generalizations, thereby, resulting in a more adequate description.

The ∅ affix is posited here as a zero or unmarked voice inflection
employed by certain classes of verb stems. These classes are identified here as psychological verbs and potential verbs. They are
distinguished by their syntactic and semantic features as well as
their morphological forms marked by the derivational affixes ma-
and maka-. For example, the verb stem makita 'to see' has an
unmarked form to indicate the objective voice, and the related form
makita?an has the affix -an to mark the locative voice. Another
stem related to this is the form kakita, also derived from the base
root kita 'visible' with the derivational affix ka-. It can be
inflected for the locative voice with the affix -an and for the
reason voice with the affix i-, thus, we have the inflected forms

kakita?an and ikakita. The other stem related to the preceding verb
stems is makakita which indicates the dative voice. It may be analyzed
as a derived stem whose base is either the root kita with the derivational affix maka-, or the derived stem kakita with the derivational
affix ma-. It seems that there is no significant difference between
the two analyses. In terms of meaning, however, the derivational
affix maka- appears to be analogous to ma- in referring to potential
or accidental events. For this reason and for simplicity and ease of
reference, the former analysis with the affix maka- has been adopted
in this study. (See Section 3.4.2.3 for a discussion of psychological
verbs.) Now, it will be observed that, like the stem makita,
makakita does not take any voice affix although it indicates a voice
inflection different from the MA-stem. The absence of a voice
inflectional affix in both the MA- and MAKA- stems has no syntactic
consequences since the unique forms of the derived stems which are
related by derivation from the same base, can adequately mark the
necessary voice distinctions. Hence, we can refer to similar forms
that do not manifest an inflectional affix yet indicate a voice inflection as being marked by ∅.

　　Compared with the preceding major classes of verbs, semantically
derived potential or accidental verb stems from action verb stems
are formed with the same affixes ma-, maka-, and ka-. For example,
we may have the following correspondences of action verbs from the
preceding section and of potential verbs:

1.a. hiram 1.a'. mahiram 1.b'. makahiram
      'borrow'   'able to be   'able to borrow'
      [-erg]   borrowed'
                       [+Derv,+pot,-act]   [+Derv,+pot,+act]
      humiram
      [-[+NM,-AGT]]   makahiram
                                             [-[+NM,-AGT]]
      hiramin   mahiram
      [-[+NM,-OBJ]]   [-[+NM,-OBJ]]

      hiraman   mahiraman
      [-[+NM,-LOC]]   [-[+NM,-LOC]]

      ihiram   maihiram
      [-[+NM,-BEN]]   [-[+NM,-BEN]]

2.a. bigay   2.a'. mabigay
      'give'   'able to be given'
      [+erg]   [+Derv,+pot,-act]

      ibigay   maibigay
      [-[+NM,-OBJ]]   [-[+NM,-OBJ]]

      bigyan   mabigyan
      [-[+NM,-LOC]]   [-[+NM,-LOC]]

3.a. pagbigay 3.a'. mapagbigay 3.b'. makapagbigay
      [-pot,+act]   [+Derv,+pot,-act]   [+Derv,+pot,+act]

      magbigay
      [-[+NM,-AGT]]   makapagbigay
                                           [-[+NM,-AGT]]

      ipagbigay   maipagbigay
      [-[+NM,-BEN]]   [-[+NM,-BEN]]

      pagbigyan   mapagbigyan
      [-[+NM,-LOC]]   [-[+NM,-LOC]]

From the above examples, we note that the MA-stems can occur with
the inflectional affixes i- or -an marking an objective, benefactive
or locative voice, as the case may be. The affix i- also marks the
instrumental voice of the derived potential instrumental verb stem,
e.g., maipanggupit 'be able to cut with'. The MA-stems, however, are
inhibited from appearing with the objective voice affix -in which
marks non-potential forms; similarly, the MAKA-stems do not occur with

either of the active voice affixes um- or m-, which mark agentive
voice or objective voice in intransitive verbs. The only explanation that seems reasonable for the Ø marking of the objective,
dative or agentive voice above is that the new stems with ma-
or maka- are distinct enough and marking them with the voice affix
would have been redundant. Maka- can be considered the active
derivational affix marking the agentive, or without an agentive
it marks the instrumental, or otherwise, the dative; ma- is typically
the passive counterpart marking the objective or with certain smaller
classes of verbs, the dative.

It is admitted that the analysis of the derived stems with ma-
and maka- adopted in this study presents a problem in connection with
the occurrence of the voice affix i- in the inner layer of the stem
where ordinarily inflectional affixes occur in the outer layer.
Some linguists who accept the criterion that anything which carries
over in derivation cannot be inflectional, can argue that i- is
a derivational affix, hence, it is carried over to the derived
potential form. Perhaps, this criterion only applies when there
is a resulting change in part of speech in the process of derivation.
When the derivation is within the same lexical category, which means
that the same inflectional features operate, then naturally the
same inflectional affixes are generally expected to appear.
Futhermore, there is no necessity that inflectional affixes be
restricted only to the outer layers. There are special cases where
the inflectional affix occurs in the inner layer and the derivational
affix on the outer layer as in the German form Kinderchen 'little

children', which derives from Kinder ' children', which shows the
plural inflectional affix -er within the word.[17] One explanation
that may be attempted to account for the occurrence of the inflectional
affix i- following the derivational affix ma- instead of the other
way around is to highlight the MA- form of the verb stem to signal
potential structure. If i- precedes the derivational affix ma-,
the resulting verb form may be confused with the ordinary non-potential
forms taking the same inflectional affix i as in imasahe 'to massage
with', imaneho 'to steer or drive s.t.', and in rare cases imatyag
or imasid 'to look or observe for'. It is of course true that there
are very few Root-stems with initial ma-, but compared with those
that have other syllable beginnings such as imulat 'to open one's
eyes', imungkahi? 'to suggest', imumog 'to gargle with', imudmod
'to distribute; to sow', etc., the potential forms with i- if they
were to appear as i- + ma-stem, say *imahiram, would have the effect
of the preceding forms and lose their distinctiveness as potential
verb stems.

Despite this minor objection, if it can be called one, the
present analysis positing a ∅ inflectional affix and derived MA-
and MAKA-stems is still considered more viable than the previous
analyses where the affixes ma-, ma- -an, mai-, and ka- -an are the
inflectional affixes, with a separate -ka- derivational affix or
simply another inflectional maka- for the reasons summarized below.

(a) As has been shown in the preceding section, only one simple
voice affix occurs in each verb stem to identify the cooccurring
subject; thus, the complex voice affixes are unnecessary additions to

the inventory of inflectional affixes.

(b) The occurrence of the voice affixes i- and -an with MA-stems marking objective, benefactive or locative voice, as they do with non-potential stems, indicates that these MA-stems are passive forms.

(c) Considering both a and b above, we cannot account for the MA- and MAKA- stems and their inflections more adequately and simply if we do not consider these two affixes derivational and a ∅ as one possible inflectional affix that these two types of verb stems take. The reason no inflectional affix is necessary is that each derived form is distinct enough to identify at least one voice inflected form.

By distinguishing inflectional and derivational affixes, we have observed some relevant generalizations pertaining to verbal lexical relations. They are summarized as follows:

(a) It is not just the verb root that is inflected for the different possible voices but, broadly, the verb stem, which may be either a root or a derived stem consisting of a derivational affix and a root or another derived stem.

(b) Each stem class has its corresponding voice inflectional paradigm which never exhausts all possible subject choices.

(c) Some morphological stem classes may be subcategorized according to their respective voice inflectional paradigm, e.g., Root-stems exemplified by hiram 'borrow' versus bigay 'give', whereas other derived stem classes, regardless of the structure of their bases, regularly take the same voice inflectional paradigm, e.g., [+ins] PANG-stem.

(d) A derived stem class may share an identical voice inflectional paradigm with a Root-stem class, e.g., the derived [+caus, +erg] PA-stem exemplified by <u>pabigay</u> 'have s.o. give' and Root-stem exemplified by <u>bigay</u>.

(e) A single root can be the basis of various derived stems, but not all roots automatically create all types of derived stems, e.g., no PAG-stem can be directly derived from the [-erg] Root-stem; the existence or non-existence of a corresponding PAG-stem can be predicted on the basis of the class of the Root-stem;

(f) The order in which the derivational affixes appear provides the key to the direction of derivation and re-derivation of stems as can be shown in some examples below, where a fletched arrow indicates a stem derivation.

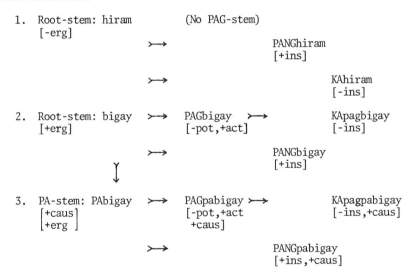

1. Root-stem: hiram   (No PAG-stem)
   [-erg]
                     ⟩—→   PANGhiram
                                            [+ins]

                     ⟩—→   KAhiram
                                                      [-ins]

2. Root-stem: bigay ⟩—→ PAGbigay ⟩—→   KApagbigay
   [+erg]   [-pot,+act]   [-ins]

                     ⟩—→ PANGbigay
                          [+ins]

3. PA-stem: PAbigay ⟩—→ PAGpabigay ⟩—→   KApagpabigay
   [+caus]   [-pot,+act   [-ins,+caus]
   [+erg]   +caus]

                     ⟩—→ PANGpabigay
                          [+ins,+caus]

3.2.2.2 Aspect Inflectional Modification

The realization of the aspect feature is inextricably linked with the voice affix associated with the morphological-voice feature of a given verb stem. As described in the preceding section, a verb stem class with a specified set of case frame, semantic and morphological features manifests its own voice paradigm marked by corresponding voice affixes. Different classes of verb stems based on these three types of features may share a common voice affix and, for convenience, they may be referred to as a general class under the label of their voice affix since their aspectual modification depends on the voice-marking affix. Thus, we can refer to six general classes of voice-marked stems identified by the voice affixes they take, namely, UM-class, M-class, IN-class, AN-class, I-class, and Ø class. The feature specifications of the various classes of verb stems that indicate to which voice paradigm and corresponding voice affix class they belong will be identified in the succeeding section, 3.4 Primary Verb Stem Subcategories.[18]

Although a voice affix is identified for each verb stem, the affix may not appear in all its aspectual forms. The overt manifestation of a given aspectual category is determined by the morphophonemic rules that realize each aspect feature, which is in turn conditioned by the voice affix class of the verb stem. This interplay between the voice and aspect realization is accounted for by the following rules referred to as voice-aspect morphophonemic rules (VAMR). The first six rules involve the UM-, IN-, AN-, and I- affix classes and the next three rules pertain to the M- and Ø affix classes.

VAMR-1: $_V[(C_1)V_1 \longrightarrow _V[(C_1)V_1(C_1)V_1 \; / \left[\begin{Bmatrix} UM- \\ IN- \\ AN- \\ I- \end{Bmatrix} class \atop \begin{Bmatrix} -beg \\ -comp \end{Bmatrix} \right]$

VAMR-2: $_V[(C_1) \longrightarrow _V[(C_1)um \; / \left[UM\text{-}class \atop \begin{Bmatrix} -fin \\ +beg \end{Bmatrix} \right]$

VAMR-3: $_V[(C_1) \longrightarrow _V[(C_1)in \; / \left[\begin{Bmatrix} IN- \\ AN- \\ I- \end{Bmatrix} class \atop +beg \right]$

VAMR-4: $]_V \longrightarrow in]_V \; / \left[IN\text{-}class \atop \begin{Bmatrix} -fin \\ -beg \end{Bmatrix} \right]$

VAMR-5: $]_V \longrightarrow an]_V \; / \; AN\text{-}class$

VAMR-6: (a) $_V[inV_1 \longrightarrow _V[iniV_1 \; / \begin{bmatrix} I\text{-}class \\ +beg \end{bmatrix}$

(b) $_V[I \longrightarrow _V[i \; / \; I\text{-}class$

VAMR-1 states that the first consonant, if any, and the first vowel of the verb stem is reduplicated when the stem belonging to either the UM-, IN-, AN- or I- affix class is marked with either [-beg] or [-comp]. By VAMR-2, the UM- affix class of stems specified further with either [-fin] or [+beg], which includes both [+comp] and [-comp], is affixed with um- after the first consonant, if any. VAMR-3 applies to the IN-, AN- or I- class marked with the feature [+beg]. It attaches the affix -in- before the first vowel of the stem. It may be stressed that this rule includes in its input the output of VAMR-1 marked [-comp], except the UM-class stems, since [-comp] is redundantly [+beg]. The fourth rule marks the [-fin] or the [-beg] forms of the IN-class stems with the suffix -in. Implicit in this rule is that the [+beg] forms of the IN-class never show the suffix -in. In contrast, all four aspectual forms of the AN-class are marked by the suffix -an by VAMR-5. Similarly, all aspectual forms of the I-class are marked by the affix i-. VAMR-6 which a-counts for this affixation consists of two disjunctively ordered subrules. The first subrule, VAMR-6.a, applies to the [+beg] forms, resulting from the application of VAMR-3, with the phonological shape in- prefix before the verb stem with an initial vowel. To this input, VAMR-6.a infixes i- between in- and V_1. All other forms of the I-class which do not meet the conditions specified in the first subrule are subject to the second subrule, VAMR-6.b, which prefixes i- to each form.

VAMR-7: (a) $_V[C_1V_1\{^g_{ng}\}(C_2)V_2 \longrightarrow _V[C_1V_1\{^g_{ng}\}(C_2)V_2(C_2)V_2$ /

$$\begin{bmatrix} \text{M-class} \\ \{^{-beg}_{-comp}\} \end{bmatrix}$$

(b) $_V[C_1V_1(C_2)V_2 \longrightarrow _V[C_1V_1(C_2)V_2(C_2)V_2$ /

$$\begin{bmatrix} \emptyset\text{-class} \\ \{^{-beg}_{-comp}\} \end{bmatrix}$$

VAMR-8: (a) $_V[\longrightarrow _V[m$ / M-class

(b) $_V[mp \longrightarrow _V[m$

VAMR-9: (a) $_V[\longrightarrow _V[n$ / $\begin{bmatrix} \{^{M-}_{\emptyset-}\}\text{class} \\ \text{+beg} \end{bmatrix}$

(b) $_V[nm \longrightarrow _V[n$

The process of partial reduplication of the stem is characteristic of the [-beg] and the [-comp] forms. The M-class and $\emptyset$-class stems, however, differ from the preceding affix classes in reduplicating the second consonant, if any, and the second vowel of the verb stem, not

counting the final -g or -ng of the derivational affix of M-class
stems, as stated in VAMR-7.a. VAMR-8 has two conjunctively ordered
rules. The first marks all forms of the M-class with the prefix m-
and the second indicates the full assimilation of the initial p-
of the stem to the prefix m-. VAMR-9 also consists of two conjunctively ordered rules which apply to the [+beg] forms of either the
M- or ∅ class. The first rule prefixes n- to the stem and the second
effects full assimilation of the initial m- of the stem to the
n- prefix.

The following Charts 3 to 6 show examples of the six voice-
affix classes of verb stems in their four aspectual forms. Applying
the two sets of VAMR's above, the four charts identify the voice
(horizontal entries) and aspect paradigms (vertical entries in the four
charts) of each of the verb stem classes exemplified.

Voice-affix Marked Class Aspect feature Verb stem class	UM-class [-fin]	M-class [-fin]	IN-class [-fin]	AN-class [-fin]	I-class [-fin]	Ø-class [-fin]
1. hiram 'borrow' [-erg]	humiram		hiramin	hiraman	ihiram	
2. bigay 'give' [+erg]				bigyan	ibigay	
3. pagbigay 'give' [-pot, +act]		magbigay		pagbigyan	ipagbigay	
4. pangbigay 'give' [+ins]					ipangbigay	
5. kapagbigay 'give' [-ins]					ikapagbigay	
6. makakita 'see' [+pot,+act]						makakita
7. makita 'see' [+pot,-act]						makita

Chart 3. Examples of voice-affix-marked classes of verb stems marked [-fin]

Voice-affix Marked Class	UM-class [-beg]	M-class [-beg]	IN-class [-beg]	AN-class [-beg]	I-class [-beg]	Ø-class [-beg]
Aspect feature Verb stem class						
1. hiram	hihiram		hihiramin	hihiraman	ihihiram	
2. bigay				bibigyan	ibibigay	
3. pagbigay		:magbibigay		pagbibigyan	ipagbibigay	
4. pangbigay [+ins]					ipapangbigay$_{19}$ / ipangbibigay	
5. kapagbigay					ikakapagbigay / ikapapagbigay / ikapagbibigay	
6. makakita						makakakita / makakikita
7. makita						makikita
8. kakita				kakakita?an / kakikita?an	ikakakita / ikakikita	

Chart 4. Examples of voice-affix-marked classes of verb stems marked [-beg].

Voice-affix Marked Class / Aspect feature	UM-class [+comp]	M-class [+comp]	IN-class [+comp]	AN-class [+comp]	I-class [+comp]	Ø-class [+comp]
Verb stem class						
1. hiram	humiram		hiniram	hiniraman	inihiram	
2. bigay				binigyan	ibinigay	
3. pagbigay		nagbigay		pinagbigyan	ipinagbigay	
4. pangbigay [+ins]					ipinangbigay	
5. kapagbigay					ikinapagbigay	
6. makakita						nakakita
7. makita						nakita
8. kakita				kinakita'an	ikinakita	

Chart 5. Examples of voice-affix-marked classes of verb stems marked [+comp]

Voice-affix Marked Class	UM-class	M-class	IN-class	AN-class	I-class	Ø-class
Aspect feature	[-comp]	[-comp]	[-comp]	[-comp]	[-comp]	[-comp]
Verb stem class						
1. hiram	humihiram		hinihiram	hinihiraman	ihinihiram inihihiram	
2. bigay				binibigyan	ibinibigay	
3. pagbigay		nagbibigay		pinagbibigyan	ipinagbibigay	
4. pangbigay					ipinapangbigay ipinangbibigay	
5. kapagbigay					ikinakapagbigay ikinapapagbigay ikinapagbibigay	
6. makakita						nakakakita nakakikita
7. makita						nakikita
8. kakita				kinakakitaan kinakikitaan	ikinakakita ikinakikita	

Chart 6. Examples of voice-affix-marked classes of verb stems marked [-comp]

3.4 Primary Verb Stem Subcategories

As has been defined earlier, a verb stem is that element to which verb inflection applies, and the inflectional features which characterize the verbal category are voice and aspect. These features trigger the modification of the phonological representation of the lexical entry or lexeme. A verb lexical entry or lexeme abbreviates the inflected forms of a verb stem; it serves as the underlying form of the set of inflected forms.[20] Verb stems appear in different morphological shapes. The structure may be a root, a stem consisting of a root and a derivational affix, or a stem with a derivational affix and another affixed stem as base. Besides its morphological feature, a verb stem is also characterized by a set of case frame features and certain semantic features. Basically, the case frame features specify the restrictions on the cooccurring case relations. However, they may include corresponding case form features to indicate particular constraints on the realization of certain case relations. Based on these three kinds of features, the verb stem's voice paradigm can be defined. A voice form, say, agentive, cannot be realized if the case frame features do not specify a [+[+AGT]]. If it does, there must be no feature in the matrix which prohibits the occurrence of a nominative agent, i.e., [-[+NM,+AGT]]. In addition, certain semantic features provide information about the proper interpretation of some cooccurring case relations or of the meaning of the verb itself. Moreover, the verb's morphological features relate to its particular stem form and its range of voice inflection. To account for the various

distinctions made in the verb's voice inflection, verb stems are
subcategorized according to three dimensions: a) case frame
features, b) semantic features, and c) morphological-voice-related
features.

For efficiency of analysis and economy of description, an
arbitrary distinction between primary and secondary verb stems has
been adopted. The major subcategorization accounts only for what
is referred to as primary verb stems. Two criteria which have to do
with case frame, semantic and voice features are used to identify
primary verb stems. Both conditions stated below must be met.

(a) A verb stem is 'primary' if it belongs to one of the major
case frame and semantic subcategories and it manifests a distinctive
voice paradigm different from the other morphological classes of the
same case frame and semantic subcategory. A primary verb stem may
be a root or an affixed stem. It may be an underived verb root or
a root derived from a N or a Adj or another lexical category.[21]
It may also be a derived affixed stem from a verb root or another
affixed verb stem, or from a root or affixed N or Adj. For example,
the verbs hiram 'borrow', bigay 'give' and bagsak 'fall' are
root-stems each belonging to a different major syntactic-semantic
subcategory. Likewise, the root-stems anay as in anayin 'be
infested by/with termites' derived from the noun anay 'termite'
and payat as in pumayat 'become thin' derived from the adjective
payat 'thin' belong to two different semantic classes of a major
case frame subcategory, hence, two different subcategories. The
stems malanta 'become wilted' from the Adj lanta 'wilted' and

pagdoktor as in magdoktor 'be a doctor' from the N doktor 'doctor'
illustrate affixed primary verb stems derived from other lexical
catetories.

(b) A verb stem which is derived from another verb stem is
primary if it manifests an identical case frame-semantic subcategory
as its source stem and at the same time exhibits a voice paradigm
different from that of its source stem. Thus, pagbigay, derived
from the verb root bigay, is a primary verb stem since it belongs to
the same case frame-semantic subcategory as bigay, namely, location
goal verbs; it has a voice paradigm consisting of the agentive and
the predictable benefactive voice which is distinct from the voice
paradigm of its source, which consists of the objective and the
locative voices. On the other hand, a derived verb stem such as
panghiram 'borrow, [+dist]', from the root-stem hiram, which manifests
a case frame identical to its source differs from it in terms of
semantic features. Whereas the derived stem has the feature [+dist]
to mean distributive, the source stem does not. Furthermore, both
stems have the same voice paradigms. (See page 145 for comparison.)
As a result, this derived panghiram is not a primary verb stem. It
will be referred to as a semantically derived secondary verb stem.
Another type of derived verb stem from a verb stem source may be
illustrated by the causative form pabigay 'have s.t. be given to
s.o. else'. This stem is derived from the root bigay 'give',
but its case frame features include a cooccurring [+DAT] which is
negatively specified on the source stem. Moreover, the derived stem
has the semantic feature [+caus] for causative which the source
stem does not carry. Lastly, its voice paradigm, consisting of

the objective and locative voice, is identical to that of the source
stem. Therefore, this derived verb stem is not a primary verb stem
either but a syntactically derived secondary one.

Using these two criteria, primary verbs can be set apart from
other derived stems which are labelled secondary verbs. By isolating
the primary verb stems and describing their syntactic, semantic and
morphological features, we can show how verbal inflection and derivation operate. Moreover, by making such a distinction, we can relate
the secondary stems that derive from the primary stems more economically and adequately, as will be shown in the next chapter.

The two conditions above although quite effective in distinguishing a sizeable majority of primary from non-primary verb stems
are not always sufficient for distinguishing all verb stems.
It is recognized that there are borderline cases which must be
identified on the basis of some other essential factors. For
instance, the verb stems bili 'buy' and pagbili 'sell' are morphologically, syntactically, and to a certain extent, semantically related.
Morphologically, it is plausible to consider bili as the source
stem of pagbili, the simpler form of two similar and 'related'
items being the more basic in general. Syntactically, both have
identical case relation features and voice paradigms, and on these
bases, pagbili is rejected as a primary verb stem, similar to the
distributive stem panghiram. Probing into the semantic content
of the two forms, we know that both involve the meaning 'transaction'.
The essential difference, however, is in the direction of the [+OBJ]
actant involved in the transaction. Both are verbs of location,

which as a subcategory is further specified as either [+goal] or
[-goal]. The stem bili is [-goal] while pagbili is [+goal].
Such a distinction does not obtain in the pair hiram and panghiram
[+dist]. Since this semantic feature distinction is relevant to the
entire verbal subcategorization, differentiating classes such as
kuha 'take' and lagay 'put', punta 'go to', and alis 'depart from',
it may also be used as another basis for defining a primary verb
stem. Hence, on this ground, pagbili, although presumed to be
historically related to bili, is also considered a primary verb
stem different from bili.

3.4.1 Subcategorization of Primary Verb Stems in Terms of Major
Case Frame Features

The first set of features that subcategorize primary verb stems
refers to the case relations that cooccur with the verbs. These
features are expressed as contextual (case frame) features. Certain
verbs with inherent semantic features which restrict the grammatical
presence or absence of particular case relations are also subcategorized according to these case-related features.

The eight case relations which may cooccur with a primary verb
stem marking the verb's case frame features are the [+OBJ], [+AGT],
[+DAT], [+LOC], [+INS], [+BEN], [+RSN] and [+COM]. Based on these
case frame features, the primary verb stems can be broadly subcategorized according to the following case frame redundancy
(CFRR) and case frame subcategorization rules (CFSR):

CFRR-1:   [+V] $\longrightarrow$ [+[+OBJ]]

Every verb stem has a cooccurring [+OBJ] actant. Exceptions to this rule are marked in the lexical items. With this environment, a verb stem may be further specified as cooccurring with other actants or not.

CFSR-1:   [+[+OBJ]] $\longrightarrow$ $\begin{bmatrix} \pm[+AGT] \\ \pm[+DAT] \end{bmatrix}$

A verb which requires a cooccurring [+OBJ] may or may not cooccur with a [+AGT] and a [+DAT]. If it is negatively marked for [+DAT], then by the following CFSR-2, the verb may or may not be a verb of location marked by the feature [+loc].

CFSR-2:   [-[+DAT]] $\longrightarrow$ [±loc]

CFSR-3:   [+loc] $\longrightarrow$ [±strict]

CFRR-2:   [+strict] $\longrightarrow$ [+[+LOC]]

CFRR-3:   [-strict] $\longrightarrow$ [+([LOC])]

By CFSR-3, a verb that is marked with [+loc] is either marked [+strict] or non-strict [-strict].[22] According to CFRR-2, a strict location verb has to cooccur with a [+LOC]; a non-strict one, by CFRR-3, may have an optionally cooccurring [+LOC], that is, its [+LOC] actant may or may not be overtly expressed.

Verbs specified as not cooccurring with a [+AGT] and marked [-loc] may or may not cooccur with an instrumental actant by CFSR-4:

CFSR-4: $\begin{bmatrix} -[+AGT] \\ -loc \end{bmatrix}$ $\longrightarrow$ [±[+INS]]

The above rules render seven major case frame subcategories of primary verbs, which can be illustrated in the following tree diagram:

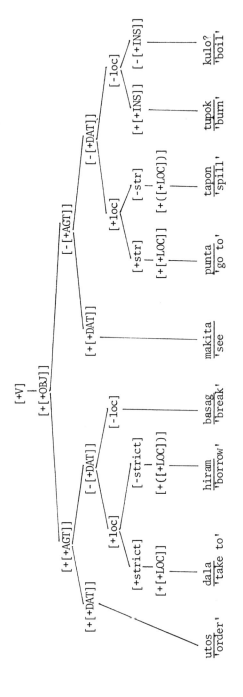

Figure 2. Major case frame subcategorization of Tagalog primary verb stems

For ease of reference, a descriptive label has been used to identify each of the seven case frame subcategories, namely:[23]

(a) information verbs, [+[+AGT], +[+DAT], +[+OBJ]]

(b) location verbs, [+[+AGT], +loc, +[+OBJ]]

(c) simple transitive verbs, [+[+AGT], -loc, +[+OBJ]]

(d) psych verbs, [-[+AGT], +[+DAT], +[+OBJ]]

(e) locomotion verbs, [-[+AGT], -[+DAT], +loc,+[+OBJ]]

(f) calamity verbs, [-[+AGT], -[+DAT], +[+INS], +[+OBJ]]

(g) simple intransitive verbs, [-[+INS], +[+OBJ]]

Furthermore, some subcategories sharing at least one identical case
relation may express other common features, hence, it is convenient
to refer to these classes by the name of their common case relation.
Those that allow a [+AGT], for instance, are agentive verbs, and
correspondingly, those without a [+AGT] are non-agentive; those that
are identified as [+loc] are locative verbs and those that are [-loc]
are non-locatives.

There are other case relations whose occurrence does not generally
serve to subcategorize the verbs but which have the potential of
cooccurring with the other basic case relations. Such case relations
may be realized in the nominative case form. It is in this form
that their cooccurring verb stem exhibits a distinct morphological
structure and corresponding voice paradigm. Thus, these case relations
become relevant to verb subcategorization when they occur in the
nominative case form. These case relations are introduced by some
redundancy rules.

Unless otherwise marked, every verb stem may allow an optionally cooccurring [+RSN] and [+COM].[24] The verbs marked for not taking

either one of these actants are identified by the following rule:

$$\text{CFRR-4:} \quad \begin{bmatrix} -[+AGT] \\ +[+INS] \end{bmatrix} \longrightarrow \begin{bmatrix} -[+RSN] \\ -[+COM] \end{bmatrix}$$

The rule states that a calamity verb does not cooccur with a [+RSN]

nor a [+COM].

Two other case relations are predictable from the presence of

another case relation by the following rules:

$$\text{CFRR-5:} \quad \begin{bmatrix} +[+AGT] \\ -[+DAT] \end{bmatrix} \longrightarrow [+([+INS])]$$

$$\text{CFRR-6:} \quad [+[+AGT]] \longrightarrow [+([+BEN])]$$

The first rule says that an agentive, non-dative verb allows the

potential cooccurrence of an instrumental actant. The second rule

marks an agentive verb with a potentially cooccurring benefactive

actant. The [+INS] indicates a tool or device employed by the agent

on the [+OBJ] in performing the action and the [+BEN] indicates for

whom the action is done.

CFRR-5 and CFRR-6 imply that verbs are generally non-instrumental,

and non-agentive verbs are predictably non-benefactives. These

generalizations can be expressed as follows:

$$\text{CFRR-7:} \quad [+V] \longrightarrow [-[+INS]$$

$$\text{CFRR-8:} \quad [-[+AGT]] \longrightarrow [-[+BEN]]$$

Compared with two previous works on Tagalog where verbs are also

classified according to their cooccurring complements or case relations,

two subcategories delineated here are analyzed differently by

Schachter and Otanes (1972) and by Ramos (1974). First of these is

the subcategory of information verbs. In Schachter and Otanes, this

class of verbs is a subclass of double object verbs whose other members
are identical to the class identified here as location verbs. This
means that what is recognized here as [+DAT] is identified by Schachter
and Otanes as a directional complement (what we mark here as [+LOC]).
In Ramos, information verbs such as _utos_ 'order', _bilin_ 'order;
requisition', _sabi_ 'say; tell', _balita?_ 'inform', _ulat_ 'report',
etc. are not accounted for in the analysis. They do not belong to
any of the fifteen major classes she sets up. Based on the occurrence
of three actants, they can be put together only with the subcategory
of location verbs (her Class 4, 1974:84), even if the information
verbs do not convey a [+OBJ] to a directional goal in the same sense
that one class of location verbs does.

Primarily, the difference in analyses lies in the distinction made
between a [+DAT] and a [+LOC] (directional actant in the two works
cited). In terms of meaning, the [+DAT] is usually the animate actant
indirectly affected by what the verb designates; the [+LOC] is the
place where the [+OBJ] actant is situated or transported. In terms
of lexical derivational possibilities, there is a difference between
the class of information verbs and that of location verbs. Under the
discussion on causative derivation (see Chapter IV), the causative
form of a verb of location which cooccurs with a [+DAT], has a meaning
similar to a verb of information. In both instances, the [+DAT]
actant performs the same role. Moreover, the causative form of a
non-location or simple transitive verb has an identical case frame
feature as the verb of information. For example:

7. nag?utos ako ng merienda sa katulong
   ask/for/ I   snack   maid
   order   [+NM] [+AC]   [+L]
   (info)   [+AGT] [+OBJ]   [+DAT]

   'I ordered the maid to prepare some snacks.'
   Lit.: 'I ordered the maid for some sancks.'

8. nagdulot ang katulong ng merienda sa mga bisita
   serve   maid   snack   guests
   (location)   [+NM]   [+AC]   [+L]
                 [+AGT]   [+OBJ]   [+LOC]

   'The maid served some snacks to the guests.'

9. nagpadulot ako sa katulong ng merienda sa mga bisita
   serve   [+NM] [+L]   [+AC]   [+L]
   (location) [+AGT] [+DAT]   [+OBJ]   [+LOC]
   [+caus]

   'I ordered the maid to serve some snacks to the guests.'

10.nagpahanda? ako ng merienda sa katulong
   prepare   [+NM] [+AC]   [+L]
   [+caus]   [+AGT] [+OBJ]   [+DAT]
   (simple trans)

   'I ordered the maid to prepare some sancks.'

If the [+DAT] and [+LOC] are not distinguished there will be a problem
of description in accounting for these two case relations cooccurring
with causative agentive verbs. Furthermore, the generalization
expressed by the [+DAT] actant of information verbs and the [+DAT]
of causative non-information agentive verbs will be unfortunately
missed.

The second subcategory analyzed differently here is what has
been labelled calamity verbs with the case frame [-[+AGT]], +[+INS],
+[+OBJ]]. This frame is also recognized in Ramos (1974:35f) under
the discussion of instrumental force. However, the same frame
illustrated therein has not been included in her list of major subcategories. The only case frame specified with a cooccurring

instrumental actant is labelled Class 13 (1974:93-94) which is also

marked with the feature [+meteorological], e.g. umulan 'it rained',

lumindol 'it quaked', etc. But the instrumental actant in this

frame is described as never occurring on the surface structure.

In Schachter and Otanes, the case frame manifested by calamity

verbs falls under one set of a subclass of what is identified as

'adjunctive' verbs which allow a cooccurring "adjunct that is

not an actor adjunct" (1972:384,387). In the present analysis, the

[+INS] is distinguished from an actor or agent actant since the

former cannot have the potential of cooccurring with another

instrumental case relation. Furthermore, unlike the [+AGT] in

the other subcategories, the [+INS] in this particular case frame is

restricted in its case form realization to the non-nominative.

Thus, the voice paradigm of this class excludes an instrumental

voice. For example:

11. giniba? ng bagyo ang maraming bahay
    destroy   storm   many   houses
$$\begin{bmatrix} +AC \\ +INS \end{bmatrix} \qquad\qquad \begin{bmatrix} +NM \\ +OBJ \end{bmatrix}$$

'Many houses were destroyed by the storm.'

This peculiar syntactic behavior of calamity verbs is expressed by

the following redundancy rule:

CFRR-9: $\begin{bmatrix} -[+AGT] \\ +[+INS] \\ +[+OBJ] \end{bmatrix} \qquad \begin{bmatrix} \begin{bmatrix} -AC \\ -[+INS] \end{bmatrix} \end{bmatrix}$

The rule states that a calamity verb does not permit its cooccurring

[+INS] to be realized in any other case form but the accusative.

As for the class of meteorological verbs set up by Ramos, that

subcategory is analyzed here as a special class of verbs marked phenomenal [+phen] because they are derived from nouns which express some natural phenomena. The [+phen] verbs are a special class because of their unique feature [-[+NM]], which means that they do not cooccur with a subject actant although they are marked by an active voice affix. It is relevant to point out that from the [+phen] class of verbs, two types of verbs can be derived, one type belongs to the simple intransitive class and the other, to the calamity class. For example:

12. uulanin   ang   parada
     rained on   parade
                          $\begin{bmatrix} +NM \\ +OBJ \end{bmatrix}$

'The parade will be overtaken by the rain.'
Lit.: 'The parade will be rained on.'

13. inulan ng punlo? ang   kuta ng mga tulisan
     attack   bullets   lair   bandits
             $\begin{bmatrix} +AC \\ +INS \end{bmatrix}$ $\begin{bmatrix} +NM \\ +OBJ \end{bmatrix}$

'The lair of the bandits was the target of bullets.'

A third distinctive case frame subcategory established in this study involves psych verb stems which are beyond the scope of Ramos' study, although they may be related in part to the subclass she describes as experiential, having only a cooccurring objective case in its case frame (Class 10, 1974:91). In Schachter and Otanes, psych verbs are classified under the object subtype of transitive verbs (1972:293-98). The reasons behind distinguishing this subcategory from that of simple transitive verbs are as follows:

(a) There is a general difference in meaning indicated by the psych verb stem class and the simple transitive verb class. This

difference is reflected in the role played by a [+DAT] actant with
a psych verb and a [+AGT] with a simple transitive verb in relation
to a cooccurring [+OBJ] actant. The [+DAT] does not affect the [+OBJ],
but the [+AGT] usually does:

(b) The derivational potential of each verb stem class in both
causative and social forms is more revealing of significant generalizations if the two subcategories are distinguished. (See the sections
on derived causative and social verbs in Chapter IV.) For example:

14. narinig   nila   ang   tugtugin   ni   Angel
    hear   they   composition
               $\begin{bmatrix} +AC \\ +DAT \end{bmatrix}$ $\begin{bmatrix} +NM \\ +OBJ \end{bmatrix}$

   'Angel's composition was heard by them.'

14.a. ipinarinig   ni   Jo   sa   kanila   ang   tugtugin   ni   Angel
      hear $\begin{bmatrix} +AC \\ +AGT \end{bmatrix}$ $\begin{bmatrix} +L \\ +DAT \end{bmatrix}$ $\begin{bmatrix} +NM \\ +OBJ \end{bmatrix}$

   'Jo made/let them hear Angel's composition.'

15. binali?   ni   Jose   ang   tubo
    break   sugarcane
               $\begin{bmatrix} +AC \\ +AGT \end{bmatrix}$ $\begin{bmatrix} +NM \\ +OBJ \end{bmatrix}$

   'The sugarcane was broken by Jose.'

15.a. ipinabali?   niya   kay   Jose   ang   tubo
      break   he
      [+caus] $\begin{bmatrix} +AC \\ +AGT \end{bmatrix}$ $\begin{bmatrix} +L \\ +DAT \end{bmatrix}$ $\begin{bmatrix} +NM \\ +OBJ \end{bmatrix}$

   'He asked Jose to break the sugarcane.'

In 14.a, the [+DAT] actant of the derived causative verb corresponds
to the [+DAT] of the source psych verb. In 15.a, the [+DAT] of the
causative verb corresponds to that of the [+AGT] of the source simple
transitive verb. In both cases, the causative verbs created from either

a psych or a simple transitive verb have a new [+AGT] actant introduced into its case frame.

There are two other subcategories here which need to be compared with similar subcategories identified in the two works mentioned above. These are the case frame subcategory of locomotion verbs, [-[+AGT], +loc, +[+OBJ]], and that of simple intransitive verbs, [-[+INS], +[+OBJ]]. The former class includes both subcategories identified in Ramos (1974:158-59) as having the case frame marked with agent and directional, (Class 7 and Class 8), and with object and directional cases (Class 15); the latter, both her subcategories identified by the occurrence of only an agent (Class 9) and of only an object (Class 14). To a certain extent, the two present subcategories are similar to those in Schachter and Otanes (1972:301-303) belonging to the general class of directional verbs, having an actor and a directional complement, and the subclass of simple intransitive verbs, respectively. The essential difference is that the two subcategories in this study are both non-agentive. The verbs of locomotion indicate that the [+OBJ] actant, without the mediation of an agent, goes to, comes from or stays in a given location [+LOC]. The verb class permits either animate or inaminate [+OBJ] referents. For example:

16. pumasok ang {bata?} sa silid
     enter   {tubig}   room
                 child/
                 water
                 $\begin{bmatrix} +NM \\ +OBJ \end{bmatrix}$ $\begin{bmatrix} +L \\ +LOC \end{bmatrix}$

     'The child/water entered the room.'

17. gumalaw ang ⎰bata?⎱
   ⎱baso ⎰
   move child/
   glass
   ⎡+NM ⎤
   ⎣+OBJ⎦

'The child/glass moved.'

Irrespective of the feature [+anim] or [-anim], the [+OBJ] referent of
locomotion verbs undergoes movement on its own in relation to a given
location. Likewise, the subclass of simple intransitive verbs that
expresses physical or bodily movement may have either type of [+OBJ]
referent. Such a description implies that 'animateness of the subject
is not syntactically relevant' (Starosta, 1971a:445). This may be
contrasted to the situation with agentive verbs where the introduction
of inanimate agents results in situationally anomalous sentences.

3.4.2 Subcategorization of Primary Verb Stems in Terms of
      Semantic Features

Most of the major case frame subcategories described in the
preceding section are further subcategorized in terms of semantic
features which indicate different meanings. A semantic feature may
provide a proper interpretation to a particular cooccurring case
relation or restrict the case form realization of certain case relations.
It may also denote the nature of the action, process or state suggested
by the verb stem. The rules that account for these features are
referred to as semantic feature subcategorization rules (SFSR).

3.4.2.1 Semantic Features of Locative Verbs, [+loc]

The first set of rules below applies to locative verbs marked by
the feature [+loc]:

SFSR-1:   [+loc] $\longrightarrow$ [±dir]

SFSR-2:   [+dir] $\longrightarrow$ [±goal]

The first rule states that locative verbs identified by the feature
[+loc], which include location and locomotion verbs, may be either
directional [+dir] or non-directional [-dir]. The former class means
transportation or movement of the cooccurring [+OBJ] referent to or
from a place designated by the cooccurring or unexpressed [+LOC].
Non-directional [-dir] verbs refer to those that do not express this
type of movement. Rather, they presuppose a particular location of
the [+OBJ] involved. For instance, the verb sulat 'to write down'
presupposes the particular location of what is to be written down,
hence, it is a [-dir] locative verb. On the other hand, a verb such
as basag 'to break' does not presuppose a location for the [+OBJ],
thus, it does not require a [+LOC] and is, therefore, a non-locative
verb.

By SFSR-2, a directional verb is further specified as either a
goal [+goal] verb or a non-goal [-goal] or source verb. The feature
[+goal] means the movement of the cooccurring [+OBJ] referent to a
place of destination which may be identified by a cooccurring or
unexpressed [+LOC]. This [+LOC] is interpreted as the goal. In
contrast, the opposite feature [-goal] indicates movement from a
place designated by the [+LOC] which means the source or place of
origin of the [+OBJ].[25]

3.4.2.2 Semantic Features of Agentive Verbs, [+[+AGT]]

The class of [-dir] verbs that cooccurs with a [+AGT] is further subcategorized according to the following rules assigning semantic features that refer to the effect of the action on the [+OBJ] involved:

$$\text{SFSR-3:} \quad \begin{bmatrix} +[+AGT] \\ -[+DAT] \\ +loc \\ -dir \end{bmatrix} \longrightarrow [\pm af]$$

$$\text{SFSR-4:} \quad [+af] \longrightarrow [\pm cs]$$

SFSR-3 states that [-dir] location verbs may be either affected [+af] or non-affected [-af]. The class [+af] means that the physical state of the cooccurring [+OBJ] is affected whereas the class [-af] means that the [+OBJ] is not affected in the same manner. The effect of a [-af] verb can be a change in the [+OBJ] referent's position in a particular location. A verb which affects the physical or substantial state of the [+OBJ] is further specified by SFSR-4 as to whether the effect is a change-of-state [+cs] or a non-physical, superficial change which effect is identified as a non-change-of-state [-cs].[26]

The case frame subcategory labelled simple transitive verbs is agentive but non-locative. It is further subcategorized following the rules below:

$$\text{SFSR-5:} \quad \begin{bmatrix} +[+AGT] \\ -[+DAT] \\ -loc \end{bmatrix} \longrightarrow [\pm extn]$$

$$\text{CFRR-10:} \quad \begin{bmatrix} +extn \\ \begin{bmatrix} +NM \\ -[+OBJ] \end{bmatrix} \end{bmatrix} \longrightarrow \begin{bmatrix} \begin{bmatrix} -L \\ -[+OBJ] \end{bmatrix} \end{bmatrix}$$

SFSR-5 marks two types of simple transitive verbs, namely, extension [+extn] and non-extension [-extn] verbs. Extension verbs denote some kind of abstract effect on the [+OBJ] referent. They are exemplified by verb stems such as _tulong_ 'help', _saklolo_ 'succor',

damay 'aid; express sympathy', or dalo 'help; attend to'. Schachter
and Otanes (1972) and Ramos (1974) classify these verbs as directional
verbs cooccurring with an agentive and a directional (locative here)
actant. In both works, these verb stems are not distinguished in
terms of case frame or complements from other members of the same
category such as punta 'go', pasok 'enter', etc. By and large, these
two groups of verbs differ in the roles played by their cooccurring
actants. Considering the first group (our [+extn] verbs), the
cooccurring [+AGT] may be said to be doing something on or for another
actant (the posited [+OBJ]). In contrast to the second group which
indicates that an actant transports itself to a place designated by a
[+LOC], the [+AGT] of the verbs of 'helping' may not necessarily be in
the place where the [+OBJ] is located. For example:

18.a.　tinutulungan　ng　mga　Amerikano　ang　mahihirap　sa
　　　　help　　　　　　　　　　Americans　　　　poor
　　　　　　　　　　　　　　　　$\begin{bmatrix} +AC \\ +AGT \end{bmatrix}$　　$\begin{bmatrix} +NM \\ +OBJ \end{bmatrix}$

　　　　ibang bansa?
　　　　other countries

　　　　'The poor in other countries are helped by the Americans.'

18.b.　tumutulong　ang　mga　Amerikano　sa　mahihirap　sa
　　　　　　　　　　　　　　　　$\begin{bmatrix} +NM \\ +AGT \end{bmatrix}$　　$\begin{bmatrix} +L \\ +OBJ \end{bmatrix}$

　　　　ibang bansa?

　　　　'The Americans help the poor in other countries.'

If the classification of the verbs in question is based on the
fact that the actant marked by sa in its non-nominative case form
qualifies it to be identified as a directional or locative actant since
if it is made the subject, the voice affix on the verb is -an, which is

is a regular affix for a locative subject, it may be argued that such ground is not compelling. From the preceding chapter, it has already been shown that the case marker sa may mark the locative case form not only of a [+LOC] case relation but a [+DAT], a [+COM], or a [+OBJ] as well. Furthermore, the voice affix -an in the verb does not only mark a cooccurring [+LOC] as subject. Depending on the verb subclass, -an can also mark a [+OBJ] or a [+DAT] subject, not to mention a [+COM].

Within the present system of verb subcategorization, the verbs of the type tulong 'help' in contrast to those of the class punta 'go to' admit in their case frame a potentially cooccurring [+BEN] and [+INS].[27] This indicates that the former class is an agentive verb and not a non-agentive like the latter class. For example:

19. tumulong si Mang Pedro ng bigas   sa mga nasunugan
     help   rice   fire victims
                   $\begin{bmatrix} +NM \\ +AGT \end{bmatrix}$ $\begin{bmatrix} +AC \\ +INS \end{bmatrix}$ $\begin{bmatrix} +L \\ +OBJ \end{bmatrix}$

     para sa kanilang samahan
     for   their   association
     [+B] $\begin{bmatrix} +L \\ +BEN \end{bmatrix}$

     'Mang Pedro helped the fire victims with rice on behalf of their association.'

By CFRR-10, a [+extn] verb which is not inflected for the objective voice realizes its cooccurring [+OBJ] only in the locative case form. In comparison, the non-nominative form of the [+OBJ] of a [-extn] verb may be realized in the accusative or the non-accusative case form. If it is in the accusative, the [+OBJ] is indefinite; if it is in the non-accusative case form, then it is definite. The non-accusative case form is also the locative case form. All these are expressed by the following rules:

CFSR-5: $\begin{bmatrix} -\text{extn} \\ \begin{bmatrix} +\text{NM} \\ - \begin{bmatrix} +\text{OBJ} \end{bmatrix} \end{bmatrix} \end{bmatrix} \longrightarrow \begin{bmatrix} \begin{bmatrix} \pm\text{AC} \\ + \begin{bmatrix} +\text{OBJ} \end{bmatrix} \end{bmatrix} \end{bmatrix}$

CFRR-11: $\begin{bmatrix} -\text{extn} \\ + \begin{bmatrix} \alpha\text{AC} \\ +\text{OBJ} \end{bmatrix} \end{bmatrix} \longrightarrow \begin{bmatrix} \begin{bmatrix} +\text{OBJ} \\ - \begin{bmatrix} \text{?}\alpha\text{def} \end{bmatrix} \end{bmatrix} \end{bmatrix}$

CFRR-12: $\begin{bmatrix} -\text{extn} \\ + \begin{bmatrix} -\text{AC} \\ +\text{OBJ} \end{bmatrix} \end{bmatrix} \longrightarrow \begin{bmatrix} \begin{bmatrix} -\text{L} \\ - \begin{bmatrix} +\text{OBJ} \end{bmatrix} \end{bmatrix} \end{bmatrix}$

The other subclass of simple transitive verbs marked [-extn] has a wider membership than the [+extn] class. It expresses an effect on the cooccurring [+OBJ] actant which is more direct and visible in character. There is a three-way distinction with regard to the manner in which the [+OBJ] referent is affected. These distinctions are identical to those expressed by the [-dir] agentive verbs, and reflect the same corresponding syntactic and morphological consequences.[28] Thus, SFSR-3 involving only [-dir] agentive verbs as input is revised as follows:

SFSR-3': $\begin{bmatrix} + [+\text{AGT}] \\ \begin{Bmatrix} -\text{dir} \\ -\text{extn} \end{Bmatrix} \end{bmatrix} \longrightarrow [\pm\text{af}]$

By SFSR-3' and SFSR-4, [-extn] verbs are further subclassified into three semantic feature subcategories, namely, [+cs], [-cs] and [-af] simple transitive verbs.

The semantic feature subcategorization of the agentive case frame subcategories may be shown in the following tree diagram.[29]

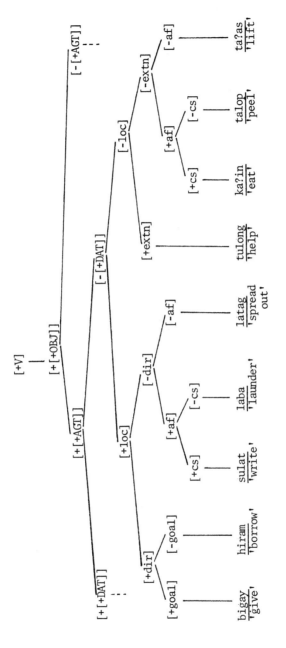

Figure 3. Case frame and semantic feature subcategorization of agentive verbs

3.4.2.3 Semantic Features of Calamity Verbs, [-[+AGT], +[+INS], +[+OBJ]]

The class of calamity verbs has a cooccurring [+INS] instead of a [+AGT] as the direct causer of an event designated by the verb. The [+INS] may be a natural force or phenomenon or a substance that affects the cooccurring [+OBJ] referent. The kind of effect the [+INS] actant leaves on the [+OBJ] referent is characterized by the same semantic features which subcategorize agentive [-dir] and [-extn] verbs. Thus, SFSR-3ʹ (the revised form of SFSR-3) is again revised below to include calamity verbs:

$$
\text{SFSR-3ʹʹ:} \quad
\left\{
\begin{array}{l}
\begin{bmatrix} +[+\text{AGT}] \\ \left\{ \begin{array}{l} -\text{extn} \\ -\text{dir} \end{array} \right\} \end{bmatrix} \\[2ex]
\begin{bmatrix} -[+\text{AGT}] \\ +[+\text{INS}] \end{bmatrix}
\end{array}
\right\}
\longrightarrow \quad [\pm\text{af}]
$$

By this rule and SFSR-4, calamity verbs are also subcategorized into the subclasses [+cs], [-cs] and [-af].

3.4.2.4. Semantic Features of Simple Intransitive Verbs, [-[+INS], +[+OBJ]]

The verb stems in this subcategory are varied. They are identified by semantic features which further subcategorize them as follows:

SFSR-6: $\begin{bmatrix} -[+\text{INS}] \\ +[+\text{OBJ}] \end{bmatrix}$ $\longrightarrow$ [±inch]

SFSR-7: [+inch] $\longrightarrow$ [±term]

SFSR-8: [-inch] $\longrightarrow$ [±affl]

SFSR-9: [+affl] $\longrightarrow$ [±cs]

The rules above subcategorize simple intransitive verbs into five subclasses, namely: (a) inchoative, terminal [+inch, +term], (b) inchoative, non-terminal [+inch, -term], (c) non-inchoative, afflicted, with change-of-state [-inch, +affl, +cs], (d) non-inchoative, afflicted, without change-of-state [-inch, +affl, -cs], and (e) non-inchoative, non-afflicted [-inch, -affl].

Inchoative [+inch] verbs express a process of 'becoming' whereas those marked non-inchoative [-inch] express an action, an activity or an event. The feature [+term] refers to a terminal or permanent change or transformation; the opposite feature [-term] means non-terminal or transient state. The feature [+affl] denotes that something external to the [+OBJ] referent afflicts it resulting in some form of change-of-state specified with the feature [+cs] or of a superficial change-of-state identified by the feature [-cs]. These features are similar to those marking the agentive verbs of [+af]. To capture this similarity, SFSR-4 which applies only to agentive and calamity verbs may be revised as follows to incorporate and, hence, eliminate, SFSR-9:

$$\text{SFSR-4}': \quad \left\{\begin{matrix} [+af] \\ [+affl] \end{matrix}\right\} \quad \longrightarrow \quad [\pm cs]$$

The verbs of affliction are similar to calamity verbs in that being derived from phenomenal nouns pertaining to diseases, illnesses or discomforts or nouns that have destructive effects, they express the external factor affecting the [+OBJ] referent. Other verbs of this class derive from adjectives and they express certain dispositions towards some activity. For example:

20. inulan ang parada kahapon
    rain   parade yesterday
    $\begin{bmatrix} -\text{inch} \\ +\text{cs} \end{bmatrix}$ $\begin{bmatrix} +\text{NM} \\ +\text{OBJ} \end{bmatrix}$

    'The parade was overtaken by the rain yesterday.'
    Lit.: 'The parade was rained on yesterday.'

21. pinapawisan   ang bata?
    perspire   child
    $\begin{bmatrix} \text{-inch} \\ \text{-cs} \end{bmatrix}$ $\begin{bmatrix} \text{+NM} \\ \text{+OBJ} \end{bmatrix}$

'The child is perspiring.'

Verbs that are marked [-affl] express activities or events without any external factor affecting the [+OBJ] referent, e.g., pumutok 'explode', mahulog 'fall, drop'.

In sum, the subcategories of non-agentive non-dative verbs consisting of locomotion, calamity, and simple intransitive types are represented with their semantic feature subcategorization in the following tree diagram:

191

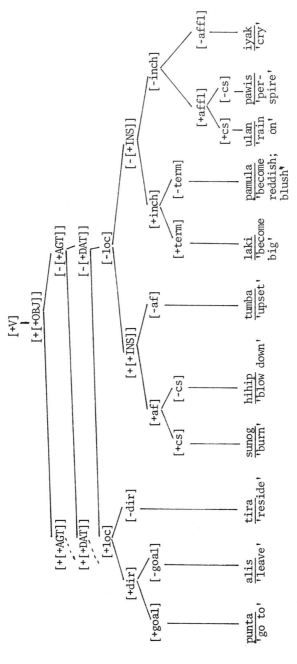

Figure 4. Case frame and semantic feature subcategorization of non-agentive non-dative verbs

3.4.2.5 Semantic Features of Psych Verbs, [-[+AGT], +[+DAT], +[+OBJ]]

The last case frame subcategory identified by the presence of a cooccurring [+DAT] and [+OBJ] and the absence of a [+AGT] is generally associated with verbs referring to a psychological state or condition.[30] Its [+DAT] actant is the experiencer or perceiver of the [+OBJ] referent. Psych verbs are classified according to the following semantic features:

SFSR-9: $\begin{bmatrix} -[+AGT] \\ +[+DAT] \\ +[+OBJ] \end{bmatrix}$ $\longrightarrow$ [±per]

SFSR-10: [+per] $\longrightarrow$ [±cog]

SFSR-11: [-per] $\longrightarrow$ [±emo]

SFSR-12: [-emo] $\longrightarrow$ [±assm]

SFSR-13: [-assm] $\longrightarrow$ [±attd]

Rule SFSR-9 divides psych verbs into perception [+per] and non-perception [-per] verbs. If it is marked [+per], then by SFSR-10, it is further marked either as cognition [+cog] or non-cognition [-cog]. On the other hand, if it is marked [-per], then it is either an emotion [+emo] or a non-emotion [-emo] verb by rule SFSR-11. Non-emotion verbs are further subdivided by SFSR-12 into verbs of assessment [+assm] or non-assessment [-assm]. And finally, SFSR-13 marks [-assm] verbs as either an attitude [+attd] or a non-attitude [-attd] verb.

The class of verbs marked [+cog] may be referred to as verbs of cognition. They include such verbs as ma?alam 'know', malimot 'to forget', matuto 'learn', etc. The class of [+per, -cog] verbs may simply be referred to as perception verbs. Like cognition verbs, they do not express duration. They are exemplified by verbs such as makita 'see', <u>marinig</u> 'hear', and <u>mabatid</u> 'know; be aware of'.

In general, psych verbs, unlike agentive verbs, do not cooccur with an instrumental case relation. However, a few verbs of perception such as 'seeing' and 'hearing' allow their cooccurring [+OBJ] referent to be perceived through an instrument. The instrumental actant may be one that is inalienably possessed by the [+DAT] perceiver, e.g., his eyes or his ears, or it may be some tool or device for visual or auditory perception, e.g., binoculars, magnifying glass, stethoscope, etc. For example:

22. nakita ko ng mga mata ko   lang ang kometa
    see   I   eyes mine only   comet
    [-cog] $\begin{bmatrix} +AC \\ +DAT \end{bmatrix}$ $\begin{bmatrix} +AC \\ +INS \end{bmatrix}$ $\begin{bmatrix} +NM \\ +OBJ \end{bmatrix}$

    'The comet was seen by me with my bare eyes.'

23. narinig ng bata? ng 'stethoscope' ang tibok ng
    hear   child   beat
    [-cog] $\begin{bmatrix} +AC \\ +DAT \end{bmatrix}$ $\begin{bmatrix} +AC \\ +INS \end{bmatrix}$ $\begin{bmatrix} +NM \\ +OBJ \end{bmatrix}$

    puso   niya
    heart his

    'His heartbeat was heard by the child with/through a stethoscope.'

To account for this fact, the particular verbs are individually marked for a potential cooccurrence of an [+INS] actant. Since this feature is not a regular part of the case frame features of psych verbs, there is no specific verb stem which manifests an instrumental voice.

Another characteristic of [+per, -cog] verbs, which is more general in nature, is that they permit the cooccurrence of a non-strict inner locative actant. Since the verb denotes an event experienced by the

[+DAT] referent, the [+LOC] can only be viewed as the location of the [+OBJ] perceived. Thus, the redundancy rule:

CFRR-13: [-cog] $\longrightarrow$ $\begin{bmatrix} \text{-strict} \\ \text{-dir} \end{bmatrix}$

The rule states that a perception verb marked [-cog] is redundantly marked with the features [-strict] and [-dir]. By CFRR-3, the feature [+([+LOC])] is added to the verb's case frame features. For example:

24. nakita ng doktor sa pasyente ang isang malaking tumor
    see   doctor   patient   one   big   tumor
    [-cog] $\begin{bmatrix} +AC \\ +DAT \end{bmatrix}$ $\begin{bmatrix} +L \\ +LOC \end{bmatrix}$ $\begin{bmatrix} +NM \\ +OBJ \end{bmatrix}$

'A big tumor was seen by the doctor in the patient.'

This generality is matched by the existence of a locative voice form in which the corresponding voice inflection is marked with the regular locative affix -an as in:

24.a. nakita?an ng doktor ang pasyente ng isang malaking
                   $\begin{bmatrix} +AC \\ +DAT \end{bmatrix}$ $\begin{bmatrix} +NM \\ +LOC \end{bmatrix}$

tumor
$\begin{bmatrix} +AC \\ +OBJ \end{bmatrix}$

'The patient was seen by the doctor as having a big tumor.'

The classes of non-perception verbs differ from perception verbs in realizing their cooccurring [+OBJ] in the locative case form instead of the accusative when it is not the subject of the sentence. Thus, the following redundancy rule applies:

CFRR-14: $\begin{bmatrix} \text{-per} \\ -\begin{bmatrix} +NM \\ +OBJ \end{bmatrix} \end{bmatrix}$ $\longrightarrow$ $\begin{bmatrix} -\begin{bmatrix} -L \\ +OBJ \end{bmatrix} \end{bmatrix}$

Verbs of emotion marked [+emo] are essentially directed to

objects. It is not possible to be ashamed without being ashamed of something in particular, neither is it possible to be delighted without knowing what is delighting one. There may be no reason for being afraid, but one is afraid of something (Kenny, 1969:60-62). For this reason, verbs of emotion are considered as having the basic case frame features [+[+DAT], +[+OBJ]]. Very often, this class of verbs is described as objectless, hence, the only cooccurring case frame feature ascribed to it is the experiencer. (Cf. Ramos, 1974:91.) For example, compare the following pair of sentences:

25.a. natakot ang bata? sa aso
      fear   child   dog
      [+emo] $\begin{bmatrix} +NM \\ +DAT \end{bmatrix}$ $\begin{bmatrix} +L \\ +OBJ \end{bmatrix}$

'The child was afraid of the dog.'

25.b. natakot ang bata?
                  $\begin{bmatrix} +NM \\ +OBJ \end{bmatrix}$

'The child became fearful/afraid.'

The present analysis differentiates the case frame features of the two homophonous forms of the verb matakot. In 25.a, it is a verb of emotion which requires a cooccurring [+DAT] and [+OBJ] whereas in 25.b, it is a derived non-afflicted verb which requires only a cooccurring [+OBJ]. The two verbs are lexically related by means of a derivation rule which creates the form in 25.b from that of 25.a. (See SVDR-3, Chapter IV.) Each of these two forms has a different morphological stem membership with correspondingly different voice paradigms.

The class of non-emotion verbs is subdivided into verbs of assessment [+assm] and non-assessment [-assm]. The former denotes the experiencer's assessment or judgment of the quality of the [+OBJ] referent involved. Unlike the three preceding classes of psych verbs, verbs of assessment manifest only one morphological stem form which in turn inflects only for the dative voice.[31] Thus, the redundancy rule below marks all [+assm] verbs as taking only a [+DAT] subject.

CFRR-15:   [+assm] $\longrightarrow$ $\left[- \begin{bmatrix} +NM \\ -DAT \end{bmatrix} \right]$

For example:

26. nadali?an   siya   sa   eksamen
     consider easy   he   examination
     [+assm] $\begin{bmatrix} +NM \\ +DAT \end{bmatrix}$ $\begin{bmatrix} +L \\ +OBJ \end{bmatrix}$

'He considered the examination easy.'

Non-assessment verbs are further specified either as verbs of attitude [+attd] or non-attitude [-attd]. As the name implies, the former expresses the attitude of the cooccurring experiencer towards an object referent. The latter denotes the intentional exhibition of the trait or behavior indicated by the adjective base of the verb, hence, it may be referred to as verbs of enactment. Both classes of [-assm] verbs are derived from Adj's, but they are of different morphological structures and they display different voice paradigms and corresponding voice affixes.

The semantic feature subcategorization of the non-agentive dative case frame subcategory may be represented in the following tree diagram:

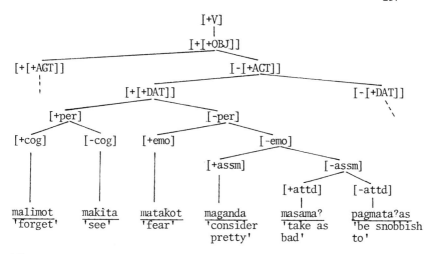

Figure 5. Case frame and semantic feature subcategorization of non-agentive dative or psych verbs

3.4.3 Subcategorization of Primary Verb Stems in Terms of Morphological and Voice-Related Features

The verb stems manifesting the seven major case frame subcategories and the twenty-six semantic classes therein appear in different morphological structures. Each morphological form is associated with the set of cooccurring case relations that can be realized in the nominative case form, thus indicating the stem form's voice inflectional paradigm. On one extreme, one type of morphological form allows a maximum of four voice inflected forms and, on the other, certain types exhibit one and only one voice form. Still other morphological types restrict their range of voice inflection to two or three forms. This new added dimension to the subcategorization of verb stems is necessary in order to explain the operation of voice inflection marked by a simple set of inflectional affixes. Past studies, which have always

ignored this particular aspect of subcategorization and which have
emphasized the classification of roots instead of stems, unfortunately
end up with a complex and redundant system of voice affixation. At
the same time, they fail to relate systematically classes of derived
verb stems with their sources as well as with other derived and
obviously related stems.

The rules that account for the subcategorization of the verb stems
according to their morphological-voice-related features given below are
labelled MVRSR's.

MVRSR-1: [+V] $\longrightarrow$ [±root]

A verb stem is either a root [+root] or a non-root [-root] by
MVRSR-1. As described earlier (see section 3.3.2), a root is a minimal
unanalyzable form. In contrast, a non-root is a derived stem analyzable
into a derivational affix and a base, which may be a root or another
derived stem. All primary verb stems are either roots or derived
stems.

MVRRR-1: [+root] $\longrightarrow$ $\begin{bmatrix} -\begin{bmatrix} -AC \\ +INS \end{bmatrix} \\ -\begin{bmatrix} -R \\ +RSN \end{bmatrix} \\ -\begin{bmatrix} -C \\ +COM \end{bmatrix} \end{bmatrix}$

MVRRR-1 states that a [+root] verb stem does not allow a cooccurring
[+INS], [+RSN] or [+COM] to be realized in any other form except in
their respective non-nominative case form. This implies that not one
of these three case relations is included in the voice paradigm of a
[+root] stem.

MVRSR-2: [+root] $\longrightarrow$ [±erg]

When the verb is marked [+root], it may be either ergative [+erg] or non-ergative [-erg]. The term ergative verb has been defined as one which may have a [+AGT] or a [+INS] in its case frame for some types, but whose unmarked subject choice is [+OBJ]. It contrasts with an accusative or a non-ergative verb whose unmarked subject choice is determined according to the Fillmorean hierarchy of AGT-DAT-INS-OBJ, i.e., the unmarked subject choice is [+AGT] if there is a cooccurring [+AGT] in its case frame; [+DAT] if there is no [+AGT], etc. (Starosta, 1974:10-11). For our purposes, these two terms are adopted here with a slight modification in meaning. Since every subject choice is marked, [+erg] is marked for not allowing a cooccurring [+AGT] or [+INS] to be realized in the nominative case form. Thus,

$$\text{MVRRR-2:} \quad [+\text{erg}] \longrightarrow \begin{bmatrix} -\begin{bmatrix} +\text{NM} \\ +\text{AGT} \end{bmatrix} \\ -\begin{bmatrix} +\text{NM} \\ +\text{INS} \end{bmatrix} \end{bmatrix}$$

The above redundancy rule implies that a [+erg] verb paradigm consists of at most the dative or locative and objective voices. In addition, if an agentive verb does not permit a nominative agentive, then by the following redundancy rule, it does not permit a nominative benefactive either:

$$\text{MVRRR-3:} \quad \begin{bmatrix} +[+\text{AGT}] \\ -\begin{bmatrix} +\text{NM} \\ +\text{AGT} \end{bmatrix} \end{bmatrix} \longrightarrow \begin{bmatrix} -\begin{bmatrix} +\text{NM} \\ +\text{BEN} \end{bmatrix} \end{bmatrix}$$

A [-erg] verb, on the other hand, is not marked for similar voice restrictions. This means then that its voice paradigm consists of the maximum of four, namely, agentive, dative or locative, objective and benefactive, where the case frame specifications include all these case relations.

MVRSR-3: [-root] $\longrightarrow$ $\begin{bmatrix} \pm\text{pot} \\ \pm\text{act} \end{bmatrix}$

By MVRSR-3, a non-root verb is further specified as either potential [+pot] or non-potential [-pot] and active [+act] or non-active [-act]. Verbs that are marked [-pot, -act] are further specified as either instrumental [+ins] or non-instrumental [-ins] by the following rule:

MVRSR-4: $\begin{bmatrix} -\text{pot} \\ -\text{act} \end{bmatrix}$ $\longrightarrow$ [$\pm$ins]

MVRSR-3 and MVRSR-4 describe five subclasses of derived verb stems which are identified by the derivational affixes maka- for the [+pot, +act], ma- for the [+pot, -act], pag- for the [-pot, +act], pang- for the [-pot, -act, +ins] and ka- for the [-pot, -act, -ins]. These subclasses have the following restrictions on their voice paradigm:

MVRRR-4: $\left\{\begin{matrix} [+\text{pot}] \\ \begin{bmatrix} -\text{pot} \\ +\text{act} \end{bmatrix} \end{matrix}\right\}$ $\longrightarrow$ $\begin{bmatrix} -\begin{bmatrix} +\text{NM} \\ +\text{INS} \end{bmatrix} \\ -\begin{bmatrix} +\text{NM} \\ +\text{RSN} \end{bmatrix} \end{bmatrix}$

MVRRR-5: $\begin{bmatrix} +\text{pot} \\ +\text{act} \end{bmatrix}$ $\longrightarrow$ $\begin{bmatrix} -\begin{bmatrix} +\text{NM} \\ +\text{OBJ} \end{bmatrix} \end{bmatrix}$

MVRRR-6: [+ins] $\longrightarrow$ $\begin{bmatrix} -\begin{bmatrix} +\text{NM} \\ -\text{INS} \end{bmatrix} \end{bmatrix}$

MVRRR-7: $\begin{bmatrix} +[+\text{AGT}] \\ -\text{ins} \end{bmatrix}$ $\longrightarrow$ $\begin{bmatrix} -\begin{bmatrix} +\text{NM} \\ -\text{RSN} \end{bmatrix} \end{bmatrix}$

MVRRR-8: $\begin{bmatrix} -[+\text{AGT}] \\ -\text{ins} \end{bmatrix}$ $\longrightarrow$ $\begin{bmatrix} -\begin{bmatrix} +\text{NM} \\ +\text{DAT} \end{bmatrix} \end{bmatrix}$

MVRRR-4 states that potential and non-potential active stems do not allow either an instrumental or a reason voice in their voice paradigm. By MVRRR-5, potential active verbs are marked for not inflecting in the objective voice. MVRRR-6 specifies only an instrumental voice for the [+ins] stem. On the other hand, the [-ins] stem of agentive verbs realizes only the reason voice by MVRRR-7, but there are syntactic and semantic classes which permit an objective or a locative, besides the reason voice. Thus, MVRRR-8 provides that a non-agentive [-ins] stem excludes the dative voice in its paradigm.

Each of these morphological verb stem classes is associated with voice marking affixes it takes in its paradigm, which paradigm is in turn linked to its case frame and semantic features. A [+erg] stem takes only the passive voice affixes -in, -an or i- to mark the objective and the locative or dative voice. A [-erg], which follows the accusative verb subject choice hierarchy, signals its 'preferred' subject with the active voice affix um- and the other 'less preferred' case relations, if any, with the passive voice affixes.

The two subclasses of derived stems marked [+pot] take distinct derivational affixes maka- and ma-. The active or maka-class manifests only one voice form and it is always marked by a zero or ∅ affix; the non-active or ma-class may take a ∅, -an or i- for its voice paradigm. The [-pot] class subdivided into the [+act] and [-act] subclasses are also restricted in the voice affixes that they take. The [-pot, +act] which is usually marked by the derivational affix pag- marks its preferred subject with the active affix m- and the non-preferred ones with the passive affixes -an or i-. Both the [+ins] and [-ins] stems, having the derivational affixes pang- and ka-, respectively, take the voice affix i-, and, with certain non-agentive semantic classes, the [-ins] stem can also take -an to mark either a locative or an objective voice in its paradigm.

The seven morphological-voice-related subcategories of verb stems cross-classify the major case frame and semantic feature subcategories described in the preceding sections. These cross-classifications can be shown in tree-intersecting diagrams.

3.4.3.1 Cross-classification of Agentive Verb Stems

The tree-intersecting diagram which follows (see Figure 6, p.203) shows the cross-classification of information, location and simple transitive verbs.

Some generalizations that can be stated concerning the cross-classification of the [-root] subcategory are as follows:

(a) Information verbs lack the [+ins] stem class.

(b) Of the [+root] stems, [+goal] location verbs are manifested only by the [+erg] class; conversely, [-goal] verbs are manifested only by the [-erg] class.

(c) The absence of [-erg] stems manifesting the [-cs] and [-af] subcategories of [-dir] location verbs is matched in the same semantic subcategories of the [-extn] simple transitive verbs.

(d) The [-root] stem classes derive from the [+root] and other [-root] classes. The [-pot, +act] class derives from the [+erg] and never from the [-erg] class (which is why there are no [+act, -goal] stems) and, unless otherwise marked, it has the derivational affix pag-.[32] The [+ins] class derives from both [+erg] and [-erg] classes

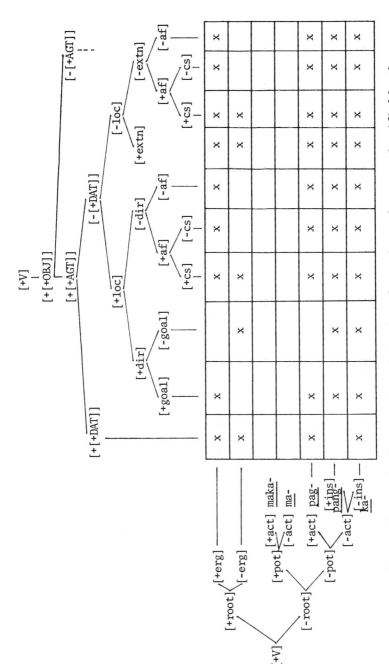

Figure 6. Case frame and semantic feature subcategorization of agentive verbs cross-classified by the morphological-voice-related feature subcategorization

and is always prefixed by the derivational affix pang-. The [-ins]
class which may be redundantly referred to as the reason stem derives
from the [-erg] and the [-pot, +act] classes, and is prefixed by
the derivational affix ka-.

Depending on its case frame and semantic subcategory, a [+erg]
stem has basically two voice forms in its paradigm, an objective and a
dative or a locative; a [-erg] consists of an agentive, an objective,
a dative or a locative, and a benefactive, where the [+BEN] is allowed
to cooccur; a [-pot, +act] normally consists of an agentive and a
benefactive, but when it is marked [+af, -cs], it can also include a
locative voice in its paradigm. The agentive [+ins] and [-ins]
classes are marked for manifesting only one voice form each, the
instrumental and the reason voice, respectively. There are, however,
non-agentive verb classes in which the [-ins] form can include other
voice forms.

In terms of listing the agentive verbal lexemes in the lexicon,
the predictable regularity of the derived or [-root] primary verb
stem classes indicates that the relevant entries are those marked
[+erg] and [-erg]. The derived verb stems can be accounted for by the
derivation rules included in the lexicon.

Each of the [+erg] and [-erg] stem subcategories under the major
agentive case frame and semantic subcategories is exemplified below.
For the derived or [-root] stem classes, only a sentence is used
to illustrate each of them.

3.4.3.1.1 Information Verbs, [+[+AGT], +[+DAT], +[+OBJ]]

Since information verbs generally express oral communication, the
medium is understood to be the mouth. Hence, these verbs do not
usually have a potentially cooccurring [+INS], unlike other types of
agentive verbs. If the agent requires an intermediary, it uses the
complex form of the instrumental actant which never gets realized in
the nominative case form. One other way of expressing this idea of
an intermediary is through the employment of a causative verb.
Consequently, there is no morphological class of instrumental verbs
among the information verbs. One other characteristic of these verbs
is the limited membership in the [-erg] class.

(a) [+[+AGT], +[+DAT], +[+OBJ], +erg][33]

   sabi 'say'   ʔutos 'order'   turoʔ 'teach'

   banggit 'mention' bilin 'requisition' balitaʔ 'inform'

   tanong 'ask'   ʔulat 'report'   kuwento 'narrate'

27. ibinalitaʔ niya sa nanay ang buong nangyari
     relate   he   mother   whole happening
               [+AC]   [+L]   [+NM]
               [+AGT]   [+DAT]   [+OBJ]

'The entire happening was related by him to mother.'

(b) [+[+AGT], +[+DAT], +[+OBJ], -erg]

   sulat 'inform by   daʔing 'express supplication;
        writing'   complain'

   ungot 'express
      some whim'

28. dumaʔing siya sa nanay ng sakit ng ulo
     complain she   mother   ache   head
           [+NM]   [+L]   [+AC]
           [+AGT]   [+DAT]   [+OBJ]

'She complained to mother of a headache.'

(c) [+[+AGT], +[+DAT], +[+OBJ], -pot, +act]

29. naghilín si Rode ng libro sa kaniyang kaibigan
    order   book   her   friend
    $\begin{bmatrix} +NM \\ +AGT \end{bmatrix}$ $\begin{bmatrix} +AC \\ +OBJ \end{bmatrix}$ $\begin{bmatrix} +L \\ +DAT \end{bmatrix}$

    'Rode requested her friend to get her a book.'

(d) [+[+AGT], +[+DAT], +[+OBJ], -ins]

30. ikinapag?utos niya ng meriyenda sa katulong ang
    order   she   snacks   maid
    $\begin{bmatrix} +AC \\ +AGT \end{bmatrix}$ $\begin{bmatrix} +AC \\ +OBJ \end{bmatrix}$ $\begin{bmatrix} +L \\ +DAT \end{bmatrix}$

    pagdating ng ilang bisita
    arrival   some visitor
    $\begin{bmatrix} +NM \\ +RSN \end{bmatrix}$

    'The arrival of some visitors made her order the maid to
    get some snacks.'

Besides a concrete noun, a [+OBJ] case relation cooccurring with
any of the subclasses of information verbs may also be an abstract
noun, a prepositional phrase, or a nominalization. For example:

31.a. binanggit ng guro sa prinsipal ang panganga?ilangan
      mention   teacher principal   need
      $\begin{bmatrix} +AC \\ +AGT \end{bmatrix}$ $\begin{bmatrix} +L \\ +DAT \end{bmatrix}$ $\begin{bmatrix} +NM \\ +OBJ \end{bmatrix}$

      niya ng libro
      her   book

      'Her need for books was mentioned by the teacher to
      the principal.'

31.b. babanggitin ng guro sa prinsipal na kailangan
                                            S
      $\begin{bmatrix} +AC \\ +AGT \end{bmatrix}$ $\begin{bmatrix} +L \\ +DAT \end{bmatrix}$

      niya ng libro

      'The teacher will mention to the principal that she
      needs books.'

3.4.3.1.2 Location Verbs, [+[+AGT], +loc, +[+OBJ]]

The five semantic subclasses of locative verbs cross-classified by morphological classes are illustrated as follows:

(1.a) [+[+AGT], +loc, +[+OBJ], +goal, +erg]

    tapon 'throw'   bigay 'give'   dala 'take to'

    lagay 'put'   alay 'offer'   sa?uli? 'return to'

    sabit 'hang'   kabit 'attach'   suksok 'thrust into'

32. ibibigay niya sa mga estudyante ang marka bukas
    give   he   student   grade tomorrow
              $\begin{bmatrix} +AC \\ +AGT \end{bmatrix}$ $\begin{bmatrix} +L \\ +LOC \end{bmatrix}$ $\begin{bmatrix} +NM \\ +OBJ \end{bmatrix}$

'The grades will be given by him to the students tomorrow.'

(1.b) [+[+AGT], +loc, +[+OBJ], +goal, -pot, +act]

33. magsasabit siya ng kurtina sa bintana?
    hang   she   curtain   window
               $\begin{bmatrix} +NM \\ +AGT \end{bmatrix}$ $\begin{bmatrix} +AC \\ +OBJ \end{bmatrix}$ $\begin{bmatrix} +L \\ +LOC \end{bmatrix}$

'She will hang curtains at the windows.'

(1.c) [+[+AGT], +loc, +[+OBJ], +goal, +ins]

34. ipinangdikit niya ng larawan sa album   ang
    paste with   she   picture   photo album
                 $\begin{bmatrix} +AC \\ +AGT \end{bmatrix}$ $\begin{bmatrix} +AC \\ +OBJ \end{bmatrix}$ $\begin{bmatrix} +L \\ +LOC \end{bmatrix}$

'Scotch tape'
$\begin{bmatrix} +NM \\ +INS \end{bmatrix}$

'The Scotch tape was used by her for pasting the pictures in the album.'

(1.d) [+[+AGT], +loc, +[+OBJ], +goal, -ins]

35. ikinapagbigay niya ng balato   sa mga kapatid
     give   he   'windfall'   sister/brother
                    [+AC]   [+AC]   [+L]
                    [+AGT]   [+OBJ]   [+LOC]

     niya ang pananalo niya sa 'sweepstakes'
     his   [+NM]
                [+RSN]

     'His winning in the sweepstakes was the reason for his
     giving away a gift to his sisters.'

(2.a) [+[+AGT], +loc, +[+OBJ], -goal, -erg]

     bili 'buy'   kuha 'take from; get' hiram 'borrow'

     pitas 'pick from' abot 'reach for'   hingi? 'ask for'

     tanggap 'receive' pulot 'pick'   salok 'fetch from'

This class also includes verbs of pulling such as <u>hugot</u> 'pull

out; draw', <u>bunot</u> 'pluck', <u>hila</u> 'drag', which are [-strict] verbs.

36. bumili sila ng bahay sa 'Nu-West Realtors'
     buy   they   house
             [+NM]   [+AC]   [+L]
             [+AGT]   [+OBJ]   [+LOC]

     'They bought a house from Nu-West Realtors.'

(2.b) [+[+AGT], +loc, +[+OBJ], -goal, +ins]

37. ipinangpitas ni Jun ng niyog   sa puno? ang kawayan
     pick   coconut   tree   bamboo pole
                   [+AC]   [+AC]   [+L]   [+NM]
                   [+AGT]   [+OBJ]   [+LOC]   [+INS]

     'The bamboo pole was used by Jun to pick coconuts from
     the tree.'

(2.c) [+[+AGT], +loc, +[+OBJ], -goal, -ins]

38. ikinakuha niya ng pera sa bangko ang pagbili ng bahay
    take from he   money   bank   purchase   house
    $\begin{bmatrix} +AC \\ +AGT \end{bmatrix}$ $\begin{bmatrix} +AC \\ +OBJ \end{bmatrix}$ $\begin{bmatrix} +L \\ +LOC \end{bmatrix}$ $\begin{bmatrix} +NM \\ +RSN \end{bmatrix}$

   'Their purchase of a house caused him to withdraw money from the bank.'

(3.a) [+[+AGT], +loc, +[+OBJ], +cs, +erg]

   luto? 'cook'   tunaw 'dissolve'   bayo 'pound'

   ihaw 'broil'   biling 'grind'   tadtad 'chop'

   laga? 'boil'   prito 'fry'   halo? 'mix in'

39. iihawin niya ang karne (sa pugon)
    broil   he   meat   oven
    $\begin{bmatrix} +AC \\ +AGT \end{bmatrix}$ $\begin{bmatrix} +NM \\ +OBJ \end{bmatrix}$ $\begin{bmatrix} +L \\ +LOC \end{bmatrix}$

   'He will broil the meat (in the oven).'

It will be observed that most of the verbs in this class pertain to cooking or the preparation of food.

(3.b) [+[+AGT], +loc, +[+OBJ], +cs, -erg]

   sulat 'write down'   lilok 'sculpture'

   ukit 'carve'

40. lumilok siya ng mukha ni Hesu Kristo (sa marbol)
    sculpture he   face   Jesus Christ   marble
    $\begin{bmatrix} +NM \\ +AGT \end{bmatrix}$ $\begin{bmatrix} +AC \\ +AC \end{bmatrix}$ $\begin{bmatrix} +L \\ +LOC \end{bmatrix}$

   'He sculptured the face of Jesus Christ (in marble).'

(3.c) [+[+AGT], +loc, +[+OBJ], +cs, -pot, +act]

41. mag?iihaw siya ng karne (sa pugon)
    broil   he   meat   oven
    $\begin{bmatrix} +NM \\ +AGT \end{bmatrix}$ $\begin{bmatrix} +AC \\ +OBJ \end{bmatrix}$ $\begin{bmatrix} +L \\ +LOC \end{bmatrix}$

   'He will broil meat (in the oven).'

(3.d) [+[+AGT], +loc, +[+OBJ], +cs, +ins]

42. ipinangtunaw niya ng harina (sa mangkok) ang tubig
    dissolve he flour bowl water
    $\begin{bmatrix} +AC \\ +AGT \end{bmatrix}$ $\begin{bmatrix} +AC \\ +OBJ \end{bmatrix}$ $\begin{bmatrix} +L \\ +LOC \end{bmatrix}$ $\begin{bmatrix} +NM \\ +INS \end{bmatrix}$

'The water was used by him to dissolve the flour (in the bowl).'

(3.e) [+[+AGT], +loc, +[+OBJ], +cs, -ins]

43. ikinalilok niya ng mukha ni Hesu Kristo (sa marbol)
    sculpture he face Jesus Christ marble
    $\begin{bmatrix} +AC \\ +AGT \end{bmatrix}$ $\begin{bmatrix} +AC \\ +OBJ \end{bmatrix}$

ang inspirasyon na nakuha niya sa kaniyang paniniwala?
    inspiration derive his faith
    $\begin{bmatrix} +NM \\ +RSN \end{bmatrix}$

sa Diyos
in God

'The inspiration he derived from his faith in God caused him to sculpture the face of Jesus Christ (in marble).'

(4.a) [+[+AGT], +loc, +[+OBJ], -cs, +erg]

laba 'launder' banlaw 'rinse' banli? 'scald'

hugas 'wash' paligo? 'bathe' almirol 'starch'

44. hinugasan niya ang mga baso (sa palanggana)
    wash she glass basin
    $\begin{bmatrix} +AC \\ +AGT \end{bmatrix}$ $\begin{bmatrix} +NM \\ +OBJ \end{bmatrix}$ $\begin{bmatrix} +L \\ +LOC \end{bmatrix}$

'The glasses were washed by her (in the basin).'

(4.b) [+[+AGT], +loc, +[+OBJ], -cs, -pot, +act]

45. naghugas siya ng mga baso (sa palanggana)
    wash she glass basin
    $\begin{bmatrix} +NM \\ +AGT \end{bmatrix}$ $\begin{bmatrix} +AC \\ +OBJ \end{bmatrix}$ $\begin{bmatrix} +L \\ +LOC \end{bmatrix}$

'She washed the glasses (in the basin).'

(4.c) [+[+AGT], +loc, +[+OBJ], -cs, +ins]

46. ipinanglaba niya ng mga puti?an   ang mainit
    wash with   she   white clothes   hot
                 $\begin{bmatrix} +AC \\ +AGT \end{bmatrix}$ $\begin{bmatrix} +AC \\ +OBJ \end{bmatrix}$ $\begin{bmatrix} +NM \\ +INS \end{bmatrix}$

    na tubig
        water

    'The hot water was used by her in laundering white garments.'

(4.d) [+[+AGT], +loc, +[+OBJ], -cs, -ins]

47. ikinapaglaba ni Rosa ng damit   ang pag?alis   ng
    launder   clothes   departure
                  $\begin{bmatrix} +AC \\ +AGT \end{bmatrix}$ $\begin{bmatrix} +AC \\ +OBJ \end{bmatrix}$ $\begin{bmatrix} +NM \\ +RSN \end{bmatrix}$

    katulong nila
    maid   their

    'The departure of their maid is the reason for Rosa's
    washing the clothes.'

(5.a) [+[+AGT], +loc, +[+OBJ], -af, +erg]

       latag 'spread out'   sandal 'lean against'

       upo? 'sit s.t.'   tihaya? 'lay s.t. face up'

       higa? 'lay down'   salansan 'file one on top of another'

       tali? 'tie to'   ta?ob 'turn upside down'

       pasok 'take in'

48. inilatag   niya ang banig (sa araw)
    spread out   he   mat   sun
                 $\begin{bmatrix} +AC \\ +AGT \end{bmatrix}$ $\begin{bmatrix} +NM \\ +OBJ \end{bmatrix}$ $\begin{bmatrix} +L \\ +LOC \end{bmatrix}$

    'The mat was spread out by him (in the sun.)'

As in the preceding class of [-dir, -cs] verb stems, we find no

morphological class of [-erg] manifesting the [-dir, -af] subcategory.

(5.b) [+[+AGT], +loc, +[+OBJ], -af, -pot, +act]

49. naglatag   siya ng banig (sa araw)
    spread out   he   mat   sun
                 $\begin{bmatrix} +NM \\ +AGT \end{bmatrix}$ $\begin{bmatrix} +AC \\ +OBJ \end{bmatrix}$ $\begin{bmatrix} +L \\ +LOC \end{bmatrix}$

'He spread out the mat (in the sun).'

(5.c) [+[+AGT], +loc, +[+OBJ], -af, +ins]

50. ipinangtali? niya ng suhay   (sa bahay) ang
    he   support   house
                 $\begin{bmatrix} +AC \\ +AGT \end{bmatrix}$ $\begin{bmatrix} +AC \\ +OBJ \end{bmatrix}$ $\begin{bmatrix} +L \\ +LOC \end{bmatrix}$

alembrang ·makapal
wire   thick
$\begin{bmatrix} +NM \\ +INS \end{bmatrix}$

'The thick wire was used by him to tie the support to the house.'

(5.d) [+[+AGT], +loc, +[+OBJ], -af, -ins]

51. ikinapagsalansan   niya ng mga damit
    file one on top of another   she   clothes
                                    $\begin{bmatrix} +AC \\ +AGT \end{bmatrix}$ $\begin{bmatrix} +AC \\ +OBJ \end{bmatrix}$

(sa aparador) ang pagkahulog   ng mga ito
     closet   falling off   this
     $\begin{bmatrix} +L \\ +LOC \end{bmatrix}$ $\begin{bmatrix} +NM \\ +RSN \end{bmatrix}$

'The clothes fell off so she had to arrange them back (in the closet).'

3.4.3.1.3 Simple Transitive Verbs, [+[+AGT], -loc, +[+OBJ]]

Like the other agentive verbs, the four semantic subclasses of simple transitive verbs are also manifested by five morphological subclasses, namely, the two types of [+root] and the three [-pot] classes of [-root]. It will be noted that only the [+extn] and [+cs] subclasses have both [+erg] and [-erg] verb stems as submembers.

(1.a) [+[+AGT], -loc, +[+OBJ], +extn, +erg]

    alaga? 'take care of'   abang 'watch for'

    matyag 'follow up'   parangal 'honor; fete'

    masid 'watch'   bantay 'guard'

    anyaya 'invite'

52. inalaga?an ng misyonaryo ang sundalong nasugatan
    take care of   missionary   soldier   wounded
                    $\begin{bmatrix}+AC\\+AGT\end{bmatrix}$ $\begin{bmatrix}+NM\\+OBJ\end{bmatrix}$

    'The wounded soldier was taken care of by the missionary.'

(1.b) [+[+AGT], -loc, +[+OBJ], +extn, -erg]

    tulong 'help'   ambag 'share with'   tutol 'oppose'

    damay 'aid'   abuloy 'contribute'   halik 'kiss'

    saklolo 'succor'   ayuda 'support'   susog 'amend'

53. tumutol   ang mga guro?   sa plano ng konseho
    oppose/reject   teachers   plan   council
                    $\begin{bmatrix}+NM\\+AGT\end{bmatrix}$ $\begin{bmatrix}+L\\+OBJ\end{bmatrix}$

    'The teachers rejected the council's plan.'

(1.c) [+[+AGT], -loc, +[+OBJ], +extn, -pot, +act]

54. nagparangal ang buong bayan kay Kapitan Pepe
    honor   whole town
                    $\begin{bmatrix}+NM\\+AGT\end{bmatrix}$ $\begin{bmatrix}+L\\+OBJ\end{bmatrix}$

    'The whole town honored Capt. Pepe.'

(1.d) [+[+AGT], -loc, +[+OBJ], +extn, +ins]

55. ipinangsaklolo niya sa batang nalulunod ang salbabida
    succor   he   child   drowning   life-saver
                  $\begin{bmatrix}+AC\\+AGT\end{bmatrix}$ $\begin{bmatrix}+L\\+OBJ\end{bmatrix}$ $\begin{bmatrix}+NM\\+INS\end{bmatrix}$

    'The life-saver was used by him for saving the drowning child.'

(1.4) [+[+AGT], -loc, +[+OBJ], +extn, -ins]

56. ikinapag?abuloy niya sa paaralan ang pangangailangan nito
    contribute   he   school   needs   this

                  $\begin{bmatrix}+AC\\+AGT\end{bmatrix}$ $\begin{bmatrix}+L\\+OBJ\end{bmatrix}$ $\begin{bmatrix}+NM\\+RSN\end{bmatrix}$

'Its needs made him contribute to the school.'

It may be stressed that the feature [+extn] is too limited to be able to unify the more specific semantic features expressed by the various members of the entire subclass. It should be interpreted as some action which leaves a non-physical effect on the [+OBJ] referent.

(2.a) [+[+AGT], -loc, +[+OBJ], -extn, +cs, +erg]

    pisa? 'squeeze' hiwa? 'cut; slice' basag 'break'

    pitpit 'crush'   lukot 'crumple'   sira? 'tear'

    sibak 'split;   hampas 'strike' tiba? 'cut down'
        chop'

57. sinira? niya ang larawan
    tear   he   picture

        $\begin{bmatrix}+AC\\+AGT\end{bmatrix}$ $\begin{bmatrix}+NM\\+OBJ\end{bmatrix}$

'The picture was torn by him.'

(2.b) [+[+AGT], -loc, +[+OBJ], -extn, +cs, -erg]

    ka?in 'eat   inom 'drink'   gawa? 'make'

    lulon 'swallow' tungga? 'gulp down' patay 'kill'

    higop 'sip'   sipsip 'suck'   tahi? 'sew'

58. tinungga? ng lasenggo ang isa pang boteng serbesa
    gulp down   drunkard   one more bottle beer

              $\begin{bmatrix}+AC\\+AGT\end{bmatrix}$ $\begin{bmatrix}+NM\\+OBJ\end{bmatrix}$

'One more bottle of beer was emptied/gulped down by the drunkard.'

Similar to the [-goal] type of location verbs, most members of the

class of [-erg] change-of-state transitive verbs denote actions
toward the agent. They express termination, consumption, use or
creation of the [+OBJ] referent.

(2.c) [+[+AGT], -loc, +[+OBJ], -extn, +cs, -pot, +act]

59. nagsibak si Sepa ng kahoy
    chop   wood
              [+NM]   [+AC]
              [+AGT]   [+OBJ]

    'Sepa chopped some firewood.'

(2.d) [+[+AGT], -loc, +[+OBJ], -extn, +cs, +ins]

60. ipinanggulpi ng tulisan sa bihag ang latigo
    beat   bandit   captive   whiplash
                [+AC]   [+L]   [+NM]
                [+AGT]   [+OBJ]   [+INS]

    'The whiplash was used by the bandit to beat up the captive.'

(2.e) [+[+AGT], -loc, -extn, +cs, -ins]

61. ikinapaghiwa? ng nanay ng isa pang papaya ang
    slice   mother   one more
                 [+AC]   [+AC]
                 [+AGT]   [+OBJ]

    madaling pagka?ubos nito
    immediate consumption this
              [+NM]
              [+RSN]

    'Its immediate consumption caused mother to slice another
    papaya.'

(3.a) [+[+AGT], -loc, +[+OBJ], -extn, -cs, +erg]

    talop 'peel'   bukas 'open'   pintas 'find fault'

    punas 'mop;   balat 'remove   kapkap 'frisk'
     wipe off'   skin'

    burda 'embroider'   kaliskis 'scale,   sugat 'wound'
                          as of fish'

62. kinapkapan ng pulis   ang mga binata?
    frisk   policeman   young men
                $\begin{bmatrix} +AC \\ +AGT \end{bmatrix}$ $\begin{bmatrix} +NM \\ +OBJ \end{bmatrix}$

'The young men were frisked by the policeman.'

(3.b) [+[+AGT], -loc, +[+OBJ], -extn, -cs, -pot, +act]

63. ipinagtalop niya   ng dalandan ang maysakit
    peel   she   orange   patient
             $\begin{bmatrix} +AC \\ +AGT \end{bmatrix}$ $\begin{bmatrix} +AC \\ +OBJ \end{bmatrix}$ $\begin{bmatrix} +NM \\ +BEN \end{bmatrix}$

'She peeled an orange for the patient.'

(3.c) [+[+AGT], -loc, +[+OBJ], -extn, -cs, +ins]

64. ipinangbukas ng mga magnanakaw ng 'kaha de yero'
    open   burglar   safe
                   $\begin{bmatrix} +AC \\ +AGT \end{bmatrix}$ $\begin{bmatrix} +AC \\ +OBJ \end{bmatrix}$

ang ilang paputok
   some   explosive
         $\begin{bmatrix} +NM \\ +INS \end{bmatrix}$

'Some explosives were used by the burglars to open the safe.'

(3.d) [+[+AGT], -loc, +[+OBJ], -extn, -cs, -ins]

65. ikinapagbukas ng tatay ng lahat ng bintana? ang
    open   father all   window
               $\begin{bmatrix} +AC \\ +AGT \end{bmatrix}$ $\begin{bmatrix} +AC \\ +OBJ \end{bmatrix}$

matinding init kagabi
extreme   heat last night
         $\begin{bmatrix} +NM \\ +RSN \end{bmatrix}$

'The extreme heat last night caused father to open all the windows.'

(4.a) [+[+AGT], -loc, +[+OBJ], -extn, -af, +erg]

ladlad 'unfurl'   labas 'put out' kaway 'wave at'

ayos 'fix; arrange' bukas 'open'   baba? 'lower; put
                                          down'

pikit 'close one's ta?as 'raise'   sara 'close'
eyes'

66. ipinikit ng bata? ang isang mata niya
    shut   child   one   eye his
                 ⌈+AC ⌉   ⌈+NM ⌉
                 ⌊+AGT⌋   ⌊+OBJ⌋

'One of his eyes was shut by the child.'

(4.b) [+[+AGT], -loc, +[+OBJ] -extn, -af, -pot, +act]

67. nagta?as ang mga kompaniya ng kotse ng halaga
    raise   company   car   price
                     ⌈+NM ⌉   ⌈+AC ⌉
                     ⌊+AGT⌋   ⌊+OBJ⌋

'The car companies raised their prices.'

(4.c) [+[+AGT], -loc, +[+OBJ], -extn, -af, +ins]

68. ipinangta?as niya ng kotse ang "jack"
    raise   he   car
                 ⌈+AC ⌉ ⌈+AC ⌉   ⌈+NM ⌉
                 ⌊+AGT⌋ ⌊+OBJ⌋   ⌊+INS⌋

'The jack was used by him in raising the car.'

Some of the [+erg] stems do not have corresponding [+ins] forms
because they are not, under normal conditions, performed with the use
of an outside instrument or tool, e.g. pikit 'close one's eyes.'

(4.d) [+[+AGT], -loc, +[+OBJ], -extn, -af, -ins]

69. ikinapag?ayos niya kaagad ng bahay ang pagdating
    arrange   she at once   house   arrival
                  ⌈+AC ⌉   ⌈+AC ⌉   ⌈+NM ⌉
                  ⌊+AGT⌋   ⌊+OBJ⌋   ⌊+RSN⌋

ng panauhin
   guest

'The arrival of a guest made her put the house in order at once.'

3.4.3.2 Cross-classification of Non-agentive, Non-dative Verb Stems

The three case frame subcategories under the non-agentive, non-dative group of verbs are the locomotion, calamity and simple intransitive verb stems. Their morphological cross-classification is represented in the following tree-intersecting diagram:

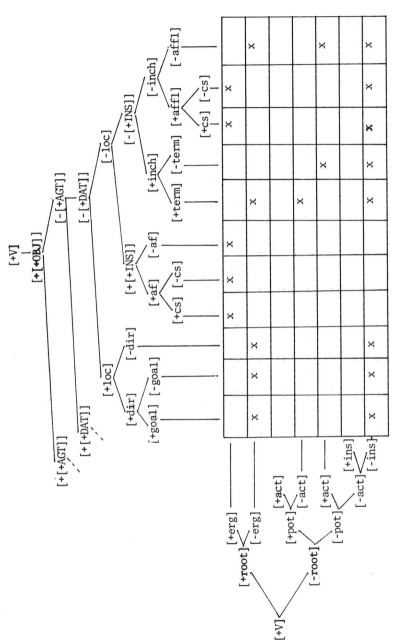

Figure 7. Case frame and semantic feature subcategorization of non-agentive, non-dative verbs cross-classified by the morphological-voice-related feature subcategorization.

The observable generalizations pertaining to the cross-classification of non-agentive, non-dative verb stems may be summarized as follows:

(a) Only the subcategory of calamity and simple intransitive verbs of affliction manifest the morphological class of [+erg] stems, which suggests their relation or similarity to agentive verbs in implying an external initiator.

(b) Of the non-agentive, non-dative verbs, only the [+inch, +term] manifests both the [-erg] and [+pot, -act] forms. On the other hand, only the [-affl] class manifests both the [-erg] and the [-pot, +act] form, the latter being likewise manifested by the [+inch, -term] class.

(c) Similar to agentive verbs, the [-ins] stem, whatever classes it manifests in the non-agentive non-dative subcategory, derives from the [-erg] and [-pot, +act] classes. It can also be derived from the noun or adjective source of the [+pot, -act] derived class, still identified by the same derivational affix ka-.

Based on their cooccurring case frame features, the three subclasses of non-agentive non-dative verbs imply corresponding voice paradigms as follows:

(a) The voice paradigm of the class of calamity verbs, which are all marked [+erg], consists only of the objective voice. By CFRR-7, the cooccurring [+INS] can only be realized in the non-nominative case form, hence, no stem form manifests the instrumental voice.

(b) Verbs of locomotion marked [-erg] have both the objective and locative voices.

(c) Simple intransitive verbs, whether [+erg], [-erg], [+pot, -act] or [-pot, +act] can only manifest the objective voice.

Each of the major case frame and semantic subcategories cross-classified by the morphological-voice-related feature subcategories is exemplified below.

3.4.3.2.1 Locomotion Verbs, [-[+AGT], -[+DAT], +loc, +[+OBJ]]

The three semantic subclasses of locomotion verbs, namely, [+goal], [-goal] and [-dir] are exemplified according to their morphological class manifestations as follows:

(1.a) [-[+AGT], -[+DAT], +loc, +[+OBJ], +goal, -erg]

This class indicates motion of a [+OBJ] referent toward a goal denoted by the cooccurring or unexpressed [+LOC].

punta 'go to'	lapit 'go near to'
pasok 'enter'	tungo 'go to'
bagsak 'fall on'	akyat 'climb'
kabit 'attach to'	balik 'return to'

70. pumasok ang tubig sa loob ng bahay namin
    enter   water   inside house our
           [+NM]   [+L]
           [+OBJ]   [+LOC]

'The water went inside our house.'

(1.b) [-[+AGT], -[+DAT], +loc, +[+OBJ], +goal, -ins]

71. ikinakapasok ng tubig   sa loob ng bahay namin ang
    enter   water   inside   house our
                       ⌈+AC ⌉   ⌈+L ⌉
                       ⌊+OBJ⌋   ⌊+LOC⌋

    malakas na ulan
    strong   rain
                 ⌈+NM ⌉
                 ⌊+RSN⌋

'The strong rain causes water to enter our house.'

(2.a) [-[+AGT], -[+DAT], +loc, +[+OBJ], -goal, -erg]

This class expresses motion of the [+OBJ] from a source location.

alis 'depart from'	hiwalay 'separate from; stay away from'
takas 'escape from'	labas 'get out of'
layo? 'go away from'	kalag 'break away from'
tiwalag 'resign from'	baba? 'go down from'

72. hiniwalayan niya ang asawa niya
    separate   he   spouse his
                  ⌈+AC ⌉   ⌈+NM ⌉
                  ⌊+OBJ⌋   ⌊+LOC⌋

'He divorced his spouse.'
Lit.: 'He separated from his spouse.'

(2.b) [-[+AGT], -[+DAT], +loc, +[+OBJ], -goal, -ins]

73. ikinahiwalay ni Jose sa kaibigan ang pagsisinu-
    separate   friend   lying
                  ⌈+AC ⌉   ⌈+L ⌉   ⌈+NM ⌉
                  ⌊+OBJ⌋   ⌊+LOC⌋   ⌊+RSN⌋

    ngaling nito
             this

'His friend's lying made Jose stay away from him.'

(3.a) [-[+AGT], -[+DAT], +loc, +[+OBJ], -dir, -erg]

The verbs in this class denote motion designated by the verb in a given place.

higa? 'lie down'	langoy 'swim in'	tira 'reside in'
dapa? 'lie face down'	takbo 'run in a place'	tigil 'stop at'
dagan 'lie on'	upo? 'sit on'	hinto? 'stop by'
sakay 'ride on'	sandal 'lean against'	silong 'take shelter in'

74. sumilong   sila   sa   tindahan   habang   umuulan
    take   they   store   while   raining
    shelter   [+NM]   [+L]
               [+OBJ]   [+LOC]

'They took shelter at the store while it was raining.'

(3.b) [-[+AGT], -[+DAT], +loc, +[+OBJ], -dir, -ins]

75. ikinasilong   nila   sa   tindahan   ang   biglang   pag?ulan
    take shelter   they   store   sudden   raining
                   [+AC]   [+L]   [+NM]
                   [+OBJ]   [+LOC]   [+RSN]

'The sudden downpour of rain made them take shelter
at the store.'

As far as the morphological structure and voice marking of the verbs of locomotion are concerned, three semantic subclasses are identical. The semantic features [+goal] and [-goal] become relevant in connection with the optional cooccurrence of another related [+LOC] which must be introduced by a preposition. As described in the preceding chapter (see Chapter II, p.49), directional locomotion verbs are permitted to have a cooccurring [+LOC] which expresses the point of origin of a [+goal] verb or the destination of a [-goal] verb. This property is expressed by the following redundancy rule:

CFRR-14:   [αgoal]   ⟶ $\begin{bmatrix} +P \\ -\begin{vmatrix} \alpha goal \\ +[+LOC] \end{vmatrix} \end{bmatrix}$

The rule states that a directional verb stem may allow a potentially cooccurring locative actant marked by a preposition which indicates the opposite direction indicated by the verb.

3.4.3.2.2 Calamity Verbs, [-[+AGT], -[+DAT], -loc, +[+INS], +[+OBJ]]

The three subclasses of calamity verbs can only express the objective voice and they are manifested by the same morphological type, the [+erg]. However, each semantic subclass is marked by a different objective voice affix.

(1)   [-[+AGT], -[+DAT], -loc, +[+INS], +[+OBJ], +cs, +erg]

sunog 'burn'	tupok 'char; burn'	wasak 'destroy'
sira? 'tear'	giba? 'ruin; demolish'	bali? 'break'
tuklap 'blow off'	tangay 'carry away'	lipad 'blow away'

76.   tinangay   ng   agos   ang   tsinelas   ni   Rizal
      carry   water   slipper
      away   current
                     $\begin{bmatrix} +AC \\ +INS \end{bmatrix}$ $\begin{bmatrix} +NM \\ +OBJ \end{bmatrix}$

'Rizal's slipper was carried away by the current.'

(2)   [-[+AGT], -[+DAT], -loc, +[+INS], +[+OBJ], -cs, +erg]

abot 'overtake'	dapo? 'alight'	dampi? 'touch lightly'
hihip 'blow'	baling 'turn to'	buhos 'drench'
kapit 'afflict; hold on'	sakit 'shine on'	

77. inabutan sila ng malakas na ulan
    overtake they   heavy   rain
          $\begin{bmatrix} +NM \\ +OBJ \end{bmatrix}$ $\begin{bmatrix} +AC \\ +INS \end{bmatrix}$

'They were overtaken by a heavy rain.'

(3) [-[+AGT], -[+DAT], -loc, +[+INS], +[+OBJ], -af, +erg]

ta?ob 'turn over'   sadsad 'cause to   lubog 'sink'
                           be grounded'

buwal 'blow down'   tumba 'upset'   hapay 'tilt; cause
                                             to lean'

78. ibinuwal ng bagyo ang punong mangga namin
    blow down   storm   tree   mango   our
              $\begin{bmatrix} +AC \\ +INS \end{bmatrix}$ $\begin{bmatrix} +NM \\ +OBJ \end{bmatrix}$

'Our mango tree was blown down by the storm.'

Each of the above verb stems is closely associated with the natural force or phenomenon marked [+INS] which usually can carry out what is designated by the verb. The same verb stems which can be physically possible for an agent to perform also appear as agentive verbs, which verbs may be said to have been derived from calamity verbs. In such cases, the agentive verbs may cooccur with a potential [+INS].

3.4.3.2.3 Simple Intransitive Verbs, [-[+AGT], -[+DAT], -loc, -[+INS], +[+OBJ]]

The five subclasses of simple intransitive verbs based on their semantic and morphological cross-classification are exemplified below. The subclass labelled [+inch] may be marked [+term], which expresses a permanent or terminal change of state, or [-term], which means a temporary or transient change of state. The [+term] class is realized by the [-erg] and [+pot, -act] forms, not to mention the [-ins]. The [-erg] and [+pot, -act] classes are generally derived   from the category of adjective and noun roots. Manifesting a morphological structure distinct from each other, each subclass requires a different voice marker.

(1.a) [-[+INS], +[+OBJ], +inch, +term, -erg]

    laki 'become big; increase   payat 'become thin'
      in size'

    bigat 'become heavy'   sariwa? 'become fresh'

    tamis 'become sweet'   tahimik 'become quiet'

    ba?it 'become good'   laganap 'become widespread'

79. humina? ang benta ng asukal nang tuma?as ang
     become   sale   sugar   rise
     weak

$$\begin{bmatrix} +NM \\ +OBJ \end{bmatrix}$$

halaga nito
price   this

'The sale of sugar slowed down when its price rose.'
Lit.: 'The sale of sugar became weak when its price went up.'

The terminal inchoative verbs of this class have two derivational sources. The examples in the first column derive from the class of noun roots which also serve as the base for derived adjectives prefixed by the derivational affix ma-. For example:

laki]$_N$ 'bigness; size; $\longmapsto$ malaki]$_{Adj}$ 'big'

                        $\longmapsto$ laki]$_V$ 'become big; increase in size'
                                (lumaki is the inflected
                                form)

It is universally accepted that inchoative verbs derive from adjectives. However, a specific type of derivation such as evidenced by the morphological structure of the first type of inchoative verbs illustrated in the first column shows that they can also be derived from noun roots. It is easy to relate this subclass of inchoative verbs with the corresponding ma-adjectives because they have a common source. With this relation, it is tempting to posit a general inchoative verb derivation from adjectives alone, but such an account would present difficulties in explaining the deletion of the derivational prefix ma-. For instance, if the verb <u>lumaki</u> derives from the adjective <u>malaki</u>, then the affix <u>ma</u>- in the source has to be deleted. By introducing a 'subtraction' rule in this particular process of derivation, we will be losing the important generalization that derivational affixes always carry over in derivation and, at the same time, we will be adding an unnecessary power to the theory. On the other hand, deriving verbs from noun roots is quite a general process, too. The irregularity and unpredictability of derivation is observable in the range of classes into which the verbs derived from them can be classified. Largely, the classification rests on the semantic content of the source noun and the meaning introduced in the verb in the process of derivation. (See Chapter IV for a more thorough discussion of derivation from noun roots, adjective roots and verb roots.)

The inchoative verbs in the second column derive from adjective roots. Appearing in identical morphological forms, both derivations are marked by the active voice affix, um-.

(1.b) [-[+INS], +[+OBJ], +inch, +term, +pot, -act]

mabulag 'become blind'   mabaliw 'become insane'

mahilo 'become dizzy'   matuyo? 'become dry'

matunaw 'become melted'   mahinog 'become ripe'

                                 mabasa? 'become wet'

                                 malanta 'become withered'

                                 mamatay 'become dead'

80. nabulok   ang   saging
      become rotten   banana
                          $\begin{bmatrix} +NM \\ +OBJ \end{bmatrix}$

'The banana became rotten.'

The source adjectives of this class of inchoative verbs are simple, root forms usually accented on the final syllable, e.g., bulók 'rotten', patáy 'dead', baliw 'crazy', etc., indicating natural states. This [+pot, -act] terminal inchoative class denotes the natural process undergone by the [+OBJ] resulting in the state denoted by the source adjective. The derived verb stems are marked by the derivational affix ma-.[34] In some cases, the final syllable accent in the source stem retracts to the penultimate syllable, as in the verbs in the first column, but, generally, the accent remains on the final syllable, as in the second column.

(1.c) [-[+INS], +[+OBJ], +inch, +term, -ins]

81. ikinahina? ng benta ng asukal ang pagta?as ng
      become weak   sale   sugar   rise
                        $\begin{bmatrix} +AC \\ +OBJ \end{bmatrix}$ $\begin{bmatrix} +NM \\ +RSN \end{bmatrix}$

      halaga nito
      price   this

'The rise in the price of sugar caused its sale to drop.'

229

82. ikinabulok ng mga saging ang pagkabasa? nito
    rot   banana   getting wet this
                  [+AC]   [+NM]
                  [+OBJ]   [+RSN]

'Their getting wet caused the bananas to become rotten.'

It will be observed that the terminal inchoative [-ins] class
derives from the [-erg] class. However, the [+pot, -act] counterpart
derives directly from the source form of the [+pot, -act] which is the
simple adjective form. As will be seen later, this direction of
derivation is true for all other [-ins] forms with a [+pot] counterpart.

The class of inchoative verbs marked [-term] can be realized
only in the [-pot, +act], identified by the derivational prefix
pang-, and the [-ins] forms.

(2.a) [-[+INS], +[+OBJ], +inch, -term, -pot, +act]

panlaki 'turn big; swell'   panariwa 'turn fresh'

pamigat 'turn heavy'   panahimik 'quiet down'

panghina? 'turn weak'   pamayat 'become thin'

pangitim 'turn blackish'   pangalog 'turn shaky'

83. nangalog ang tuhod ng matanda dahil sa pagod niya
    turn shaky   knee   old man because   fatigue his
               [+NM]   [+R]   [+L]
               [+OBJ]   [+RSN]

'The old man's knees became shaky because of fatigue.'

(2.b) [-[+INS], +[+OBJ], +inch, -term, -ins]

84. ikinapangalog ng tuhod ng matanda ang pagod niya
    turn shaky   knee   old man   fatigue his
                 [+AC]   [+NM]
                 [+OBJ]   [+RSN]

'His fatigue caused the old man's knees to shake.'

The next two subclasses of simple intransitive verbs are marked
[-inch] and further specified as either afflicted [+affl] or

non-afflicted [-affl]. The [+affl] verbs are either [+cs] or [-cs]
to refer to the type of affliction on the [+OBJ] referent. Each
subclass is exemplified below.

(3.a) [-[+INS], +[+OBJ], -inch, +cs, +erg]

ulan 'be overtaken by   umaga 'be overtaken by morning'
  rain'

sipon 'be afflicted with   hika? 'be seized by asthma'
   cold'

amag 'have mildew'   langgam 'be infested by ants'

tamad 'feel lazy'   malas 'experience bad luck'

85. lalagnatin ang mga bata?   dahil sa laganap na 'flu'
  have fever   children because of widespread
      $\begin{bmatrix} +NM \\ +OBJ \end{bmatrix}$ [+R] $\begin{bmatrix} +L \\ +RSN \end{bmatrix}$

  'The children will be afflicted with fever because of the
  flu epidemic.'

86. kakalawangin ang kutsara kung ibabad sa suka?
  have rust   spoon   if   soaked   vinegar
      $\begin{bmatrix} +NM \\ +OBJ \end{bmatrix}$

  'The spoon will turn rusty if it is soaked in vinegar.'

(3.b) [-[+INS], +[+OBJ], -inch, +cs, -ins]

87. ikinakalawang ng kutsara ang pagkababad nito sa suka?
  turn rusty   spoon   being soaked this in vinegar
      $\begin{bmatrix} +AC \\ +OBJ \end{bmatrix}$ $\begin{bmatrix} +NM \\ +RSN \end{bmatrix}$

  'Its being soaked in vinegar made the spoon rusty.'

(4.a) [-[+INS], +[+OBJ], -inch, -cs, +erg]

This class has a limited membership. It denotes the appearance
on the [+OBJ] referent of what is referred to by the noun from which
the verb derives.

pawis 'perspire'   kilabot 'have goose pimples'

kati 'have itch;   alibadbad 'get nauseated'
    feel itchy'

88. pinapawisan tayo kung tag?init
    perspire   we   when summer
$$\begin{bmatrix} +NM \\ +OBJ \end{bmatrix}$$

'We perspire in summer.'

(4.b) [-[+INS], +[+OBJ], -inch, -cs, -ins]

89. ikinaalibadbad ko ang amoy ng gasolina
    get nauseated I   smell   gasoline
$$\begin{bmatrix} +AC \\ +OBJ \end{bmatrix} \quad \begin{bmatrix} +NM \\ +RSN \end{bmatrix}$$

'The smell of gasoline caused me to get nauseated.'

The last subclass of simple intransitive verbs marked [-affl] is realized in three different morphological types. Each is exemplified as follows:

(5.a) [-[+INS], +[+OBJ], -inch -affl, -erg]

This class has a wide membership. It refers to bodily actions or movements or to active processes.

tawa 'laugh'   takbo 'run'   kulo? 'boil'

iyak 'cry'   ikot 'rotate'   putok 'explode'

dilat 'open one's   tungo 'bow;   sikat 'shine'
    eyes'   stoop'

idlap 'doze'   tikwas 'tilt' litaw 'appear; surface'

90. pumutok ang bulkang Mauna Loa
    erupt   volcano
$$\begin{bmatrix} +NM \\ +OBJ \end{bmatrix}$$

'Mauna Loa volcano erupted.'

(5.b) [-[+INS], +[+OBJ], -affl, -pot, +act]

This class of [-pot, +act] verbs is like that of agentive verbs

in taking the derived forms preceded by the derivational affix pag-.
However, it differs from the latter in that it does not derive from
another verbal subclass of a simpler morphological form. Rather, the
broad class of [-aff, -pot, +act] verb stems consists of various semantic
subtypes which derive generally from nouns and they are identified by
their respective derivational affixes. All these affixes such as pag-,
pagsa-, pagpaka-, pagpati- and pagka- in verb stems take identical
voice marking. Hence, they are treated here just as one class.
Examples of stems in this subclass are as follows:

pagdoktor 'be a doctor'	pagbunga 'bear fruit'
pagpayong 'use an umbrella'	pag?asin 'develop salt crystals'
pagsapusa 'act like a cat'	pagpakaba?it 'try to be good'
pagsakastila 'behave like a Spaniard'	pagpakata?o 'try to be civil; act like a human being'
pagkatihulog 'let one's self fall'	pagkabahay 'acquire a house'
pagpatiwakal 'commit suicide'	pagkasuwerte 'acquire a fortune'

91. nagsapulubi   ang   binatang   mayaman
     be like a beggar   bachelor   rich
                              $\begin{bmatrix} +NM \\ +OBJ \end{bmatrix}$

'The rich bachelor put on a beggar's appearance.'

(5.c) [-[+INS], +[+OBJ, -aff1, -ins]

This class derives from both the [-erg] and the [-pot, +act]
classes.

92. ikinaiyak ng bata? ang pag?alis ng kaniyang nanay
    cry   child   departure   his   mother
              $\begin{bmatrix} +AC \\ +OBJ \end{bmatrix}$ $\begin{bmatrix} +NM \\ +RSN \end{bmatrix}$

'His mother's departure caused the child to cry.'

93. ikinapagpatiwakal ng dalaga ang kaniyang pagkasawi?
    commit suicide   maiden   her   misfortune
                        $\begin{bmatrix} +AC \\ +OBJ \end{bmatrix}$ $\begin{bmatrix} +NM \\ +RSN \end{bmatrix}$

'Her misfortune made the maiden commit suicide.'

3.4.3.3 Cross-classification of Non-agentive, Dative Verb Stems

The only case frame subcategory which is non-agentive dative is
marked [-[+AGT], +[+DAT], +[+OBJ]]. It has been labelled here as
psych verbs, and it is further subcategorized into six semantic
classes, namely, [+cog], [-cog], [+emo], [+assm], [+attd] and [-attd].
The morphological cross-classification of these six classes is
represented in the following diagram (see Figure 8, p.234).

The subclass of non-agentive dative or psych verbs reveals the
following generalizations:

(a) Both types of perception verbs manifest three morphological
subclasses, the [+pot, +act], [+pot, -act] and [-ins]. Verbs of
emotion and of assessment do not have a [+pot, +act] that corresponds
to their [+pot, -act] forms.

(b) The [+pot] and [-ins] forms of psych verbs generally derive
directly from their non-verbal source stems; the [-ins] class of [-attd]
verbs, however, derives from the [-pot, +act] class and not from the
source stems of the latter class.

(c) The subclasses marked [+assm] and [+attd] are unique in

234

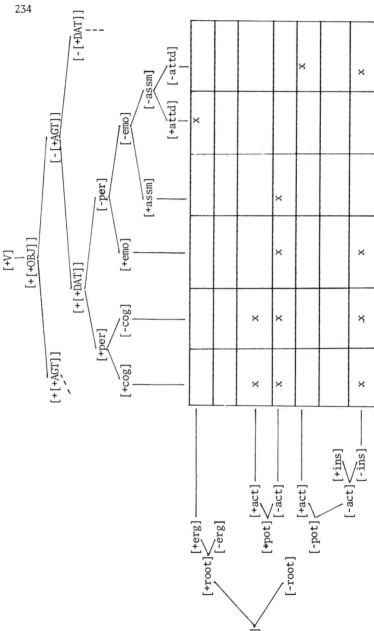

Figure 8. Case frame and semantic feature subcategorization of psych verbs cross-classified by the morphological-voice-related feature subcategorization

being manifested only by one stem class, the [+pot, -act] and the [+erg], respectively.

(d) The verbs of [+attd] and [-attd] stand isolated in the entire set of psych verbs in that they do not manifest a [+pot] form. Instead, their forms can be closely associated with agentive stems. In terms of meaning, these two classes differ from the other psych verbs and resemble the agentive and simple intransitive classes in expressing intention.

In terms of the corresponding voice paradigm of each morphological class of a given set of case frame and semantic features, the following may be stated:

(a) In general, the [+pot, -act] class of [+per] verbs inflects only for the objective voice; that of [-per] verbs, only for the dative voice. However, when the [+pot, -act] is also marked [-cog], it can also include a locative voice.

(b) The class of [+pot, +act] stems consists only of the dative voice.

(c) The [+erg] class includes only an objective voice while the [-pot, +act] includes both dative and objective voice.

(d) The [-ins] class always expresses a reason voice. In addition, if the stem is marked [-cog], it also inflects for the locative voice, and if it is marked [+emo] it also inflects for the objective voice.

Each of the subclasses of psych verbs may be exemplified as follows:

(1.a) [-[+AGT], +[+DAT], +cog, +pot, -act]

ma?intindi 'understand'   ma?alam 'know'

ma?unawa? 'comprehend'   maramdam 'sense; feel'

matanda? 'remember'   malimot 'forget'

94. nalaman ng maraming tao   ang iskandalo tungkol
    know   many   people   scandal   about
$$\begin{bmatrix} +AC \\ +DAT \end{bmatrix} \qquad \begin{bmatrix} +NM \\ +OBJ \end{bmatrix}$$

sa 'Watergate'

'The scandal about Watergate came to be known to many people.'

(1.b) [-[+AGT], +[+DAT], +cog, +pot, +act]

maka?intindi 'understand'   maka?alam 'know'

maka?unawa? 'comprehend'   makaramdam 'sense; feel'

makatanda? 'remember'   makalimot 'forget'

95. sa wakas, naka?intindi rin ang mga bata? ng
      end   understand also   child
$$\begin{bmatrix} +NM \\ +DAT \end{bmatrix}$$

paliwanag   niya
explanation his
$$\begin{bmatrix} +AC \\ +OBJ \end{bmatrix}$$

'Finally, the children understood his explanation.'

(1.c) [-[+AGT], +[+DAT], +[+OBJ], +cog, -ins]

96. ikina?alam ng maraming tao   ang iskandalo tungkol
    know   many   people   scandal
                         $\begin{bmatrix} +AC \\ +DAT \end{bmatrix}$ $\begin{bmatrix} +AC \\ +OBJ \end{bmatrix}$

    sa "Watergate" ang masugid na pagbabalita na mga
                         close   reporting
                                     $\begin{bmatrix} +NM \\ +RSN \end{bmatrix}$

    mamamahayag
    newspapermen

    'The close news-reporting by newspapermen made many people
    know of the scandal about "Watergate".'

As stated in other subcategories manifesting a [+pot] class,
a corresponding [-ins] class also derives from the same stem source
as the [+pot]. It is characteristic of the subcategories illustrated
above for all the three stem classes [+pot, +act], [+pot, -act] and
[-ins] to derive from one stem source, which usually belongs to another
lexical category. Each of these three morphological stem classes is
marked by specific derivational affixes maka-, ma- and ka-, respectively,
to identify their morphological structure each of which is in turn
associated with its corresponding voice inflectional paradigm. It
appears that the [+pot, -act] class, which manifests four of the six
subcategories of psych verbs, is the most widely used form. Thus, it
is mentioned first in the examples. Derivation being selective and
non-automatic, we find a few members of a subcategory having a
[+pot, -act] form but not a corresponding [+pot, +act] form. For
example, matuto 'learn' marked [+cog, +pot, -act] does not have a
corresponding [+cog, +pot, +act] form   *makututo, which class
normally inflects for the dative voice. Instead the [+pot, -act]

form which generally inflects only for the objective voice, manifests both dative and objective voices in the forms <u>matuto</u> and <u>matutuhan</u>, respectively. Compare the following sentences:

97.a. natuto si Irma ng Pranses
       learn
              $\begin{bmatrix} +NM \\ +DAT \end{bmatrix}$ $\begin{bmatrix} +AC \\ +OBJ \end{bmatrix}$

      'Irma learned French.'

97.b. natutuhan ni Irma ang Pranses
                $\begin{bmatrix} +AC \\ +DAT \end{bmatrix}$ $\begin{bmatrix} +NM \\ +OBJ \end{bmatrix}$

      Lit.: 'French was learned by Irma.'

Such verbs are individually marked as exceptions.

(2.a) [-[+AGT], +[+DAT], +[+OBJ], -cog, +pot, -act]

    makita 'see'   maʔamoy 'smell'   mabatid 'be aware of'

    marinig 'hear'   maʔaninaw 'see   mahalataʔ 'perceive'
                    vaguely'

   matanaw 'see   mabanaʔag 'catch   mapuna 'notice'
     from a   a glimpse of'
     distance'

98. nakita ng mga bataʔ ang salamangkero
    see   child   magician
                 $\begin{bmatrix} +AC \\ +DAT \end{bmatrix}$ $\begin{bmatrix} +NM \\ +OBJ \end{bmatrix}$

    'The magician was seen by the children.'

(2.b) [-[+AGT], +[+DAT], +[+OBJ], -cog, +pot, +act]

    makakita 'see'   makaʔamoy 'smell'   makabatid 'be aware
                                      of'

    makarinig 'hear'   makaʔaninaw 'see   makahalataʔ
                    vaguely'   'perceive'

99. nakakita ang mga ḅata? ng salamangkero
$$\begin{bmatrix} +NM \\ +DAT \end{bmatrix} \qquad \begin{bmatrix} +AC \\ +OBJ \end{bmatrix}$$

'The children saw a magician.'

(2.c) [-[+AGT], +[+DAT], +[+OBJ], -cog, -ins]

100. ikinabatid niya ng nangyaring sakuna?
be aware of he happen accident
$$\qquad\qquad\quad \begin{bmatrix} +AC \\ +DAT \end{bmatrix} \quad \begin{bmatrix} +AC \\ +OBJ \end{bmatrix}$$

ang pagbabalita? ni Pedro
reporting
$$\begin{bmatrix} +NM \\ +RSN \end{bmatrix}$$

'Pedro's reporting made him aware of the accident that
occurred.'

As had been mentioned before, [-cog] verbs allow the optional

cooccurrence of a [+LOC], and that actant can occur in the nominative

case form. When it does, it can be expressed either by the [+pot, -act]

form or the [-ins]. Compare sentence 24.a (p.194) repeated below with

24.b.

24.a. nakita?an ng doktor ang pasyente ng isang
see doctor patient one
$$\qquad\qquad\quad \begin{bmatrix} +AC \\ +DAT \end{bmatrix} \qquad \begin{bmatrix} +NM \\ +LOC \end{bmatrix}$$

malaking tumor
big tumor
$$\qquad\quad \begin{bmatrix} +AC \\ +OBJ \end{bmatrix}$$

'The patient was seen by the doctor as having a big tumor.'

24.b. kinakita?an ng doktor ang pasyente ng isang
      $\begin{bmatrix} +AC \\ +DAT \end{bmatrix}$ $\begin{bmatrix} +NM \\ +LOC \end{bmatrix}$

malaking tumor
$\begin{bmatrix} +AC \\ +OBJ \end{bmatrix}$

'The patient was seen as having a big tumor by the doctor.'

There appears to be no discernible difference semantically nor syntactically between the two locative voice forms in the [+pot, -act] and [-ins] stems.

(3.a) [-[+AGT], +[+DAT, +[+OBJ], +emo, +pot, -act]

matakot 'afraid of'   mayamot 'feel annoyed'

matuwa? 'be delighted   ma?inis 'feel irritated'
         with'

mahina? 'feel   masabik 'be eager'
       embarrassed'

magalit 'be angry with/ masuklam 'be loathful of'
           at'

101. natakot ang mga mamamayan sa mga tulisan
     afraid   townfolk   bandit
                           $\begin{bmatrix} +NM \\ +DAT \end{bmatrix}$ $\begin{bmatrix} +L \\ +OBJ \end{bmatrix}$

'The townspeople were afraid of the bandits.'

(3.b) [-[+AGT], +[+DAT], +[+OBJ], +emo, -ins]

102. ikinatakot ng mga mamamayan sa mga tulisan ang
     afraid of   townfolk   bandit
                         $\begin{bmatrix} +AC \\ +DAT \end{bmatrix}$ $\begin{bmatrix} +L \\ +OBJ \end{bmatrix}$

kawalang?awa? ng mga ito
ruthlessness   this
$\begin{bmatrix} +NM \\ +RSN \end{bmatrix}$

'The bandits' ruthlessness made the townpeople fear them.'

103. kinatakutan ng mga mamamayan ang mga tulisan
                  $\begin{bmatrix} +AC \\ +DAT \end{bmatrix}$ $\begin{bmatrix} +NM \\ +OBJ \end{bmatrix}$

'The bandits were feared by the town people.'

The [-ins] form of [-cog] verbs under 2.c and [+emo] verbs under 3.b may be compared in terms of the case relation it marks as subject with the affix -an. With the former semantic class, it marks a [+LOC] and with the latter, it marks a [+OBJ]. This shows that the [-ins] class is not limited to the reason voice alone; it can include two other voices in its paradigm.

(4) [-[+AGT], +[+DAT], +[+OBJ], +assm, +pot, -act]

malaki 'consider big'   mamura 'consider cheap'

maganda 'consider pretty'   mamahal 'consider expensive'

ma?alat 'consider salty'   mabigat 'consider heavy'

madali? 'consider easy'   mahirap 'consider difficult'

104. nagandahan siya sa palabas sa TV kagabi
     consider   she   show   last night
     pretty $\begin{bmatrix} +L \\ +OBJ \end{bmatrix}$
                  $\begin{bmatrix} +NM \\ +DAT \end{bmatrix}$

'She considered the show on TV last night good.'

(5) [-[+AGT], +[+DAT], +[+OBJ], +attd, +erg]

masama? 'take as bad'   dakila? 'honor; exalt'

mali?it 'take as trivial'   mahal 'value; love'

malaki 'take as enormous'   gusto 'like; desire'

105. minasama? niya ang tulong ng politiko
     take as bad   he   help   politician
                 $\begin{bmatrix} +AC \\ +DAT \end{bmatrix}$ $\begin{bmatrix} +NM \\ +OBJ \end{bmatrix}$

'He took the politician's help in a bad light.'

(6.a)   [-[+AGT], +[+DAT], +[+OBJ], -attd, -pot, +act]

pagmaginoo 'be a gentleman   pagmabuti 'act kindly to'
to s.o.'

pagmarahas 'be aggressive   pagmasungit 'be ill-tempered
to s.o.'   to s.o.'

pagmata?as 'be snobbish'   pagmaramot 'be stingy/selfish
toward s.o.'

106.a. nagmasungit   ang   bata?   sa mga kalaro   niya
       be ill-tempered   child   playmate   her
                               $\begin{bmatrix} +NM \\ +DAT \end{bmatrix}$ $\begin{bmatrix} +L \\ +OBJ \end{bmatrix}$

'The child was ill-tempered towards her playmates.'

106.b. pinagmasungitan ng   bata ang mga kalaro niya
                        $\begin{bmatrix} +AC \\ +DAT \end{bmatrix}$ $\begin{bmatrix} +NM \\ +OBJ \end{bmatrix}$

(6.b)   [-[+AGT], +[+DAT], +[+OBJ], -attd, -ins]

107. ikapagmamasungit   ng   bata sa mga kalaro   niya ang
     be ill-tempered   child   playmates
                             $\begin{bmatrix} +AC \\ +DAT \end{bmatrix}$ $\begin{bmatrix} +L \\ +OBJ \end{bmatrix}$

kakulangan nito   sa   tulog
lack   this   sleep
$\begin{bmatrix} +NM \\ +RSN \end{bmatrix}$

'The child's lack of sleep will cause him to be ill-tempered
toward his playmates.'

3.4.4 Voice-marking Affixes of Primary Verb Stem Classes

Given the case frame, semantic and morphological-voice-related
features of primary verb stem classes, each class manifests a
corresponding voice inflectional paradigm marked by corresponding
voice affixes. The following chart presents each verb stem class with
its respective voice paradigm identified by the case relation or

case relations entered horizontally and matched vertically by the
corresponding affix marking the verbal voice inflection.

CF-SF-MVF Verb Stem Classes	Voice Inflectional Paradigm and Corresponding Affixes					
	UM-	M-	IN	I-	-AN	∅
1. Information Verbs, [+[+AGT], +[+DAT] +[+OBJ]]						
(a) [+erg]				OBJ	DAT	
(b) [-erg]	AGT			OBJ/ BEN	DAT	
(c) [-pot, +act]		AGT		BEN	DAT	
(d) [-ins]				RSN		
2. Location Verbs [+[+AGT], +loc, +[+OBJ]]						
(a) [+goal, +erg]				OBJ	LOC	
(b) [+goal, -pot, +act]		AGT		BEN	LOC	
(c) [-goal, -erg]	AGT		OBJ	BEN	LOC	
(d) [+cs, +erg]			OBJ			
(e) [+cs, -erg]	AGT		OBJ	BEN	LOC	
(f) [-cs, +erg]					OBJ	
(g) [-af, +erg]				OBJ		
(h) [-dir, -pot, +act]		AGT		BEN	LOC	
(i) [+ins]				INS		
(j) [-ins]				RSN		
3. Simple Transitive Verbs, [+[+AGT], -loc, +[+OBJ]]						
(a) [+extn, +erg]					OBJ	

CF-SF-MVF Verb Stem Classes	Voice Inflectional Paradigm and Corresponding Affixes					
	UM-	M-	-IN	I-	-AN	∅
(b) [+extn, -erg]	AGT			BEN	OBJ	
(c) [+extn, -pot, +act]		AGT		BEN		
(d) [+cs, +erg]			OBJ			
(e) [+cs, -erg]	AGT		OBJ	BEN		
(f) [-cs, +erg]					OBJ	
(g) [-af, +erg]				OBJ		
(h) [-extn, -pot, +act]		AGT		BEN		
(i) [+ins]				INS		
(j) [-ins]				RSN		
4. Locomotion Verbs, [-[+AGT], -[+DAT], +loc, +[+OBJ]]]						
(a) [-erg]	OBJ				LOC	
(b) [-ins]				RSN		
5. Calamity Verbs, [-[+AGT], -[+DAT], +[+INS], +[+OBJ]]]						
(a) [+cs, +erg]			OBJ			
(b) [-cs, +erg]					OBJ	
(c) [-af, +erg]				OBJ		
6. Simple Intransitive Verbs, [-[+AGT], -[+DAT], -[+INS], +[+OBJ]]]						
(a) [+term, -erg]	OBJ					
(b) [+term, +pot, -act]						OBJ
(c) [-term, -pot, +act]		OBJ				

CF-SF-MVF Verb Stem Classes	Voice INflectional Paradigm and Corresponding Affixes					
	UM-	M-	-IN	I-	-AN	∅
(d) [+cs, +erg]			OBJ			
(e) [-cs, +erg]					OBJ	
(f) [-affl, -erg]	OBJ					
(g) [-affl, -pot, +act[		OBJ				
(h) [-ins]				RSN		
7. Psych Verbs, [-[+AGT], +[+DAT], +[+OBJ]]						
(a) [+per, +pot, +act]						DAT
(b) [+cog, +pot, -act]					OBJ	
(c) [-cog, +pot, -act]					LOC	OBJ
(d) [-cog, -ins]				RSN	LOC	
(e) [+emo, +pot, -act]						DAT
(f) [+assm, +pot, -act]					DAT	
(g) [+attd, +erg]			OBJ			
(h) [-attd, -pot, +act]		DAT			OBJ	
(i) [-ins]				RSN		
(j) [+per, +erg, +ntn]			OBJ			

Chart 7. Voice inflectional paradigm and corresponding affixes of primary verb stem classes

The same correspondences between the voice paradigm and the voice marking affixes of each verb stem class shown in Chart 7 can be presented in a similar chart below in which the morphological instead of the case frame features serve as the primary basis for subcategorization.

MVF-CF-SF Verb Stem Classes	Voice Inflectional Paradigm and Corresponding Affixes					
	UM-	M-	-IN	I-	-AN	∅
1. [+erg]						
(a) [+[+AGT], +[+DAT], +[+OBJ]]				OBJ	DAT	
(b) [+[+AGT], +loc, +[+OBJ]]						
(1) [+goal]				OBJ	LOC	
(2) [+cs]			OBJ			
(3) [-cs]					OBJ	
(4) [-af]				OBJ		
(c) [+[+AGT], -loc, +[+OBJ]]						
(1) [+extn]					OBJ	
(2) [+cs]			OBJ			
(3) [-cs]					OBJ	
(4) [-af]				OBJ		
(d) [-[+AGT], -[+DAT], +[+INS], +[+OBJ]]						
(1) [+cs]			OBJ			
(2) [-cs]					OBJ	
(3) [-af]				OBJ		
(e) [-[+AGT], -[+DAT], -[+INS], +[+OBJ]]						
(1) [+cs]			OBJ			
(2) [-cs]					OBJ	
(f) [-[+AGT], +[+DAT], +[+OBJ]]						

MVF-CF-SF Verb Stem Classes	Voice Inflectional Paradigm and Corresponding Affixes					
	UM-	M-	-IN	I-	-AN	Ø
(1) [+attd]			OBJ			
(2) [+per, +ntn]			OBJ			
2. [-erg]						
(a) [+[+AGT], +[+DAT], +[+OBJ]]	AGT			OBJ	DAT	
(b) [+[+AGT], +loc, +[+OBJ]]						
(1) [-goal]	AGT		OBJ	BEN	LOC	
(2) [+cs]	AGT		OBJ	BEN	LOC	
(c) [+[+AGT], -loc, +[+OBJ]]						
(1) [+extn]	AGT			BEN	OBJ	
(2) [+cs]	AGT		OBJ	BEN		
(d) [-[+AGT], -[+DAT], +loc, +[+OBJ]]	OBJ				LOC	
(e) [-[+AGT], -[+DAT], -[+INS], +[+OBJ]]						
(1) [+term]	OBJ					
(2) [-affl]	OBJ					
3. [-pot, +act]						
(a) [+[+AGT], +[+DAT], +[+OBJ]]		AGT		BEN	DAT	
(b) [+[+AGT], +loc, +[+OBJ]]						
(1) [+goal]		AGT		BEN	LOC	
(2) [-dir]		AGT		BEN	LOC	

MVF-CF-SF Verb Stem Classes	Voice Inflectional Paradigm and Corresponding Affixes					
	UM-	M-	-IN	I-	-AN	Ø
(c) [+[+AGT], -loc, +[+OBJ]]	:	:	:	:	:	:
(1) [+extn]	:	: AGT	:	: BEN	:	:
(2) [-extn]	:	: AGT	:	: BEN	:	:
(d) [-[+AGT], -[+DAT], -[+INS], +[+OBJ]]	:	:	:	:	:	:
(1) [-term]	:	: OBJ	:	:	:	:
(2) [-affl]	:	: OBJ	:	:	:	:
(e) [-[+AGT], +[+DAT], +[+OBJ], -attd]	:	: DAT	:	:	: OBJ	:
4. [+ins]	:	:	:	:	:	:
(a) [+[+AGT], +loc, +[+OBJ]]	:	:	:	: INS	:	:
(b) [+[+AGT], -loc, +[+OBJ]]	:	:	:	: INS	:	:
5. [-ins]	:	:	:	:	:	:
(a) [+[+AGT], +[+DAT], +[+OBJ]]	:	:	:	: RSN	:	:
(b) [+[+AGT], +loc, +[+OBJ]]	:	:	:	: RSN	:	:
(c) [+[+AGT], -loc, +[+OBJ]]	:	:	:	: RSN	:	:
(d) [-[+AGT, -[+DAT], +loc, +[+OBJ]]	:	:	:	: RSN	:	:
(e) [-[+AGT], -[+DAT], -[+INS], +[+OBJ]]	:	:	:	: RSN	:	:
(f) [-[+AGT], +[+DAT], +[+OBJ]]	:	:	:	: RSN	:	:
(1) [-cog]	:	:	:	: RSN	: LOC	:

MVF-CF-SF Verb Stem Classes	Voice Inflectional Paradigm and Corresponding Affixes					
	UM-	M-	-IN	I-	-AN	∅
6. [+pot, +act]						
(a) [-[+AGT], +[+DAT], +[+OBJ], +per]						DAT
7. [+pot, -act]						
(a) [-[+AGT], -[+DAT], -[+INS], +[+OBJ], +term]						OBJ
(b) [-[+AGT], +[+DAT], +[+OBJ]]						
(1) [+cog]					OBJ	
(2) [-cog]					LOC	OBJ
(3) [+emo]						DAT
(4) [+assm]					DAT	

Chart 7.a. Voice inflectional paradigm and corresponding affixes of primary verb stem classes (with morphological features highlighted)

Chart 7.a shows readily the restrictions on the general range of the inflectional paradigm and the corresponding affixes of each morphological stem class. For instance, the [-erg] is the only class that manifests the maximum of four inflected forms and the [-pot, +act], the maximum of three. Only these two classes can take an active voice affix in one of their inflected forms; all others are marked by a passive affix(es) or by ∅. On the other hand, the two non-potential classes which are generally restricted to only one voice inflection are the [+ins] and the [-ins], manifesting the instrumental and the reason voice, respectively. Likewise, the [+pot, +act] class manifests only

one inflected voice form, the dative of perception verbs, whereas the
[+pot, -act] class manifests one or two inflected forms of varying
paradigms depending on the case frame and semantic feature
specifications.

3.5 Conclusion

From the foregoing, we find that case frame, semantic and
morphological-voice-related features on verb stems are germane to
their subcategorization. To determine the maximum possible range of
voice forms which can be manifested by a particular verb stem and the
corresponding voice marking affix or affixes it takes, we need to
refer not only to its case frame and semantic features, but also to its
morphological features. These three types of features bear relevant
information as to the case form realization of the verb's cooccurring
actants, thereby indicating the verb's characteristic voice paradigm.
All together, these features trigger the assignment of the corresponding
affix for each voice inflected form. The chart showing the voice
paradigm and corresponding affixes of each verb stem class reveals two
important characteristics of verb stems. (a) Each verb stem class is
distinguished from every other class by at least one distinct feature,
either case frame, semantic or morphological; and (b) Each stem class
manifests its own voice paradigm and corresponding voice affix or
affixes according to its distinguishing features. Where a stem class
of a given case frame subcategory shares an identical set of morphological
and voice-related features with another stem class in the same case
frame subcategory, the two stem classes must differ in their semantic

subcategorization. If a stem class belongs to the same case frame
and semantic feature subcategory as another stem class and they
manifest different voice paradigms, then the two stem classes must
differ in their morphological and voice-related features. Finally, two
stem classes that exhibit identical voice paradigms and morphological
and semantic features must differ in their case frame features.

By subcategorizing verb stems according to their case frame,
semantic and morphological features, as described here, we are able to
isolate the invariant forms of the active and passive voice inflectional
affixes and to recognize the characteristic stem forms that these
affixes cooccur with to mark specific voices. For instance, we find
that with primary verb stems the active affixes um- and m- are in
complementary distribution with two morphological classes. Um- occurs
only with the [-erg] root stems whereas m- goes only with the derived
[-pot, +act] form. Both affixes mark either the agentive voice of
agentive verbs or the objective voice of non-agentive non-dative
verbs. The affix m- also marks the dative voice of the [-attd] class
of psych verbs. The passive affix -in attaches itself only to the root
stems [+erg] and [-erg] and marks only the objective voice of primary
verb stems. The passive affix -an goes with more forms; it can cooccur
with the [+erg] or the [-erg] and the [-pot, +act] form of non-psych
verbs. With psych verbs, it can be affixed to the [+pot, -act] and
also to one semantic class of the [-ins] form. This affix marks
either dative, locative or objective voice. Of the three passive
affixes, i- is accommodated by the most number of morphological
forms. It cooccurs with the [+erg] to mark objective voice, with the

[-erg] to mark benefactive or sometimes objective voice, with the
[-pot, +act] to mark benefactive voice, with the [+ins] to mark
instrumental voice, and with the [-ins] to mark reason voice.

It has been mentioned that some of the stem classes under a given
case frame subcategory are derivable from other stem classes. For
instance, [-pot, +act] is usually derived from [+erg], [-ins] from
[-erg] and [-pot, +act], and [+ins] from [+erg] and [-erg]. This
creative property of morphological forms indicates that such predictable
stem classes may be accounted for economically by means of derivation
rules. The output of 100% productive derivation rules need not be
entered in the lexicon. Only those stem classes that derive from
verb stem classes and other lexical categories by means of semi-
productive derivation rules are identified in the lexicon. It may
be added that verb stems which deviate from the general rules of voice-
marking have to be marked individually for their respective idiosyncracies.

Being underived from other verb stem classes, the [+erg], [-erg],
[+pot, -act], and certain members of the [-pot, +act] forms may be
regarded as basic among the primary verb stem classes. Interestingly,
these four classes express their preference for a particular cooccurring
case relation to be realized as subject. The [+erg] class always
manifests the objective voice; the [-erg] manifests the objective and
the agentive voices if the latter case relation is specified positively
in the case frame; the [+pot, -act] manifests the objective or the
dative voice; and the [-pot, +act] form that derives from a non-verbal
lexical category manifests either an objective or a dative voice. Based

on these manifestations, Tagalog may be described quite generally as
an ergative language, one whose subject choice preference ranks the
[+OBJ] case relation first. However, it is not accurate to ascribe
the ergative system to Tagalog as a whole in view of the presence of
[-erg] and [+pot] forms which cooccur with subjects other than a [+OBJ]
actant. Furthermore, the existence of a derived stem class, from
another verb stem class, which functions to subjectivize agents, i.e.,
[-pot, +act] from [+erg], supports the thesis that Tagalog, or
Philippine languages in general, is neither completely ergative nor
accusative. Seemingly, Tagalog creates a balance between the use
of these two systems. Thus, in terms of subject choice, Tagalog may
be properly described as exhibiting a mixed ergative and accusative
system depending on its verb stem classes.

254

Footnotes to Chapter III

[1]Other works which will be referred to in this chapter, although not included in the review, are Lopez (1939), Institute of National Language (1950), Kess (1967) and Schachter and Otanes (1972).

[2]See Blake, F., "Review of Bloomfield's Tagalog," in Hockett, C.F., A Leonard Bloomfield Anthology. Bloomington: Indiana University Press, 1970: 88.

[3]With instrumental passives, in particular, Bloomfield states that roots with the prefix pang- correspond to the active with mang- (1917: 250). There are, however, a good number of such forms with the prefix pang- and the prefix i- which do not have any corresponding active forms with mang-, e.g., ipangdilig 'use for watering,' ipanghalo? 'use for mixing,' ipangtagpi? 'use for patching,' ipangbukas 'use for opening,' ipanghukay 'use for digging', etc. This means that the instrumental passive forms with the prefix pang- do not necessarily correspond to active forms with mang- alone. They may also correspond to active forms with um- or mag-. Moreover, the form ipamili 'use for shopping,' which corresponds to mamili 'shop' can also be rendered as ipangpamili 'use for shopping.'

[4]Actually the verb forms with i- regularly correspond to ma-forms with the same affix i-, e.g., ma?ikuha 'able to get s.t. for s.o.; ma?itapon 'able to throw s.t.'.

[5]In fact in some works, Bloomfield has been identified along with SIL linguists as saying that "an affix indicates one and only one grammatical relation" (Constantino, 1971:55: Ramos, 1974:3).

[6]An examination of the 'recent past' form of the verb, however, reveals that it has a unique syntactic behavior which the other three forms do not manifest. Thus, it is treated in this study as a derived form (see pp. 142-44).

[7]As a variable, tension is closely tied to a given voice. In effect, it is the affix associated with a particular voice. A morphophonemic rule designating an affix for each voice can take care of this realization, and the set or paradigm consisting of the non-finite and finite forms, excluding the absolute form since it is non-verbal, can be accounted for by the variable aspect. Therefore, the tension actualizing functor can be dispensed with.

[8]This type of classification is in effect similar to what Kess (1967) suggests in his conclusion that the system should cross classify its verbs both as to which verbal affixes they occur with as well as which particular case relationship these verbal affixes happen to mark.

[9]A similar process of subjectivalization is described by Constantino (1970:6).

[10]The classes of verbs cooccurring with nominalized sentences or sentential complements have not been included in this study because sentential complements unlike nominal complements are not marked for either case relation or case form.

[11]It will be noted that the sentence structure exemplified in 4 is not generated by the Phrase Structure Rules in Chapter II because the rewrite rule for NP does not include the alternant Comp S for the constituents complement and sentence, respectively. This aspect has not been treated here because it is not relevant to the main problem of this study. The category of the predicate marked [+Adj] here is analyzed either as a Verb or as an Adjective in many related languages. This problem certainly needs investigation.

[12]Llamzon labels this subcategory 'immediate past'.

[13]This is one of the problematic verb forms mentioned in the preceding chapter which may turn out to belong to the class of nomina-lizations, particularly if the criterion used for the subcategorization of verb stems is that the subject actant involved is also a necessary complement appearing in its non-nominative form with the other verb forms in the paradigm. This form differs in meaning from the corresponding locative ergative form in that it is the medium through which the object given and intended for someone else is transmitted. Tentatively, however, this form is analyzed here as a verbal form.

[14]The PANG-stems marked [-pot, +act, +dist] are derived by a semantic DR rather than a syntactic DR, hence, they are not accounted for in this study. The investigation here deals only with syntactic derivation of verb stems. They have been cited here to show the various possibilities of verb stem derivation.

[15]The causative instrumental is not illustrated above. See causative derivation in Chapter IV.

[16]Cf. Schachter and Otanes (1972).

[17]Bloomfield, L. Language. New York:Holt, Rinehart and Winston, 1933: 226.

[18]One problem of formalization which needs further investigation
is the assignment of the voice affixes for the corresponding forms
in the voice paradigm of each stem class. The problem is that there
is no specific feature that refers to one unique voice affix manifested
by various stem classes. For instance, no single feature unifies
the different syntactic, semantic and morphological classes that
manifest a voice form, either dative, locative or objective, marked
by the affix -an. This feature is necessary for aspect inflection.
When a verb stem is inflected for aspect, the rule looks to the
particular voice affix the stem takes, and operates on the entire
affix-class, regardless of what case relation the affix marks.

Provisionally, Charts 7 and 7.a, which appear at the end of
this chapter, simply display the voice inflectional paradigm of each
primary verb stem class and the corresponding voice affix that marks
each voice form. All voice forms marked by the affix -in are said to
belong to the IN-class; those marked by um- fall under the UM-class,
etc.

[19]Each alternant form showing the first CV of the root or of
the first derivational affix instead of simply the first CV of the
verb stem has not been accounted for in the morphophonemic rules
due to complications they entail in their formalization. To account
for them, boundaries between bases and affixes or roots and derivational affixes have to be marked. Inasmuch as this aspect of the
analysis is not relevant to the main thesis of the study, this area
has been left for further investigation.

[20]For further distinctions between lexeme and word or word-form,
see Matthews (1974:20f.).

[21]Verb derivation from other lexical categories covered in
this study includes only those coming from simple N's and Adj's.

[22]These features are adopted from Kullavanijaya (1974: 58).

[23]It will be observed that in the case frame specifications
of each subcategory, a feature that is implied by another is no
longer specified. For instance, the feature [+loc] or [-loc]
implies a [-[+DAT]], a [+[+INS]] or [-[+INS]] implies a [-loc]
and a [-[+DAT]], hence, these implied features need not be marked.
The reason the predictable [+[+OBJ]] feature is retained is to see
readily the basic cooccurring case relations.

[24]See constraints on the cooccurrence of a [+COM] discussed in Chapter II, pp. 70f. and the section on social verb derivation in Chapter IV, pp. 369f. It will be recalled that the [+COM] can only be realized in the non-nominative case form when cooccurring with a primary verb, hence in the succeeding discussion of primary verb stem subcategories, this case relation will not be mentioned anymore. In spite of this restriction, it has been introduced here to emphasize the fact that it can be a possible subject of a secondary verb stem indentified by the feature social [+soc].

[25]The features [±dir] indicate the same meaning implied by Ramos' [±ter] features on the one hand and [±dir] on the other, and [±goal] correspond to her [±cf]. She used [±goal] to identify two types of directional (our locative [+LOC]) case relations. See Ramos, 1974: 45, 47-48, and 30f.

[26]The features [+cs], change of state, and [-cs], no change of state, have been adopted from Ramos (1974: 47) with some modification in meaning.

[27]It is recognized here that this observation is compatible, with Schachter and Otanes' and Ramos' agentive-directional analysis. However, we have shown earlier that this agentive-directional subcategory can be analyzed more accurately as belonging to the objective-directional or objective-locative subcategory.

[28]As will be shown later in the following section, these features are also shared by calamity verbs.

[29]Note that no semantic features subcategorize the class of information verbs. Likewise, note that the features [+strict] and [-strict] which pertain to the obligatory and optional cooccurrence, respectively, of the [+Loc] actant have been assumed in the tree since they do not affect the semantic feature subcategorization.

[30]Similar verbs are identified by Lakoff (1970:121) as stative verbs and by Chafe (1970:145) as experientail verbs. However, the class of psych verbs posited here do not include adjectives which Chafe classifies as state verbs (1970:98).

[31]This class should be distinguished from the set of secondary verb stems designated as indirect effect verbs. The latter has the same morphological structure as the former and it takes the same voice inflection marker -an to denote a dative subject. The difference lies in their semantic content and their derivational history. Indirect effect verbs denote the effect on an experiencer of an event undergone by a [+OBJ] referent. The experiencer is indirectly affected because the [+OBJ] actant involved is related to it as an alienable or inalienable possession. For example, na-sumugan sila ng bahay 'They lost their house in a fire,' Moreover, indirect effect verbs derive from simple intransitive verbs.

[32]Subclasses of the [-pot, +act] class can be derived either
syntactically or semantically, and they are usually identified by
corresponding derivational affixes. Verbs from the [+erg] and
[-erg] classes, for instance, which denote an action which is characterized as being hostile, unfavorable, harmful and usually performed
on an adversary, voluntarily and deliberately, derive into the
class of [-pot, +act] further specified as adversive or adversative
[+advr]. For example, panghampas 'to strike', pambatok 'to hit on
nape', pandagan 'to lie on to compress'. Similar to the distributive
[+dist] subclass, the [+advr] class is neither a primary verb class
nor a syntactically derived class, hence, it is not included in
this study.

[33]The first two examples in the first column are exceptions to
the voice inflectional affixes presented on p. 243. Instead of the
regular i- for the objective voice, these verbs take -in.
Lawrence Reid (personal communication) states that such a subclassification depends on the type or nature of the [+OBJ] involved.

[34]This class of inchoative verbs is not identified as a separate
subcategory in Ramos (1974). She states that "there are very few
examples of verbs marked [+inchoative, -transient] that take ma-.
The writer knows of only one exception. The verb is mamatay 'to die'"
(p. 141). On the contrary, it has been shown here that the class
has a wider membership than that. The reasons for setting up this
class of [+inch, +term, +pot, -act] are its similarity in meaning
with the [+inch, +term, -erg] class and its difference from it in
morphological form. Having different morphological forms, their
corresponding voice affixes are different.

CHAPTER IV

SYNTACTIC DERIVATION OF TAGALOG VERBS

4.1 Derivation and Lexical Relations

Derivation is the process of creating a new stem on the basis of an existing one. A stem is new if it differs from its related source in at least one syntactic, semantic or morphological feature which is not freely variable with other stems of the same class. The derived stem may or may not differ from its source form in syntactic categorization. When a syntactic or morphological feature modification, having to do with a case feature, is involved in the process, then it is a syntactic derivation and this results in a change in syntactic categorization or subcategorization. If the syntactic features remain unchanged and what is introduced or modified in the derived form is a semantic feature only, then it is a semantic derivation without a corresponding change in syntactic categorization or subcategorization. This study treats only of the more interesting type of lexical derivation, that which is referred to here as syntactic derivation of verb stems. It is interesting in the sense that it is relevant to the theoretical questions pertaining to case relations and to the clarification of the distinction between inflectional and derivational affixes of Tagalog verb stems.

In the preceding chapter, the primary verb stems are subcategorized according to their case frame, semantic and morphological-voice-related features and each subclass exhibits its own voice paradigm matched by the corresponding affixes that mark its voice inflection. It has been observed that an inflectional affix marking a particular voice may be appended to verb stems of different morphological structures. For instance, the root [-erg] stem kuha 'take s.t. to' is inflected for the benefactive voice by affixing i-, hence, ikuha 'take s.t. for s.o.' and the [-pot, +act] stem pagbigay 'give s.t. to' is inflected for the same voice as ipagbigay 'give s.t. for s.o.'. The [-pot, +act] form pagbigay corresponds to the [+erg] form bigay which does not allow the agentive voice inflection and, consequently, the benefactive voice. The stems bigay and pagbigay are closely related in that they share identical case frame and semantic features but they differ in their morphological features and, concomitantly, in their range of voice inflectional paradigm. This relationship, notwithstanding the difference, can be captured by means of a formal statement called a derivation rule in which a [-pot, +act] verb stem can possibly be created from a [+erg] verb stem. Similarly, other primary verb stem classes such as those marked [+ins] and [-ins] are also related to certain corresponding verb stem classes and their properties can also be accounted for by appropriate derivation rules. On the other hand, there are primary verb stem classes which do not derive from other verb stem classes, but instead they correspond to roots or stems belonging to a Noun or an Adjective category. For example, the verb sipon 'be afflicted with cold' and the source N sipon 'cold'; the verb mabulók 'rot' and the Adj bulók 'rotten'. On the basis of their shared semantic features, such verb stems cannot but be related to their non-verbal counterparts. Again, this relationship can be formalized in terms of derivation rules that account for the formation of lexically derived primary verb stems from nouns or adjectives. Such a process of verb formation is undeniably a universal property of natural languages.

In this chapter, it will be shown how these two kinds of primary verb stems, those derivable from other primary verb stems and those originating from the noun and adjective categories, are lexically related to their corresponding sources and how they differ from them in their feature specifications. In addition, non-primary or secondary verb stems derived from primary verb stem classes via a syntactic derivation rule are also formally accounted for. The major concern in the latter type of verb stem derivation is to determine the 'new' and/or 'related' case frame subcategories with their attendant semantic and morphological features which characterize the derived forms. Needless to say, the features of each secondary stem class include certain semantic features governing its own case frame features, its morphological-voice-related features and corresponding affix markers. Given their syntactic, semantic and morphological features, the secondary verb stem classes are subject to voice and aspect inflection following the same general voice-aspect morphophonemic rules stated in the preceding chapter.

4.2 Form of Derivation Rules

The various types of derived stems with their corresponding lexical relation to the source forms are accounted for by means of a set of rules known in the lexicase framework as derivation rules (DR's). A derivation rule can change, add or delete syntactic, semantic or phonological features to produce new lexical entries or lexemes. These rules, in comparison with transformation rules, are more restrained in their application since they operate on lexical entries and not on trees. This implies that derivation cannot perform permutations, additions, deletions or any other changes in syntactic bracketing or labelling.

Starosta (1971b) and Taylor (1971) have formalized these rules and they,
along with others (Li, 1973; Kullavanijaya, 1974; Lee, 1974; Clark, 1975
and Ikranagara, 1975), have demonstrated that derivation rules can best
capture generalizations about lexical relations. These rules account
systematically for the variety of relationships which hold between
lexical entries without adding to the generative power of the grammar.
Unlike the devices used by transformationalists and generative semanticists
where certain lexical items are derived from underlying sentences or from
a complex of semantic primes represented in a hierarchy of branching
nodes, derivation rules avoid the unnecessary complications encountered
by the former accounts and at the same time prevent the grammar from
increasing its generative power (Starosta, 1971d).

Derivation rules are part of the lexicon component of a grammar.
Each one shows that a class of items constituting the output of the rule
is formally and historically related to the class characterized by the
input. The rules operate with varying degrees of generality and, as
mentioned previously, the derived stems created by these rules are
subject to the same inflection or inflections of the underived members
of the class into which they have been derived. The rules that apply
quite generally are referred to as productive DR's, those that are
fairly restricted in their application are semi-productive, and those
that are strictly limited may be called idiomatic. Except for 100%
productive rules, such as gerundive nominalization in English and
abstract noun formation in Tagalog, every instance of derivation of a
lexical item is a separate event which must be separately recorded in
the lexicon. The DR's state relationships between sets of items and
even after a rule has ceased being used as the basis of forming new items,

the relationship may remain. For instance, the stem pagbili 'sell'
exhibits a strong semantic relationship with the stem bili 'buy'.[1] Both
stems are marked by the same case frame features [+[+AGT], +loc,+[+OBJ]].
However, they differ in the marking of the direction of transportation
of the [+OBJ] referent. The former stem is [+goal] whereas the latter
is [-goal]. Furthermore, pagbili is identical in structure with other
[+goal] stems marked [-pot, +act], e.g., pagbigay 'give', whereas bili
belongs to the [-erg] stem class, and, consequently, their respective
agentive voice affix differs. The former is marked by m- and the latter
by um-. These outstanding differences tend to widen the gap between the
two stems, for seemingly they overrule any kind of suggestion in favor
of establishing a formal relation between them. However, there are a
few other pairs of verb stems which denote the same similarities and
contrasts. They are as follows:

umabot 'reach for'	mag?abot 'hand over'
umupa 'rent s.t. from s.o.'	magpa?upa 'have s.t. rented'[2]
humiram 'borrow'	magpahiram 'lend'
umutang 'take a loan'	magpa?utang 'grant a loan'

All these pairs indicate that certain [-pot, +act] stems may be derived
from [-goal, -erg] stems through one or more DR's which show among others
the correspondence between the original feature [-goal] and the opposite
feature [+goal] on the derived stem. Presently, however, this rule is
no longer used to create new lexical items; yet, native speakers continue
to respond positively to this particular type of lexical relationship.

Derivation as a process of word or stem formation is admittedly
notoriously sporadic and unpredictable. Even a DR which may be productive

cannot account for certain identical morphological forms which develop a special meaning deviating from the meaning of the regularly derived forms. For example, Starosta (1971c) gives the item <u>destroyer</u> meaning a type of warship of a particular size and armament as an example of a form different from the item <u>destroyer</u> which means 'a person or device that destroys things' which can be predicted regularly by a derivation rule. These two items are separate lexical items with different derivational histories. The second form derives from the verb <u>destroy</u> via a productive DR which accounts for the nominal class of the form X-er meaning 's.o. or s.t. that Xs'. Because of its predictability, this form need not be fully specified as a lexical entry. In contrast, the first <u>destroyer</u> presumably derives from the second <u>destroyer</u> with predictable features, as attested by the meaning carried over from the source form, but it is specified with all other idiosyncratic semantic features. For a number of sporadic changes occurring in certain derived items in which the meanings that develop are so removed from the original or source meaning, the derived forms are lexicalized, to mean that they form new lexical items (Matthews, 1974:33-35). For example, <u>alat</u> in Tagalog means 'saltiness' and, curiously enough, an identical form means 'bad luck'. From the latter, the same form <u>alat</u> is derived to mean in colloquial speech 'policeman', and this form because of the unpredictability and distinctiveness of its features is lexicalized. It is entered as an independent, underived lexeme. In this study, however, the concern is on verb derivations that are more general and predictable.

The form of a derivation rule may be illustrated as follows:

VDR: Affliction Verbs

$$[+\text{N}] \quad \succ\!\!\!\rightarrow \quad \begin{bmatrix} +\text{V} \\ +\text{Derv} \\ -[+\text{INS}] \\ +[+\text{OBJ}] \\ +\text{affl} \\ +\text{cs} \\ +\text{erg} \end{bmatrix}$$

A fletched arrow, $\succ\!\!\!\rightarrow$, indicates a derivation rule. Any feature specified on the left side of the arrow which does not appear on the right side means that the feature is absent in the new item or it has been changed to a new but comparable one, e.g., [+N] to [+V]. A feature that appears only on the right side of the arrow refers to a new feature created for the item as a result of the derivation, e.g., case frame and syntactic-semantic features. All other features not mentioned by the rule which are carried over to the derived form but which do not have any syntactic consequences may be said to be embodied in the meaning that the new item acquires. The feature [+Derv] signifies that the output or the new item is a derived form and is therefore lexically related to its source form. The above rule, for example, applies to the noun root _lagnat_ 'fever' giving the derived verb stem _lagnat_ 'be afflicted with fever' without any corresponding morphophonemic change. The class of simple intransitive stems marked [+cs] take the objective voice affix -_in_, hence, the form _lagnatin_.

In general, every derivation rule is accompanied by a corresponding morphophonemic rule which identifies the derivational affix attached to the relevant portion of the source stem or the phonological shape which the derived stem assumes. The rule corresponding to a verb derivation rule (VDR) is marked VDMR to mean verb derivation morphophonemic rule.

To illustrate, a PAG-stem derivation rule involving a change to the feature [-pot, +act] has the following form of morphophonemic rule:[3]

$$\text{VDMR:} \quad _V[\quad \longrightarrow \quad _V[pag$$

The rule states that the derived stem created by a particular VDR, which is taken here as the rule that forms [-pot, +act] stems, is prefixed with pag-. Some derivation rules which carry over the exact form of the source item without any morphophonemic modification, as in the sample VDR above, do not require VDMR's.

The pairs of items related by a DR which is not 100% productive are listed in the lexicon of a competence-type grammar. For instance, the example lagnat is entered as a noun with its idiosyncratic syntactic, semantic and phonological features while the derived verb stem is entered with the syntactic feature [+V], denoting that it belongs to the verbal category, and the features [+Derv] and [+affl]. These features suffice to direct one to look for the DR which formally states that the entry is related to an identical or similar form and which provides it with its relevant syntactic, semantic and morphological and consequent phonological features, if any is specified. In effect, productive DR's make the claim that the lexical relations expressed by them form part of the native speaker's knowledge about the words in his language.

4.3 Verb Derivation Rules in Tagalog

Having identified the voice inflectional affixes um- or m-, -in, i-, -an and ∅ and the aspect inflectional affixes -in- for the [+beg] forms of some classes and $(C_1)V_1(C_1)V_1$ of the root or stem for the [-comp] and [-beg] forms, we can strip them off from the verbs and deal with the verb stems. All other affixes occurring in these verb stems are derivational

affixes. Tagalog as a typical agglutinating language makes extensive
use of derivation especially with its verbs. As can be observed in the
examples given under each verbal subcategory, Tagalog verb stems assume
varied morphological forms. There are simple roots manifested by stems
marked with the feature [+erg] or [-erg] and affixed stems marked with
[-pot, +act], [+ins], [-ins], etc. An affixed stem may vary in complexity of structure according to the number and type of derivations it has
undergone. Bloomfield (1933:222) refers to this process as a ranking of
construction. For instance, a complex stem such as pagsipagpabigay which
appears in the form magsipagpabigay when expressing agentive voice and
non-finite aspect meaning 'cause s.o. to give, [-[+AGT,-pl], +loc,
+[+DAT], -pot, +act, +caus]' shows the root bigay 'give' preceded by a
chain of affixes identifiable as pagsi-, pag-, and pa-. This complex
form is analyzed here as a derived stem involving the affixation of
pagsi- to its source stem pagpabigay 'cause to give, [-pot, +act, +caus]'
to create a plural [+pl] agentive form of the causative stem. In turn,
pagpabigay derives from the stem pabigay 'cause to give, [+erg]' to create
an active stem counterpart, which process necessitates the affix pag-
on the derived stem. Lastly, the stem pabigay is also a derived stem
from the simple underived root bigay 'give, [+erg]' to create a causative form which requires the affixation of pa-, with the resulting
derived stem also marked [+erg]. This ranking of morphological constructions may be shown as follows:

Root-stem 1:   bigay 'give, [+erg]'

PA-stem 2:   pa + bigay 'cause to give,[+caus, +erg]'

PAG-stem 3:   pag + pabigay 'cause to give,[+caus,-pot,+act]'

PAGSI-stem 4: pagsi + pagpabigay 'cause to give,[-[+AGT,-pl]]'

From the above illustration, the base of a stem is not necessarily always a root. It may be a root, as in PA-stem 2, or an affixed stem, as in PAG-stem 3 and PAGSI-stem 4.

At this juncture, it is relevant to point out that each of the derived stems, stem 2 to 4 above, is formed by a DR whose input is specified with a particular feature and so is its output. The rules that derive these three stems operate quite generally and below they are shown to apply to either or both underived and derived stems.

(a) bigay   pagbigay   pagsipagbigay
     [+erg]   [-pot,+act]   [-[+AGT,-pl],
                                                  -pot,+act]

        ⋏
     Caus-DR   ⊱[+act]-DR→   ⊱[+pl]-DR→
        ↓
     pabigay   pagpabigay   pagsipagpabigay
     [+caus,   [-pot,+act,   [-[+AGT,-pl],
      +erg]   +caus]   -pot,+act,+caus]

(b) kuha   ∅   pagsikuha
     [-erg]   [-[+AGT,-pl],
        ⋏   -pot,+act]
        |
     Caus-DR   ⊱[+pl]-DR→
        ↓
     pakuha   ⊱[+act]-DR→ pagpakuha   pagsipagpakuha
     [+caus,   [-pot,+act,   [-[+AGT,-pl],
      +erg]   +caus]   -pot,+act,+caus]

The causative derivation rule, Caus DR, applies to both simple roots marked [+erg] in a and [-erg] in b. The active DR, [+act] DR, however, applies only to stems that carry the feature [+erg] regardless of whether the stem is also specified [+caus]. It does not apply to [-erg] stems, hence, *pagkuha as a verb stem is ungrammatical. On the contrary, the plural DR, [+pl] DR, has a wider application. It takes in [-pot, +act], either marked [+caus] or not, and [-erg] stems. What it is restricted from applying to is [+erg] stems, and thus when we hear *magsibigay,

*magsipabigay and *magsipakuha, these are detected as ungrammatical.
The expected correct forms are magsipagbigay, magsipagpabigay and
magsipagpakuha.

The given capacity of DR's to apply to various types of stems, as
specified in their input, results in the formation of distinct classes
of stems. These classes are identified by particular features and,
usually, by given derivational affixes. The members of each of these
classes have stem bases of varying complexities. The following classes
of causative, active, and plural stems show this property of DR's more
vividly:

   (a) PA-stems:

        pa + bili 'cause to buy'

        pa + pag-luto? 'cause to cook'

        pa + pa-kulo? 'cause s.o. to boil s.t.'

   (b) PAG-stems:

        pagbili 'sell'

        pag + pa-bili 'cause s.o. to buy'

        pag + pa-pagbili 'cause s.o. to sell'

        pag + paki-bili 'request s.o. to do the buying of s.t.'

        pag + paki-pa-bili 'request s.o. to cause s.o. else
                            to buy'

        pag + paka-ba?it 'exert effort to be good'

   (c) PAGSI-stems:

        pagsi + bili 'buy, [+pl]'

        pagsi + pag-pa-bili 'ask s.o. to buy, [+pl]'

        pagsi + pag-paki-bili 'request s.o. to do the
                            buying, [+pl]'

Instead of treating a complex affix in a linear fashion such that pagsipagpa- in pagsipagpabili is one affix involving one type of deriva- tion distinct from the affix pagsi as in pagsibili and from pagsipag- as in pagsipagluto? or that pagpa- as in pagpaluto? is distinct from pag- as in pagluto?, the present analysis deviates from this usual approach common in most of the previous studies and considers a kind of hierarchical derivation as a more adequate, accurate and less redundant account of affixed verb stems. By hierarchical derivation, we mean deriving a class of stems, usually identified by its particular affix and a corresponding feature, from a class of stems which may be either roots or affixed stems. If the base is an affixed stem, then it can be traced back to its source, thus, making it possible to determine the stages of derivation of a given base. As each derivation of a class of stems corresponds to a specific relationship existing between the source and the derived form, a hierarchical type of derivation also provides an explanation for the complex of syntactic and/or semantic features of the resulting derived form.

There are two basic types of verb derivation rules based on the resultant changes in features effected by the process on the derived stem, namely, (a) syntactic derivation rules and (b) semantic derivation rules. A syntactic derivation rule changes the lexical categorization or verb subcategorization of a given stem. It provides the case frame, semantic, and morphological-voice-related features and other idiosyn- cratic semantic features of a newly created verb stem from another lexical category. On a stem derived from another verb stem subcategory, it modifies either the case frame or the morphological-voice-related features of the source stem, or both, thus creating a new verbal subcategory or forming a new class of members of an already existing subcategory. Along with these syntactic feature changes, a semantic feature may also be introduced by the rule. In contrast, a semantic derivation does not involve a change in case frame features. Rather, the modification is only in the complex of the idiosyncratic semantic features and in the morphological structure of the stem. The latter type of DR's covers the formation of such semantically derived stem classes identified as plural agentive or objective, multiple or simultaneous plural, intensive, moderative, ability-accidental, insistent, involuntary action, accidental result, distributive/repetitive, recreational, seasonal and requestive.[4] This particular area, however, has not been included in the scope of this investigation. This study focuses only on syntactic derivation of verb stems.

The two types of syntactic derivation rules formulated in this study are distinguished primarily by the change effected on the lexical categorization or the verbal subcategorization of the source stem class. The first type applies to the lexical categories N(oun) and Adj(ective).[5] The second type applies to primary verb stem subcategories.

4.3.1 Syntactic DR's That Change Lexical Categories

The first set of derivation rules involves N's as input and the next set, Adj's.

4.3.1.1 Verb Stems Derived from Nouns

In deriving verbs from N's or Adj's, it is often difficult to determine the precise semantic feature or features that characterize the input. Perhaps, these categories are sometimes best left unmarked, to leave the possibilities of derivation open. It may suffice to say that

certain features F_x of the input are carried over to the derived form.
The features adopted here, which may be considered provisional,
represent, however, the important regularities that are to be captured
about the input and output classes. The semantic feature in the input,
where specified, provides the criterion for determining which N's can
undergo the rule.

VDR-1: Phenomenal Verbs

$$\begin{bmatrix} +N \\ +phen \end{bmatrix} \succ\!\!\longrightarrow \begin{bmatrix} +V \\ +Derv \\ -[+NM] \\ +([+OBJ]) \\ -erg \end{bmatrix}$$

A subclass of verbs derives from nouns marked phenomenal [+phen]
such as <u>ulan</u> 'rain', <u>bagyo</u> 'storm', <u>baha?</u> 'flood', <u>kulog</u> 'thunder',
<u>lindol</u> 'earthquake', <u>kidlat</u> 'lightning' and other natural occurrences.
These verbs mean the occurrence of an event involving the natural
phenomena designated by the N. Unlike other verbs, they are marked for
not cooccurring with a nominative actant. This means that the sentences
in which they occur are subjectless sentences. However, even without
a subject, these verbs have the potential for cooccurring with an
accusative objective actant. The [+OBJ] when it occurs refers to something other than the phenomenal noun itself. It is a kind of 'factive'
OBJ referent that results from the event. The meaning of the derived
stem suggests whether or not an optional OBJ is situationally possible.

This small set of derived verbs is also marked [-erg] to indicate
that it is a root form and that it takes the active voice affix <u>um-</u>
without an associated nominative actant. The class manifests a
syntactic subcategory which contains no underived members. For example:

1. umu?ulan
   rain

   'It is raining.'

2. bumaha? ng dugo? sa digma?an
   flood   blood   war
              $\begin{bmatrix} +AC \\ +OBJ \end{bmatrix}$
   'There was bloodshed in the war.' (Lit.: It flooded blood
      in the war.)

This DR does not involve any morphophonemic change, hence, no VDMR

accompanies it. The derived verb stems remain roots.[6]

VDR-2: Affliction Verbs

$$[+N] \quad \longmapsto \quad \begin{bmatrix} +V \\ +Derv \\ -[+INS] \\ +[+OBJ] \\ +affl \\ +erg \end{bmatrix}$$

Another set of verbs can be derived from nouns that usually refer

to insects or creatures that infest, to any natural phenomena that may

afflict, or to inanimate nouns that leave a harmful effect on certain

objects. In general, the meaning of these verbs is 'to be infested or

afflicted by/with N'. They belong to the case frame subcategory of

simple intransitive verbs. These verbs are further subclassified into

change-of-state [+cs] and non-change-of-state [-cs] verb stems. The

former class regularly takes the affix -in to mark its objective voice

and the latter, the affix -an.

(a) [+affl, +cs]

(a.1) From nouns referring to insects or creatures

    langaw 'fly'   anay 'termite'   ipis 'cockroach'

    bulati 'worm'   surot 'bedbug'   langgam 'ant'

3. lalanggamin diyan ang tinapay
   ant   there   bread
                         $\begin{bmatrix} +NM \\ +OBJ \end{bmatrix}$
'The bread will be ant-infested there.'

(a.2) From phenomenal nouns

     ulan 'rain'   bagyo 'storm'   hangin 'wind'

     baha? 'flood'   alon 'wave'   lindol 'earthquake'

4. inulan ang parada kahapon
   rain on   parade   yesterday
              $\begin{bmatrix} +NM \\ +OBJ \end{bmatrix}$
'The parade was overtaken by rain yesterday.'

(a.3) From inanimate nouns

     sipon 'cold'   amag 'mold'   antok 'drowsiness'

     lagnat 'fever' kalawang 'rust' malat 'hoarseness'

5. sinipon siya at minalat noong isang linggo
   cold   he and hoarse   last one   week
          $\begin{bmatrix} +NM \\ +OBJ \end{bmatrix}$
'He suffered from cold and hoarseness last week.'

(Lit.: He was stricken with cold and hoarseness last week.)

(b) [+affl, -cs]

The limited number of verbs derived in this class has been listed previously (see p. 230, Chapter III). The following may be added:

     kabag 'gas pain'   kaba 'palpitation'

6. kinabagan ang bata? sa ka?iiyak
   gas pain   child   crying
                $\begin{bmatrix} +NM \\ +OBJ \end{bmatrix}$
'The child suffered gas pain from crying too much.'

There is a small set of nouns referring to measurement or measurable qualities which can be verbalized. The derived verbs require the cooccurrence of a nominative objective actant and an appropriate accusative. objective. These two actants are coreferential in the sense that the accusative objective refers to a number or quantity of a unit of measure characterizing or describing the nominative objective referent. Thus,

VDR-3: Verbs of Measure

$$\begin{bmatrix} +N \\ +meas \end{bmatrix} \longrightarrow \begin{bmatrix} +V \\ +Derv \\ -[+INS] \\ -[+NM, -OBJ] \\ -[+AC, +OBJ, -qty] \\ -affl \\ -erg \end{bmatrix}$$

This class may be identified as a subclass of the simple intransitive subcategory. Like the [-affl] class of non-inchoative verb stems, the objective voice form of these verbs of measure is marked by <u>um-</u>. For example:

sukat 'measure'   timbang 'weigh'   ta?as 'grow by'

tagal 'last for'   bigat 'be heavy by'   laki 'be big by'

7. tumagal ang miting namin ng dalawang oras
   last for   meeting our   two   hours
   $$\begin{bmatrix} +NM \\ +OBJ \end{bmatrix}$$ $$\begin{bmatrix} +AC \\ +OBJ \\ +qty \end{bmatrix}$$

   'Our meeting lasted for two hours.'

VDR-4: Active Inchoative Verbs

$$\begin{bmatrix} +N \\ +root \end{bmatrix} \longrightarrow \begin{bmatrix} +V \\ +Derv \\ -[+INS] \\ +[+OBJ] \\ +term \\ -erg \end{bmatrix}$$

Certain abstract noun roots serve as the source of inchoative verbs that express 'grow or develop' in what is designated by the N. It expresses a terminal change in the [+OBJ] rather than a temporary one.

The root derived stems are marked by the active voice affix um-. For example:

> ganda 'grow in beauty; become beautiful'

> dunong 'develop in intelligence; become intelligent'

> laki 'increase in size; become big'

> taba? 'become stout; develop fatness'

> hina? 'become weak; develop weakness'

> ba?it 'become good; develop goodness'

8. lumaki   na   ang halamang ibinigay mo sa akin
   become already   plant   give   you me
    big $\begin{bmatrix} +NM \\ +OBJ \end{bmatrix}$

'The plant you gave me has grown.'

Other classes of primary verbs that derive from certain noun roots, but which largely derive from adjective roots, are accounted for by DR's in the following section. The rules show both Adj's and N's as the sources of the derived verb stems. Thus, VDR-4 is also reflected in VDR-14. (See also VDR-15, 16, 20, 21 and 24 which derive potential terminal inchoative, non-terminal inchoative, provocation, assessment, and exertion verbs, respectively, from both N's and Adj's.)

VDR-5: Verbs of Use

$$[+N] \longrightarrow \begin{bmatrix} +V \\ +Derv \\ +[+AGT] \\ -loc \\ +[+OBJ] \\ -extn \\ +cs \\ +erg \end{bmatrix}$$

This rule creates verb stems that fall under the same class as the [-extn, +cs, +erg] type of simple transitive verbs, hence, they are also marked by the voice affix -in in the objective voice. These verbs denote three general ideas which are situationally determined:

(a) making or turning the OBJ referent into what is designated by the base N; (b) using the OBJ referent for the function designated by the base N; or (c) using the tool N on the OBJ referent. Each meaning depends on the external knowledge about the situational behavior of the referents of the source N's. For example:

(a) Making N

adobo 'braised dish'   matamis 'dessert'

litson 'roast dish'   ensalada 'salad'

saya 'long skirt'   punda 'pillow case'

9. aadobohin ng nanay ang manok
   braised-   mother   chicken
       dish $\begin{bmatrix} +AC \\ +AGT \end{bmatrix}$ $\begin{bmatrix} +NM \\ +OBJ \end{bmatrix}$

   'Mother will cook chicken-adobo.' (Lit.: The chicken will be made into adobo by mother.)

(b) Use as N substitute

kahoy 'firewood'   kumot 'blanket'   balabal 'shawl'

unan 'pillow'   mesa 'table'   meryenda 'snack'

10. uunanin niya ang almohadon
    pillow   he   cushion
          $\begin{bmatrix} +AC \\ +AGT \end{bmatrix}$ $\begin{bmatrix} +NM \\ +OBJ \end{bmatrix}$
    'The cushion will be used by him as pillow.'

(c) Use N on something

araro 'plow'   martilyo 'hammer'

gunting 'scissors'   makina 'sewing machine'

karit 'scythe'   suklay 'comb'

11. aararuhin niya bukas   ang isang bahagi ng bukid
    plow   he   tomorrow   one   part   field
          $\begin{bmatrix} +AC \\ +AGT \end{bmatrix}$ $\begin{bmatrix} +NM \\ +OBJ \end{bmatrix}$

    'A part of the field will be plowed by him tomorrow.'

VDR-6: Verbs of Affect

$$[+N] \longrightarrow \begin{bmatrix} +V \\ +Derv \\ +[+AGT] \\ -loc \\ +[+OBJ] \\ -extn \\ -cs \\ +erg \end{bmatrix}$$

One other subclass of verb stems derived by VDR-6 belongs to the class of [-extn, -cs, +erg] simple transitive verbs. It takes the affix -an to indicate its objective voice. It means the application or extraction of what the N base designates on or from the OBJ referent. For example:

pinta 'paint'	tali? 'tie'	laso 'put a ribbon on'
benda 'bandage'	asin 'put some salt'	bakod 'fence'
ganda 'make pretty'	talbos 'pick young shoots'	balat 'skin'
gatas 'milk'	laki 'enlarge'	tamis 'sweeten'

12. binendahan ng manlalaro? ang kaniyang tuhod
    bandage   player   his   knee
    $\begin{bmatrix} +AC \\ +AGT \end{bmatrix}$ $\begin{bmatrix} +NM \\ +OBJ \end{bmatrix}$

   'The player bandaged his knee.'

13. gagatasan ni Juan ang kanilang kambing
    milk   their   goat
    $\begin{bmatrix} +AC \\ +AGT \end{bmatrix}$ $\begin{bmatrix} +NM \\ +OBJ \end{bmatrix}$

   'Juan will milk their goat.'

While the verb stems derived through the first six DR's are morphologically identical to their source N's, the stems which are created by the succeeding DR's require the presence of certain derivational affixes.

VDR-7: Time Verbs

$$\begin{bmatrix} +N \\ \begin{Bmatrix} +\text{time of day} \\ +\text{season} \\ +\text{occasion} \end{Bmatrix} \end{bmatrix} \longmapsto \begin{bmatrix} +V \\ +\text{Derv} \\ -[+NM] \\ -[+OBJ] \\ -\text{pot} \\ +\text{act} \end{bmatrix}$$

VDMR-7: $_V[\longrightarrow {}_V[\text{pag}$

VDR-7 states that a time verb can be derived from a noun which pertainssto the time of day, season or occasion. Like derived phenom-enal verbs, time verbs are marked for not cooccurring with a nominative actant nor any other obligatory actant. The nouns are usually non-roots, and the derived verb stems are marked [-pot, +act] and they require the prefixing of the affix pag- as indicated by the accompanying VDMR-7. Being a PAG-stem, the time verb stem class is marked by the active affix m-, instead of um-. For example:

pag?umaga 'become morning'   pagtag?ulan 'be rainy season'

pagmadaling-araw 'be dawn'   pagdapit-hapon 'be twilight'

pagbukang-liwayway 'be sun-   pag?ala-una 'be one o'clock'
    rise time'

14. magbubukang-liwayway   na
     sunrise   already

     'It will be sunrise soon.'

VDR-8: Verbs of Occupation or Trade

$$[+N] \longmapsto \begin{bmatrix} +V \\ +\text{Derv} \\ -[+INS] \\ +[+OBJ] \\ -\text{affl} \\ -\text{pot} \\ +\text{act} \end{bmatrix}$$

VDMR-8: $_V[\longrightarrow {}_V[\text{pag}$

One class of simple intransitive verbs derived by VDR-8 denotes doing something to be in a particular profession or occupation, or engaging in a trade expressed by the base N. The stems in this class are prefixed by pag- and marked by the active voice affix m-. For example:

pagdoktor 'to be a doctor'   pagmanok 'be in the chicken business'

pagpulis 'to be a policeman'   pagbigas 'be in the rice trade'

pagpare? 'to be a clergyman'   paghampas-lupa? 'be a vagabond'

15. magmemestra ang anak ni Mang Ado
     be a teacher   child
                   $\begin{bmatrix} +NM \\ +OBJ \end{bmatrix}$

'Mang Ado's child will study to be a teacher.'

Another set of verb stems belonging to a similar subcategory as above derives by the following rule:

VDR-9: Verbs of Growth

$$[+N] \longrightarrow \begin{bmatrix} +V \\ +Derv \\ -[+INS] \\ +[+OBJ] \\ -([-AC, +OBJ])^7 \\ -affl \\ -pot \\ +act \end{bmatrix}$$

VDMR-9: $_V[\longrightarrow {}_V[pag$

This set of verbs derived by VDR-9 denotes growth. It may optionally cooccur with a [+OBJ] which can be expressed only in the accusative case form and some of whose features are shared by the base N. The accusative objective is interpreted as an inalienable part of the nominative objective referent. These two actants are said to be coreferential and, therefore, the cooccurrence of two identical case relations is permitted.

If the item selected for the role of the accusative is identical to the base N, meaning that the verb already expresses it, the sentence is rejected by the speakers not because it is ungrammatical, but rather because it is totally redundant and thus carries no information; it has no use in communicating anything. The verbs of growth are also sub-classified under the [-pot, +act] stems, hence, they exhibit the derivational affix pag- and take the voice affix m-. For example:

pagbunga 'bear fruit'   pagdalantao 'bear a child; be pregnant'

pagbulaklak 'bear flowers; paglaman 'grow tissue'
    blossom'

pag?usbong 'grow shoots'   pag?asin 'develop salt crystals'

16. hindi? magbubunga ng talong ang kamatis
    not   bear fruit   eggplant   tomato (plant)
$$\begin{bmatrix} +AC \\ +OBJ \end{bmatrix} \quad \begin{bmatrix} +NM \\ +OBJ \end{bmatrix}$$

  'The tomato plant will not bear eggplants.'

VDR-10: Verbs of Wearing or Utilizing

$$[+N] \quad \longmapsto \quad \begin{bmatrix} +V \\ +Derv \\ +[+AGT] \\ -loc \\ +[+OBJ] \\ -[+NM, -AGT] \\ -[-AC, +OBJ] \\ -affl \\ -pot \\ +act \end{bmatrix}$$

VDMR-10: $_V[\quad \longrightarrow \quad _V[pag$

Any noun the speaker conceives of as possible to wear or utilize either internally, i.e., consume, or externally may serve as base for VDR-10. The derived verb stems express the wearing or utilizing of what is designated by the base N. These verbs may cooccur with an optional [+OBJ] actant which Jespersen (1924:133) refers to as cognate object.

In general, this actant is unexpressed although implied. When it is
manifested, it refers to a specific subtype or brand of what is designated by the base N. This situation is similar to the preceding verbs
of growth where the OBJ referent is already expressed by the verb base.
This [-pot, +act] class of verbs of wearing can be distinguished from
the [+erg] verbs of using derived by VDR-4 in that the former's over-
riding meaning is that of a continued or repeated activity rather than
a single instance of an action, which is what the latter indicates.
Like other PAG-stems, this derived set of [-pot, +act] verbs takes the
m- marker to indicate its agentive voice. For example:

pagsapatos 'wear shoes'	pagpabango 'wear perfume'
pagbarong-tagalog 'wear barong-Tagalog shirt'	pag-'make-up' 'wear make-up'
pagsaging 'eat a banana'	pagkuwintas 'wear a necklace'
pagpurga 'take laxative'	pag?eroplano 'take an airplane'

17. nagpapabango siya pagkapaligo? (ng 'Worth')
     wear perfume she after-bath
              $\begin{bmatrix} +NM \\ +AGT \end{bmatrix}$ $\begin{bmatrix} +AC \\ +OBJ \end{bmatrix}$

'After bathing, she wears Worth perfume.'

18. mag?eeroplano   siya (ng 'Western') pagpunta niya
     take an airplane she   going-to she
                 $\begin{bmatrix} +NM \\ +AGT \end{bmatrix}$ $\begin{bmatrix} +AC \\ +OBJ \end{bmatrix}$

sa'Morgantown'

'She will take a (Western Airlines) airplane when she
goes to Morgantown.

VDR-11: Verbs of Acquisition

$$[+N] \quad \succ\!\!\longrightarrow \quad \begin{bmatrix} +V \\ +Derv \\ -[+INS] \\ +[+OBJ] \\ -affl \\ -pot \\ +act \end{bmatrix}$$

VDMR-11: $_V[\quad \longrightarrow \quad _V[pagka$

Verb stems can be derived from N's which designate objects that can be acquired by a OBJ referent. They express the meaning 'appearance or development of the N on a OBJ referent' or the unexpected occurrence of 'having N'. The OBJ referent is not cognate with the N in the verb base and the event is beyond the control of the OBJ actant. This class is a member of the subclass of simple intransitive verbs.

The corresponding morphophonemic rule VDMR-11 attaches the derivational affix pagka- to the N base. Rather than treat the affix as a composite of two separate units pag- and -ka- (see Bloomfield, 1917: 268-69 and Llamzon, 1968:178,195) and label -ka- as distinct from other instances of the same affix, the present analysis follows Blake (1925) in part in considering it a single unit which is a member of the [-pot, +act] affixes. It expresses the meaning acquisition. The rationale behind this approach is that the stem forms, in any of its related or inflected variety, never occur with this -ka- without the accompanying pag-. Moreover, this is the preferable analysis since it offers the advantage of a simpler, more direct reference to rule formulation without any loss in generalization. Like PAG-stems, PAGKA-stems are also marked by the voice affix m-. For example:

pagkapera 'acquire money'   pagkasakit 'come to have illness' pagkalamat 'develop a crack'   pagkasugat 'come to have a wound'

pagkasuwerte 'come to be   pagkabukol 'come to have a boil'
  fortunate'

19. nagkalamat   ang baso   nang buhusan ko
    develop a crack   glass   when pour   I
                        $\begin{bmatrix} +NM \\ +OBJ \end{bmatrix}$

    ng ma?init na tubig
       hot   water

'The glass developed a crack when I poured hot water in it.'

Where an unexpected event is not attributed to a OBJ referent, but simply occurs, the derived verb stem is referred to as an 'event' verb. The rule that accounts for this limited class of verbs is as follows:

VDR-12: Event Verbs

$$\begin{bmatrix} +N \\ +event \end{bmatrix} \rightarrowtail \begin{bmatrix} +V \\ +Derv \\ -[+OBJ] \\ -[+NM] \\ -pot \\ +act \end{bmatrix}$$

VDMR-12: $_V[\longrightarrow _V[pagka$

For example:

pagkagera 'have a war'   pagkagulo 'have trouble'

pagkasalot 'have pestilence' pagkasakuna? 'have an accident'

pagkasunog 'have a fire'   pagka?aksidente 'have an accident'

20. nagkagulo   sa plasa   kagabi
    have trouble   town-square   last night

    'There was trouble at the town-square last night.'

Event verbs are similar to phenomenal and time verbs in being subjectless. On the basis of this feature, all three classes may belong together.[8] It is interesting to note that both acquisition and event verbs are related in meaning to one type of special verb, the verb

pagkaro?on 'come to have; come to occur' which is in turn related to
another special verb, the existential verb mayro?on 'have; exist'. The
verb pagkaro?on expresses the meaning acquisition or event as in the
following sentences:

19.a. nagkaro?on   ng lamat   ang baso
      come to have   crack   glass
$$\begin{bmatrix} +AC \\ +OBJ \end{bmatrix} \quad \begin{bmatrix} +NM \\ +OBJ \end{bmatrix}$$

'The glass came to have/developed a crack.'

20.a. nagkaro?on   ng gulo   (sa plasa kagabi)
      there occur   trouble
$$\begin{bmatrix} +AC \\ +OBJ \end{bmatrix}$$

'There was trouble (at the town-square last night).'

Syntactically, the verb pagkaro?on is marked for two coreferential
OBJ's, the accusative one being interpreted as part of or is contained
in the nominative OBJ. In both acquisition and event verbs, this
accusative OBJ referent does not cooccur because the verbs themselves
already express the 'occurrence' of what is indicated by their bases
derived from corresponding N's.

VDR-13: Verbs of Imitation

$$[+N] \quad \rightarrowtail \quad \begin{bmatrix} +V \\ +Derv \\ -[+INS] \\ +[+OBJ] \\ -affl \\ -pot \\ +act \end{bmatrix}$$

VDMR-13: $_V[\quad \rightarrow \quad _V[pagsa$

Nouns that depict a peculiar behavior can be verbalized to mean
'pretend to be or behave like N'. The noun may be a profession or
occupation, a nationality, an animal or creature, a social class, etc.

These verbs are referred to as verbs of imitation acted out by the cooccurring OBJ referent. They belong to the class of simple intransitive verbs and to the morphological type [-pot, +act] marked by the derivational affix pagsa-. Like the other subtypes of [-pot, +act], these verbs of imitation also take the voice affix m-. For example:

pagsapari? 'pretend to be or act like a priest'

pagsakastila? 'act like a Spaniard'

pagsapulubi 'pretend to be a beggar'

pagsatengang-kawali? 'pretend to be deaf' (Lit.: pretend to have ears like a frying pan)

21. nagsamangingisda? pretend to be a fisherman

ang espiya spy
$$\begin{bmatrix} +NM \\ +OBJ \end{bmatrix}$$

'The spy posed as a fisherman.'

The affix pagsa- is treated as a whole unit rather than as consisting of two individual affixes pag- and sa- attached to the stems by two derivational processes because the affix sa- never occurs as a separate verb derivational affix. Similar to ka- in pagka- and si- in pagsi-, discussed previously, sa- is considered an inextricable part of pag-. These three affixes having the distinct initial syllable pag- are related to the active stem marker pag-. They all belong to the morphological class [-pot, +act] and thus all take the active inflectional affix m-.

4.3.1.2 Verb Stems Derived from Adjectives

4.3.1.2.1 Adj Category in Contrast with N and V Categories

To say that a verb stem derives from an adjective instead of from a noun implies a distinction between the lexical categories Adj and N.

Adjectives are usually affixed and they may be derived from noun or verb stems. When they are simple roots, it is sometimes difficult to determine whether they are Adj's or N's since both can occur in certain identical contexts. However, there are other constructions which admit only Adj's and not N's and vice versa. The forms that can serve as test structures for Adj's are as follows:

(a) An adjective can be fully reduplicated with the linker na/-ng between the items to denote an intense degree of the quality expressed by the adjective base. For example:

> payat 'thin'   payat na payat 'very thin'
>
> pihikan 'fastidious'   pihikang-pihikan 'very fastidious'
>
> pangit 'ugly'   pangit na pangit 'very ugly'
>
> dakila? 'great; sublime' dakilang-dakila? 'very great'

(b) An adjective referring to a quality or characteristic takes the prefix pinaka- to indicate a superlative form. For example:

> pinakapayat 'thinnest'   pinakapihikan 'most fastidious'
>
> pinakapangit 'ugliest'   pinakadakila? 'greatest; most
>   sublime'

(c) A degree adjective occurs in the construction with mas/ lalo-ng/ higit na ... sa/kaysa sa to express comparison of quality which is ascribed more to one object than to another. For example:

> mas mahal 'more expensive'   higit na bantog 'more popular'
>
> lalong tamad 'more lazy'   mas bago 'newer'

Neither nouns with objective referents nor abstract nouns can occur in the above constructions. Thus, the following forms are ungrammatical:

> *bahay na bahay (bahay 'house)   *dunong na dunong
>   (dunong 'wisdom')

*pinakabahay (to mean *most   *pinakadunong
  house)

*mas bahay   *mas dunong

In contrast, there is a structure which allows the occurrence of
abstract nouns, roots or derived nouns, but never adjective roots or
stems. Compare the following pairs of sentences:

22.a.   balita?   sa kapayatan   ang batang iyan
          popular   thinness   child   that

     'That child is known for his thinness.'

22.b.   balita?   sa kadunungan   ang batang iyan
                  intelligence

     'That child is known for his intelligence.'

In the nominal position occupied by the abstract nouns kapayatan
'thinness', derived from the adjective payat 'thin', and kadunungan
'intelligence; wisdom', derived from the noun dunong 'intelligence',
only the root dunong can occur unaffixed with the same meaning as the
derived abstract noun.[9] Thus,

23.a.   *balita? sa payat ang batang iyan

23.b.   balita? sa dunong ang batang iyan

If both payat and dunong belong to either Adj or N, then we would
expect them to occur in identical environments. From the illustrations
above, we observe that where payat occurs, as in a, b and c, dunong
does not; and where dunong occurs, as in 23.b, payat does not. These
contextual restrictions are evidences which justify a categorial
distinction between N roots and Adj roots. The identical structure of
the two abstract nouns in 22.a and 22.b is brought about by a derivation rule operating on both N and Adj root inputs to derive abstract
noun forms with the affix ka- -an. These forms now belong to the class

of abstract nouns which already contains the underived member dunong.

The noun root dunong, however, just like other abstract and concrete nouns can be the source of derived adjectives. The most common formation is with the affix ma- which may be historically connected with may 'to have'. Hence, with the adjective form madunong 'intelligent', we can predict the corresponding forms:

    (a)   madunong na madunong 'very intelligent'

    (b)   pinakamadunong 'most intelligent'

    (c)   mas/lalong/ higit na madunong 'more intelligent'

To show that the two categories N and Adj differ from the category V, for verbs, we have to cite instances where verb roots occur but N or Adj roots do not. Generally, verbs must occur with a voice inflectional affix and an aspectual manifestation. On this count, the roots payat and dunong do not qualify as verbs since they can freely occur unaffixed. In addition, in the limited contexts where verb roots can serve as alternant forms of voice and aspect inflected forms, as in the two instances below, the N and Adj roots in question cannot occur. These two instances pertain to imperative [+imp] and repetitive [+rep] forms. For example:

    24.a.   tumayo?   ka
              stand up   you
              [+imp]

              'Stand up.'

    24.b.   tayo?   ka
              [+imp]

              'Stand up.'

25.a. kuma?in kayo ng saging
      eat   you   banana
      [+imp]

'Eat some bananas.'

25.b. ka?in kayo ng saging
      [+imp]

'Eat some bananas.'

The [-comp] aspect form of a verb stem such as <u>iyak</u> 'cry' <u>umi?iyak</u>.
To express a [-comp], [+rep] form, the verb root is fully reduplicated
with the particle <u>nang</u> between them. For example:

26. iyak nang iyak ang bata?
    cry   child
    [+rep]

'The child keeps crying/The child is crying incessantly.'

27. ka?in nang ka?in ang bata? ng saging
    eat   child   banana
    [+rep]

'The child keeps eating bananas.'

Being qualities, it is evident that neither <u>payat</u> nor <u>dunong</u> can
take the imperative form. Under a special situation where a command is
used for some hypnotic stunt, these two roots can occur but only with
an accompanying voice affix <u>um-</u> as in the following:

28. pumayat   ka
    become thin you

'Grow thin.'

29. dumunong   ka
    become wise you

'Grow wise.'

Similarly, the only way to express a [+rep] process of becoming thin
or becoming wise is by using the affixed forms as in:

30. pumayat nang pumayat ang bata?
    become thin   child

'The child grew thin increasingly.'

31. dumunong nang dumunong ang bata?
    become knowledgeable   child

'The child increasingly became knowledgeable.'

The non-occurrence in verbal position of payat and dunong as

independent roots (cf. 24.b, 25.b, 26 and 27 above) indicates that they

are not basically verb roots. However, they can serve as base for

derived verb stems. From the adjective root payat, we can regularly

derive the verb pumayat 'become thin' (see VDR-14). Within the

derived form dumunong 'become wise', it could have come from either the

noun root dunong or from the derived adjective stem madunong. Based on

the semantic feature [+inch], which generally means 'become', shared by

derived verbs pumayat and dumunong, it is reasonable to suppose that

both derive from their adjective counterparts payat and madunong.

Without regard to the difference in morphological structure of their

source stems, such an analysis may look more convincing because of the

fact that a rule deriving [+inch] verbs from either underived or derived

adjectives states a wider generalization rather than if the class comes

from two different lexical categories. However, the morphological

structure of the derived verb stems provides evidence for the more

plausible and tenable analysis of two separate derivations, one from

the Adj root class and another from the N root class. (See pp.226-28,

Chapter III, for reasons for preferring the latter analysis.) This is

to propose that where a ma-Adj can be derived from a N, a [+inch] verb

can be potentially derived from the same N, too. A descriptive Adj in root form also provides a potential source for inchoative verbs. Thus,

(a) [+N] $\rightarrowtail$ [+Adj]

dunong $\rightarrowtail$ madunong
'intelligence'   'intelligent'

(b) [+N] $\rightarrowtail$ [+V]

dunong $\rightarrowtail$ dunong   (dumunong is the voice-
                                    [+inch]   inflected form)
                                    'become intelligent;
                                    develop in intelligence'

(c) [+Adj] $\rightarrowtail$ [+V]

payat $\rightarrowtail$ payat   (pumayat is the voice-
'thin'   [+inch]   inflected form)
                                    'become thin'

The above examples show the existence of three distinct categories
N, Adj and V.

One other piece of evidence to show the difference between verb
roots and noun roots is the presence of two types of derived adjectives
with the affix ma-. McGinn (1970) cites one form mabili 'marketable/
saleable' from the verb bili 'buy' as an instance of an adjective
derived from a verb. To this one, we can add a few other examples such
as magalaw 'easily moved; unsteady' from the verb galaw 'move', mabuwal
'easily toppled; unstable' from the verb buwal 'fall headlong', malikot
'restless' from likot 'meddle with; tamper with'. This class of
adjectives meaning 'be V-ed or able to V' expresses the capacity or
quality of the cooccurring objective referent to undergo a process or
perform an action. It differs from the class which derives from noun
roots, e.g., marunong 'wise' from dunong 'wisdom', malakas 'strong'
from lakas 'strength', matinik 'thorny' from tinik 'thorn', etc. The
latter set denotes adjective stems meaning 'having the quality

designated by N' or 'being abundant in what the N indicates'. The
semantic difference between these two sets of derived adjective stems
supports the hypothesis that their respective sources do not belong to
the same class. Another type of adjectives that derive from verb stems
does not take the affix ma-. Instead, it is marked by an accent shift.
For example: tunaw 'melted; dissolved' from tunaw 'to dissolve', durog
'crushed; pulverized' from durog 'to crush', basag 'broken; cracked'
from basag 'to break', etc.

The preceding discussion has shown in one sense a kind of symbiotic
relationship that exists among the different lexical categories whereby
one category makes itself available as a base to create new items in
another category. This relationship can best be depicted by the
following diagram:

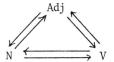

Thus, while N's and Adj's provide bases for derived V's, so do N's and
V's for derived Adj's, and, likewise, Adj's and V's for derived N's.
It is this dynamic process of lexical derivation which all languages
employ to a considerable extent which accounts for the presence of one
identifiable root in various morphological forms which correspond to
certain specifiable functions.

4.3.1.2.2 DR's with Adj Input

Having justified the existence of the category Adj, we can now
proceed with the rules for deriving verb stems from adjectives.

VDR-14: Active Inchoative Verbs

$$\begin{bmatrix} \left\{ \begin{matrix} +Adj \\ +N \end{matrix} \right\} \\ +root \end{bmatrix} \rightarrowtail \begin{bmatrix} +V \\ +Derv \\ -[+INS] \\ +[+OBJ] \\ +term \\ -erg \end{bmatrix}$$

From underived descriptive adjectives or abstract nouns, usually expressing quality or color, verbs of becoming can be derived with the features [+inch, +term] and [-erg]. Similar to the inchoative verbs derived from N's, this set of verbs means that the OBJ referent undergoes the process of becoming what the Adj indicates in a permanent or terminal nature. For example:

pula 'become red'	sariwa? 'become fresh'	dunong 'increase in intelligence'
itim 'turn black'	pangit 'become ugly'	laki 'grow in size'
puti? 'turn white'	bata? 'become young'	bigat 'increase in weight'

32. bumata?   si Pat   nang manggaling sa 'Australia'
     look young   when come-from
                 $\begin{bmatrix} +NM \\ +OBJ \end{bmatrix}$

'Pat looked younger when she arrived from Australia.'

Another class of inchoative verbs derive from unaffixed adjectives or nouns. These adjectives are characteristically accented on the final syllable. The derived verb stems are identified as potential inchoative verbs. Unlike the preceding active inchoative verbs, the potential ones are marked by the derivational prefix ma-, but the same meaning of terminal process of change-of-state is expressed. The process of getting into or being in a changed state may be gradual or cumulative or, on the other hand, it may be instantaneous, a transformation from one state to another occurring in a moment of time.

This set is accounted for by the following rule:

VDR-15: Potential Inchoative Verbs

$$\begin{bmatrix} \begin{Bmatrix} +Adj \\ +N \end{Bmatrix} \\ +root \end{bmatrix} \longmapsto \begin{bmatrix} +V \\ +Derv \\ -[+INS] \\ +[+OBJ] \\ +term \\ +pot \\ -act \end{bmatrix}$$

VDMR-15: $_V[\longrightarrow _V[ma$

The resulting class of [+pot, -act] inchoative stems identified by the affix ma- does not require any affix to indicate its objective voice. For example:

mabuhay 'become alive'   malanta 'become wilted'

magutom 'become hungry'   matuyo? 'become dry'

mapagod 'become tired'   mabulok 'become rotten'

mahibang 'become   mabaliw 'become crazy'
    delirious'

33. nalanta ang mga halaman sa tindi   ng init
     wither   plant   intense   heat
                     [+NM
                      +OBJ]

'The plants withered due to the intense heat.'

Both classes of inchoative verbs may be related semantically to the special intransitive verb paging 'become' whose inflected objective voice form is maging, affixed with m-. It requires a cooccurring adjective or noun complement that expresses the state or form into which the nominative objective actant transforms. For example:

34. naging maliwanag ang paningin niya (cf. lumiwanag 'become
     become clear   vision   his   clear')
        [+Adj]   [+NM
                          +OBJ]

'His vision became clear.'

35. magiging mahal   daw ang kape   (cf. <u>mamahal</u> 'become
    become   expensive   coffee   expensive')
             [+Adj] $\begin{bmatrix} +NM \\ +OBJ \end{bmatrix}$

'It is said that coffee will become expensive.'

36. naging prinsipe ang palaka?
    become prince   frog
           $\begin{bmatrix} +AC \\ +OBJ \end{bmatrix}$ $\begin{bmatrix} +NM \\ +OBJ \end{bmatrix}$

'The frog turned into a prince.'

A third set of inchoative verbs can be derived from some of the
sources of the active inchoative verbs and of the potential inchoative
verbs. In contrast to the two preceding types of inchoative verbs,
this class expresses a non-terminal or temporal change-of-state or
becoming.[10] It belongs to the class of [-pot, +act] form class manifesting the derivational affix <u>pang-</u> and the active voice affix <u>m-</u>.
The examples below show the resulting forms after the nasal assimilation
rule has applied on the final nasal of the affix and the initial sound
of the base.

    pamula 'turn reddish'   panlaki 'turn big'

    pangitim 'turn blackish'   panghina? 'turn weak'

    pamuti? 'turn white'   pangalog 'turn shaky'

37. namula   ang mukha niya nang mapahiya? siya
    turn red   face his   embarrass he
              $\begin{bmatrix} +NM \\ +OBJ \end{bmatrix}$

'He blushed when he got embarrassed.'

The rule that accounts for this class is as follows:

VDR-16: Non-terminal Inchoative Verbs

$$
\begin{bmatrix} \begin{Bmatrix} +Adj \\ +N \end{Bmatrix} \\ +root \end{bmatrix} \longmapsto \begin{bmatrix} +V \\ +Derv \\ -[+INS] \\ +[+OBJ] \\ -term \\ -pot \\ +act \end{bmatrix}
$$

VDMR-16: $_V[\longrightarrow _V[pang$

The classes of perception and emotion verbs are also analyzed as having been derived from adjective and/or noun roots. The following rules account for these verb stems:

VDR-17: Perception Verbs

$$
\begin{bmatrix} +Adj \\ +root \\ \alpha cog \end{bmatrix} \longmapsto \begin{bmatrix} +V \\ +Derv \\ -[+AGT] \\ +[+DAT] \\ +[+OBJ] \\ \alpha cog \\ \begin{Bmatrix} +pot,+act \\ +pot,-act \\ -ins \end{Bmatrix} \end{bmatrix}
$$

VDMR-17: (a) $_V[\longrightarrow _V[maka \; / \; [+act]$

(b) $_V[\longrightarrow _V[ma \quad / \; [-act]$

(c) $_V[\longrightarrow _V[ka \quad / \; [-ins]$

VDR-18: Verbs of Emotion

$$
\begin{bmatrix} \begin{Bmatrix} +Adj \\ +N \end{Bmatrix} \\ +root \\ +emo \end{bmatrix} \longmapsto \begin{bmatrix} +V \\ +Derv \\ -[+AGT] \\ +[+DAT] \\ +[+OBJ] \\ +emo \\ \begin{Bmatrix} +pot,-act \\ -ins \end{Bmatrix} \end{bmatrix}
$$

VDMR-18: (a) $_V[\longmapsto _V[ma \quad / \; [-act]$

(b) $_V[\longmapsto _V[ka \quad / \; [-ins]$

Based on the meaning of the source stems, the derived stems are marked either as [+cog] or [-cog], and, likewise, as [+emo]. The morphological-voice features on the verb trigger the assignment of their corresponding derivational affixes. (For examples, see pp.238-42 , Chapter III.)

Two other classes of verbs can be derived from the same sources of perception and emotion verb classes. They are labelled intentional perception verbs and verbs of provocation.

VDR-19: Intentional Perception Verbs

$$
\begin{bmatrix} +Adj \\ +root \\ \alpha cog \end{bmatrix} \longmapsto \begin{bmatrix} +V \\ +Derv \\ -[+AGT] \\ +[+DAT] \\ +[+OBJ] \\ -[+NM,-OBJ] \\ \alpha cog \\ +ntn \\ +erg \end{bmatrix}
$$

The intentional perception verbs derived through VDR-19 differ from the output of VDR-17 in three ways: (a) they inflect only for the objective voice as restricted by the feature [-[+NM,-OBJ]]; (b) they manifest only one morphological form, the [+erg]; and (c) they denote intention indicated by the feature [+ntn] which accounts for the semantic difference between verbs such as <u>listen</u> versus <u>hear, look</u> versus <u>see,</u> and the like.[11] Below are pairs of perception and intentional perception verbs in their objective voice inflected forms for comparison.

(a) [+cog] Verbs	(a') Intentional [+cog] Verbs
malaman 'know'	alamin 'try to know; find out'
ma?unawa?an 'comprehend'	unawa?in 'try to comprehend'
ma?intindihan 'understand'	intindihin 'try to understand'
malimutan 'forget'	limutin 'try to forget'

(b)   [-cog] Verbs   (b')   Intentional [-cog] Verbs

madinig 'hear'   dinggin 'listen to'

matanaw 'see from a   tanawin 'look at from a
   distance'   distance'

mapuna 'notice'   punahin 'try to notice'

ma?amoy 'smell'   amuyin 'try to smell'

38.a. malalaman mo   rin ang problema niya
       know   you too   problem his
$$\begin{bmatrix} +AC \\ +DAT \end{bmatrix} \qquad \begin{bmatrix} +NM \\ +OBJ \end{bmatrix}$$

'You will know of his problem, too.'

38.b. aalamin mo   ba ang problema niya
      find out you   problem his
$$\begin{bmatrix} +AC \\ +DAT \end{bmatrix} \qquad \begin{bmatrix} +NM \\ +OBJ \end{bmatrix}$$

'Will you find out what his problem is?'

VDR-20: Verbs of Provocation

$$\begin{bmatrix} \begin{Bmatrix} +Adj \\ +N \end{Bmatrix} \\ +root \\ +emo \end{bmatrix} \longrightarrow \begin{bmatrix} +V \\ +Derv \\ +[+AGT] \\ -[+DAT] \\ -[+OBJ,-hum] \\ +cs \\ +erg \end{bmatrix}$$

The class of verbs of provocation derived via VDR-20 differs from the class of emotion verbs derived by VDR-18 in that the former belongs to the case frame subcategory of simple transitive verbs. Although the agentive actant intends to provoke an emotional change-of-state in the objective referent, as designated by the verb base, the [+OBJ] actant, being human, may be indifferent to the action, and, thus, not necessarily experiencing a change in emotional state. Pairs of examples are listed below to show contrast between verbs of emotion and verbs of provocation.

(a) Verbs of Emotion   (a') Verbs of Provocation

matakot 'be afraid of s.t.'   takutin 'scare s.o.'

ma?inis 'be irritated   inisin 'irritate s.o.'
with s.t.'

magalit 'be angry at s.t.   galitin 'make s.o. angry'
or with s.o.'

magulat 'be surprised   gulatin 'surprise s.o.'
with s.t.'

39.a. nagulat si Boombie kay Grace
be surprised

$$\begin{bmatrix} +NM \\ +DAT \end{bmatrix} \qquad \begin{bmatrix} +L \\ +OBJ \end{bmatrix}$$

'Boombie was surprised with Grace.'

39.b. ginulat ni Grace si Boombie
surprise

$$\begin{bmatrix} +AC \\ +AGT \end{bmatrix} \qquad \begin{bmatrix} +NM \\ +OBJ \end{bmatrix}$$

'Grace surprised Boombie.'

Adjective roots and abstract noun roots denoting quality such as appearance, size, color, taste, abstract quality, etc. can also be the source of another class of derived verb stems which may be referred to as verbs of assessment.

VDR-21: Verbs of Assessment

$$\begin{bmatrix} \begin{Bmatrix} +Adj \\ +N \end{Bmatrix} \\ +root \end{bmatrix} \quad \longmapsto \quad \begin{bmatrix} +V \\ +Derv \\ -[+AGT] \\ +[+DAT] \\ +[+OBJ] \\ +assm \\ +pot \\ -act \end{bmatrix}$$

VDMR-21: $_V[\quad \longrightarrow \quad _V[ma$

This class can be distinguished from the active inchoative verbs not only in its syntactic and semantic features but in its morphological

form as well. In comparison with potential inchoatives, whose morphological form is identical to the verbs of assessment, the latter has a
different set of case frame features. By CFRR-13 (see p.194 ,
Chapter III), this class is marked as taking only the [+DAT] as its
subject and manifesting its [+OBJ] only in the locative case form. The
single voice form in its paradigm is marked by -an.

Verbs of assessment, as mentioned before, express the [+DAT]
actant's judgment or assessment of the quality ascribed to a definite
[+OBJ] actant. When the verb refers to natural conditions such as the
weather, the [+OBJ] is usually unexpressed. For example:

    ma?init 'consider hot'   mali?it 'consider small'

    malamig 'consider cold'   mapayat 'consider thin'

    masansang 'consider as   mamahal 'consider expensive'
       strong-scented'

40. nagandahan   kami sa palabas sa TV kagabi
     consider pretty we   show   last night

$$\begin{bmatrix} +NM \\ +DAT \end{bmatrix} \quad \begin{bmatrix} +L \\ +OBJ \end{bmatrix}$$

'We considered the TV show last night good.'

Two other subclasses of psych verbs derived from adjectives, roots
or derived forms, are more limited than those created by the preceding
VDR's. They are labelled verbs of attitude and verbs of enactment.

VDR-22: Verbs of Attitude

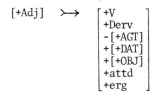

$$[+Adj] \quad \longrightarrow \quad \begin{bmatrix} +V \\ +Derv \\ -[+AGT] \\ +[+DAT] \\ +[+OBJ] \\ +attd \\ +erg \end{bmatrix}$$

Adjectives which may designate an attitude a [+DAT] experiencer may take towards a OBJ referent, be it a person or a state of affairs, may have corresponding derived verbs of attitude. In this class, the full form of the adjective, unaffixed or ma- affixed, is carried over to the derived stem. They belong to the [+erg] morphological class. Its voice paradigm consists of only the objective voice and it is marked by the affix -in. For example:

dakila? 'honor; exalt'   mabuti 'take as good'

masama? 'take as adverse'   mabigat 'take as insurmountable'

mali?it 'take as trivial'   mahal 'take as valuable; love'

malaki 'take as enormous'   mahalaga 'take as precious'

41. dinadakila?   ng mga Pilipino si Rizal
    consider great   Filipino
                           $\begin{bmatrix} +AC \\ +DAT \end{bmatrix}$ $\begin{bmatrix} +NM \\ +OBJ \end{bmatrix}$

    'Rizal is considered great by the Filipinos.'

42. mamatamisin   pa niya ang mamatay kaysa sa pumatay
    take as sweet he   die   kill
                   $\begin{bmatrix} +AC \\ +DAT \end{bmatrix}$ $\begin{bmatrix} +NM \\ +OBJ \end{bmatrix}$

    'For him to die rather than to kill is considered by him
    sweeter.'

This class of verbs, having the feature [+erg] and taking the -in affix, can be easily confused with agentive verbs of the same morphological structure and taking the same voice affix. For instance, compare the following:

43. mamabutihin   niya ang tulong mo
    take as good   he   help   your
                    $\begin{bmatrix} +AC \\ +DAT \end{bmatrix}$ $\begin{bmatrix} +NM \\ +OBJ \end{bmatrix}$
    'Your help will please him..' (Lit.: Your help will be
    taken by him as good.)

44. babasagin niya ang bote
      break   he   bottle

$$\begin{bmatrix} +AC \\ +AGT \end{bmatrix} \quad \begin{bmatrix} +NM \\ +OBJ \end{bmatrix}$$

'The bottle will be broken by him.'

The two constructions are identical in form except for their case relation and semantic features. The features on the former class are accounted for by VDR-22, without which it would have been difficult to distinguish the two classes and relate the [+attd] to other [-emo] verbs.

VDR-23: Verbs of Enactment

$$[+Adj] \quad \rightarrowtail \quad \begin{bmatrix} +V \\ +Derv \\ -[+AGT] \\ +[+DAT] \\ -[+OBJ,-def] \\ -attd \\ -pot \\ +act \end{bmatrix}$$

VDMR-23: $_V[\quad \rightarrow \quad _V[pag$

Verbs marked [-attd] are verbs of enactment. They derive from Adj's that refer to a personal trait or quality. They mean the intentional performance or display of the trait indicated by the Adj base. The behavior exhibited by the [+DAT] actant is always in relation to a definite [+OBJ] actant. This means that in the non-nominative case form, the [+OBJ] is realized in the locative. The stem form of this class is the [-pot, +act] and its paradigm consists of the dative voice marked by m- and the objective voice marked by -an. For example:

pagmata?as 'be snobbish'   pagmabuti 'act kindly'

pagmasama? 'behave badly'   pagmaba?it 'behave well'

pagmarahas 'act aggressively' pagmasungit 'be ill-tempered'

45.a. nagmamaba?it na ang anak ni Rosa sa mga kalaro? niya
     be good   child   playmates his

$$\begin{bmatrix} +NM \\ +DAT \end{bmatrix} \qquad\qquad\qquad \begin{bmatrix} +L \\ +OBJ \end{bmatrix}$$

'Rosa's child is now behaving well towards his playmates.'

45.b. pinagmamaba?itan na ng anak ni Rosa ang mga kalaro? niya

$$\qquad\qquad\qquad \begin{bmatrix} +AC \\ +DAT \end{bmatrix} \qquad\qquad\qquad\qquad \begin{bmatrix} +NM \\ +OBJ \end{bmatrix}$$

Related to the preceding class of verbs of enactment is a similar
set which expresses the exertion of effort to appropriate for one's self
the personal quality or characteristic designated by the source noun or
adjective. These verbs are referred to as verbs of exertion, and they
are derived as follows:

VDR-24: Verbs of Exertion

$$\begin{bmatrix} \begin{Bmatrix} +Adj \\ +N \end{Bmatrix} \\ +root \end{bmatrix} \longmapsto \begin{bmatrix} +V \\ +Derv \\ -[+INS] \\ +[+OBJ] \\ -affl \\ -pot \\ +act \end{bmatrix}$$

VDMR-24: $_V[\longrightarrow {}_V[pagpaka$

VDR-24 shows that only root adjectives and nouns can be the source of
these derived verb stems preceded by the affix <u>pagpaka-</u>. Belonging to
the PAG-stem class, these verbs take the affix <u>m-</u> to mark the objective
voice. Since these verbs express deliberateness, intention or volition
in attaining the quality indicated by the verb base to the utmost, the
OBJ referent can only be a human actant. This class belongs to the
broad class of [-affl, -pot, +act] simple intransitive verbs. For
example:

pagpakabanal 'exert effort
    to be virtuous'

pagpakatino? 'exert effort to be
    righteous'

pagpakababa? 'exert effort
    to be humble'

pagpakatatag 'exert effort to be
    stable'

pagpakasikap 'exert effort   pagpakahinahon 'exert effort to
  to be diligent'   be calm'

46. nagpapakaba?it na kaya? ang bilanggo?
      try to be good   prisoner
$$\begin{bmatrix} +NM \\ +OBJ \end{bmatrix}$$

'Could the prisoner be exerting effort to be good?

Although there is a strong resemblance between verbs of enactment and verbs of exertion in the sense that both involve a deliberate or conscious display of a personal quality, they cannot be equated. The former involves a [+OBJ], grammatically present or not, to whom the quality exhibited is directed. With the latter, there is no such requirement. One may strive to be virtuous for its own sake. Also, we cannot posit that verbs of exertion derive from verbs of enactment, granted that they have identical case features, for two reasons. First, such an account will entail a morphophonemic complexity which is not at all felicitous. It will be necessary for the morphophonemic rule to delete the ma- given in the verbs of enactment and in its place sub-stitute paka- while retaining the prefix pag- to account for the proper form of the verbs of exertion. Second, there are forms resulting from VDR-24 which do not have counterparts in the class derived by VDR-23, e.g., *magbanal, *magmababa? are both non-occurrent but magpakabanal and magpakababa? are. In view of these differences, verbs of exertion are considered as being directly derived from Adj's and N's.

4.3.2 Syntactic DR's That Change Verb Subcategories

The bases for subcategorizing primary verb stems in this study are the characteristic case frame, semantic and morphological-voice feature

specifications on their matrices. It has been observed in the preceding
chapter that some verb stems which differ from other related stems only
in their morphological structure and associated voice inflectional
paradigm can be derived from the more 'basic' verb stem form. The term
'basic' refers to the morphologically simplest stem form as compared
with the same stem plus an affix, e.g. bigay 'give' is basic; the
related affixed stem pagbigay can be derived from the basic form. These
two stem forms may be related by a derivation rule in which the only
difference lies in their morphological-voice features which correspond
to the individual stem's voice inflectional paradigm and voice marking.
This new feature introduced by the DR, then, indicates a new subcategory,
separate from but related to the subcategory of the basic source form.
The DR's that account for this type of lexical relation among verb stems
may be referred to as DR's that do not change the array of case relation
features. What they do is create a new stem class that manifests a
voice paradigm different from its source.

On the other hand, there are verb stems which derive from a primary
verb stem subcategory already established whose case relation features
differ from their source. The difference lies in one of the following
ways:

(a) A case relation feature is deleted without loss of semantic
implication.

(b) A case relation is incorporated in another.

(c) A new case relation feature is introduced without altering
the case features carried over from the source stem.

(d) A new case relation feature is introduced and the original case features carried over are altered.

The DR's that account for this second type of syntactic derivation are referred to as DR's that change case features.

4.3.2.1 DR's That Change Morphological-voice Features

The seven major case frame subcategories set up for primary verb stems are each further specified by semantic and morphological-voice features. The last set of features are identified as [+erg], [-erg], [-pot, +act], [+ins], [-ins], [+pot, +act] and [+pot, -act]. Although each of these classes represents a morphological structure corresponding to its own voice paradigm and voice affixes, some of them are related to a more basic stem class. The bases for determining which of two stem classes is more basic are as follows:

(a) its voice paradigm includes a major case relation, i.e., one which is not predictable from the occurrence of another case relation, e.g., [+OBJ], [+AGT], [+DAT] or [+LOC], and

(b) its morphological structure is the simplest of all stems manifesting a given root.

Of the seven morphological stem classes identified in the various case frame and semantic subcategories, the [+erg] and [-erg] are the basic classes from which some of the other non-root classes derive. From the different subclasses of agentive verbs, it can be observed that the [+erg] form does not allow the [+AGT] to cooccur as its subject. What it allows as subject is either the [+OBJ] or the [+LOC], if the latter is also specified. In comparison to this highly selective property of the [+erg], the [-erg] form is rather permissive and impartial to its cooccurring case relations. Each of its major case relations,

including a minor, one, the [+BEN], can be realized as subject. It is
marked by either the active or the passive affix. The active affix um-
marks the agentive voice while each of the passive affixes -in, -an and
i- marks the objective, locative or dative, and benefactive voice. The
class of [-pot, +act], which is marked by certain derivational affixes
pag- or pang- and other prefixes with initial pag- or pang-, complements
the corresponding [+erg] class in allowing its cooccurring [+AGT] to
become subject. It takes the active affix m- to mark its agentive
voice. In this respect, the [-pot, +act] class is related to the [+erg].
If it is not related to a [+erg], it may be any one of the following
manifesting its own case frame:

(a) analogically formed with an affix and a base which is non-
existent as an independent verb stem, e.g., paghilom 'heal' with the
base *hilom;

(b) lexically derived from another lexical category, e.g.,
pagbunga 'bear fruit', pagsakastila? 'pretend to be a Spaniard',
pagkapera 'acquire money'; and

(c) a form with a petrified affix, whose base does not exist
as an independent form, e.g., pano?od 'watch', pakinig 'listen'.

With the basic stems [+erg] and [-erg], we will show how the other
non-psychological, non-potential verb stem classes marked [-pot, +act],
[+ins] and [-ins] are derived. The derivation rules that account for
these stem classes are identified as primary verb derivation rules
(PVDR's).

4.3.2.1.1   [-pot, +act] Stem Class

The [+erg] class of agentive verbs derive into the class of
[-pot, +act] verbs by the following rule:

PVDR-1:   [-pot, +act] Stem Class

$$
\begin{bmatrix} +[+AGT] \\ +erg \\ \alpha F_i \end{bmatrix} \longmapsto \begin{bmatrix} +V \\ +Derv \\ +[+AGT] \\ -pot \\ +act \\ \alpha F_i \end{bmatrix}
$$

PVDMR-1: $_V[\ \longrightarrow \ _V[pag$

The rule states that an agentive verb marked [+erg] corresponds to
a derived verb whose features are the same as its source except for the
features [-pot, +act] which replace the feature [+erg]. The new features mean that the verb allows its cooccurring [+AGT] to be realized
in the nominative case form marked by the active affix m-. The features
αF_i indicate that all other syntactic and semantic features in the input
are carried over to the output. The accompanying morphophonemic rule
states that the verb stem is prefixed with pag-.

With this rule, all subclasses of agentive verbs marked [+erg] can
predictably have a corresponding [-pot, +act] form. Thus, the classes
of information verbs, of [+goal] and [-dir] subclasses of location verbs,
and of the subclasses of simple transitive verbs, each of which manifests
a [+erg] form, need not list separately their [-pot, +act] forms because
the rule is 100% productive.

4.3.2.1.2   [+ins] Stem Class

The [+ins] stem class manifests only the subclasses under the
location and simple transitive verb subcategories. As has been mentioned

previously, the [+INS] actant as a tool employed by the cooccurring [+AGT] in the performance of an action is a minor case relation. As specified by CFRR-5, its presence is conditioned by the case features [+[+AGT], -[+DAT]]. The [+ins] stem class can be derived from the [+erg] and [-erg] classes of the same case feature specifications.

PVDR-2: [+ins] Stem Class

$$\begin{bmatrix} +[+AGT] \\ -[+DAT] \\ +root \\ \alpha F_i \end{bmatrix} \longmapsto \begin{bmatrix} +V \\ +Derv \\ +[+AGT] \\ -[+DAT] \\ +[+INS] \\ +ins \\ \alpha F_i \end{bmatrix}$$

PVDMR-2: $_V[\longmapsto \ _V[pang$

By PVDR-2, [+ins] stems are created from either the [+erg] or the [-erg] class of location and simple transitive verb subcategories. Other features specified under each source, indicated by αF_i, are carried over to the derived stem. By PVDMR-2, the instrumental stem is prefixed with pang-.

In some instances, the [+ins] form is observed to be used by native speakers without the derivational affix pang-, especially when the objective voice of the source stem is not marked by the affix i-. Thus, one hears the inflected forms itulong 'use for helping', ihiwa? 'use for slicing', ibunot 'use for plucking', ipunas 'use for wiping', ibato 'use for hitting' substituting for the expected forms, based on the given rule above, ipantulong, ipanghiwa?, ipambunot, ipampunas, or ipambato, respectively. Allowing a free alternation between the pang- affixed and the simplified (unaffixed) form of the [+ins] results in the ambiguity of a good number of [+erg] and [-erg] stems. For example:

47. itutulong niya ito sa mga mahihirap
    help   he   this   poor
                  [+NM]

  (a) 'This is what he will help the poor for./
      This is for whom he will help the poor.'
      (With benefactive voice meaning)

  (b) 'This is what he will help the poor with.'
      (With instrumental voice meaning)

48. ibukas mo ito
    open   you this
              [+NM]

  (a) 'Open this.' (With objective voice meaning)

  (b) 'Open with this.' (With instrumental voice meaning)

While it is true that there are stems which may permit the absence of
the affix pang- and still express the meaning of an instrumental stem
unambiguously, there are many others that cannot be used without pang-
which do not become ambiguous, e.g., tapon 'throw; use for throwing',
?abot 'hand over; use for handing over', etc. It will be observed,
however, that every abbreviated [+ins] stem form has a corresponding
form with the affix pang- which is categorically unambiguous. This
situation shows the development of a competing DR which allows the non-
application of PVDMR-2 creating [+ins] stems without the affix pang-.
This process is an evidence of the tendency for the speakers to use the
simpler stem form to the degree where ambiguity is tolerable.

  Another point that needs clarification in connection with [+ins]
verb stems is the distinction that must be made between two similar
pang- stem forms both of which express the meaning 'use something'.
Compare the following sentences:

49. ipampapano?od niya ng karera ang larga-bistang ito
    watch   he   race   binoculars   this
                $\begin{bmatrix} +AC \\ +AGT \end{bmatrix}$ $\begin{bmatrix} +AC \\ +OBJ \end{bmatrix}$ $\begin{bmatrix} +NM \\ +INS \end{bmatrix}$

'These binoculars will be used by him to watch the race.'

50. ipambabahay niya ang tsinelas na iyan
    house-wear he   slippers   that
                $\begin{bmatrix} +AC \\ +AGT \end{bmatrix}$ $\begin{bmatrix} +NM \\ +OBJ \end{bmatrix}$

'Those slippers will be used by him in the house.'
Lit.:'Those slippers will be house-worn by him.'

The two verbs in the examples above are identical in morphological
structure except that 49 has a verb base pano?od 'watch' and 50 has a
noun base bahay 'house'. The pang-form pampano?od 'use for watching'
is related to the verb stem pano?od but pambahay 'use for housewear'
does not show precisely the same type of relationship with the base
bahay which is the noun 'house'. Their respective case frames are also
different; 49 consists of a cooccurring [+AGT], [+OBJ] and [+INS] which
is shared by it source stem, and 50, by the meaning of the stem itself,
does not permit a cooccurring [+INS]. These stems are marked for not
cooccurring with [+INS]. The latter verb stem cannot express an agentive voice unless it is derived as a [-pot, +act] stem. Thus,

50.a. nagpambahay siya ng tsinelas
      house-wear   he   slippers
                   $\begin{bmatrix} +NM \\ +AGT \end{bmatrix}$ $\begin{bmatrix} +AC \\ +OBJ \end{bmatrix}$

'He used slippers for housewear.' (Lit.: He house-wore
slippers.)

The correspondence indicates that the verb stem pambahay 'use for
housewear' is not an instrumental stem in the same sense that pampano?od
is. It is analyzed as a derived [+erg] stem from the noun bahay and
affixed with pang- which in turn derives into the noun pambahay

'housewear'.[12] This type of verb stem derivation is beyond the scope of the present study, however.

4.3.2.1.3 [-ins] Stem Class

Unless otherwise marked, a verb stem can cooccur with a [+RSN] actant, and as such it can be predicted that there is a form which expresses the reason voice. This stem is marked with the feature [-ins], and it can be derived directly from a basic stem class or from another derived stem class. As has been shown previously, [-ins] verbs of perception and emotion derive from Adj and/or N roots, hence, the following rule applies only to the morphological and semantic verb classes specified as follows:

PVDR-3:   [-ins] Stem Class

$$\begin{bmatrix} \begin{Bmatrix} \text{-erg} \\ \text{-pot, +act} \\ \text{+ins} \end{Bmatrix} \\ \alpha F_i \end{bmatrix} \longmapsto \begin{bmatrix} +V \\ +Derv \\ -ins \\ \alpha F_i \end{bmatrix}$$

PVDMR-3: $_V[\longrightarrow _V[ka$

PVDR-3 means that a derived [-ins] or reason stem can be created from either the basic stem class [-erg] or the derived stem class [-pot, +act] or even a [+ins]. The case frame and semantic features specified in any of these classes, identified by αF_i, are carried over to the derived stem class. PVDMR-3 states that every derived stem form carried over from its source is prefixed with the derivational affix ka-. As has been observed in the preceding chapter, the verb stem classes indicating a cooccurring [+RSN] or the two other minor case relations [+BEN] and [+INS] as subject, are invariably marked by the voice affix i-. By this DR, instances of actually occurring verbs such as <u>ikabigay</u>, <u>ikalaba</u>, supposedly derived directly from the [+erg] stems <u>bigay</u> 'give' and <u>laba</u> 'launder', respectively, are labelled anomalous. Apparently, they are analogical reductions of the grammatical forms derived from the corresponding [-pot, +act] forms <u>ikapagbigay</u> and <u>ikapaglaba</u>. Simplification of these forms must have been motivated by the general resemblance of the [+erg] and the [-erg] morphological structure and by the fact that such a reduction does not result in a form which is homophonous with preexisting forms.

It is interesting to note that through this DR, we can account for the various kinds of bases the derived [-ins] stems acquire from their sources, thereby showing how certain combinations of affixes grow or expand. For example:

    (a) From [-erg] class:

        (1) tawag 'call up for s.t.' ⊶ katawag

        (2) hiram 'borrow' ⊶ kahiram

        (3) punta 'go to' ⊶ kapunta

    (b) From [-pot, +act] class:

        (1) pagsabi 'tell' ⊶ kapagsabi

        (2) pamili 'shopt' ⊶ kapamili

        (3) pano?od 'watch' ⊶ kapano?od

        (4) pagkakotse 'acquire a car' ⊶ kapagkakotse

        (5) pagpakasikap 'work diligently' ⊶ kapagpakasikap

    (c) From [+ins] class:

        (1) panghiram 'use for borrowing' ⊶ kapanghiram

        (2) pangluto? 'use for cooking' ⊶ kapangluto?

        (3) pansibak 'use for chopping' ⊶ kapansibak

4.3.2.2 DR's That Change Case Relation Features

The second type of syntactic DR's affect the case relation features
registered in the source verb in one of four different ways. These
changes are described under the following headings: (a) DR's that
delete DR, (b) DR's that incorporate CR, (c) DR's that add CR without
changing CR of source, and (d) DR's that add CR and change CR of source.
Each of these rules is referred to as a secondary verb derivation rule
(SVDR) because the input or source is a primary verb stem of a given
case frame subcategory and the output or derived stem is of a different
case frame subcategory, which may or may not be a major case frame
subcategory. Its accompanying morphophonemic rule, if any, is identified as a secondary verb derivation morphophonemic rule (SVDMR).

4.3.2.2.1 DR's That Delete CR

SVDR-1: Derived Potential Process Verbs

$$\begin{bmatrix} +V \\ +[+AGT] \\ -[+DAT] \\ +[+OBJ] \\ +cs \\ +root \\ \alpha F_i \end{bmatrix} \rightarrowtail \begin{bmatrix} +V \\ +Derv \\ -[+INS] \\ +[+OBJ] \\ -affl \\ +pot \\ -act \\ \alpha F_i \\ \beta F_x \end{bmatrix}$$

SVDMR-1: $_V[\longrightarrow _V[ma$

The rule states that the class of agentive verbs marked [+cs] in
root form corresponds to a class of derived simple intransitive verbs
marked [-affl] with the morphological features [+pot, -act] and identified by the derivational affix ma-. From the array of case relation
features, only the [+OBJ] actant in the input corresponds to the same

actant in the output. The derived verb no longer expresses an agentive referent responsible for bringing about the changed state of the [+OBJ] referent. The agent is merely implied or presupposed. The features αF_i represent other feature constraints in the source verb which also apply to the derived stem and βF_x in the latter form are certain other features sporadically developed in the derivation. In the other succeeding rules, these last two types of features--αF_i and βF_x--will not be indicated in the feature matrices, but they will be presumed. Some examples of derived potential process verbs are as follows:

masibak 'be chopped'	magawa? 'be made'
masulat 'be written'	masira? 'be torn'
maluto? 'be cooked'	matahi? 'be sewn'

51. magagawa? na ang bahay ni Del
    make   house
                  $\begin{bmatrix} +NM \\ +OBJ \end{bmatrix}$

'Del's house will soon be built/finished.'

Having a morphological form and case frame identical to that of the [+inch, +term, +pot, -act] class, the new set of derived process verbs can be distinguished in terms of its meaning. Whereas the feature [+inch] expresses 'becoming' or developing into another state, the derived [-affl] means 'to be V-ed'. It is semantically similar to the primary class of [-inch, -affl, -erg] in expressing a process or event undergone by the object involved. It may be noted further that the class of [+inch] verbs in contrast to the derived [-affl] verbs do not have a corresponding primary agentive form. Thus, mahinog 'become ripe' does not have an underived agentive counterpart *hinog, which indicates that this verb is not intrinsically an agentive verb. However, an agentive form can be derived from the same source of the verb mahinog, which is the adjective hinog, through a causative derivation resulting in the form pahinog 'allow to ripen'.

The rule above exemplifies the process referred to as intransitivization. Like the agentive verb input, calamity verbs and non-emotion psych verbs may also derive into the same class of potential intransitive verbs.

SVDR-2: Derived Potential Calamity Verbs

$$
\begin{bmatrix} +V \\ -[+AGT] \\ +[+INS] \\ +[+OBJ] \\ +cs \end{bmatrix} \longrightarrow \begin{bmatrix} +V \\ +Derv \\ -[+INS] \\ +[+OBJ] \\ -affl \\ +pot \\ -act \end{bmatrix}
$$

SVDMR-2: $_V[\longrightarrow {}_V[ma$

Similar to the preceding rule, SVDR-2 states that a simple non-inchoative, non-afflicted intransitive verb can be derived from a calamity verb marked [+cs]. By SVDMR-2, the derived stem is prefixed with ma-. For example:

matupok 'be charred'   mawasak 'be destroyed'

mabali? 'be broken'   masunog 'be burned'

matuklap 'be blown off'   malipad 'be blown away'

52. nasunog   ang pabrika
    burn   factory
              $\begin{bmatrix} +NM \\ +OBJ \end{bmatrix}$

'The factory was burned.'

SVDR-3: Derived Intransitive Psych Verbs

$$
\begin{bmatrix}
+V \\
-[+\text{AGT}] \\
+[+\text{DAT}, \ \alpha F_i] \\
+[+\text{OBJ}] \\
\begin{bmatrix} +\text{emo} \\ +\text{pot}, -\text{act} \end{bmatrix} \\
\begin{bmatrix} -\text{attd} \\ -\text{pot}, +\text{act} \end{bmatrix}_1
\end{bmatrix}
\ \longmapsto \
\begin{bmatrix}
+V \\
+\text{Derv} \\
-[+\text{INS}] \\
-[+\text{OBJ}, \ -\alpha F_i] \\
-\text{affl} \\
\begin{bmatrix} [+\text{pot}, -\text{act}] \\ [-\text{pot}, +\text{act}] \end{bmatrix}_1
\end{bmatrix}
$$

SVDR-3 states that either a verb of emotion marked [+pot, -act] or
a verb of non-attitude or enactment marked [-pot, +act] can be the
source of simple intransitive verbs marked [-affl] whose [+OBJ] corresponds to the [+DAT] of the source verb. The [+OBJ] in the source does
not correspond to any actant in the output. The exact morphological
features of the source verb are carried over unchanged to the derived
verb. For example:

(a) [+pot, -act] Verbs   (b) [-pot, +act] Verbs

matakot 'be afraid'   pagmata?as 'be snobbish'

matuwa? 'be joyful'   pagmabuti 'pretend to be good'

magalit 'be angry'   pagmaramot 'be selfish'

53. natatakot ka   pa   ba
     afraid   you   still
            $\begin{bmatrix} +\text{NM} \\ +\text{OBJ} \end{bmatrix}$

'Are you still afraid?'

54. nagmamata?as na siya   ngayon
     be snobbish   he   now
              $\begin{bmatrix} +\text{NM} \\ +\text{OBJ} \end{bmatrix}$

'He is snobbish now.'

In the last rule, there has been not only a deletion of a case
relation but also a change in the marking of an original case relation,

i.e., the original [+DAT] corresponds to the [+OBJ] in the derived form.

4.3.2.2.2 DR's That Incorporate CR

A SVDR may have the effect of eliminating a case frame feature specified in the input on account of its being absorbed by or incorporated with another dominant case relation. In some cases, a CR that has been incorporated has the option of being expressed overtly but in a different role specified as [+COM] functioning as an attributive to the head N marked for the dominant case relation. In this function, however, the [+COM] is not part of the verb's case frame. The incorporation rule applies to verbs whose lexical content denotes an action which can be performed mutually by two agents or a psychological process which can be undergone mutually by two experiencers. The stems derived by this kind of rule are referred to as reciprocal verbs meaning 'to V each other'.

In view of the different case relations incorporated in each of the classes of agentive verbs, two separate DR's account for reciprocal agentive verbs. Another rule accounts for reciprocal psych verbs because they cooccur with a different dominant case relation which incorporates the meaning of the [+OBJ] referent and they manifest a different derivational affix.

SVDR-4: Reciprocal Transitive Verbs

$$
\begin{bmatrix}
+V \\
+[+AGT,\ \alpha F_i] \\
\begin{Bmatrix} +[+DAT,\ \alpha F_i] \\ +[+LOC,\ \alpha F_i] \end{Bmatrix} \\
+[+OBJ] \\
+root
\end{bmatrix}
\longmapsto
\begin{bmatrix}
+V \\
+Derv \\
-[+AGT,\ -pl] \\
-[+AGT,\ -\alpha F_i] \\
-[+DAT] \\
-[+LOC] \\
+[+OBJ] \\
+recip \\
-pot \\
+act
\end{bmatrix}
$$

SVDMR-4: (a) $]_V \longrightarrow an]_V$

(b) $_V[\longrightarrow _V[pag$

The rule states that a verb exemplifying an information or a location subcategory can have a corresponding derived reciprocal verb whose [+AGT] must always be plural and must have the same selectional features as the actants identified in the source verb to indicate the combined meanings of the [+AGT] and the [+DAT] or [+LOC] in the original verb. Since the original DAT or LOC has been transformed, a new [+DAT] or [+LOC] is now prohibited from cooccurring with the derived verb. The derived verb is further specified with the semantic feature reciprocal [+recip] and the morphological features [-pot, +act].

SVDMR-4 comes in two parts. The first rule attaches to the root the affix -an, which signifies reciprocation, and the second attaches the regular active derivational affix pag-.[13]

The derived reciprocal verbs exhibit only the agentive voice marked by the affix m-.[14] The examples below show the sources and their corresponding derived forms.

(a) Information Verbs	(a') Reciprocal Transitive Verbs
balita? 'give news report'	pagbalita?an 'exchange news'
kuwento 'narrate stories'	pagkuwentuhan 'exchange stories'
tanong 'ask'	pagtanungan 'ask each other'
sulat 'inform by writing'	pagsulatan 'write letters to each other'

55.a. ikinuwento niya kay Maria ang nangyari
      narrate   she   happening
      $\begin{bmatrix} +AC \\ +AGT \end{bmatrix}$ $\begin{bmatrix} +L \\ +DAT \end{bmatrix}$ $\begin{bmatrix} +NM \\ +OBJ \end{bmatrix}$

'The happening was narrated by her to Maria.'

55.b. nagkuwentuhan   sila (ni Maria) ng nangyari
  tell each other they   happening
        $\begin{bmatrix} +NM \\ +AGT \end{bmatrix}$ $\begin{bmatrix} +AC \\ +OBJ \end{bmatrix}$

  'They (with Maria) told each other what had happened.'

(b) Location Verbs   (b') Reciprocal Transitive Verbs

  hiram 'borrow'   paghiraman 'borrow from
                each other'

  utang 'take a loan'   pag?utangan 'take a loan
                from each other'

  bigay 'give'   pagbigayan 'give each
                other s.t.'

  palit 'exchange; trade'   pagpalitan 'trade s.t.
                with each other'

  wisik 'spray s.t. on s.o.' pagwisikan 'spray s.t. on
                each other'

56.a. ipapalit ko ang selyo ko kay Mel
  exchange I stamp my
     $\begin{bmatrix} +AC \\ +AGT \end{bmatrix}$ $\begin{bmatrix} +NM \\ +OBJ \end{bmatrix}$ $\begin{bmatrix} +L \\ +LOC \end{bmatrix}$

  'I will trade my stamp with Mel.' (Lit.: I will exchange
  my stamp with Mel's.)

56.b. magpapalitan kami (ni Mel) ng selyo
  exchange we   stamp
  with each $\begin{bmatrix} +NM \\ +AGT \end{bmatrix}$ $\begin{bmatrix} +AC \\ +OBJ \end{bmatrix}$
  other

  'Mel and I will exchange stamps.'

SVDR-5: Reciprocal Intransitive Verbs

$$\begin{bmatrix} +V \\ +[+AGT, \ \alpha F_i] \\ -[+DAT] \\ -loc \\ +[+OBJ, \ \alpha F_i] \\ +root \end{bmatrix} \longrightarrow \begin{bmatrix} +V \\ +Derv \\ -[+INS] \\ -[+OBJ, -pl] \\ -[+OBJ, -\alpha F_i] \\ +recip \\ -pot \\ +act \end{bmatrix}$$

SVDMR-5: (a) $]_V \longleftrightarrow$ an$]_V$

(b) $_V[\longleftrightarrow _V[\text{pag}$

With a simple transitive verb stem as input, the derived reciprocal stem becomes an intransitive verb. The original [+AGT] and [+OBJ] together correspond to the [+OBJ] of the derived verb which is thus required to occur only in the plural form. This OBJ incorporates the selectional features of the original AGT and OBJ identified by αF_i. The semantic and morphological features that specify the derived verb further are identical with those in the preceding rule. Likewise, SVDMR-5 is identical to SVDMR-4. The only member of the voice paradigm of the derived reciprocal intransitive, which is the objective voice, is marked also by the active affix m-. For example:

(a) Simple Transitive Verbs

hampas 'hit s.o.'

suntok 'give s.o. a fist blow'

hintay 'wait for s.o.'

tulong 'help s.o.'

halik 'kiss s.o.'

takot 'scare s.o.'

(a') Reciprocal Intransitive Verbs

paghampasan 'hit each other'

pagsuntukan 'exchange fist blows'

paghintayan 'wait for each other'

pagtulungan 'help each other'

paghalikan 'kiss each other'

pagtakutan 'scare each other'

57.a. kinamayan niya ang ka?ibigan niya
shake hands he   friend   his
$\begin{bmatrix} +AC \\ +AGT \end{bmatrix}$ $\begin{bmatrix} +NM \\ +OBJ \end{bmatrix}$

'He shook his friend's hand.'

57.b. nagkamayan sila (ng ka?ibigan niya)
shake hands they
with each $\begin{bmatrix} +NM \\ +OBJ \end{bmatrix}$
other

'They (with his friend) shook hands with each other.'

SVDR-6: Reciprocal Psych Verbs

$$
\begin{bmatrix}
+V \\
-[+AGT] \\
+[+DAT,\ \alpha F_i] \\
+[+OBJ,\ \alpha F_i] \\
+per \\
+ntn
\end{bmatrix}
\ \rightarrowtail\
\begin{bmatrix}
+V \\
+Derv \\
-[+INS] \\
-[+OBJ,\ -pl] \\
-[+OBJ,\ -\alpha F_i] \\
+recip \\
+per \\
-pot \\
+act \\
+ntn
\end{bmatrix}
$$

SVDMR-6: (a) $]_V \ \longrightarrow\ an]_V$

(b) $_V[\ \longrightarrow\ _V[pag$

By SVDR-6, intentional perception verbs can derive into intentional reciprocal psych verbs. Based on their case frame, the resulting derived verbs fall under the subcategory of simple intransitive verbs. The constraints on the [+OBJ] in the output are precisely the same as those in SVDR-5. In the above rule, however, the [+OBJ] in the derived verb corresponds to the combined original [+DAT] and [+OBJ]. Furthermore, the derived verb reflects the feature [+ntn] carried over from the source verb. The derived verb means that each pair of members of the [+OBJ] referents tries to do a mutual action which leaves on both members the psychologicàl experience designated by the verb base. By SVDMR-6, the morphological structure of the new stem becomes identical to the preceding derived sets. It is also marked with the active affix m- to indicate its objective voice.

It will be noted that no reciprocal verbs can be derived from psych verbs of assessment nor verbs of attitude. However, there is a separate but similar rule as SVDR-6 which applies to non-attitude verbs (see VDR-23) to derive another set of reciprocal psych verbs. The only difference is that the accompanying morphophonemic rule does not need part b since the input already carries the affix pag-. Because of this similarity, the rule for this particular verb subclass need not be shown. Its application is illustrated in the examples given below under c'.

(a) [+cog, +ntn] Verbs   (a') Reciprocal [+cog] Verbs

intindi 'understand s.t.'   pag?intindihan 'try to
                                       understand each other'

limot 'forget s.t.'   paglimutan 'try to forget
                                       each other'

alala 'remember s.t.'   pag?alalahan/pag?alalahanan
                                       'remember each other'

58.a. uunawa?in   ng nanay   ang tatay
       understand   mother   father
                    [+AC]   [+NM]
                    [+DAT]   [+OBJ]

'Mother will try to understand father.'

58.b. nag?unawa?an ang nanay at tatay
       understand   mother   father
        each other   [+NM]
                      [+OBJ]

'Mother and father tried to understand each other.'

(b) [-cog, +ntn] Verbs   (b') Reciprocal [-cog] Verbs

tanaw 'take a glimpse   pagtanawan 'try to take a
   at s.t.'   glimpse of each other'

aninaw 'try to see s.t.'   pag?aninawan 'try to see
                                       each other'

puna 'notice'   pagpunahan 'take notice of
                                       each other'.

59.a. tinanaw ni Loty si Nene
       look at   [+AC]   [+NM]
                   [+DAT]   [+OBJ]

'Loty looked at Nene.'

59.b. nagtanawan sila (ni Nene)
       look at   they
        each other [+NM]
                    [+OBJ]
       'They looked at each other.'

(c) [-attd] Verbs   (c') Reciprocal [-attd] Verbs

pagmata?as 'be snobbish   pagmata?asan 'snub each other'
  to s.o.'

pagmabuti 'act kindly   pagmabutihan 'show kindness
  towards s.o.'   to each other'

pagmarahas 'act harshly   pagmarahasan 'act harshly to
  toward s.o.'   each other'

60.a. nagmata?as si Rosa sa kamag?aral niya
       snub   classmate her
                  [+NM]   [+L   ]
                  [+DAT]   [+OBJ]

       'Rosa snubbed her classmate.'

60.b. nagmata?asan sila   (ng kamag?aral niya)
       snub each   they
         other   [+NM]
                     [+OBJ]

       'They snubbed each other.'

4.3.2.2.3 DR's That Add a CR Without Changing CR of Source

Two productive rules for deriving secondary verb stems without
causing a change in the case feature specifications on the source stem
may be referred to as 'transitivization'. The term is used to mean
adding either a [+AGT] or a [+DAT] case feature in the case frame where
there used to be none. The verb stem derived with an added [+AGT]
expresses that what is indicated by the verb is now instigated or performed by an agent. The process or action is under the agent's control.
These derived verb stems become new members of the agentive subcategory.
On the other hand, a verb stem derived with an added [+DAT] actant
expresses that the change of state undergone by a [+OBJ] as indicated
by the verb base is suffered by the [+DAT] referent. These new stems
fall under the subcategory of psych verbs.

SVDR-7: Derived Location and Simple Transitive Verbs

$$
\begin{bmatrix} +V \\ -[+AGT] \\ -[+DAT] \\ +[+OBJ] \\ \begin{bmatrix} +loc \\ -affl \end{bmatrix}_1 \\ -erg \end{bmatrix} \longmapsto \begin{bmatrix} +V \\ +Derv \\ +[+AGT] \\ -[+DAT] \\ +[+OBJ] \\ \begin{bmatrix} +loc \\ -af \end{bmatrix}_1 \\ +erg \end{bmatrix}
$$

The rule states two sources of derived agentive verbs. They are the set of locomotion verbs marked [+loc] and the subclass of non-afflicted [-affl] verbs, both further marked [-erg]. With the introduction of a [+AGT], the corresponding derived stems have case relation features identical to those classified under location and simple transitive verbs. The syntactic and semantic features of the locomotion verbs identified as [+loc] are carried over to the derived stem, while the feature [-affl] of the intransitive input is replaced by [-af]. These derived stems, which originally are marked [-erg], are now marked [+erg].

In the following examples, the objective voice inflected forms rather than the stems are given to show readily and more vividly the distinction between the source and the derived forms.

(a) Locomotion Verbs

pumasok 'enter'

bumalik 'return to'

lumayo? 'go away from'

humiwalay 'separate from'

humiga? 'lie down'

sumakay 'ride on'

(a') Derived Location Verbs

ipasok 'take s.t. in'

ibalik 'return s.t. to'

ilayo? 'take s.t. away from'

ihiwalay 'separate s.t. from'

ihiga? 'lay s.t. down'

isakay 'put s.t. on a vehicle; take s.t. for a ride'

61.a. tumakas ang bilanggo sa bilibid
     escape   prisoner   prison
     [-erg] $\begin{bmatrix} +NM \\ +OBJ \end{bmatrix}$ $\begin{bmatrix} +L \\ +LOC \end{bmatrix}$

     'The prisoner escaped from prison.'

61.b. itinakas niya ang bilanggo sa bilibid
     [+erg] $\begin{bmatrix} +AC \\ +AGT \end{bmatrix}$ $\begin{bmatrix} +NM \\ +OBJ \end{bmatrix}$ $\begin{bmatrix} +L \\ +LOC \end{bmatrix}$

     'He took the prisoner away from prison.'

(b) Simple Intransitive   (b') Derived Simple Transitive
    Verbs, [-affl]   Verbs, [-af]

    bumukas 'open'   ibukas 'open s.t.'

    umikot 'rotate; turn'   i?ikot 'turn s.t. around'

    tumungo 'bow; bend'   itungo 'bend s.t.'

    tumakbo 'run'   itakbo 'run s.t. away'

62.a. bumagsak ang mga libro
     fall   book
     [-affl] $\begin{bmatrix} +NM \\ +OBJ \end{bmatrix}$

     'The books fell.'

62.b. ibinagsak niya ang mga libro
     drop   he   book
     [-af] $\begin{bmatrix} +AC \\ +AGT \end{bmatrix}$ $\begin{bmatrix} +NM \\ +OBJ \end{bmatrix}$

     'The books were dropped by him.'

At this point, it may be instructive to call attention to the direction of derivation that has been adopted in this analysis as stated by SVDR-7. While this rule says that location and simple transitive verbs can be derived from locomotion and simple intransitive verbs, respectively, it is also conceivable to have a rule stating a derivation in the reverse direction. Such a rule will entail the deletion of the AGT actant. As two equally plausible possibilities, both directions of

of derivation must be assessed on the basis of their semantic and
syntactic implications as well as their relationship with other DR's.
Semantically speaking, the meaning conveyed by the locomotion and simple
intransitive verbs is that the process or event can occur without the
intervention of an agent, i.e., the OBJ is capable of undergoing the
process by itself, the process being a natural one. It is possible to
conceive of an object falling as in bumagsak without any agent dropping
it or causing it to fall. With an added AGT, the derived verb is saying
that it is now an action performed by someone on an object. Thus, the
derived form ibagsak means to drop something.[15] By following the direction of derivation as given in SVDR-7, it can be expected that some
process verbs will not undergo the DR, since it is not 100% productive,
and these verbs are those without any corresponding derived forms. For
example, pumunta 'go to' has no corresponding *ipunta or lumisan 'depart'
has no *ilisan. These lexical gaps reveal the limitations on the application of the derivation rule. If the direction of derivation were from
the agentive verb to the locomotion or simple intransitive verb with a
concomitant agent deletion, we cannot account for the existence of the
latter forms which do not correspond to any source or agentive forms.

It will be recalled that in DR's where a case relation is deleted
(see SVDR-1 to SVDR-3), the derived stem continues to imply the role of
the actant that has been deleted. If this is true of all types of
deletions, then we would expect the same condition for the proposed
agentive actant deletion. Reviewing the examples given above as input
and considering them as the supposed output of the proposed alternative
rule, we find that they do not convey even the slightest suggestion of

the role of a deleted AGT. For this reason, these verbs are considered inherently intransitive in the sense of being non-agentive. These two counter-arguments to the proposal indicate that the present analysis is much more convincing.

The relation established by SVDR-7 between the locomotion-location and simple intransitive-simple transitive correlates can be shown to differ from the inchoative-simple transitive verbs which may erroneously be identified as resulting from SVDR-7. The inchoative verbs marked [+term, -erg] and those marked [+term, +pot, -act] have been shown through VDR-4, VDR-14 and VDR-15 to derive from N and Adj roots. Similarly, by VDR-6, simple transitive verbs marked [-cs, +erg] are derived from N roots. The few transitive verbs marked [+cs, +erg] that derive from Adj roots have not been accounted for here by a DR. These VDR's show an indirect relationship between the inchoative and simple transitive verbs that have a common base. The direction of derivation may be shown as follows:

(a) N >—→ Intransitive Verb
[+inch, +term, -erg]

laki 'size'   lumaki 'increase in size; become big'

ganda 'beauty'   gumanda 'grow in beauty; become pretty'

Adj >—→ Intransitive Verb
[+inch, +term, -erg]

payat 'thin'   pumayat 'become thin'

$\begin{Bmatrix} N \\ Adj \end{Bmatrix}$ >—→ Transitive Verb

laki   lakihan 'enlarge s.t.'

ganda   gandahan 'make s.t. pretty'

payat   payatan 'make s.t. thin'

N   ⟩⟶   Adj

laki   malaki 'big'

ganda   maganda 'pretty; beautiful'

(b)   Adj   ⟩⟶   Intransitive Verb
                            [+inch, +term, +pot, -act]

hinog 'ripe'   mahinog 'become ripe'

lanta 'wilted'   malanta 'become wilted'

Adj   ⟩⟶   Transitive Verb

hinog   *hinugin (pahinugin 'allow to ripen, [+caus]'

lanta   lantahin 'make s.t. wilted; cause s.t.
                     to wilt'

In a, both intransitive and transitive verbs are shown to derive directly from N or Adj roots and adjectives can derive from N roots as well. In b, they derive directly from Adj roots. By this manner of derivation, we find that each intransitive or transitive form is derived independently of the other. This account looks appealing especially when we consider the morphological structure in b of the three forms lanta, malanta and lantahin. It is more efficient to derive lantahin from the Adj lanta than from the verb malanta [+term] since as we have stated previously the latter derivation will entail the more complex process of subtracting the derivational affix ma- from the source. The former analysis lends support to the system of derivation illustrated in a where both intransitive and transitive verbs appear in the same stem form as their source N or Adj. Thus, these primary verbs can be distinguished from the secondary verbs derived in SVDR-7.

Finally, the account as described above is the only approach that is closely related to the other DR's that similarly introduce a case relation feature. As will be seen more clearly in the derivation of causative and social verbs, the direction from intransitive to transitive agentive can explain more adequately the linear arrangement of derivational affixes.

SVDR-8: Derived Psych Verbs

$$\begin{bmatrix} +V \\ -[+INS] \\ +[+OBJ,\ \alpha F_i] \\ \begin{Bmatrix} +inch \\ -affl \end{Bmatrix} \\ \begin{bmatrix} -erg \\ +pot,\ -act \\ -pot,\ +act \end{bmatrix}_1 \end{bmatrix} \;\succ\!\!\longrightarrow\; \begin{bmatrix} +V \\ +Derv \\ -[+AGT] \\ +[+DAT] \\ -[+OBJ,\ -\alpha F_i] \\ -[-AC,\ +OBJ] \\ +exp \\ \begin{bmatrix} +erg \\ +pot,\ -act \\ -pot,\ +act \end{bmatrix}_1 \end{bmatrix}$$

SVDR-8 states that a simple intransitive verb marked [+inch] or [-affl] and [-erg], [+pot, -act] or [-pot, +act] corresponds to a psych verb marked experience [+exp] showing a [+DAT] which has been added and a [+OBJ] carried over from the source verb. It denotes that the DAT referent suffers from or is affected by what the cooccurring OBJ referent undergoes as indicated by the verb base. The experience is usually adverse in terms of physical, emotional or psychological disposition. This effect arises from the fact that the OBJ is the alienable or inalienable possession of the DAT. This derived class imposes the implication that the DAT suffers from what happens to the OBJ. The [+OBJ] can only be realized in the accusative form which implies that the only voice the stem can inflected in is the dative. Each verb stem form carried over from the source is marked by the voice affix -an to indicate the dative voice. For example:

(a) Simple Intransitive   (a') Derived Psych Verbs, [+exp]
Verbs, [+inch]

    sumakit 'become painful'   sakitan 'pain on'

    lumaki 'increase in size'   lakihan 'become big on'

    mabulok 'become rotten'   mabulukan 'suffer rotting
                                        of s.t.'

    mangatog 'tremble'   pangatugan 'suffer trembling'

    mangitim 'turn black and blue'   pangitiman 'suffer bruising'

63.a. sumakit ang ulo   ni Bobby
      pain   head
                    [+NM]
                    [+OBJ]

     'Bobby's head ached.'

63.b. sinakitan si Bobby ng ulo
      [+exp]   [+NM]   [+AC]
               [+DAT]   [+OBJ]

     'Bobby suffered a headache.'

(b) Simple Intransitive   (b') Derived Psych Verbs, [+exp]
Verbs, [-affl]

    pumutok 'burst'   putukan 'suffer from a
                                    bursting of s.t.'

    tumagas 'leak; spill'   tagasan 'suffer from a leak
                                    of s.t., usually a hemor-
                                    rhage'

    masunog 'be burned'   masunugan 'suffer burning
                                    of s.t.'

    masira? 'be broken'   masira?an 'suffer breaking
                                    of s.t.'

    mabali? 'be broken/fractured'   mabali?an 'suffer a fracture
                                    of s.t.'

64.a. pumutok ang apendisitis niya
      burst   appendix   his
                  [+NM]
                  [+OBJ]

     'His appendix burst.'

64.b.   pinutukan siya   ng apendisitis
       [+exp] $\begin{bmatrix} +NM \\ +DAT \end{bmatrix}$ $\begin{bmatrix} +AC \\ +OBJ \end{bmatrix}$

'His appendix burst on him.'

The derived stems in this class are always passive in meaning. The cooccurring DAT as an affected participant should be distinguished from a OBJ actant that is directly affected by a cooccurring INS in similar derived verbs.[16]

4.3.2.2.4 DR's That Add CR and Change CR of Source

The sets of DR's that involve the addition of a case relation feature and at the same time a change in the case feature specifications of the source stem as they are carried over to the derived stem create three classes of derived verb stems, namely, (a) derived calamity and transitive verbs, (b) derived causative verbs, and (c) derived social verbs.

4.3.2.2.4.1 Derived Calamity Verbs

SVDR-9:   Derived Calamity Verbs

$$
\begin{bmatrix} +V \\ -[+INS] \\ +[+OBJ, \alpha F_i] \\ -affl \\ -erg \end{bmatrix} \longmapsto \begin{bmatrix} +V \\ +Derv \\ -[+INS, -\alpha F_i] \\ +[+OBJ] \\ -cs \\ +erg \end{bmatrix}
$$

The rule states that verb stems specified with case frame features manifesting calamity verbs and further specified with the features [-cs, +erg] can be derived from simple intransitive verbs marked [-affl, -erg]. The derived stem has a new [+OBJ] actant introduced while the original [+OBJ] identified by the features αF_i assumes the role of a INS. Meeting the case feature specifications in the input

of CFRR-9 (see p. 177, Chapter III), the derived verb stem is marked
[-[-AC, +INS]] which implies that the only member of its voice paradigm
is the objective voice. The root stem is carried over to the derived
stem and it takes the voice affix -an. It usually expresses an event
which is adverse, and it is usually rederived and is more commonly
occurring in the semantically derived accidental or unexpected form.
For example:

(a) Simple Intransitive   (a') Derived Calamity Verbs, [-cs]
    Verbs, [-affl]

    kumulo? 'boil'   kulu?an 'be boiled over'

    pumutok 'burst; explode'   putukan 'be hit by an
                                              explosion'

    bumagsak 'fall'   bagsakan 'be fallen over'

    gumulong 'roll over'   gulungan 'be rolled over'

    sumingaw 'steam'   singawan 'be steamed by'

    umiyak 'cry'   iyakan 'be cried on'

65.a. pumutok ang rebentador
       explode   firecracker
                    $\begin{bmatrix} +NM \\ +OBJ \end{bmatrix}$

       'The firecracker exploded.'

65.b. pinutukan ng rebentador ang silya namin
       [-cs] $\begin{bmatrix} +AC \\ +INS \end{bmatrix}$ $\begin{bmatrix} +NM \\ +OBJ \end{bmatrix}$

       'The firecracker blew up our chair.'

Based on the morphological-voice form and case form cooccurrences,
the derived calamity verbs are identical to the derived psych verbs
discussed above. The difference between the two classes becomes more
apparent when the [+DAT] actant of the psych verb is compared with the
[+OBJ] actant of the calamity verb. The former actant is indirectly

affected by what happens to a related [+OBJ] actant, except when the OBJ is its inalienable possession, while the latter is directly affected by the cooccurring external [+INS].

Another type of DR accounts for similar derived calamity verbs when the input is a locomotion verb subcategory. It is stated as follows:

SVDR-10: Derived Calamity Verbs (without a CR added)

$$
\begin{bmatrix}
+V \\
-[+AGT] \\
-[+DAT] \\
+[+LOC,\ \alpha F_i] \\
+[+OBJ,\ \beta F_x] \\
+goal \\
-erg
\end{bmatrix}
\longmapsto
\begin{bmatrix}
+V \\
+Derv \\
-[+INS,\ -\beta F_x] \\
-[+OBJ,\ -\alpha F_i] \\
+cs \\
+erg
\end{bmatrix}
$$

By SVDR-10, a more limited set of calamity verbs can be derived from the [+goal, -erg] locomotion verbs without the necessity of adding a new case relation feature as given in SVDR-9. What happens is that the two original case relations specified in the input assume different roles in the output. The former [+OBJ] actant becomes a [+INS], their correspondence being marked by βF_x, and the former [+LOC] acts as a [+OBJ], both identified by αF_i. The [+OBJ] of the derived stem denotes that which is directly affected by the event designated by the verb base, and, at the same time, it implies that it is the terminal goal or location of the [+INS]. Unlike the output of SVDR-9, the stems derived by SVDR-10 are marked by -in to indicate the objective voice. For example:

	(a) Locomotion Verbs, [+goal]	(a') Derived Calamity Verbs , [+cs]
	pumasok 'go in; enter'	pasukin 'enter in; break in'
	umakyat 'climb'	akyatin 'be climbed on'

tumakbo 'run'   takbuhin 'be run'

lumakad 'walk'   lakarin 'be walked, as of
                                 a distance'

66.a. pumasok ang tubig sa sapatos niya
       go in   water   shoes   his
                 $\begin{bmatrix} +NM \\ +OBJ \end{bmatrix}$ $\begin{bmatrix} +L \\ +LOC \end{bmatrix}$

       'The water went into his shoes.'

66.b. pinasok ng tubig ang sapatos niya
       [+cs] $\begin{bmatrix} +AC \\ +INS \end{bmatrix}$ $\begin{bmatrix} +NM \\ +OBJ \end{bmatrix}$

       'His shoes were drenched with water.' (Lit.: His shoes
       were into by the water.)

4.3.2.2.4.2 Derived Causative Verbs

Most productive of all syntactic derivation rules is the set that
creates verb stems labelled causative, [+caus]. Causative verbs in
Tagalog are morphologically marked. They can be distinguished from
their non-causative counterparts in having the affix pa-. Syntactically,
they differ from their non-causative source forms in having a 'new'
agentive actant in their case frames. While the source verb may or may
not have a cooccurring AGT, the derived causative verb always has one.
The AGT introduced by the rule is referred to as the causer or director
of the action, event or state characterized by the verb base. With
this particular case feature, all causative verbs may be said to be
transitive verbs, and, in fact, based on the case features of their
corresponding source verbs, different types of transitive causative
verbs are created. As has been noted previously, some items that meet
the specifications on the input for the rule that derives transitive
verbs do not undergo the rule. Instead, these elements which may be

either Adj or N roots or primary and simple intransitive verbs undergo
the causativization rule. The causative derived stems denote an 'indirect action' (Schachter and Otanes, 1972:321) with a [+AGT] causing,
directing or allowing the occurrence of what is designated by the verb
base. The reason for setting up a separate rule for deriving the
causative stem is not only for its characteristic form and meaning but
also for the generality of its application. It has been observed that
a derived causative verb from a locomotion or simple intransitive verb
source can also express the idea of 'indirect' or passive control which
is different from the meaning of a non-derived or derived transitive
verb. We can compare a derived transitive verb (by SVDR-7) and a
derived causative verb from the same source as follows:

67.a.　itutumba　niya　ang lata
　　　　upset　　　he　　　tin can
　　　　$\begin{bmatrix} +Derv \\ -af \end{bmatrix}$　$\begin{bmatrix} +AC \\ +AGT \end{bmatrix}$　$\begin{bmatrix} +NM \\ +OBJ \end{bmatrix}$

　　　　'He will upset the tin can.'

67.b.　patutumbahin niya　ang lata
　　　　upset　　　　$\begin{bmatrix} +AC \\ +AGT \end{bmatrix}$　$\begin{bmatrix} +NM \\ +OBJ \end{bmatrix}$
　　　　[+caus]

　　　　'He will $\begin{Bmatrix} \text{cause} \\ \text{let} \end{Bmatrix}$ the tin can $\begin{Bmatrix} \text{to tumble} \\ \text{be upset} \end{Bmatrix}$.'

Both verbs in the examples above are derived from the intransitive verb
tumba 'tumble' as in tumumba ang lata 'The tin can tumbled'. In 67.a,
the meaning implied by the verb is that the agent will handle the tin
can and put it in a lying position. In 67.b where the derived verb is
causative, the agent will do something that will cause the can to
tumble, e.g. jar the table on which the tin can sits, throw something
at the can, or even exercise some magical influence on the tin can.

In a sense, the distinction rests on the agent's direct control of the action in the first sentence in contrast to its indirect control in the second. In the former case, performing the action implies the successful attainment of the changed stated of the object involved, which is not necessarily true of the latter case. If one says that he did what is expressed by 67.a, it cannot be the case that the tin can was not upset. On the contrary, if one says that he did 67.b, it is logically possible to ask whether or not the tin can did in fact get upset. It is emphasized, however, that the two classes of derived stems exemplified above are syntactically identical and both of them belong to the simple transitive case frame subcategory. The first causativization rule, like SVDR-7, introduces a case relation feature but does not change the case frame features carried over from the source.

4.3.2.2.4.2.1 Causative Verbs Derived from Non-agentive, Non-dative Verb Stems

SVDR-11: Causative Transitive Verbs

$$
\begin{bmatrix} +V \\ -[+AGT] \\ -[+DAT] \\ \begin{bmatrix} \langle +loc \rangle \\ -affl \end{bmatrix}_1 \\ +[+OBJ, \ \alpha F_i] \\ \begin{Bmatrix} -erg \\ -pot, \ +act \end{Bmatrix} \end{bmatrix} \ \longmapsto \ \begin{bmatrix} +V \\ +Derv \\ +[+AGT] \\ -[+DAT] \\ \begin{bmatrix} \langle +loc \rangle \\ -af \end{bmatrix}_1 \\ -[+OBJ, \ -\alpha F_i] \\ +caus \\ +erg \end{bmatrix}
$$

SVDMR-11: $_V[\ \longrightarrow \ _V[pa$

The rule states that a locomotion verb, where the feature within angled brackets is included, corresponds to a derived causative verb of location, and a simple intransitive verb marked [-affl] corresponds

to a derived causative [-af] simple transitive verb. The source verbs
are further specified with either [-erg] or [-pot, +act] which features
are replaced by [+erg] in the derived stem. In both instances, a AGT
is introduced in the case frame which is carried over from the source
stem. The derived stem expresses causation, direction or permission
by the AGT as indicated by the feature [+caus]. The feature [+erg]
indicates that its voice paradigm consists of only the objective voice
or the objective and locative, as the case may be. By SVDMR-11, the
derived stem is marked by the derivational affix pa-. The objective
voice marker of the derived stem is -in, and the locative voice marker
is -an. For example:

(a)	Locomotion Verbs	(a')	Derived Causative Location Verbs
	pumunta 'go to'		papuntahin 'cause to go to'
	bumalik 'return to'		pabalikin 'cause to return to'
	lumayo? 'go away from'		palayu?in 'cause to go away from'
	humiga? 'lie down'		pahiga?in 'cause to lie down'

68.a. umalis ang pusa sa sopa
       leave   cat   sofa
              $\begin{bmatrix} +NM \\ +OBJ \end{bmatrix}$ $\begin{bmatrix} +L \\ +LOC \end{bmatrix}$

      'The cat departed from the sofa.'

68.b. pa?alisin mo   ang pusa sa sopa
       leave   you   cat   sofa
       [+caus] $\begin{bmatrix} +AC \\ +AGT \end{bmatrix}$ $\begin{bmatrix} +NM \\ +OBJ \end{bmatrix}$ $\begin{bmatrix} +L \\ +LOC \end{bmatrix}$

      'Drive the cat away from the sofa.' (Lit.: Make the cat
      leave the sofa.)

In most cases, the locative voice requires the cooccurring [+OBJ]
to be realized in the locative form, thus:

69. pinatirahan ni Jay   sa katiwala? ang bahay nila sa bukid
     live in   overseer   house their   farm
     [+caus] $\begin{bmatrix} +AC \\ +AGT \end{bmatrix}$ $\begin{bmatrix} +L \\ +OBJ \end{bmatrix}$ $\begin{bmatrix} +NM \\ +LOC \end{bmatrix}$

'Jay had/let the overseer live in their house on the farm.'

(b) Simple Intransitive   (b') Derived Causative
     Verbs, [-affl]   Transitive Verbs, [-af]

     gumalaw 'move'   pagalawin 'cause to move'

     umiyak 'cry'   pa?iyakin 'cause to cry'

     tumakbo 'run'   patakbuhin 'cause to run'

     pumutok 'explode'   paputukin 'cause to explode'

     pagdoktor 'study to be   papagdoktorin 'cause to/let
       a doctor'   s.o. study to be a doctor'

     pagpakaba?it 'try to be   papagpakaba?itin 'cause to/
       good'   let s.o. try to be good'

     pagkaswerte 'have some   papagkaswertehin 'cause s.o.
       fortune'   to have good fortune'

70.a. naghilom na ang tahi? sa kaniyang kamay
       heal   stitches   her   hand
                          $\begin{bmatrix} +NM \\ +OBJ \end{bmatrix}$

'The stitches on her hand have healed.'

70.b. pinapaghilom ng doktor ang tahi? sa kaniyang kamay
       [+caus] $\begin{bmatrix} +AC \\ +AGT \end{bmatrix}$ $\begin{bmatrix} +NM \\ +OBJ \end{bmatrix}$

'The stitches on her hand were caused/allowed to heal
by the doctor.'

It may be stressed that DR's do not apply automatically to all members of a given class; each derivation of a new stem is a separate historical event that takes place when there is a need for the new item.

Within the class of derived simple intransitive verbs of affliction (see VDR-2), certain verbs which indicate events that can be subjected to an agent's control have entered the lexicon via SVDR-11.

Some of these causative simple transitive verbs can mean either direct or indirect action, e.g., pa?ulanin 'cause to rain' as can be used, say, to denote what a rainmaker can do, and certain others can only mean 'allow/let the event occur', e.g., palamukin 'allow to be swarmed by mosquitoes'.

The observable lexical gaps which the rules cannot account for are by no means an indication of the rule's shortcoming. What they suggest is that the expected derived counterparts have not entered the lexicon, perhaps, due to some extra-linguistic factors, but the possibility of their formation as the need for them arises is guaranteed by the rule. Partly for this reason, Starosta (1974:8) claims that "causatives are not and cannot be derived by a synchronic rule of grammar. Each one enters the lexicon at a different period of time and all must be listed in the lexicon," that is, the lexicon of a competence-grammar.

4.3.2.2.4.2.2 Causative Verbs Derived from Agentive Verb Stems

SVDR-12: Causative Ditransitive Verbs

$$
\begin{bmatrix}
+V \\
+[+AGT, \; \alpha F_i] \\
-[+DAT] \\
+[+OBJ, \; \beta F_x] \\
\begin{bmatrix} +erg \\ \begin{cases} -erg \\ -pot, \; +act \end{cases} \end{bmatrix}_1
\end{bmatrix}
\longmapsto
\begin{bmatrix}
+V \\
+Derv \\
+[+AGT] \\
-[+DAT, \; -\alpha F_i] \\
-[+OBJ, \; -\beta F_x] \\
+caus \\
\begin{bmatrix} +erg \\ +dat \end{bmatrix}_1
\end{bmatrix}
$$

SVDMR-12: $_V[\;\; \rightarrow \;\; _V[pa$

SVDR-12 states that agentive non-dative verbs marked [+erg], [-erg] or [-pot, +act] correspond to derived causative verbs whose case frame features are similar to those of information verbs in having at least

a cooccurring [+AGT], [+DAT] and [+OBJ]. For lack of a better term,
we will refer to this characteristic case frame as the broad class of
ditransitive verbs. As in the preceding causativization rule, the
derived verb stem is marked with the feature [+caus] to denote the
meaning of a causative verb. Likewise, it also adds a new [+AGT], the
actant which directs or orders the performance of the action designated
by the verb base. The directed actant is realized as the [+DAT] which
corresponds to the [+AGT] in the source verb, the correspondence of
these two case relations being marked by αF_i. The shift to this particular role is semantically and syntactically motivated. As the
actant directed or ordered to do something, it is similar to the [+DAT]
of information verbs in receiving what is being communicated. Similar
to the [+DAT] of psych verbs, it experiences being given a direction,
command or permission. When occurring with a causative verb, this
actant in question is marked by the locative case form in its non-
nominative form which is similar to the marking of the non-nominative
[+DAT] of information verbs. Thus, the following redundancy rule applies:

$$\text{CFRR-17:} \quad \begin{bmatrix} +\text{caus} \\ +\text{erg} \\ +[+\text{AGT}] \\ +[+\text{DAT}] \\ -\begin{bmatrix} +\text{NM} \\ +\text{DAT} \end{bmatrix} \end{bmatrix} \quad \rightarrow \quad \begin{bmatrix} -\begin{bmatrix} -\text{L} \\ +\text{DAT} \end{bmatrix} \end{bmatrix}$$

The above rule states that when the causative verb is not inflected
for the dative voice, the [+DAT] can only be realized in the locative
case form.

All other case relation features in the source verb are carried
over to the derived stem, e.g., the [+LOC] where the input is a location
verb and/or the [+OBJ]. The derived form is marked [+erg] when the

source is [+erg], but it is marked [+dat], for dative, when the source is either [-erg] or [-pot, +act]. The derived [+caus, +erg] does not allow a dative voice inflection whereas the derived [+caus, +dat] does, as implied by the following redundancy rule:

MVRRR-9: $\begin{bmatrix} +caus \\ +dat \end{bmatrix} \longrightarrow \begin{bmatrix} - \begin{bmatrix} +NM \\ +AGT \end{bmatrix} \\ - \begin{bmatrix} +NM \\ +INS \end{bmatrix} \\ - \begin{bmatrix} +NM \\ +RSN \end{bmatrix} \end{bmatrix}$

SVDMR-12 marks the derived stem with the causative derivational affix pa-. To indicate the dative voice, the stem takes -in; it takes -an to mark the locative voice. The objective voice form maintains at least two major distinctions, namely, those marked [+extn] and [-cs] in the source continue to take the -an affix and all other subclasses take only the affix i-. In the following examples of causative ditran-sitive verbs, the objective voice inflected forms are cited.

(a) Location Verbs

    ibigay 'give'

    itapon 'throw away'

    kunin 'take'

    bilhin 'buy'

(a') Causative Ditransitive Location Verbs

    ipabigay 'cause s.t. to be given by s.o. to s.o. else'

    ipatapon 'cause s.t. to be thrown away by s.o.'

    ipakuha 'cause s.t. to be taken by s.o. from some place'

    ipabili 'cause s.t. to be bought by s.o.'

71.a. ibibigay ni Ruby ang Bibliya kay Lynn
    give $\qquad\qquad$ Bible
$$\begin{bmatrix} +AC \\ +AGT \end{bmatrix} \quad \begin{bmatrix} +NM \\ +OBJ \end{bmatrix} \quad \begin{bmatrix} +L \\ +LOC \end{bmatrix}$$

    'The Bible will be given to Lynn by Ruby.'

344

71.b. ipapabigay ni Jim   kay Ruby   ang Bibliya kay Lynn
       [+caus] $\begin{bmatrix} +AC \\ +AGT \end{bmatrix}$ $\begin{bmatrix} +L \\ +DAT \end{bmatrix}$ $\begin{bmatrix} +NM \\ +OBJ \end{bmatrix}$ $\begin{bmatrix} +L \\ +LOC \end{bmatrix}$

'Jim will have Ruby give the Bible to Lynn.'

(b) Simple Transitive Verbs, [+extn]	(b') Causative Ditransitive Verbs, [+extn]
tulungan 'help'	patulungan 'cause s.o. to be helped by s.o. else'
daluhan 'attend to; succor'	padaluhan 'cause s.o. to be attended to by s.o. else'
bantayan 'guard; look after'	pabantayan 'cause s.o./s.t. to be looked after by s.o. else'

72.a. binabantayan ni Onya si Melinda
       look after $\begin{bmatrix} +AC \\ +AGT \end{bmatrix}$ $\begin{bmatrix} +NM \\ +OBJ \end{bmatrix}$

'Melinda is being looked after by Onya.'

72.b. pinabantayan ni Clara kay Onya si Melinda
       [+caus] $\begin{bmatrix} +AC \\ +AGT \end{bmatrix}$ $\begin{bmatrix} +L \\ +DAT \end{bmatrix}$ $\begin{bmatrix} +NM \\ +OBJ \end{bmatrix}$

'Clara had Onya look after Melinda.'

72.c. $\begin{Bmatrix} \text{papagbabantayin} \\ \text{papapagbantayin} \end{Bmatrix}$ ni Clara si Onya kay Melinda
                      $\begin{bmatrix} +AC \\ +AGT \end{bmatrix}$ $\begin{bmatrix} +NM \\ +DAT \end{bmatrix}$ $\begin{bmatrix} +L \\ +OBJ \end{bmatrix}$

'Onya will be asked by Clara to look after Melinda.'

(c) Simple Transitive Verbs, [+cs] or [-af]	(c') Causative Ditransitive Verbs
lutu?in 'cook'	ipaluto? 'cause s.t. to be cooked by s.o.'
gawa?in 'make'	ipagawa? 'cause s.t. to be made by s.o.'
hampasin 'strike'	ipahampas 'cause s.t. to be struck by s.o.'
ilatag 'spread out'	ipalatag 'cause s.t. to be spread out by s.o.'

isara 'close'
[-cs]

ipasara 'cause s.t. to be closed by s.o.'

labhan 'launder'

palabhan 'cause s.t. to be laundered by s.o.'

hugasan 'wash'

pahugasan 'cause s.t. to be washed by s.o.'

talupan 'peel'

patalupan 'cause s.t. to be peeled by s.o.'

73.a. kaka?inin ni Melissa ang mansanas
      eat   apple
      $\begin{bmatrix} +AC \\ +AGT \end{bmatrix}$ $\begin{bmatrix} +NM \\ +OBJ \end{bmatrix}$

'The apple will be eaten by Melissa.'

73.b. $\begin{Bmatrix} \text{ipapakain} \\ \text{ipakaka?in} \end{Bmatrix}$ ni Pete   kay Melissa ang mansanas
      [+caus] $\begin{bmatrix} +AC \\ +AGT \end{bmatrix}$ $\begin{bmatrix} +L \\ +DAT \end{bmatrix}$ $\begin{bmatrix} +NM \\ +OBJ \end{bmatrix}$

73.c. $\begin{Bmatrix} \text{papaka?inin} \\ \text{pakaka?inin} \end{Bmatrix}$ ni Pete   si Melissa ng mansanas
      [+caus] $\begin{bmatrix} +AC \\ +AGT \end{bmatrix}$ $\begin{bmatrix} +NM \\ +DAT \end{bmatrix}$ $\begin{bmatrix} +AC \\ +OBJ \end{bmatrix}$

'Pete will have/let Melissa eat an apple.'

From the examples given above to illustrate the application of rules SVDR-11 and SVDR-12, we can observe the changes in the subcategorization of the verb base as a result of the addition of a new [+AGT] actant. Note the shift from a non-causative verb stem subcategory to the causative verb stem subcategory as follows:

(a) a simple intransitive stem becomes a simple transitive stem;

(b) a locomotion stem becomes a location stem;

(c) a simple transitive becomes a ditransitive; and

(d) a location becomes a ditransitive location stem.

These modifications imply two things: 1) there are causative verb stems that belong to already existing case frame subcategories, e.g.,

a and b; c may be identical to the case frame subcategory of information
verbs but they differ in their meanings, hence, they should be distinguished, and 2) a new subcategory manifested by the secondary verb class
d which consists of the case relations [+AGT], [+DAT], [+OBJ] and [+LOC]
must be set up. To this subcategory may be added another class of
secondary verb stems. They are the causative stems that correspond to
the class of information verbs which are accounted for by the following
rule:

SVDR-13: Causative Ditransitive Information Verbs

$$
\begin{bmatrix}
+V \\
+[+AGT,\ \alpha F_i] \\
+[+DAT,\ \beta F_x^i] \\
\begin{bmatrix} +erg \\ \begin{Bmatrix} -erg \\ -pot,\ +act \end{Bmatrix} \end{bmatrix}_1
\end{bmatrix}
\longrightarrow
\begin{bmatrix}
+V \\
+[+AGT] \\
-[+DAT,\ -\alpha F_i] \\
-[+LOC,\ -\beta F_x^i] \\
+\ caus \\
\begin{bmatrix} +erg \\ +dat \end{bmatrix}_1
\end{bmatrix}
$$

SVDMR-13: $_V[\longrightarrow {}_V[pa$

When the input is a verb of information which is identified by a
cooccurring [+AGT] and [+DAT] and further marked by [+erg], [-erg] or
[-pot, +act], the corresponding output in the causative form avoids
duplication of case relations by assigning them to the [+DAT] and [+LOC]
roles, respectively. Both new roles manifest the semantic selectional
features of the original case relations identified by αF_i and βF_x,
respectively. This derived stem denotes causing or letting someone, the
[+DAT] referent, pass on some information to someone else, the [+LOC]
referent. The features [+erg] and [-erg] or [-pot, +act] signifying the
classes of basic forms of the source become [+erg] or [+dat], respectively. The features on the derived causative stem also trigger the appli-

cation of CFRR-17 on the class of causative information verbs. The derived [+erg] class like its [+erg] source has a voice paradigm consisting of the objective and locative voices. If the source is a [-erg], the voice paradigm of the derived [+dat] consists of the objective, locative and dative. With a [-pot, +act] source, the only voice of the derived [+dat] stem is the dative. The objective voice is always marked by i-, the locative by -an, and the dative by -in. For example:

(a) Information Verbs, [+erg]

    i?utos 'order; command'

    i?ulat 'give a report'

    ibalita? 'inform'

    ituro? 'teach'

(a') Causative Ditransitive Information Verbs, [+crg]

    ipa?utos 'cause s.t. to be ordered by s.o.'

    ipa?ulat 'cause s.t. to be reported by s.o.'

    ipabalita? 'cause s.t. to be relayed by s.o.'

    ipaturo? 'cause s.t. to be taught by s.o.'

74.a.
ibinalita	niya	sa nanay	ang nangyari
relate	she	mother	happening
[+erg]	$\begin{bmatrix}+AC\\+AGT\end{bmatrix}$	$\begin{bmatrix}+L\\+DAT\end{bmatrix}$	$\begin{bmatrix}+NM\\+OBJ\end{bmatrix}$

'The happening was related to mother by her.'

74.b.
ipinabalita	ni Pepe	sa kaniya	sa nanay	ang nangyari
$\begin{bmatrix}+caus\\+erg\end{bmatrix}$	$\begin{bmatrix}+AC\\+AGT\end{bmatrix}$	$\begin{bmatrix}+L\\+DAT\end{bmatrix}$	$\begin{bmatrix}+L\\+LOC\end{bmatrix}$	$\begin{bmatrix}+NM\\+OBJ\end{bmatrix}$

'Pepe asked her to relate the happening to mother.'

Since there is no formal difference between the case forms of the [+DAT] and [+LOC] actants when they are non-nominative, only the preferred ordering indicates that the [+DAT] comes right after the [+AGT]. However, if either the [+DAT] or the [+LOC] is not overtly expressed, only the context of situation can provide the proper interpretation for

for the actant marked by the locative case form, for it may very well

be either one of these actants.

(b) Information Verbs,   (b') Causative. Ditransitive
     [-erg]   Information Verbs,
                                       [+dat]

    isulat 'inform s.o. by   ipasulat 'cause s.t. to be
      writing'   related to s.o. by
                                writing'

    itawag 'inform s.o. by   ipatawag 'cause s.t. to be
      calling up'   related to s.o. over
                                the phone'

75.a. isinulat niya sa tatay ang kaniyang problema
      write   she   father   her   problem
      [-erg]   [+AC]   [+L]   [+NM]
             [+AGT] [+DAT]   [+OBJ]

      'She wrote her father about her problem.'

75.b. ipinasulat ko   sa kaniya sa tatay niya
      [+caus]   [+AC]   [+L]   [+L]
      [+dat]   [+AGT] [+DAT] [+LOC]

      ang kaniyang problema
                 [+NM]
                 [+OBJ]

      'I told her to write her father about her problem.'

75.c. pasusulatin ko   siya sa tatay tungkol sa kaniyang
      [+caus]   [+AC] [+NM]   [+L] [+P]
      [+dat]   [+AGT] [+DAT] [+LOC] [+AC]

      problema
      [+L]
      [+OBJ]

      'I will tell her to write father about her problem.'

(c) Information Verbs,   (c') Causative Ditransitive
     [-pot, +act]   Information Verbs, [+dat]

    mag?utos 'order'   papag?utusin 'cause s.o.
                                to order'

    mag?ulat 'give a report'   papag?ulatin 'cause s.o.
                                  to give a report'

magbalita 'inform'   papagbalita?in 'cause s.o.
                                       to inform'

magturo? 'teach'   papagturu?in 'cause s.o.
                                       to teach'

76.a.   magtuturo? si Jimmie ng Bibliya sa kabata?an
        teach   Bible   youth
                          $\begin{bmatrix} +NM \\ +AGT \end{bmatrix}$ $\begin{bmatrix} +AC \\ +OBJ \end{bmatrix}$ $\begin{bmatrix} +L \\ +DAT \end{bmatrix}$

        'Jimmie will teach the Bible to the youth.'

76.b.   papagtuturu?in ng pastor si Jimmie ng Bibliya
                          pastor
        [+caus] $\begin{bmatrix} +AC \\ +AGT \end{bmatrix}$ $\begin{bmatrix} +NM \\ +DAT \end{bmatrix}$ $\begin{bmatrix} +AC \\ +OBJ \end{bmatrix}$

        sa kabata?an
        $\begin{bmatrix} +L \\ +LOC \end{bmatrix}$

        'Jimmie will be asked by the pastor to teach the Bible
        to the youth.'

4.3.2.2.4.2.3. Causative Verbs Derived from Intentional Perception
                Verb Stems

One other source of derived causative verbs is the class of derived
intentional perception verbs. (See VDR-19, pp. 298-99). The following
rule accounts for what may be labelled 'causative perception verbs'
whose case frame features are identical to non-causative psych verbs
except for the additional [+AGT], which feature is characteristic of all
other causative verbs.

SVDR-14:   Causative Perception Verbs

$$
\begin{bmatrix}
+V \\
+Derv \\
-[+AGT] \\
+[+DAT, \alpha F_i] \\
+[+OBJ, \beta F_x] \\
-[+NM, -OBJ] \\
\gamma cog \\
+ntn \\
+erg
\end{bmatrix}
\longmapsto
\begin{bmatrix}
+V \\
+Derv \\
+[+AGT] \\
-[+DAT, -\alpha F_i] \\
-[+OBJ, -\beta F_x] \\
-caus \\
\gamma cog \\
+erg
\end{bmatrix}
$$

SVDMR-14: $_V[\longrightarrow {}_V[pa$

With an intentional perception verb as input to SVDR-14, we can derive a corresponding causative perception verb which denotes 'to have or let someone, the [+DAT] referent, perceive or recognize something, the [+OBJ] referent'. Like the causative ditransitive verbs derived from agentive verbs by SVDR-12, this class of causative perception verbs also undergoes CFRR-17 which realizes its cooccurring [+DAT] in no other case form but the locative when the verb is not in the dative voice.

This class of causative verbs can express the objective and the more rarely used dative voice. Similar to the other causative verbs, the objective voice is marked by i- and the dative by -in, except the subclass of [-cog] verbs and some other irregular forms which are marked by -an. For example:

(a)   Intentional [+cog]
     Verbs

     alamin 'try to know'

     limutin 'try to forget'

     $\begin{cases} alalahin \\ alalahanin \end{cases}$ 'remember'

(a')   Causative [+cog] Verbs

     ipa?alam 'cause s.o. to know'

     ipalimot 'cause s.o. to forget'

     ipa?alala 'cause s.o. to remember or recall'

unawa?in 'try to comprehend'   ipa?unawa? 'cause s.o. to
                                       comprehend'

77.a. aalamin   ko   ang problema niya
       try to know   I   problem   his
       [+Derv]   [+AC]   [+NM]
       [+cog]   [+DAT]   [+OBJ]

       'I will find out what his problem is.'

77.b. ipina?alam ni Lucy sa akin   ang problema niya
       let know   me
       [+caus]   [+AC]   [+L]   [+NM]
       [+cog]   [+AGT]   [+DAT]   [+OBJ]

       'Lucy let me know of her problem.'

From the examples above, we can detect the close similarity between
the subclass of [+cog] causative verbs and the class of non-causative
information verbs in terms of their syntactic features as well as the
meaning of their case relations. Both subclasses belong to the case
frame consisting of cooccurring [+AGT],[+DAT] and [+OBJ].

(b) Intentional [-cog]   (b') Causative [-cog] Verbs
     Verbs

     din(i)gin 'listen to'   ipadinig 'let s.o. hear
                                          s.t.'

     tanawin 'look at from a   ipatanaw 'let s.o. view
        distance'   s.t.'

     halata?in 'take notice'   ipahalata? 'let s.o.
                                          notice s.t.'

     *kita?in   ipakita 'show s.o.s.t.'

78.a. didinggin namin ang awit ni Charito
       listen to we   song
                        [+AC]   [+NM]
                        [+DAT]   [+OBJ]

       'We will listen to Charito's song.'

78.b. ipapadinig niya   sa amin   ang awit : ni Charito
      let hear   he   us
      [+caus]   ⎡+AC ⎤ ⎡+L ⎤   ⎡+NM ⎤
                  ⎣+AGT⎦ ⎣+DAT⎦   ⎣+OBJ⎦

'He will let us hear Charito's song.'

78.c. papadinggan niya   kami   ng awit   ni Charito
      [+caus]   ⎡+AC ⎤ ⎡+NM ⎤   ⎡+AC ⎤
                   ⎣+AGT⎦ ⎣+DAT⎦   ⎣+OBJ⎦

The non-occurrent form *kita?in above is considered a lexical gap.
There is no need for this particular item to be used because of the
presence of an equivalent item tingnan 'look at'. The non-occurrence
of *kita?in, however, did not prevent the formation of its corresponding
causative forms ipakita and pakita?an.

To the four case frame subcategories of derived causative verbs
from primary verb classes, we can add a fifth, the set of causative
perception verbs created from a class of secondary verb stems. This
last set manifests the case frame subcategory identical to what has
been labelled 'causative ditransitive' verbs derived from the simple
transitive subcategory. Altogether, there are now three subtypes of
verbs belonging to the 'ditransitive', i.e. [+[+AGT], +[+DAT], +[+OBJ]],
subcategory. To illustrate this syntactic identity, compare the
following sentences:

79.a. itinanong niya   sa pastor ang kahulugan ng mga
      ask   he   pastor   meaning
      [+erg]   ⎡+AC ⎤ ⎡+L ⎤   ⎡+NM ⎤
                ⎣+AGT⎦ ⎣+DAT⎦   ⎣+OBJ⎦

      karanasan   niya
      experiences his

'He asked the pastor the meaning of his experiences.'

79.b.   ipinaguhit niya   sa pintor ang larawan ng kaniyang
       draw   he   painter   picture   his
       [+caus] $\begin{bmatrix}+AC \\ +AGT\end{bmatrix}$ $\begin{bmatrix}+L \\ +DAT\end{bmatrix}$ $\begin{bmatrix}+NM \\ +OBJ\end{bmatrix}$

       ama
       father

       'He had the artist paint his father's portrait.'

79.c.   ipina?alala ng politiko   sa madla ang katapatan
       remind   politician   public   sincerity
       $\begin{bmatrix}+caus \\ +cog \\ +erg\end{bmatrix}$ $\begin{bmatrix}+AC \\ +AGT\end{bmatrix}$ $\begin{bmatrix}+L \\ +DAT\end{bmatrix}$ $\begin{bmatrix}+NM \\ +OBJ\end{bmatrix}$
       ng kaniyang layon
         his   intention

       'The politician reminded the public of the sincerity
       of his intentions.'

In all three sentences, the [+DAT] actant is directed by the agent to do
or experience what is designated by the verb. It is interesting to note
that through the process of lexical derivation, basic primary verb stems
which are classified under different syntactic subcategories, e.g.,
tanong 'ask' [+[+AGT], +[+DAT], +[+OBJ]], guhit 'draw' [+[+AGT], -[+DAT],
+[+OBJ]], and a verb stem alala 'remember' [-[+AGT], +[+DAT], +[+OBJ]]
derived from another lexical category can all end up in one case frame
subcategory when derived into causative verbs. The same observation
can be noted of verbs derived from N's and Adj's being subcategorized
with underived simple intrasitive verbs and simple transitive or psych
verbs. Thus, in the final accounting of all verb stems, primary and
non-primary, we find various morphological types and differing types
of bases manifesting a single case frame subcategory. It is also because of this powerful derivational capacity of verbs that a subcategorization by verb roots, rather than by verb stems, can obscure rather than

reveal regularities and generalizations.

One other significant characteristic of syntactic derivation rules, besides the possibility of changing the syntactic subcategories of their inputs, is their ability to accommodate more than just basic primary stems. In general, derived verbs which become members of an existing subcategory can be rederived, that is, be able to go through another derivation, by means of a DR other than that which created them. This productive process, or perhaps, more appropriately, reproductive process can be seen actively operating on newly derived basic stem classes. For instance, a simple transitive verb derived from a simple intransitive verb can serve as a new input to other DR's that create a new morphological stem class manifesting a voice paradigm different from its source's, and a new syntactic stem class manifesting a different case frame subcategory. To illustrate:

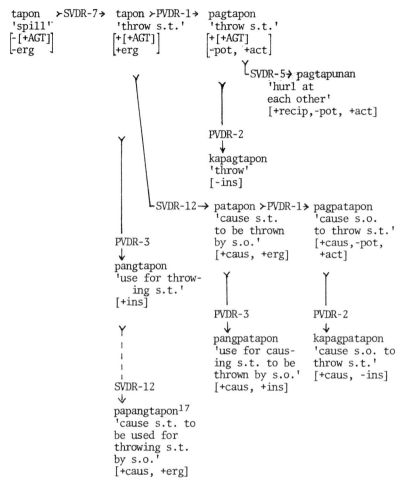

tapon ＞SVDR-7→ tapon ＞PVDR-1→ pagtapon
'spill'   'throw s.t.'   'throw s.t.'
[- [+AGT]]   [+ [+AGT]]   [+ [+AGT]
[-erg   ]   [+erg   ]   [-pot, +act]

        ∟SVDR-5→ pagtapunan
                 'hurl at
                 each other'
                 [+recip,-pot, +act]

        PVDR-2
        ↓
        kapagtapon
        'throw'
        [-ins]

        ∟SVDR-12→ patapon ＞PVDR-1→ pagpatapon
                  'cause s.t.   'cause s.o.
                  to be thrown   to throw s.t.'
        PVDR-3   by s.o.'   [+caus,-pot,
        ↓   [+caus, +erg]   +act]
        pangtapon
        'use for throw-
          ing s.t.'
        [+ins]

                  PVDR-3   PVDR-2
                  ↓   ↓
        SVDR-12   pangpatapon   kapagpatapon
        ↓   'use for caus-   'cause s.o. to
        papangtapon[17]   ing s.t. to be   throw s.t.'
        'cause s.t. to   thrown by s.o.' [+caus, -ins]
        be used for   [+caus, +ins]
        throwing s.t.
        by s.o.'
        [+caus, +erg]

Further accentuating this creative, productive power of DR's in
which the output of one rule feeds another rule is the rederivation of
causative verb stems. When a causativization DR applies to an input
which is already a causative stem, the corresponding output is what is
referred to as a double causative stem. By examining the requirements
of SVDR-11 through SVDR-13, we find the following correspondences as
potential rederivations:

I. Intransitive [-[+INS]] [+[+OBJ]]	II. Transitive [+[+AGT]] [-[+DAT]] [+[+OBJ]]	III. Ditransitive [+[+AGT]] [+[+DAT]] [+[+OBJ]]	IV. Causative Ditransitive [+[+AGT]] [+[+DAT]] [+[+LOC]] [+[+OBJ]]
Intransitive >SVDR 11->	Causative transitive >SVDR 12->	Causative ditransitive >SVDR 13->	Double causative ditransitive
kulo? 'boil'	pakulo? 'cause s.t. to boil'	papakulo? 'cause s.t. to be boiled by s.o.'	papapakulo? 'cause s.o. to have s.t. be boiled by s.o. else'
	Simple transitive >SVDR 12->	Causative ditransitive >SVDR 13->	Double causative ditransitive
	luto? 'cook s.t.'	paluto? 'cause s.t. to be cooked by s.o.'	papaluto? 'cause s.o. to have s.t. be cooked by s.o. else'
		Causative psych	Causative psych ditransitive >SVDR 13->
		pakita 'show s.t. to s.o.'	papakita 'cause s.o. to show s.t. to s.o. else'
		Information >SVDR 13->	Causative information ditransitive
		tanong 'ask s.t. to s.o.'	patanong 'cause s.t. to be asked by s.o.'

Every DR that is boxed shows the correspondence between a causative

source and a double causative output. Some sample sentences with

double causative verbs follow:

80.a.   pinakulo? ni Gloria ang tubig para sa kape
        boil   water for   coffee
        [+caus] $\begin{bmatrix} +AC \\ +AGT \end{bmatrix}$ $\begin{bmatrix} +NM \\ +OBJ \end{bmatrix}$

        'Gloria boiled the water for coffee.'

80.b.   ipinapakulo? niya kay Gloria ang tubig para sa kape
        cause to boil
        [+caus] $\begin{bmatrix} +AC \\ +AGT \end{bmatrix}$ $\begin{bmatrix} +L \\ +DAT \end{bmatrix}$ $\begin{bmatrix} +NM \\ +OBJ \end{bmatrix}$

        'He let Gloria boil the water for coffee.'

81.a.   ipinaluto? ni Del kay Virgie ang manok
        cause to cook   chicken
        [+caus] $\begin{bmatrix} +AC \\ +AGT \end{bmatrix}$ $\begin{bmatrix} +L \\ +DAT \end{bmatrix}$ $\begin{bmatrix} +NM \\ +OBJ \end{bmatrix}$

        'Del had Virgie cook the chicken.'

81.b.   ipinapaluto? niya kay Del   kay Virgie ang manok
        cause s.o. to   he
        have s.o. else $\begin{bmatrix} +AC \\ +AGT \end{bmatrix}$ $\begin{bmatrix} +L \\ +DAT \end{bmatrix}$ $\begin{bmatrix} +L \\ +LOC \end{bmatrix}$ $\begin{bmatrix} +NM \\ +OBJ \end{bmatrix}$
        cook
        [+caus]

        'He had Del ask Virgie to cook the chicken.'

82.a.   ipinakita ng guro? sa mga magulang ang marka
        show   teacher   parents   grades
        [+caus] $\begin{bmatrix} +AC \\ +AGT \end{bmatrix}$ $\begin{bmatrix} +L \\ +DAT/LOC \end{bmatrix}$ $\begin{bmatrix} +NM \\ +OBJ \end{bmatrix}$

        ng anak nila
           child their

        'The teacher showed the parents their child's grades.'

82.b. ipinapakita   ng guro   sa mga magulang ang marka
       cause to show
       [+caus]   ⎡+AC ⎤   ⎡+L   ⎤   ⎡+NM ⎤
                           ⎣+AGT⎦   ⎢+DAT⎟   ⎣+OBJ⎦
                                        ⎣+LOC⎦

       ng anak nila

       (1) 'The teacher had the parents ([+DAT]) show the grades
            of their child to s.o.'

       (2) 'The teacher had s.o. show the parents ([+LOC]) the
            grade of their child.'

SVDR-13 appearing after the boxed SVDR-12 in the first row is a
grammatically possible derivation although it is not acceptable for
performance reasons. Conceptually, it is possible to have someone ask
someone else to boil something. However, if such a situation occurs
and the form above papapakulo? is used, performance is greatly impeded.
Firstly, keeping track of the number of uninterrupted series of the
same syllable can prove rather taxing on one's memory. Secondly, as has
been pointed out in the discussion of SVDR-13, the cooccurrence of
identical case forms representing different case relations, e.g.,
[+DAT] and [+LOC], that do not have any outstanding semantic features
which may contrast them is rather confusing even to the speaker himself.
Thus, when the lexical item or the syntactic structure becomes encumbered so that it impedes the efficient functioning of performance, this
item or structure is imply avoided. To express the same message carried
by the phonologically unappealing lexical item papapakulo?, not to
mention the possible appearance of another pa- to indicate [-comp]
aspect inflection, one uses a simpler form in a more complex sentence.
It may be said that Tagalog has a perceptually motivated 'word structure
constraint' that marks triple causatives, i.e., two causative rederiva-

tions of a single causative stem, as anomalous. To combat the second
difficulty, one of the two actants with identical case forms in
LOC-DAT ditransitives may be suppressed from occurring overtly. For
the resulting sentence structure, only the context of situation provides
the proper interpretation of the remaining locative case form.

4.3.2.2.4.2.4. Double Causative Ditransitive Information Verbs

Similar to SVDR-12 and SVDR-13 which can create single and double
causative stems depending on their inputs, another causativization rule
can account for a set of double causative stems whose input is a
causative stem derived from information verbs. This is stated as
follows:

SVDR-15: Double Causative Ditransitive Information Verbs

$$
\begin{bmatrix}
+V \\
+[+AGT, \alpha F_i] \\
+[+DAT, \beta F_x] \\
+[+LOC] \\
+[+OBJ]
\end{bmatrix}_x
\rightarrowtail
\begin{bmatrix}
+V \\
+Derv \\
+[+AGT] \\
-[+DAT, -\begin{Bmatrix} \alpha F_i \\ \beta F_x \end{Bmatrix}] \\
+[+LOC] \\
+[+OBJ] \\
+caus \\
+erg
\end{bmatrix}
$$

SVDMR-15: $_V I \quad \longrightarrow \quad _V Ipa$

Interestingly, when all four major case relations are participating
as specified in the input, no other case relation is available which can
be assigned to one of the two identical [+DAT] actants resulting from
the process. One principle in case grammar is that no two identical
case relations with different referents in one clause can be allowed
to cooccur. In this case then, the only recourse is to permit only one
of the [+DAT] actants to be overtly expressed.[18] With this obligatory
suppression of one dative actant, the context of situation again has

to provide the means for interpreting the [+DAT] chosen to occur. Even
with this deletion, the meaning of double causativization is kept intact
in the morphological structure of the stem. It carries another pa- as
affixed by SVDMR-15. Going by the demands of performance simplification, one of the remaining locative case forms of this set of double
causative stems may or may not be overtly expressed either. For
example:

83.a.   ipatanong mo   kay Niki   sa Mama   ang kapanganakan
     cause to   you   mother   birthdate
     ask $\begin{bmatrix} +AC \\ +AGT \end{bmatrix}$ $\begin{bmatrix} +L \\ +DAT \end{bmatrix}$ $\begin{bmatrix} +L \\ +LOC \end{bmatrix}$ $\begin{bmatrix} +NM \\ +OBJ \end{bmatrix}$
     [+caus]

     ng Lolo
       grandfather

     'Have Niki ask Mother Grandfather's birthdate.'

83.b.   ipapatanong   mo   (kay Mike/kay Niki)   (sa Mama)
     cause s.o. $\begin{bmatrix} +AC \\ +AGT \end{bmatrix}$ $\begin{bmatrix} +L \\ +DAT \end{bmatrix}$ $\begin{bmatrix} +L \\ +DAT \end{bmatrix}$ $\begin{bmatrix} +L \\ +LOC \end{bmatrix}$
     to have s.o.
     ask s.t.
     [+caus]

     ang kapanganakan ng Lolo
       $\begin{bmatrix} +NM \\ +OBJ \end{bmatrix}$

    (1)   'Have Mike ask s.o. to ask Mama Grandfather's
         birthdate.'

    (2)   'Have s.o. ask Niki to ask Mama Grandfather's
         birthdate.'

    (3)   'Have Mike ask Niki to ask s.o. Grandfather's
         birthdate.'

With SVDR-15 available, it is possible to rederive new classes from
the double causative sets resulting from the application of SVDR-13 as
exemplified above. Nevertheless, for the same reasons that warrant the
non-occurrence of such outputs as *papapakulo? derived by SVDR-13,
SVDR-15 is utilized only with causative stem inputs which originate from

information verbs. This implies that the most a causative verb can be derived into is a double causative. The same constraint seems to apply in Hindi, where morphologically-marked causative verbs do not go beyond expressing a double causative. (See Balachandran, 1971.)

The following summary chart containing an example from each class shows schematically the morphological expansion of the basic primary stem classes and one secondary stem class in terms of acquiring derivational affixes by undergoing causativization. The examples are in their objective voice forms since all basic stems include this voice in their paradigm.

I. Intransitive	II. Transitive	III. Ditransitive	IV. Causative Ditransitive	V. Double Causative Ditransitive

A.
$$\begin{bmatrix} -[+AGT] \\ -[+DAT] \\ -[+INS] \\ +[+OBJ] \end{bmatrix} \text{>SVDR}$$

11→ [+caus]   12→ [+caus]   >SVDR

(1) [+loc]

pumunta >→
'go to'

papuntahin >→
'cause s.t.
to go to;
to send'

ipapapunta
'cause s.o. to
have s.t. go
to; cause s.o. to
send s.t.'

(2) [-affl]

gumalaw >→
'move'

pagalawin >→
'cause s.t.
to move'

ipapagalaw
'cause s.o.
to move s.t.'

magdoktor >→
'study to
be a doctor'

papagdoktorin >→
'cause s.o. to
study to be a
doctor'

ipapapagdoktor (rare)
'cause s.o. to
have s.o. else
study to be a
doctor'

magpakaba?it >→
'try to be
good'

papapakaba?itin >→
'cause s.o. to
try to be good'

papapagpakaba?itin (rare)
'cause s.o. to have s.o.
else try to be good.'

I. Intransitive	II. Transitive	III. Ditransitive	IV. Causative	V. Double Causative Ditransitive
	B. $\left[\begin{matrix} +[+AGT] \\ -[+DAT] \\ [+OBJ] \end{matrix}\right]$ $\overset{\text{SVDR}}{\underset{12\rightarrow}{\searrow}}$ [+caus]	$\overset{\text{SVDR}}{\underset{13\rightarrow}{\searrow}}$ [+caus]		
	(1) [+loc]			
	(a) [+goal]			
	ibigay $\nearrow$ 'give'	ipabigay 'cause s.t. to be given by s.o.'	ipapabigay 'cause s.o. to have s.o. else give s.t.'	
	(b) [−goal]			
	kunin $\nearrow$ 'take, get from'	ipakuha 'cause s.t. to be taken by s.o.'	ipapakuha 'cause s.o. to ask s.o. else to have s.t. taken'	
	(c) [−dir]			
	isulat $\nearrow$ 'write on'	ipasulat 'cause s.o. to have s.t. written on'	ipapasulat 'cause s.o. to ask s.o. else to write s.t.'	

I. Intransitive	II. Transitive	III. Ditransitive	IV. Causative Ditransitive	V. Double Causative Ditransitive
	(2) [-loc]			
	(a.1) [+cs]			
	lutu?in 'cook s.t.' →	ipaluto? 'cause s.o. to cook s.t.' →	ipapaluto? 'cause s.o. to have s.o. else cook s.t.'	
	(a.2) [+cs, +caus]			
	pahinugin 'cause to/let s.t. ripen' →	ipapahinog 'cause s.o. to let s.t. ripen'		
	palakihin 'cause to/ let s.t. become big or grow' →	ipapalaki 'cause s.o. to let s.t. grow or become big'		
	(b) [-cs]			
	hugasan 'wash s.t.' →	pahugasan 'have s.t. washed by s.o.' →	papahugasan 'cause s.o. to ask s.o. else to wash s.t.'	

I. Intransitive	II. Transitive	III. Ditransitive	IV. Causative Ditransitive	V. Double Causative Ditransitive
	(c) [-af]			
	ilatag 'spread out s.t.' $\longrightarrow$	ipalatag 'have s.o. spread out s.t.' $\longrightarrow$	ipapalatag 'cause s.o. to ask s.o. else to spread s.t.'	
	(d) [+extn]			
	tulungan 'help s.o.' $\longrightarrow$	patulungan 'cause s.o. to help s.o. else' $\longrightarrow$	papatulungan 'cause s.o. to ask s.o. else to help another'	

C. $\begin{bmatrix} - \begin{bmatrix} +\text{AGT} \\ +\text{DAT} \\ +\text{OBJ} \end{bmatrix} \\ +\text{per} \\ +\text{ntn} \end{bmatrix}$ $\xrightarrow{\text{SVDR}}$ 14→ [+caus] $\xrightarrow{\text{SVDR}}$ 13→ [+caus]

(1) [+cog]

alamin $\longrightarrow$ ipa'alam $\longrightarrow$ ipapa'alam
'try to know' 'cause to/let 'cause s.o.
s.o. know s.t.' to have s.o.
else know s.t.'

I. Intransitive	II. Transitive	III. Ditransitive	IV. Causative Ditransitive	V. Double Causative Ditransitive
	(2) [-cog]			
	dinggin 'listen' ⇉→	ipadinig 'let s.o. hear s.t.' ⇉→	ipapadinig 'cause s.o. to let s.t. be heard by s.o. else'	

D. [+[+AGT] +[+DAT] +[+OBJ]]

$\succ$SVDR 13→ [+caus] $\succ$SVDR 15→ [+caus]

(1) [+erg]

i?utos 'order s.o. s.t.' ⇉→ ipa?utos 'cause s.t. to be ordered by s.o.' ⇉→ ipapa?utos 'cause s.o. to order s.o. s.t.'

(2) [-erg]

itawag 'relay s.t. to s.o, by phone' ⇉→ ipatawag 'cause s.t. to be relayed to s.o. over the telephone' ⇉→ ipapatawag 'cause s.o. to have s.t. relayed over the phone by s.o. else to another person'

The first four column divisions in the chart represent the four general subcategories on which causativization operates. The fifth subcategory, although showing a distinct morphological class of double causative ditransitive stems, manifests a case frame identical to its input which is a causative ditransitive. It is set up here for morphological comparison of structures. In effect, therefore, the last subcategory falls together syntactically with the fourth subcategory. The first subcategory labelled 'intransitive' is identified by the case frame $[-[+AGT], -[+DAT], -[+INS], +[+OBJ]]$ which consists of two subclasses, one with and the other without a cooccurring $[+LOC]$ actant. The verb stems in this subcategory may be underived or derived from N's or Adj's but all of them are non-causative. From these verbs there is a potential of creating corresponding causative forms which are characterized by the second subcategory of 'transitive' verbs. This is possible through the application of SVDR-11, which does not give any importance to whether the intransitive source has a cooccurring $[+LOC]$ actant or not. The resulting causative stems fall together with other underived verbs identified by the case frame $[+[+AGT], -[+DAT], +[+OBJ]]$ with or without a cooccurring $[+LOC]$ actant, as in B. The column of 'transitive' verbs also includes the class of $[-[+AGT], +[+DAT], +[+OBJ]]$ verbs under C derived directly from Adj's through VDR-19. These three general subclasses of transitive verbs--II.A,II-B,II.C--can correspond to another type of causative verbs through the application of SVDR-12 and SVDR-14. Each of these new causative stems, III.A, III.B. and III.C allows a directed performer or experiencer identified as $[+DAT]$. With this feature, in particular, they fall under the third subcategory labelled 'ditransitive' and belong with the underived verbs of information, as in III.D and the derived causative perception verbs in III.C. While all four sets of verbs under the subcategory of ditransitive verbs exhibit the same syntactic structure, not considering a [+LOC] that may or may not cooccur, they differ from each other in the presence or absence of the semantic feature [+caus] as well as in their morphological structure. For instance, verbs under III.D are primary information verbs and do not have the feature [+caus] while those under III.A through III.C are marked [+caus]. Although the causative verbs in III.A derive from existing causative verbs in II.A, the feature [+caus] from the source stem is simply carried over to the derived stem since the same meaning of causativization is conveyed by that feature. Thus, there is no difference between these two stem classes in terms of the semantic feature [+caus]. Morphologically, the stems under III.D are roots, those under III.B, except 2.a [+cs, +caus] subclass which derives from Adj or N, and III.C are single causatives. They have one instance of the derivational causative affix pa- indicating that their source stems are not causative verbs. On the other hand, the stems under III.A and III.B, 2.a [+cs, +caus] show a pa- prefixed before another pa- stem indicating that these verbs have undergone two causativization rules, hence, they are referred to as double causative stems. Having similar case features as III.D, the single causative stems under III.B and III.C can undergo SVDR-13 creating double causative stems IV.B and IV.C. The same rule accounts for single causative stems IV.D from III.D. These new derived classes via SVDR-13 belong to the syntactic subcategory identified as 'causative ditransitive'. Since performance efficiency discourages application of any of the causativization rules on double causative stems, only IV.D can undergo SVDR-15 which results in a set labelled 'double causative ditransitive' but whose syntactic structure manifested is identical to the fourth class.

From the preceding, we have formally accounted for the syntactic, semantic and morphological relationships between corresponding verb stem classes under I and II, those under II and III, those under III and IV and, lastly, those under IV and V. Concomitantly, we find derived stems being syntactically related to underived members of the particular subcategory the new stems are derived into. Furthermore, following the direction of derivations, as illustrated in the above chart and on p.355, we can account systematically for the affixal layering or build-up in derived stems derivation after derivation.

4.3.2.2.4.3. Derived Social Verbs

A general class of verb stems labelled 'social' can be derived from either transitive or intransitive verbs that may or may not cooccur with a [+LOC]. The derived social verbs express 'joining in or participating' in the action or process designated by the source verb as performed or undergone by the original [+AGT] or [+OBJ] referent. The three types of social verbs derived under separate DR's are identified as Social Agentive Verbs, Social Reciprocal Verbs, and Social Intransitive Verbs, all of which are marked with the redundant feature intention [+ntn] predictable from the feature social [+soc].

4.3.2.2.4.3.1 Social Verbs Derived from Non-reciprocal

Agentive Verb Stems

A set of verbs identified as social agentive can be derived from the non-reciprocal agentive class of verb stems by introducing a new [+AGT] actant. The original [+AGT] corresponds to the role of a [+COM] in the newly created stem. The rule for deriving this type of social verbs is stated as follows:

SVDR-16: Social Agentive Verbs

$$
\begin{bmatrix}
+V \\
+[+AGT, \alpha F_i] \\
\begin{Bmatrix} -erg \\ -pot, +act \end{Bmatrix} \\
-recip^{19}
\end{bmatrix}
\rightarrowtail
\begin{bmatrix}
+V \\
+Derv \\
+[+AGT] \\
-[+COM, -\alpha F_i] \\
+soc \\
=pot \\
+act
\end{bmatrix}
$$

SVDMR-16: $_V[\longrightarrow _V[paki$

The input in the above rule specifies a non-reciprocal agentive stem which is either [-erg] or [-pot, +act]. This implies that the [+erg] stem does not undergo this rule. The derived stem is prefixed with paki- by SVDMR-16.[20] In this form, the voice paradigm of the stem consists of the agentive and the comitative voice. The former is marked by m- and the latter, by -an.[21]

As we have seen, there are various syntactic classes of agentive verbs. From the major subcategories, we have the information and the transitive subclasses, with or without a cooccurring [+LOC]. In these two broad classes are now included certain derived causative verbs. We will show by examples each of these possible sources.

(a) Agentive Non-dative
     Transitive Verbs

(a') Social Verbs

   (1) [+loc]

       paglagay 'put'

       pag?alay 'offer'

       kuha 'take'

       bili 'buy'

       pirma 'sign'

   (1) [+loc]

       pakipaglagay 'join others
       in putting s.t. on
       some place'

       pakipag?alay 'participate
       in making an offering'

       pakikuha 'join others in
       taking s.t.'

       pakibili 'join others in
       buying s.t.'

       pakipirma 'participate
       in signing s.t.'

84.a. nag?alay ang mga bata   ng bulaklak sa puntod
      offer   children   flower   grave
      [-erg] $\begin{bmatrix} +NM \\ +AGT \end{bmatrix}$ $\begin{bmatrix} +AC \\ +OBJ \end{bmatrix}$ $\begin{bmatrix} +L \\ +LOC \end{bmatrix}$

      ng mga bayani
          heroes

      'The children laid flowers on the heroes' grave.'

84.b. nakipag?alay ang ilang mga turista (sa mga bata) ng
      [+soc]   tourists   children
                        $\begin{bmatrix} +NM \\ +AGT \end{bmatrix}$ $\begin{bmatrix} +L \\ +COM \end{bmatrix}$

      bulaklak sa puntod ng mga bayani
              $\begin{bmatrix} +L \\ +LOC \end{bmatrix}$

      'A few tourists joined (with the children) in laying
      flowers on the heroes' grave.'

84.c. pinakipag?alayan ng ilang mga turista ang mga
      [+soc] $\begin{bmatrix} +AC \\ +AGT \end{bmatrix}$

      bata ng bulaklak sa puntod ng mga bayani
      $\begin{bmatrix} +NM \\ +COM \end{bmatrix}$ $\begin{bmatrix} +AC \\ +OBJ \end{bmatrix}$ $\begin{bmatrix} +L \\ +LOC \end{bmatrix}$

Lit.: 'The children were joined by a few tourists
in laying flowers on the heroes' grave.'

(2) [-loc]   (2') [=loc]

paglaro? 'play s.t.'   pakipaglaro? 'participate in
                                       playing s.t. with others'

paglinis 'clean s.t.'   pakipaglinis 'join s.o. in
                                       cleaning s.t.'

pano?od 'watch s.t.'   pakipano?od 'join s.o./others
                                       in watching s.t.'

?ani 'harvest'   paki?ani 'participate in
                                       harvesting'

basa 'read'   pakibasa 'join others in
                                       reading s.t.'

tulong 'help'   pakitulong 'participate in
                                       helping'

85.a. inani   ng mga magbubukid ang palay
       harvest   farmers   rice stalks
                            $\begin{bmatrix} +AC \\ +AGT \end{bmatrix}$ $\begin{bmatrix} +NM \\ +OBJ \end{bmatrix}$

'The rice stalks were harvested by the farmers.'

85.b. naki?ani ang 'Peace Corps Volunteer' ng palay
       [+soc] $\begin{bmatrix} +NM \\ +AGT \end{bmatrix}$ $\begin{bmatrix} +AC \\ +OBJ \end{bmatrix}$

sa mga magbubukid
   $\begin{bmatrix} +L \\ +COM \end{bmatrix}$

'The Peace Corps Volunteer joined the farmers in
   harvesting rice stalks.'

85.c. pinaki?anihan ng 'Peace Corps Volunteer' ng palay
       [+soc] $\begin{bmatrix} +AC \\ +AGT \end{bmatrix}$ $\begin{bmatrix} +AC \\ +OBJ \end{bmatrix}$

ang mga magbubukid
   $\begin{bmatrix} +NM \\ +COM \end{bmatrix}$

'The farmers were joined in by the Peace Corps
   Volunteer in harvesting rice.'

(b) Information Verbs   (b') Social Verbs

pagbalita? 'inform'   pakipagbalita? 'join in
                              informing'

pag?utos 'order'   pakipag?utos 'join in
                              ordering'

pagtanong 'ask'   pakipagtanong 'join in
                              asking'

pagturo? 'teach'   pakipagturo? 'participate
                              in teaching'

86.a. nagbalita? siya sa nanay ng nangyari
       inform   she   mother   happening
       $\begin{bmatrix}+NM\\+AGT\end{bmatrix}$ $\begin{bmatrix}+L\\+DAT\end{bmatrix}$ $\begin{bmatrix}+AC\\+OBJ\end{bmatrix}$

'She informed mother of the happening.'

86.b. nakipagbalita? si Jun   (sa kaniya) sa nanay
       [+soc]   her
       $\begin{bmatrix}+NM\\+AGT\end{bmatrix}$ $\begin{bmatrix}+L\\+COM\end{bmatrix}$ $\begin{bmatrix}+L\\+DAT\end{bmatrix}$

       ng nangyari
       $\begin{bmatrix}+AC\\+OBJ\end{bmatrix}$

'Jun joined (her) in informing mother of the happening.'

In the use of social verbs, three things commonly occur.

(a) When the [+COM] actant, which is realized in the locative case
form when non-subject, cooccurs with another actant in the same case
form, the [+COM] actant is usually grammatically unexpressed. Thus,
84.b and 86.b are normally rendered without the [+COM] actant. This
condition is similar to the performance restrictions observed in
causative forms of transportation and information verbs. That is, when
two cooccurring actants which are hardly distinguishable by any semantic
features are realized in identical case forms, one of them is usually
unexpressed. With causative verbs either the [+DAT] or [+LOC] may be

omitted, whereas with social verbs the preference between a [+COM] and a [+LOC] or [+DAT] is usually for the former actant to go.

(b) As a minor case relation, the [+COM] occurs more often in the non-nominative case form. However, this does not mean that it is restricted from being realized as a subject. For instance:

87.a. naglaro? ang mga bata?   ng "Monopoly"
　　　 play   children
　　　 [+act]   ⌈+NM ⌉   ⌈+AC ⌉
　　　　　　　　　 ⌊+AGT⌋   ⌊+OBJ⌋

　　　'The children played monopoly.'

87.b. pinakipaglaru?an niya ang mga bata? ng "Monopoly"
　　　 [+soc]   ⌈+AC ⌉   ⌈+NM ⌉   ⌈+AC ⌉
　　　　　　　　　　 ⌊+AGT⌋   ⌊+COM⌋   ⌊+OBJ⌋

　　　'He played monopoly with the children.'

The comitative voice can be observed to occur more commonly when the social verb stem is derived from simple transitive verbs, especially when it does not correspond to a homophonous 'request/permission' form.

(c) The reason for the rare use of the comitative voice form is probably its ambiguity with the dative or locative voice form of a request verb. For example:

88.a. nakibili ang Mama   kay Chitong ng kwintas kay Jay
　　　 [+req]   mother   necklace
　　　　　　　 ⌈+NM ⌉   ⌈+L ⌉   ⌈+AC ⌉   ⌈+L ⌉
　　　　　　　 ⌊+AGT⌋   ⌊+DAT⌋   ⌊+OBJ⌋   ⌊+LOC⌋

　　　'Mother requested Chitong to buy a necklace from Jay.'

88.b. pinakibilhan ng Mama kay Chitong ng kwintas si Jay
　　　 [+req]   ⌈+AC ⌉   ⌈+L ⌉   ⌈+AC ⌉   ⌈+NM ⌉
　　　　　　　　 ⌊+AGT⌋   ⌊+DAT⌋   ⌊+OBJ⌋   ⌊+LOC⌋

88.c. pinakibilhan ng Mama si Chitong ng kwintas kay Jay
　　　 [+req]   ⌈+AC ⌉   ⌈+NM ⌉   ⌈+AC ⌉   ⌈+L ⌉
　　　　　　　　 ⌊+AGT⌋   ⌊+DAT⌋   ⌊+OBJ⌋   ⌊+LOC⌋

89.a. nakibili ang Mama (kay Chitong) ng kwintas kay Jay
[+soc] $\begin{bmatrix} +NM \\ +AGT \end{bmatrix}$ $\begin{bmatrix} +L \\ +COM \end{bmatrix}$ $\begin{bmatrix} +AC \\ +OBJ \end{bmatrix}$ $\begin{bmatrix} +L \\ +LOC \end{bmatrix}$

'Mother bought (along with Chiton) a necklace from Jay.'

89.b. pinakibilhan ng Mama si Chitong ng kwintas
[+soc] $\begin{bmatrix} +AC \\ +AGT \end{bmatrix}$ $\begin{bmatrix} +NM \\ +COM \end{bmatrix}$ $\begin{bmatrix} +AC \\ +OBJ \end{bmatrix}$

(kay Jay)[22]
$\begin{bmatrix} +L \\ +LOC \end{bmatrix}$

To minimize confusion, the preferred form of the social verb is the
agentive voiee. Its ambiguity with a possible corresponding request
form in the agentive voice is dispelled by asking whether the [+AGT]
referent is performing what is indicated by the verb base or it is
directing or requesting someone else to do the action.

With the active form of causative verbs as input, the social verb
counterparts may have a maximal cooccurrence of three locative case
forms. For example:

90.a. nagpabigay si Fe kay Minda ng regalo sa Ate
give gift oldest sister
[+caus] $\begin{bmatrix} +NM \\ +AGT \end{bmatrix}$ $\begin{bmatrix} +L \\ +DAT \end{bmatrix}$ $\begin{bmatrix} +AC \\ +OBJ \end{bmatrix}$ $\begin{bmatrix} +L \\ +LOC \end{bmatrix}$

'Fe had Minda give a gift to my oldest sister.'

90.b. nakipagpabigay siya (kay Fe) kay Minda ng
[+soc] she
$\begin{bmatrix} +NM \\ +AGT \end{bmatrix}$ $\begin{bmatrix} +L \\ +COM \end{bmatrix}$ $\begin{bmatrix} +L \\ +DAT \end{bmatrix}$

regalo sa Ate
$\begin{bmatrix} +AC \\ +OBJ \end{bmatrix}$ $\begin{bmatrix} +L \\ +LOC \end{bmatrix}$

'She joined Fe in having Minda give a gift to
my oldest sister.'

As in the previous cases of multiple case form cooccurrences of actants
without other distinguishing semantic features, one or two are normally

omitted leaving the resulting sentence accordingly two or three ways ambiguous.

The following correspondences of active causative and social verbs are given to illustrate the affix expansion in the derived forms:

(c) Causative Verbs,   (c') Social Verbs
     [-pot, +act]

(1) pagpapasok   (1) pakipagpapasok 'participate
     'have s.o./s.t.   in having s.o./s.t. enter'
     enter'
     pagpagalaw   pakipagpagalaw 'join others
     'have s.t. move'   in having s.t. move'

(2) pagpakuha 'cause s.o.   (2) pakipagpakuha 'join others
     to take s.t.'   in having s.o. take s.t.'

     pagpagawaʔ 'have s.o.   pakipagpagawaʔ 'join others
     make s.t.'   in having s.o. make s.t.'

(3) pagpakita 'show s.o.   (3) pakipagpakita 'join others
     s.t.'   in showing s.t.'

     pagpaʔalam 'let s.o.   pakipagpaʔalam 'participate
     know s.t.'   in letting s.o. know s.t.'

(4) pagpaʔutos 'cause s.t. (4) pakipagpaʔutos 'join in
     to be ordered by   having s.t. be ordered'
     s.o.'
     pagpatanong 'cause   pakipagpatanong 'join others
     s.o. to ask s.t.'   in having s.o. ask s.t.'

4.3.2.2.4.3.2. Social Verbs Derived from Reciprocal Verb Stems

When the agentive verb is marked reciprocal, it does not undergo SVDR-16, but it can undergo a similar rule stated as follows:

SVDR-17:   Social Reciprocal Transitive Verbs

$$
\begin{bmatrix}
+V \\
-[+AGT, -pl] \\
-[+AGT, -\alpha F_i] \\
+[+OBJ] \\
+recip \\
-pot \\
+act
\end{bmatrix}
\longmapsto
\begin{bmatrix}
+V \\
+Derv \\
-[+AGT, -\alpha F_i] \\
-[+COM, -\alpha F_i] \\
+[+OBJ] \\
+soc \\
+recip \\
-pot \\
+act
\end{bmatrix}
$$

SVDMR-17: $_V[$ $\longrightarrow$ $_V[$paki

A reciprocal transitive verb denotes in part a 'social' affair in being a mutual action between the referents of the [+AGT] actant. It implies agreement of the two parties involved to do the designated action mutually. A social verb that can be derived from a reciprocal transitive verb, on the other hand, expresses a [+AGT] referent engaging someone or some others, marked [+COM], to do a mutual action with it. Structurally, the derived social verb manifests a cooccurring [+COM] which is implicit in the cooccurring [+AGT] of the reciprocal stem source. The relationship between the [+AGT] and [+COM] of the social verb with the original [+AGT] is indicated by their shared selectional features αF_i. It will be observed that the feature plural is no longer a requirement on the [+AGT] of the social verb since the [+COM] is expressed separately.

In terms of form, the reciprocal stem, which is generally identified by the derivational affixes pag- and -an, is carried over to the derived social verb and marked [-pot, +act]. By SVDMR-17, the derived social stem is prefixed with paki-. The new stem has a voice paradigm consisting of an agentive, an objective and a comitative voice, marked by m-, i- and Ø, respectively. Reciprocal verbs which are not derived via SVDR-4, but derived by other special DR's, do not have the derivational affix -an, e.g., pag?usap' talk with each other,' pag?away 'quarrel with each other,' pagtalo 'argue with each other'. The comitative voice of social verbs derived from such verb forms is then marked not by ∅ but by -an. Evidently, the ∅ marking of the comitative voice in stems that already carry the affix -an is a prohibition on the occurrence of identical affixes one after another. Below are some examples showing social reciprocal transitive verbs and their corresponding sources.

(a) Reciprocal Transitive Verbs

pagbalita?an 'exchange news'

pagtanungan 'ask each other'

pag?usap 'talk with each other'

pagpalitan 'trade with each other

paghalinhinan 'alternate with each other'

(b)) Social Reciprocal Transitive Verbs

pakipagbalita?an 'engage in exchanging news'

pakipagtanungan 'engage in asking each other s.t.'

pakipag?usap 'engage in a conversation'

pakipagpalitan 'engage in trading with each other'

pakipaghalinhinan 'engage in alternating with each other'

91.a. nagkuwentuhan sila (ni Ana) ng kanilang karanasan
tell stories they their experiences
[+recip] $\begin{bmatrix} +NM \\ +AGT \end{bmatrix}$ $\begin{bmatrix} +AC \\ +OBJ \end{bmatrix}$

'They (with Ana) told each other their experiences.'

91.b. nakipagkwentuhan siya kay Ana ng kanilang karanasan
$\begin{bmatrix} +soc \\ +recip \end{bmatrix}$ she
$\begin{bmatrix} +NM \\ +AGT \end{bmatrix}$ $\begin{bmatrix} +L \\ +COM \end{bmatrix}$ $\begin{bmatrix} +AC \\ +OBJ \end{bmatrix}$

'She engaged Ana in telling their experiences to each other.'

92.a. nag?usap ang estudyante at ang guro? tungkol
      talk   student   teacher about
      [+recip] $\begin{bmatrix} +NM \\ +AGT \end{bmatrix}$ $\begin{bmatrix} +P \\ +AC \end{bmatrix}$

      sa eksamen
         examination
         $\begin{bmatrix} +L \\ +OBJ \end{bmatrix}$

      'The student and the teacher talked about the examination.'

92.b. nakipag?usap ang estudyante sa guro? tungkol
      $\begin{bmatrix} +soc \\ +recip \end{bmatrix}$ $\begin{bmatrix} +NM \\ +AGT \end{bmatrix}$ $\begin{bmatrix} +L \\ +COM \end{bmatrix}$

      sa eksamen
      $\begin{bmatrix} +L \\ +OBJ \end{bmatrix}$

      'The student talked the examination over with the teacher.'

92.c. pinakipag?usapan ng estudyante ang guro? tungkol
      $\begin{bmatrix} +soc \\ +recip \end{bmatrix}$ $\begin{bmatrix} +AC \\ +AGT \end{bmatrix}$ $\begin{bmatrix} +NM \\ +COM \end{bmatrix}\begin{bmatrix} +P \\ +AC \end{bmatrix}$

      sa eksamen[23]
      $\begin{bmatrix} +L \\ +OBJ \end{bmatrix}$

      'The teacher was engaged in a conversation by the student about the examination.'

Two other types of social verbs can be derived from reciprocal intransitive and reciprocal psych verbs. It may be added that while reciprocal verbs express a casual exchange of what is indicated by the verb, social reciprocal verbs denote a purposeful or a more intense involvement. Similar to the preceding rule, social reciprocal intransitive verbs are derived as follows:

SVDR-18: Social Reciprocal Intransitive Verbs

$$
\begin{bmatrix}
+V \\
-[+INS] \\
-[+OBJ, \; -pl] \\
-[+OBJ, \; -\alpha F_i] \\
+recip \\
-pot \\
+act
\end{bmatrix}
\;\longmapsto\;
\begin{bmatrix}
+V \\
+Derv \\
-[+INS] \\
-[+OBJ, \; -\alpha F_i] \\
-[+COM, \; -\alpha F_i] \\
+soc \\
+recip \\
-pot \\
+act
\end{bmatrix}
$$

SVDMR-18: $_V[\;\longrightarrow\; _V[paki$

The case relation features of the social reciprocal intransitive
verbs derived by SVDR-18 consisting of [+OBJ] and [+COM] are related
to the corresponding [+OBJ] in the source verb by their common features
αF_i. Like other OBJ's in intransitive verbs, which show that this
actant can perform an action intentionally, the [+OBJ] of the social
verb here is interpreted as engaging the [+COM] referent in an exchange
of what the verb designates. SVDMR-18 is identical to SVDMR-17, thus,
the derived set above is also prefixed with paki-. The voice paradigm
manifested by this set is marked by the voice affix m- for the objective
and $\emptyset$ or -an for the comitative. The latter voice form is less commonly
used. Examples of derived social reciprocal intransitive verbs follow:

(a) Reciprocal Intran- sitive Verbs	(b') Social Reciprocal Intran- sitive Verbs
paghampasan 'hit each other'	pakipaghampasan 'engage in hitting each other'
pagsuntukan 'exchange fist blows'	pakipagsuntukan 'engage in boxing each other'
pag?away 'quarrel'	pakipag?away 'engage in quarrelling'
paghiwalay 'separate from each other'	pakipaghiwalay 'engage in separation'

93.a. nagsuntukan si Ali   at si Fraser
      fight $\begin{bmatrix} +NM \\ +OBJ \end{bmatrix}$
      [+recip]

   'Ali and Fraser fought with each other.'

93.b. nakipagsuntukan si Ali   kay Fraser
      engage in fight $\begin{bmatrix} +NM \\ +OBJ \end{bmatrix}$ $\begin{bmatrix} +L \\ +COM \end{bmatrix}$
      $\begin{bmatrix} +soc \\ +recip \end{bmatrix}$

   'Ali engaged Fraser in a fight with each other.'

93.c. pinakipagsuntukan ni Ali   si Fraser (rare)
      $\begin{bmatrix} +soc \\ +recip \end{bmatrix}$ $\begin{bmatrix} +AC \\ +OBJ \end{bmatrix}$ $\begin{bmatrix} +NM \\ +COM \end{bmatrix}$

   'It was Fraser whom Ali engaged in a fight
   with each other.'

SVDR-19: Social Reciprocal Psych Verbs

$$\begin{bmatrix} +V \\ -[+OBJ, -pl] \\ -[+OBJ, -\alpha F_i] \\ +recip \\ -pot \\ +act \end{bmatrix} \longrightarrow \begin{bmatrix} +V \\ +Derv \\ -[+AGT] \\ -[+DAT, -\alpha F_i] \\ -[+OBJ, -\alpha F_i] \\ +soc \\ +recip \\ -pot \\ +act \end{bmatrix}$$

SVDMR-19: $V_I \longrightarrow V_{[paki}$

SVDR-19 creates a subclass of psych verbs which is further identified as being reciprocal and social, thus, intentional. The actants
[+DAT] and [+OBJ] are again related to the [+OBJ] in the source
reciprocal stem as indicated by the selectional features αF_i. The
derived social reciprocal psych verb means that the [+DAT] engages the
[+OBJ] which it perceives in a mutual psychological experience. The
[+OBJ] as the object perceived by the [+DAT] is interpreted at the same
time as playing the role of a [+COM], it being the party engaged in the
psychological experience. The morphological structure of this derived

set is no different from those of the other social reciprocal verbs by
SVDMR-19. The voice paradigm of this derived class is marked by m- for
the dative and by ∅ or -an for the objective. For example:

(a) Reciprocal Psych   (b') Social Reciprocal Psych
     Verbs   Verbs

     pag?intindihan 'try   pakipag?intindihan 'engage
       to understand   s.o. in understanding
       each other'   each other'

     paglimutan 'try to   pakipaglimutan 'engage
       forget each other'   in forgetting each other'

     pagkita 'see each   pakipagkita 'arrange to
       other'   meet each other'

94.a. nagkita   kami   (ni Harmony) sa New York
       see each we
       other   [+NM]
       [+recip] [+OBJ]

       'We (Harmony and I) saw each other in New York.'

94.b. nakipagkita   ako   kay Harmony sa New York
       arrange to meet   I
       [+soc]   [+NM]   [+L]
       [+recip]   [+DAT]   [+OBJ]

       'I arranged to meet with Harmony in New York.'

94.c. pinakipagkita?an ko   si Harmony sa New York
       [+soc]   [+AC]   [+NM]
       [+recip]   [+DAT]   [+OBJ]

       'It was Harmony whom I arranged to meet with in New York'

4.3.2.2.4.3.3 Social Verbs Derived from Non-agentive,

               Non-dative Verb Stems

     A third type of social verbs derive from non-agentive, non-dative
verb stems according to the following rule:

SVDR-20: Social Intransitive Verbs

$$\begin{bmatrix} +V \\ \langle+loc\rangle \\ -[+INS] \\ +[+OBJ, \alpha F_i] \end{bmatrix} \longmapsto \begin{bmatrix} +V \\ +Derv \\ \langle+loc\rangle \\ -[+INS] \\ +[+OBJ] \\ -[^{+COM}_{+soc}, -\alpha F_i] \\ -pot \\ +act \end{bmatrix}$$

SVDMR-20: $_V[\longrightarrow {}_V[paki$

The rule states that a locomotion or a simple intransitive verb can have a corresponding social verb, marked as in other 'socialization' rules with the features [+soc, -pot, +act]. The derived stem denotes likewise, 'joining in or partipating in' an intentional action performed by a [+COM] actant. The participant that 'joins in' is the [+OBJ] that is introduced in the case frame and the actant already performing what is designated by the verb base is the [+COM] actant which corresponds to the original [+OBJ] as marked by the features αF_i. By SVDMR-20, the stem which is usually a simple root is prefixed by paki-. Although the voice paradigm includes both objective and comitative voices, the more frequently used form is the objective. It is marked by the affix m- while the comitative voice is marked by -an. For example:

(a) Locomotion Verbs	(a') Social Intransitive Verbs
silong 'take shelter'	pakisilong 'take shelter with'
sakay 'ride on'	pakisakay 'take a ride with'
pasok 'enter'	pakipasok 'enter with'
punta 'go to'	pakipunta 'go with; go to as others do'

(b) Simple Intransitive   (b') Social Intransitive Verbs
     Verbs

    takbo 'run'   pakitakbo 'join in running'

    tawa 'laugh'   pakitawa 'join in laughing'

    sigaw 'shout'   pakisigaw 'join in shouting'

    tindig 'stand'   pakitindig 'join in standing'

    iyak 'cry'   paki?iyak 'join in crying'

95.a. tumakbo ang mga bata?   nang marinig ang banda
       run   children when hear   band (music)
                      $\begin{bmatrix} +NM \\ +OBJ \end{bmatrix}$

     'The children scampered when they heard the band.'

95.b. nakitakbo si Buddy sa mga bata?
      [+soc] $\begin{bmatrix} +NM \\ +OBJ \end{bmatrix}$ $\begin{bmatrix} +L \\ +COM \end{bmatrix}$

     'Buddy ran along with the children.'

When the source stem is a verb of locomotion, the [+COM] takes
precedence over the [+LOC] in being realized as subject. Since a [+LOC]
as subject is regularly marked by the affix -an on the verb, and the
same affix already marks the [+COM], an imminent ambiguity between the
identical forms is avoided by requiring the [+LOC] actant to be
realized only in the locative case form in all social verbs as follows:

CFRR-18: $\begin{bmatrix} +soc \\ +loc \end{bmatrix}$ $\longrightarrow$ $\begin{bmatrix} -L \\ +LOC \end{bmatrix}$

Thus, we can have the following pair of sentences indicating an objective and comitative voice:

96.a. nakisakay si Cricket kay Daisy sa 'roller coaster'
      ride with
      [+soc] $\begin{bmatrix} +NM \\ +OBJ \end{bmatrix}$ $\begin{bmatrix} +L \\ +COM \end{bmatrix}$ $\begin{bmatrix} +L \\ +LOC \end{bmatrix}$

     'Cricket rode with Daisy on the roller coaster.'

96.b. pinakisakyan ni Cricket si Daisy sa 'roller coaster'
[+soc] $\begin{bmatrix} +AC \\ +OBJ \end{bmatrix}$ $\begin{bmatrix} +NM \\ +COM \end{bmatrix}$ $\begin{bmatrix} +L \\ +LOC \end{bmatrix}$

'It was Daisy with whom Cricket rode on the
roller coaster.'

However, the comitative voice where it suffers ambiguity with a
'request' form is frequently avoided.

It may also be mentioned that the semantically derived set of
'simultaneous action' verbs, e.g. magtakbuhan 'run together at the same
time', can also undergo SVDR-18 giving the corresponding form of the
type makipagtakbuhan 'engage with s.o./others in running together;
join s.o./others in running at the same time'. Likewise, these derived
forms are ambiguous with certain social reciprocal forms, e.g.,
makipagsigawan meaning 'shout together with others' or 'engage in
shouting at each other.'

4.3.3 Voice-marking Affixes of Secondary Verb Stem Classes

The following chart summarizes the derived secondary verb stem
classes indicating their respective voice inflectional paradigm and
corresponding voice-marking affixes.

CF-SF-MVF Secondary Verb Stem Classes	Voice Inflectional Paradigm and Corresponding Affixes					
	UM-	M-	-IN	I-	-AN	Ø
1. [-[+INS], +[+OBJ]]	:	:	:	:	:	:
(a) [-affl, +pot,-act]	:	:	:	:	:	: OBJ
(b) [-affl, -pot,+act]	:	: OBJ	:	:	:	:
(c) [+recip,-pot,+act]	:	: OBJ	:	:	:	:
(d) [+recip, +per, -pot, +act]	:	: OBJ	:	:	:	:

CF-SF-MVF Secondary Verb Stem Classes	Voice Inflectional Paradigm and Corresponding Affixes					
	UM-	M-	-IN	I-	-AN	Ø
2. [+[+AGT], -[+DAT], -loc, +[OBJ]]						
(a) [+recip, -pot, +act]		AGT				
(b) [-af, +erg]				OBJ		
(c) [+caus, -af, +erg]			OBJ			
3. [+[+AGT], -[+DAT], +loc, +[OBJ]]						
(a) [+dir, +erg]				OBJ		
(b) [+caus, +erg]			OBJ		LOC	
4. [+[+INS], +[+OBJ]]						
(a) [-cs, +erg]					OBJ	
(b) [+cs, +erg]			OBJ			
5. [-[+AGT], +[+DAT], +[+OBJ], +exp]						
(a) [+erg]					DAT	
(b) [+pot, -act]					DAT	
(c) [-pot, +act]					DAT	
6. [+[+AGT], +[+DAT], +loc, +[+OBJ], +caus]						
(a) [+erg]				OBJ	LOC	
(b) [+dat]			DAT	(OBJ)	(LOC)[24]	
7. [+[+AGT], +[+DAT], -loc, +[+OBJ], +caus]						
(a) [{+extn / -cs}, +erg]				`	OBJ	
(b) [+extn, +dat]			DAT		OBJ	
(c) [{+cs / -af}, +erg]				OBJ		
(d) [{+cs / -af}, +dat]			DAT	(OBJ)		

CF-SF-MVF Secondary Verb Stem Classes	Voice Inflectional Paradigm and Corresponding Affixes					
	UM-	M-	-IN	I-	-AN	Ø
(e) [+cog, +erg]			DAT	OBJ	(DAT)	
(f) [-cog, +erg]				OBJ	DAT	
8. [+[+AGT], -[+DAT], +[+OBJ], +[+COM], +soc]						
(a) [+loc, -pot, +act]		AGT			COM	
(b) [-loc, -pot, +act]		AGT			COM	
9. [+[+AGT], +[+DAT], +[+OBJ], +[+COM], +soc, -pot, +act]		AGT			(COM)	
10. [+[+AGT], +[+DAT], +loc, +[+OBJ], +[+COM], +soc, -pot, +act]		AGT				
11. [+[+AGT], -[+DAT], -loc, +[+OBJ], +[+COM], +soc, +recip, -pot, +act]		AGT			(COM)	
12. [-[+INS], +[+OBJ], +[+COM], +soc, +recip, -pot, +act]		OBJ			(COM)	
13. [-[+AGT], +[+DAT], +[+OBJ], +soc, +recip, -pot, +act]		DAT			OBJ	
14. [-[+INS], +[+OBJ], +[+COM], +soc]						
(a) [+loc, -pot, +act]		OBJ			COM	
(b) [-loc, -pot, +act]		OBJ				

Chart 8. Voice inflectional paradigm and corresponding affixes of secondary verb stem classes

4.4 Conclusion

From the foregoing description of syntactic derivation rules, we
have seen the capacity of DR's to account adequately for the syntactic,
semantic and morphological-voice relations of separate but related
lexical items. Given a set of items specified with syntactic, semantic
and/or morphological-voice features, a DR is able to create a corresponding set of items with its own matrix of features. The DR supplies
the derived stem with new features, allows some features carried over
from the source item to be modified, if necessary, and keeps intact all
other features from the source. With its accompanying morphophonemic
rule, the morphological shape of the verb stem is modified. By employing DR's, especially the productive ones, the lexicon can be greatly
simplified. For instance, each verbal entry need not be specified for
those features that are assigned by its associated DR. It is enough
to indicate what particular DR applies to the item so that one can be
directed to look to the DR for the full specification of its syntactic
and semantic features.

The DR's formulated here are able to account for the verb stems
that derive from N's and Adj's. They assign to the stems characteristic features which, in turn, qualify the stems to belong to the major
syntactic subcategories of verbs. Likewise, the other DR's account for
various types of verb stems that originate from other verb stem classes.
Some of these DR's show the relationship between basic and derived
primary verb stems whose case relation features are identical but whose
voice inflectional possibilities and morphological forms differ. Other

DR's show syntactic and at the same time semantic differences and similarities between pairs of corresponding classes of verb stems. Thus, we see the relationship between a basic primary stem and a basic secondary stem, e.g., [+erg] and [+caus, +erg]; [+erg] and [+recip, -pot, +act]. By means of DR's, many new stems are formed from one basic stem or root and as new stems are created, membership in the various syntactic, semantic and morphological-voice subcategories multiplies. Some of the major case frame subcategories increase in the semantic subclasses that manifest them. Likewise, the morphological subclasses include more and more semantic and corresponding case frame subcategories. For instance, the class of [+[+AGT], -[+DAT], -loc, +[+OBJ]] can include not only basic primary stems such as <u>inom</u> 'drink s.t.,' <u>punas</u> 'wipe off s.t.,' <u>tulong</u> 'help s.o.', and the primary stems derived from them, but also secondary stems such as <u>bagsak</u> 'drop s.t.', <u>tunaw</u> 'melt s.t.,' <u>pakulo?</u> 'boil s.t.' created through transitivization and causativization. With a few DR's, the formation of a new stem class results in the creation of a new syntactic class. For example, the syntactic class which has been labelled 'causative ditransitive' results from SVDR-13 which creates classes of stems with the case frame [+[+AGT], +[+DAT], +[+LOC], +[+OBJ]] which is not a member of the major case frame subcategories. It will be observed, however, that the three classes of verb stems under this subcategory differ in their semantic and morphological features. One is a double causative form of a former simple transitive verb, another is a double causative of a former causative perception verb, and the other is a single causative of a former information verb. Only by means of a DR can all three classes be related syntactically, semantically and morphologically in a simple, economical and elegant fashion.

Finally, without the use of DR's as formulated in this study, any account for the occurrence of such complex verb stems as pakipagpabigay and how it is related syntactically, semantically and morphologically to other existing stems such as pagpabigay, pabigay and bigay and how it may be related, although distantly, to other stems such as pagbigay, pambigay and kabigay can only render either a description of the differences in affixes, which is no explanation, or an ad hoc elaborate explanation which may still be short of being an adequate description of Tagalog verb formation.

Footnotes to Chapter IV

[1]Otanes analyzes the two verbs magbili 'sell' and bumili 'buy' as sharing the base bili 'transaction', and attributes the difference in their meanings to the difference in their affixes, mag- and -um-, respectively (1966:57). It may be mentioned, however, that the base bili when used as a nominal always expresses 'buying', e.g., mahal ang bili ko nito (Lit. 'My buying of this is expensive.'). This may suggest that the basic form is the verb stem bili 'buy' and that magbili (pagbili) with its semantic modification is derived from the former.

[2]This and the two following forms are causative stem forms.

[3]The notational conventions used here follow Starosta's (1973) formulation.

[4]Most of the classes identified by Otanes (1966: 156ff.) as 'modified verbs' are recognized here as semantically derived from verb stems. Most of the terms identifying the semantic classes are adopted from Otanes.

[5]For the purposes of this dissertation, other lexical categories which can be sources of derived verb stems have not been included. Even the N and Adj categories treated here are limited to noun roots, excluding the class of pronouns, and to adjective roots and ma-adjectives. (See Blake, 1911).

[6]The succeeding VDR's without accompanying VDMR's mean that the derived stem does not acquire an affix.

[7]This feature is interpreted as an optionally cooccurring coreferential OBJ of the subject OBJ.

[8]It will be noted that the class of subjectless verbs is not included in the major case frame subcategorization in which the subject is considered an obligatory cooccurring feature of every verb stem. They have been included in this section to illustrate their 'creation'.

[9]This observation was made by Richard McGinn in his paper "Tagalog Words and Verbs: A Probe into the Nature of Derivational Processes," for Linguistics 651, University of Hawaii, 1970.

[10]See Ramos (1974: 92) for this class which she marks [+transient].

[11]A similar distinction between intentional and non-intentional actions exists. In general, non-psych verbs are characteristically [+ntn] whereas psych verbs are [-ntn]. Thus, what are considered in the subcategorization in Chapter III are these characteristic forms of non-psych and psych verbs. Moreover, since the [+ntn] counterpart of non-psych verbs are semantically derived from the unmarked intentional primary verbs, they lie outside the scope of this study. The [+ntn] forms of psych verbs are accounted for since they derive directly from the Adj source just like the [-ntn] forms. Thus, primary verbs marked with [+[+AGT]]or -[+INS]] are redundantly [+ntn] whereas the psych verbs are marked as either [-ntn] or [+ntn].

[12]Cf. Pang-adjectives in Schachter and Otanes (1972:218-221).

[13]The derived reciprocal verb may also be shown to have derived indirectly from the source verb via a noun derivation. That is, a reciprocal noun referring to an 'exchange of action' e.g., balita?an 'an exchange of news-telling,' tanungan 'exchange of asking questions,' hiraman 'borrowing from each other,' palitan 'trading of s.t. with each other,' etc., derived from the non-reciprocal source verb, marked by the derivational affix -an (given in SVDMR-4, as the first affixation) serves as the source of the derived reciprocal verb marked by the prefix pag-. However, this alternative account is not followed here because such would not reveal the relationship in the case frames of the two types of verbs.

[14]The class of reciprocal verbs include what Schachter and Otanes label 'referential-focus' verbs (1972:317). In the present study, the 'referential-focus' verbs are the objective voice forms of underived reciprocal verbs. Note that these are also marked by the voice affix -an, e.g., pag?usapan, whose corresponding agentive voice is mag?usap 'speak with each other.' The underived reciprocal verbs in this study fall under the subcategory of information verbs, but they have not been included only because there are very few of them to warrant a sub-division of the information subclass.

[15]There is another kind of transitivization rule which applies to the same input in SVDR-7 whose resulting forms have the same syntactic features but whose semantic and morphological features differ from the forms derived through SVDR-7. This rule is labelled 'causative transitive verbs', SVDR-11.

[16]Two derived homophonous stems manifesting the case frames of a psych [+exp] verb and a calamity verb can also be distinguished by their derivational potential. Whereas the derived calamity verb can correspond to an accidental, semantically derived, form the derived psych [+exp] cannot. Compare the meaning difference, too, between 64.b and 65.b following.

[17]This possibility as designated by a broken arrow is shown here to illustrate the further capacity of SVDR-12 to accommodate a [+ins] stem instead of only a [+root] or a [-pot, +act] input. What the rule is prohibited from taking as input are [-ins] stems. However, this possibility has not been specified in the rules as formulated.

[18]It is significant to point out that lexicase makes a prediction that no new actants can be added while transformational grammar has no way of explaining why the process stops here.

[19] Like the feature [+ntn] (see footnote 11), the primary agentive verb stems are generally non-reciprocal, thus, both features [+ntn] and [-recip] can be introduced by a redundancy rule such as:

$$\begin{bmatrix} +\ V \\ +[+AGT] \\ -[+DAT] \end{bmatrix} \longrightarrow \begin{bmatrix} +ntn \\ -recip \end{bmatrix}$$

The reciprocal verbs are the marked forms and the non-reciprocal are the unmarked ones.

[20]This affix should be distinguished from the homophonous paki- which means 'to request that s.t. be done'. Stems with the request affix paki- can be related to causative verbs and they are considered here as being formed by semantic derivation rules since there is no modification in the syntactic features of the source stem in the process of derivation.

[21]In Otanes (1966:173), social verbs can occur only in actor-focus (with an agentive actant as subject). Compare her account of this type of verbs as being developed or generated by the base rule: "Asp͡ maki-S". At one point, she states that the complementation of social verbs is "fully determined by the embedded sentence, or, more precisely, by the embedded verb." Deriving social verbs directly from agentive verbs, as is done in the present study, does not necessitate "embedding;" it is simply a morphological formation.

[22]Note that the request type of the paki- verb includes locative voice, but the social type does not.

[23]An irregular verb such as this one can also indicate an objective voice, as in: pinakipag?usapan ng estudyante sa guro ang (tungkol sa) eksamen. This instance is viewed as an irregularity since the expected objective voice form, ipinakipag?usap also occurs.

[24]The parentheses mean that with certain verbs of the class identified, the specified voice is marked as such or that the voice form rarely occurs.

CHAPTER V

In addition to the works based on the lexicase framework that are cited here, this study has shown the workability of lexicase in one more language. Of particular significance in this study is the capability of lexicase to account formally for lexical relations through derivation rules. It is able to show that DR's can best capture syntactic, semantic and morphological relations between two lexical items or two lexical classes. This study demonstrates three types of syntactic relations expressed by VDR's, PVDR's and SVDR's. The first type of rules accounts for verb stems originating from other lexical categories, namely N's and Adj's. The second type accounts for verb stems derived from other verb stems whose case relation and semantic features are identical but whose morphological features are different. The last type accounts for verb stems derived from other verb stem classes whose case relation features, primarily, differ from each other. By these sets of derivation rules, a systematic overview of the various types of verb stems each being marked correspondingly by a simple set of voice and aspect inflectional affixes can be observed.

In the attempt to distinguish clearly between Tagalog verb inflection and derivation, we have come to the following conclusions which have never been arrived at in a similar fashion in previous studies. These are the major contributions of this study to Philippine linguistics in general and to Tagalog grammar in particular.

(a) The two inflectional categories of verbs are voice and aspect. A verb stem expresses at least one or no more than four of the following voices: objective, agentive, dative, locative, instrumental, benefactive, reason or comitative. Aspect inflection does not include the recent [+rec] category proposed in some studies.

(b) The verbal affixes marking voice inflection are the active affix um- or m-, the passive affixes -in, -an and i- and ∅. The two affixes that are introduced for the first time are m- and ∅.

(c) The verbal affixes marking the completed and, partially, the non-completed aspects are um-, n- or in-. Reduplication of the first consonant and vowel of the verb stem, in general, marks the begun and, partially, the non-completed aspects, except the M- and ∅-classes of stems.

(d) All affixes on the verb stem other than the inflectional affixes stated in b and c are derivational affixes, e.g., pag-, pang-, ka-, ma-, maka-, pa-, pag- -an, pagsa-, paki-, etc.

(e) Verb stems manifesting a complex of derivational affixes indicate a process of lexical rederivation which explains the hierarchical layering of derivational affixes. This is clearly illustrated particularly by the causativization, activization and socialization rules.

(f) Only a verb stem, never a root, classification reveals the simple and invariant set of voice and aspect affixes which can be distinguished from derivational affixes.

(g) The selection of the voice inflectional affixes manifesting the verb stem's voice paradigm is based not only on the syntactic and semantic features of the verb but also on its morphological features. The last type of feature is necessary because there are stems that differ only in this specification and, correspondingly, they are marked by different affixes to indicate their voice paradigm.

(h) The aspect inflectional affixes are dependent on the verb stem's voice affix which is the manifestation of the verb's complex of distinctive features as stated in g.

In addition, there are related accounts in this study which lend clarification to some syntactic problems that are not satisfactorily explained or adequately accounted for in past studies. These are the concomitant contributions of this investigation summarized as follows:

(a) Strict adherence to the lexicase grammar's use of the construction labels NP and PP as manifesting actants or verbal complements has led to the clarification of the categories Det and P which mark the case form of the cooccurring actants. This distinction has always been obscured by the practice of classifying such expressions as para sa, dahil sa, and even sa pamamagitan ng as complex 'complement or case markers' falling together with the simple markers ang, nang and sa.

(b) The analysis of case relations as one of the relevant features of verbs has led to the conclusion that positing one CR, labelled LOC, to represent both the actant identified in other works as DAT or Dir of 'give-verbs' and the LOC or Dir of 'put-verbs' achieves greater generality and simplicity of description.

(c) The analysis of [+goal] and [-goal] types of directional verbs has brought out the possibility of an optional cooccurrence of a second locative actant which complements the noun phrase [+LOC] expressing the destination or origin of the [+OBJ] of the respective verb stem. The complementary locative actant, however, must occur as a prepositional phrase specified on the preposition with a directional feature opposite that of the verb's.

(d) There are constraints on the cooccurrence of more than two

[+AC]'s or [+L]'s realizing various kinds of case relations. These constraints can be expressed as redundancy rules.

Toward defining certain universal features of verbs, this study has shown the viability of positing the following characteristics:

(a) Contextual or case frame features of verbs describe the basic sentence types of verbal sentences.

(b) Verb forms identify which cooccurring case relation must be realized as the subject of the sentence.

(c) The semantic features which subcategorize the various case frame subcategories may be true for most languages but their corresponding syntactic and/or morphological consequences are language specific.

(d) A verb derivation rule states either a syntactic and/or a semantic relation between two separate but corresponding lexical items or classes.

Finally, this study has raised questions that have not been considered before as relevant to grammatical analysis. Clarifying these questions and hinting at some possible directions for their investigation are also a contribution to further linguistic inquiry.

SEMANTIC AND CASE FEATURES OF TAGALOG

DET'S (DETERMINERS) AND PRO'S (PRONOUNS)

I. Subcategorization and Redundancy Rules for Det's

SR-1: $[+Det]$ $\longrightarrow$ $\begin{bmatrix} \pm com \\ \pm NM \end{bmatrix}$

SR-2: $[-com]$ $\longrightarrow$ $[\pm sg]$

SR-3: $[-NM]$ $\longrightarrow$ $[\pm AC]$

RR-1: $[-AC]$ $\longrightarrow$ $[+L]$

RR-2: $\begin{bmatrix} +Det \\ \alpha com \end{bmatrix}$ $\longrightarrow$ $\begin{bmatrix} - \begin{bmatrix} +N \\ -\alpha com \end{bmatrix} \end{bmatrix}$

II. Subcategoirzation and Redundancy Rules for Pro's

SR-1: $[+Pro]$ $\longrightarrow$ $\begin{bmatrix} \pm pers \\ \pm NM \end{bmatrix}$

SR-2: $[+pers]$ $\longrightarrow$ $\begin{bmatrix} \pm sg \\ \pm 1p \end{bmatrix}$

SR-3: $[-1p]$ $\longrightarrow$ $[\pm 2p]$

RR-1: $[-2p]$ $\longrightarrow$ $[+3p]$

SR-4: $\begin{matrix} +1p \\ -sg \end{matrix}$ $\longrightarrow$ $[\pm incl]$

SR-5: $[-pers]$ $\longrightarrow$ $[\pm near\ spkr]$

SR-6: $[-near\ spkr]$ $\longrightarrow$ $[+near\ hearer]$

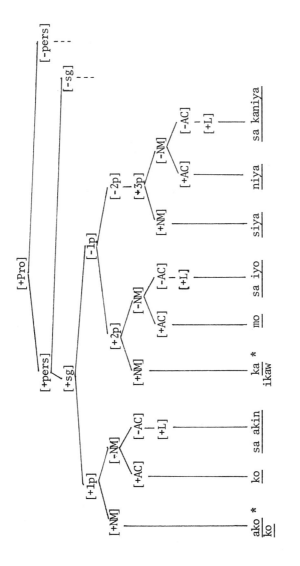

*The first entry is the regular form. Of these two variants, only the longer form, i.e., ako and ikaw, can occur in sentence initial position or as independent word responses.

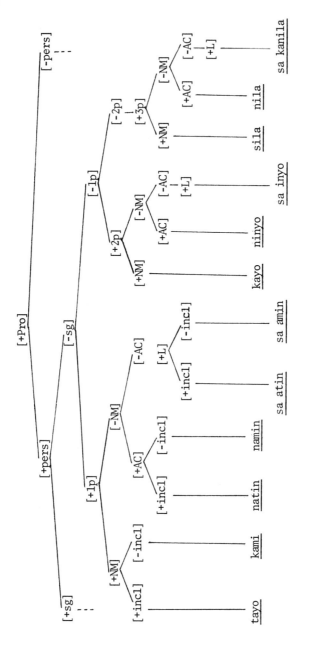

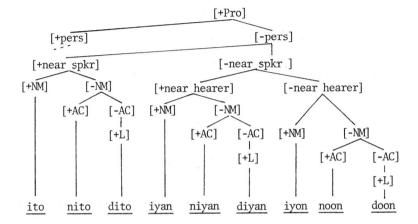

APPENDIX B

VERB INFLECTION RULES

I. Voice Redundancy and Subcategorization Rules

VRR-1: $[+V] \longrightarrow [+[+NM]]$

VRR-2: $[+V] \longrightarrow [-[+NM][+NM]]$

VSR-1: $\begin{bmatrix} +V \\ +[+NM] \end{bmatrix} \longrightarrow \begin{bmatrix} -\begin{bmatrix} +NM \\ \pm OBJ \end{bmatrix} \end{bmatrix}$

VSR-2: $\begin{bmatrix} -\begin{bmatrix} +NM \\ +OBJ \end{bmatrix} \end{bmatrix} \longrightarrow \begin{bmatrix} -\begin{bmatrix} +NM \\ \pm DAT \end{bmatrix} \end{bmatrix}$

VSR-3: $\begin{bmatrix} -\begin{bmatrix} +NM \\ +DAT \end{bmatrix} \end{bmatrix} \longrightarrow \begin{bmatrix} -\begin{bmatrix} +NM \\ \pm LOC \end{bmatrix} \end{bmatrix}$

VSR-4: $\begin{bmatrix} -\begin{bmatrix} +NM \\ +LOC \end{bmatrix} \end{bmatrix} \longrightarrow \begin{bmatrix} -\begin{bmatrix} +NM \\ \pm AGT \end{bmatrix} \end{bmatrix}$

VSR-5: $\begin{bmatrix} -\begin{bmatrix} +NM \\ +AGT \end{bmatrix} \end{bmatrix} \longrightarrow \begin{bmatrix} -\begin{bmatrix} +NM \\ \pm BEN \end{bmatrix} \end{bmatrix}$

VSR-6: $\begin{bmatrix} -\begin{bmatrix} +NM \\ +BEN \end{bmatrix} \end{bmatrix} \longrightarrow \begin{bmatrix} -\begin{bmatrix} +NM \\ \pm INS \end{bmatrix} \end{bmatrix}$

VSR-7: $\begin{bmatrix} -\begin{bmatrix} +NM \\ +INS \end{bmatrix} \end{bmatrix} \longrightarrow \begin{bmatrix} -\begin{bmatrix} +NM \\ \pm RSN \end{bmatrix} \end{bmatrix}$

VRR-3: $\begin{bmatrix} -\begin{bmatrix} +NM \\ +RSN \end{bmatrix} \end{bmatrix} \longrightarrow \begin{bmatrix} -\begin{bmatrix} +NM \\ -COM \end{bmatrix} \end{bmatrix}$

II. Aspect Subcategorization Rules

ASR-1: $[+V] \longrightarrow [\pm fin]$

ASR-2: $[+fin] \longrightarrow [\pm beg]$

ASR-3: $[+beg] \longrightarrow [\pm comp]$

III. Voice-Aspect Morphophonemic Rules

VAMR-1: $_V[(C_1)V_1 \longrightarrow {}_V[(C_1)V_1(C_1)V_1 \Big/ \begin{bmatrix} \begin{bmatrix} UM- \\ IN- \\ AN- \\ I- \end{bmatrix} class \\ \begin{Bmatrix} -beg \\ -comp \end{Bmatrix} \end{bmatrix}$

VAMR-2: $_V[(C_1) \longrightarrow {}_V[(C_1)um$ / $\begin{bmatrix} \text{UM-class} \\ \{\text{-fin}\} \\ \{\text{+beg}\} \end{bmatrix}$

VAMR-3: $_V[(C_1) \longrightarrow {}_V[(C_1)in$ / $\begin{bmatrix} \begin{Bmatrix} \text{IN-} \\ \text{AN-} \\ \text{I-} \end{Bmatrix} \text{class} \\ \text{+beg} \end{bmatrix}$

VAMR-4: $]_V \longrightarrow in]_V$ / $\begin{bmatrix} \text{IN-class} \\ \{\text{-fin}\} \\ \{\text{-beg}\} \end{bmatrix}$

VAMR-5: $]_V \longrightarrow an]_V$ / AN-class

VAMR-6: (a) $_V[inV_1 \longrightarrow {}_V[iniV_1$ / $\begin{bmatrix} \text{I-class} \\ \text{+beg} \end{bmatrix}$

(b) $_V[\longrightarrow {}_V[i$ / I-class

VAMR-7: (a) $_V[C_1V_1\begin{Bmatrix} g \\ ng \end{Bmatrix}(C_2)V_2 \longrightarrow {}_V[C_1V_1\begin{Bmatrix} g \\ ng \end{Bmatrix}(C_2)V_2(C_2)V_2$ /

$$\begin{bmatrix} \text{M-class} \\ \{\text{-beg}\} \\ \{\text{-comp}\} \end{bmatrix}$$

(b) $_V[C_1V_1(C_2)V_2 \longrightarrow {}_V[C_1V_1(C_2)V_2(C_2)V_2$ /

$$\begin{bmatrix} \emptyset\text{-class} \\ \{\text{-beg}\} \\ \{\text{-comp}\} \end{bmatrix}$$

VAMR-8: (a) $_V[\longrightarrow {}_V[m$ / M-class

(b) $_V[mp \longrightarrow {}_V[m$

VAMR-9: (a) $_V[\longrightarrow {}_V[n$ / $\begin{bmatrix} \begin{Bmatrix} \text{M-} \\ \emptyset\text{-} \end{Bmatrix}\text{class} \\ \text{+beg} \end{bmatrix}$

(b) $_V[nm \longrightarrow {}_V[n$

VERB STEM SUBCATEGORIZATION AND REDUNDANCY RULES

I. Case Frame SR's and RR's

CFRR-1:　$[+V]$　$\longrightarrow$　$[+[+OBJ]]$

CFSR-1:　$[+[+OBJ]]$　$\longrightarrow$　$\pm[+AGT]$
　　　　　　　　　　　　　　　$\pm[+DAT]$

CFSR-2:　$[-[+DAT]]$　$\longrightarrow$　$[\pm loc]$

CFSR-3:　$[+loc]$　$\longrightarrow$　$[\pm strict]$

CFRR-2:　$[+strict]$　$\longrightarrow$　$[+[+LOC]]$

CFRR-3:　$[-strict]$　$\longrightarrow$　$[+([+LOC])]$

CFSR-4:　$\begin{bmatrix} -[+AGT] \\ -loc \end{bmatrix}$　$\longrightarrow$　$[\pm[+INS]]$

CFRR-4:　$\begin{bmatrix} -[+AGT] \\ +[+INS] \end{bmatrix}$　$\longrightarrow$　$\begin{array}{c} -[+RSN] \\ -[+COM] \end{array}$

CFRR-5:　$\begin{bmatrix} +[+AGT] \\ -[+DAT] \end{bmatrix}$　$\longrightarrow$　$[+([+INS])]$

CFRR-6:　$[+[+AGT]]$　$\longrightarrow$　$[+([+BEN])]$

CFRR-7:　$[+V]$　$\longrightarrow$　$[-[+INS]]$

CFRR-8:　$[-[+AGT]]$　$\longrightarrow$　$[-[+BEN]]$

CFRR-9:　$\begin{bmatrix} -[+AGT] \\ +[+INS] \\ +[+OBJ] \end{bmatrix}$　$\longrightarrow$　$\begin{bmatrix} -AC \\ -\begin{bmatrix} +INS \end{bmatrix} \end{bmatrix}$

CFRR-10:　$\begin{bmatrix} +extn \\ +NM \\ -[+OBJ] \end{bmatrix}$　$\longrightarrow$　$\begin{bmatrix} -L \\ -\begin{bmatrix} +OBJ \end{bmatrix} \end{bmatrix}$

CFSR-5:　$\begin{bmatrix} -extn \\ +NM \\ -[+OBJ] \end{bmatrix}$　$\longrightarrow$　$\begin{bmatrix} \pm AC \\ +\begin{bmatrix} +OBJ \end{bmatrix} \end{bmatrix}$

CFRR-11:　$\begin{bmatrix} -extn \\ \alpha AC \\ +[+OBJ] \end{bmatrix}$　$\longrightarrow$　$\begin{bmatrix} +OBJ \\ -\begin{bmatrix} -\alpha def \end{bmatrix} \end{bmatrix}$

CFRR-12: $\begin{bmatrix} -\text{extn} \\ \begin{bmatrix} -\text{AC} \\ +\begin{bmatrix} +\text{OBJ} \end{bmatrix} \end{bmatrix} \end{bmatrix} \longrightarrow \begin{bmatrix} \cdot \begin{bmatrix} -\text{L} \\ - \begin{bmatrix} +\text{OBJ} \end{bmatrix} \end{bmatrix} \end{bmatrix}$

CFRR-13: $[-\text{cog}] \longrightarrow \begin{bmatrix} -\text{strict} \\ -\text{dir} \end{bmatrix}$

CFRR-14: $\begin{bmatrix} -\text{per} \\ \begin{bmatrix} +\text{NM} \\ - \begin{bmatrix} +\text{OBJ} \end{bmatrix} \end{bmatrix} \end{bmatrix} \longrightarrow \begin{bmatrix} \cdot \begin{bmatrix} -\text{L} \\ - \begin{bmatrix} +\text{OBJ} \end{bmatrix} \end{bmatrix} \end{bmatrix}$

CFRR-15: $[+\text{assm}] \longrightarrow \begin{bmatrix} \cdot \begin{bmatrix} +\text{NM} \\ - \text{DAT} \end{bmatrix} \end{bmatrix}$

CFRR-16: $[\alpha\text{goal}] \longrightarrow \begin{bmatrix} \cdot \begin{bmatrix} +\text{P} \\ \alpha\text{goal} \\ + \begin{bmatrix} +\text{LOC} \end{bmatrix} \end{bmatrix} \end{bmatrix}$

CFRR-17: $\begin{bmatrix} +\text{caus} \\ +\text{erg} \\ +[+\text{AGT}] \\ +[+\text{DAT}] \\ \begin{bmatrix} +\text{NM} \\ - [+\text{DAT}] \end{bmatrix} \end{bmatrix} \longrightarrow \begin{bmatrix} \cdot \begin{bmatrix} -\text{L} \\ - [+\text{DAT}] \end{bmatrix} \end{bmatrix}$

CFRR-18: $\begin{bmatrix} +\text{soc} \\ +\text{loc} \end{bmatrix} \longrightarrow \begin{bmatrix} \cdot \begin{bmatrix} -\text{L} \\ - [+\text{LOC}] \end{bmatrix} \end{bmatrix}$

II. Semantic SR's and RR's

SFSR-1: $[+\text{loc}] \longrightarrow [\pm\text{dir}]$

SFSR-2: $[+\text{dir}] \longrightarrow [\pm\text{goal}]$

SFSR-3'': $\left\{ \begin{bmatrix} +[+\text{AGT}] \\ -\text{dir} \\ -\text{extn} \end{bmatrix} \\ \begin{bmatrix} -[+\text{AGT}] \\ +[+\text{INS}] \end{bmatrix} \right\} \longrightarrow [\pm\text{af}]$

SFSR-4': $\left\{ \begin{matrix} [+\text{af}] \\ [+\text{aff1}] \end{matrix} \right\} \longrightarrow [\pm\text{cs}]$

SFSR-5: $\begin{bmatrix} +[+\text{AGT}] \\ -[+\text{DAT}] \\ -\text{loc} \end{bmatrix} \longrightarrow [\pm\text{extn}]$

SFSR-6: $\begin{bmatrix} -[+\text{INS}] \\ +[+\text{OBJ}] \end{bmatrix} \longrightarrow [\pm\text{inch}]$

SFSR-7:   [+inch] $\longrightarrow$ [±term]

SFSR-8: [-inch] $\longrightarrow$ [±affl]

SFSR-9: $\begin{bmatrix} - [+AGT] \\ + [+DAT] \\ + [+OBJ] \end{bmatrix}$ $\longrightarrow$ [±per]

SFSR-10: [+per] $\longrightarrow$ [±cog]

SFSR-11: [-per] $\longrightarrow$ [±emo]

SFSR-12: [-emo] $\longrightarrow$ [±assm]

SFSR-13: [-assm] $\longrightarrow$ [±attd]

III. Morphological and Voice-Related SR's and RR's

MVRSR-1: [+V] $\longrightarrow$ [±root]

MVRRR-1: [+root] $\longrightarrow$ $\begin{bmatrix} - \begin{bmatrix} -AC \\ +INS \end{bmatrix} \\ - \begin{bmatrix} -R \\ +RSN \end{bmatrix} \\ - \begin{bmatrix} -C \\ +COM \end{bmatrix} \end{bmatrix}$

MVRSR-2: [+root] $\longrightarrow$ [±erg]

MVRRR-2: [+erg] $\longrightarrow$ $\begin{bmatrix} - \begin{bmatrix} +NM \\ +AGT \end{bmatrix} \\ - \begin{bmatrix} +NM \\ +INS \end{bmatrix} \end{bmatrix}$

MVRRR-3: $\begin{bmatrix} + [+AGT] \\ - \begin{bmatrix} +NM \\ +AGT \end{bmatrix} \end{bmatrix}$ $\longrightarrow$ $\begin{bmatrix} - \begin{bmatrix} +NM \\ +BEN \end{bmatrix} \end{bmatrix}$

MVRSR-3: [-root] $\longrightarrow$ $\begin{bmatrix} ±pot \\ ±act \end{bmatrix}$

MVRSR-4: $\begin{bmatrix} -pot \\ -act \end{bmatrix}$ $\longrightarrow$ [±ins]

MVRRR-4: $\begin{Bmatrix} [+pot] \\ \begin{bmatrix} -pot \\ +act \end{bmatrix} \end{Bmatrix}$ $\longrightarrow$ $\begin{bmatrix} - \begin{bmatrix} +NM \\ +INS \end{bmatrix} \\ - \begin{bmatrix} +NM \\ +RSN \end{bmatrix} \end{bmatrix}$

MVRRR-5: $\begin{bmatrix} +pot \\ +act \end{bmatrix}$ $\longrightarrow$ $\begin{bmatrix} - \begin{bmatrix} +NM \\ +OBJ \end{bmatrix} \end{bmatrix}$

MVRRR-6: $[+\text{ins}] \longrightarrow \left[- \begin{bmatrix} +\text{NM} \\ -\text{INS} \end{bmatrix} \right]$

MVRRR-7: $\begin{bmatrix} +[+\text{AGT}] \\ -\text{ins} \end{bmatrix} \longrightarrow \left[- \begin{bmatrix} +\text{NM} \\ -\text{RSN} \end{bmatrix} \right]$

MVRRR-8: $\begin{bmatrix} -[+\text{AGT}] \\ -\text{ins} \end{bmatrix} \longrightarrow \left[- \begin{bmatrix} +\text{NM} \\ +\text{DAT} \end{bmatrix} \right]$

MVRRR-9: $\begin{bmatrix} +\text{caus} \\ +\text{dat} \end{bmatrix} \longrightarrow \left[\begin{array}{l} - \begin{bmatrix} +\text{NM} \\ +\text{AGT} \end{bmatrix} \\ - \begin{bmatrix} +\text{NM} \\ +\text{INS} \end{bmatrix} \\ - \begin{bmatrix} +\text{NM} \\ +\text{RSN} \end{bmatrix} \end{array} \right]$

BIBLIOGRAPHY

Akhmanova, Olga. 1971. Phonology, Morphonology, Morphology.
The Hague: Mouton.

Anderson, John M. 1971. The Grammar of Case: Towards a Localistic
Theory. Cambridge: Cambridge University Press.

Balachandran, Lakshmi Bai. 1971. A Case Grammar of Hindi with
special reference to the Causative Sentences. Cornell University
doctoral dissertation.

Blake, Frank R. 1906. Expression of Case by the Verb in Tagalog.
Journal of the American Oriental Society 27:183-9.

_____. 1911. Tagalog Verbs Derived from Other Parts of Speech.
American Journal of Philology 32:436-40.

_____. 1916. The Tagalog Verb. Journal of the American Oriental
Society 36:396-414.

_____. 1925. A Grammar of the Tagalog Language. New Haven:
Yale University Press.

_____. 1930. A Semantic Analysis of Case. Curme Volume of
Linguistic Studies, ed. by James T. Hatfield, et al., 34-49.
Baltimore: Waverly Press.

Bloomfield, Leonard. 1917. Tagalog Texts with Grammatical Analysis.
(University of Illinois, Studies in Language and Literature, 3.2-4)
Urbana: University of Illinois.

_____. 1933. Language. New York: Holt, Rinehart and Winston.

Capell, Arthur. 1964. Verbal System in Philippine Languages.
Philippine Journal of Science 93:231-49.

Chafe, Wallace. 1970. Meaning and the Structure of Language.
Chicago: The University of Chicago Press.

Chapin, Paul. 1967. On the Syntax of Word-Derivation in English.
Massachusetts: The MITRE Corporation.

_____. 1970. On Affixation in English. Progress in Linguistics,
ed. by Manfred Bierwisch and Karl Erick Heidolph. The Hague:
Mouton.

Chomsky, Noam. 1965. Aspects of the Theory of Syntax. Cambridge:
The MIT Press.

Cook, Walter A. 1971. Improvements in Case Grammar 1970. Languages and Linguistics 2:10-22. Washington, D. C.: Georgetown University Press.

Clark, Marybeth. 1975. Coverbs and Case in Vietnamese. University of Hawaii doctoral dissertaion.

Constantino, Ernesto. 1965. The Sentence Patterns of Twenty-six Philippine Languages. Lingua 15:71-124.

_____. 1970. The Deep Structures of the Philippine Languages. The Archives 1.2:67-79. Quezon City: University of the Philippines.

_____. 1971. Tagalog and Other Major Languages of the Philippines. Current Trends in Linguistics, ed. by Thomas A. Sebeok, Volume VIII, Linguistics in Oceania. The Hague: Mouton.

Fillmore, Charles J. 1966. A Proposal Concerning English Prepositions. Georgetown University Monograph Series 19:19-34.

_____. 1968a. The Case for Case. Universals in Linguistic Theory, ed. by Emmon Bach and Robert T. Harms, 1-88. New York: Holt, Rinehart and Winston.

_____. 1968b. Lexical Entries for Verbs. Foundations of Language 4:373-93.

_____. 1971. Some Problems for Case Grammar. Monograph Series on Languages and Linguistics 24:35-56.

Freidin, Robert. 1975. The Analysis of Passives. Language 51.2: 384-405.

Gruber, Jeffrey S. 1970. Studies in Lexical Relations. Indiana University Linguistics Club (mimeographed).

Guzman, Videa P. De. 1968. Tagalog Verbal Cooccurrence with Affixes and Complements. Term Paper for Linguistics 650, University of Hawaii.

_____. 1970. A Syntactic Comparison of Tagalog, Maori and Chamorro. The Archives 1.1:33-60. Quezon City: University of the Philippines.

Halle, Morris. 1973. Prolegomena to a Theory of Word Formation. Linguistic Inquiry 4.1:3-16.

Halliday, Michael A. K. 1967. Notes on Transitivity and Theme in English. Journal of Linguistics 3.1:37-81, and 4.3:179-215.

Huddleston, Rodney. 1970. Some Remarks on Case Grammar. Linguistic Inquiry 1.4:501-11.

410

Ikranagara, Kay. 1975. Melayu Betawi Grammar. University of Hawaii doctoral dissertation.

Institute of National Language. 1950. Balarila ng Wikang Pambansa (Grammar of the National Language). Fourth Printing. Manila: Bureau of Printing.

Jackendoff, Ray S. 1972. Semantic Interpretation in Generative Grammar. Cambridge: The MIT Press.

Jespersen, Otto. 1975. The Philosophy of Grammar. London: George Allen and Unwin Ltd. (First published in 1924.)

Kenny, Anthony. 1963. Action, Emotion and Will. London: Routledge and Kegan Paul.

Kerr, Harland B. 1965. The Case-marking and Classifying Function of Cotabato Manobo Voice Affixes. Oceanic Linguistics 4:15-47.

Kess, Joseph F. 1967. Syntactic Features of Tagalog Verbs. University of Hawaii doctoral dissertation.

Krishnamurti, B. H. 1971. Causative Constructions in Indian Languages. Indian Linguistics 32.1:18-35.

Kufner, Herbert L. 1962. The Grammatical Structures of English and German. Chicago: The University of Chicago Press.

Kullavanijaya, Pranee. 1974. Transitive Verbs in Thai. University of Hawaii doctoral dissertation.

Kuroda, S. Y. 1965. Causative Forms in Japanese. Foundations in Language 1.1:30-50.

Lakoff, George. 1970. Irregularity of Syntax. New York: Holt, Rinehart and Winston.

_____. 1971. On Generative Semantics. Semantics, ed. by Danny Steinberg and Leon A. Jakobovitz, 232-96. Cambridge: The University Press.

Lee, Gregory P. 1969. Subjects and Agents. Working Papers in Linguistics 3:36-113. Columbus, Ohio: The Ohio State University.

Lee, Keedong. 1974. Kusaiean Verbal Derivation Rules. University of Hawaii doctoral dissertation.

Li, Paul Jen-kuei. 1973. Rukai Structure. Institute of History and Philology Academia Sinica, Special Publication No. 64. Nankang, Taipei, Taiwan, Republic of China.

Llamzon, Teodoro. 1966. Main Transient Formations in Tagalog.
Philippine Journal of Science 95;143-57.

———. 1968. Modern Tagalog: A Functional-Structural Description
with Particular Attention to the Problem of Verification.
Georgetown University doctoral dissertaion.

Lopez, Cecilio. 1937. Preliminary Study of the Affixes in Tagalog.
Publications of the Institute of National Language, Volume 2.
Manila: Bureau of Printing.

———. 1941. A Manual of the Philippine National Language.
Manila: Bureau of Printing.

Lyons, John. 1968. Introduction to Theoretical Linguistics.
London: Cambridge University Press.

McCawley, James. 1968. Lexical Insertion in a Transformation Grammar
without Deep Structure. Papers Presented to the Fourth Regional
Meeting, Chicago Linguistics Society, 71-80.

———. 1972. Syntactic and Logical Arguments for Semantic
Structures. Indiana University Linguistics Club (mimeographed).

McGinn, Richard. 1970. Tagalog Words and Verbs: A Probe into the
Nature of Derivational Processes. Term Paper for Linguistics 651,
University of Hawaii.

McKaughan, Howard P. 1958. The Inflection and Syntax of Maranao Verbs.
Manila: Bureau of Printing.

———. 1962. Overt Relation Markers in Maranao. Language 38,1:
47-51.

———. 1970. Topicalization in Maranao—an addendum. Pacific
Linguistic Studies in Honour of Arthur Capell. Pacific
Linguistics, Series C, No. 13, ed. by S. A. Wurm and D. C. Laycock,
291-300. Canberra: The Australian National University.

———. 1973. Subject Versus Topic. Parangal Kay Cecilio Lopez
(Essays in Honor of Cecilio Lopez on His 75th Birthday), ed. by
Andrew B. Gonzalez,FSC, 206-13. Philippine Journal of Linguistics.
Special Monograph Issue No. 4. Quezon City: Linguistic Society
of the Philippines.

Matthews, P. H. 1974. Morphology: An introduction to the theory of
word-structure. London: Cambridge University Press.

Members of the Summer Institute of Linguistics. 1964. Papers in
Philippine Linguistics. Oceanic Linguistics 3.1.

412

Nilsen, Don Lee Fred. 1972. Toward a Semantic Specification of Deep Case. The Hague; Mouton.

Otanes, Fe T. 1966. A Contrastive Analysis of English and Tagalog Verb Complementation. University of California (Los Angeles) doctoral dissertation.

_____. 1970. Some Transformational Rules for Noun Derivation in Tagalog. Philippine Journal of Linguistics 1.1:33-73.

Pittman, Richard. 1966. Tagalog -um- and mag-. Pacific Linguistics, Series A, No. 8:9-20. Canberra: The Australian National University.

Platt, John T. 1971. Grammatical Forms and Grammatical Meaning. Amsterdam: North-Holland Publishing Company.

Ramos, Teresita V. 1974. The Case System of Tagalog Verbs. Pacific Linguistics, Series B, No. 27. Canberra: The Australian National University.

Reid, Lawrence A. 1966. An Ivatan Syntax. Oceanic Linguistics Special Publication No. 2. Honolulu: University of Hawaii Press.

Schachter, Paul and Fe Otanes. 1972. Tagalog Reference Grammar. Los Angeles: University of California Press.

Starosta, Stanley. 1971a. Review of John Lyons, "Introduction to Theoretical Linguistics." Language 47.2:429-47.

_____. 1971b. Derivation and Case in Sora Verbs. Indian Linguistics 32.3:194-206. Calcutta University.

_____. 1971c. Lexical Derivation in a Case Grammar. University of Hawaii Working Papers in Linguistics 3.8:83-101.

_____. 1972. Case in the Lexicon. Paper read at the 11th International Congress of Linguists, Bologna.

_____. 1973a. Case Forms and Case Relations in Sora. University of Hawaii Working Papers in Linguistics 5.1:133-53.

_____. 1973b. The Faces of Case. Language Sciences 25:1-14.

_____. 1974. Causative Verbs in Formosan. Paper read at the First International Conference on Comparative Austronesian Linguistics, Honolulu.

_____. (forthcoming) Generative Syntax: A Case Approach.

Stevens, Alan M. 1969. Case Grammar in Philippine Languages. Paper read at the Linguistic Society of America meeting.

Stockwell, Robert, Paul Schachter and Barbara Hall Partee. 1973. The Major Syntactic Structures of English. New York: Holt, Rinehart and Winston.

Taylor, Harvey. 1971. Case in Japanese. South Orange, New Jersey: Seton Hall University Press.

White, Alan R., ed. 1968. The Philosophy of Action. London: Oxford University Press.

Wolfenden, Elmer. 1961. A Re-statement of Tagalog Grammar. Manila: Summer Institute of Linguistics and Institute of National Language.

Videa P. De Guzman received her Ph.D. from the University of Hawaii. Her specialization and research interests are in Philippine and Austronesian linguistics. She is presently an assistant professor in the Department of Linguistics, The University of Calgary, Calgary, Alberta, Canada.